BLACK QUEER STUDIES

BLACK QUEER STUDIES

A CRITICAL ANTHOLOGY

E. PATRICK JOHNSON
AND MAE G. HENDERSON,
EDITORS

DUKE UNIVERSITY PRESS

DURHAM AND LONDON 2005

© 2005 Duke University Press
All rights reserved
Printed in the United States
of America on acid-free paper ∞
Designed by Amy Ruth Buchanan
Typeset in Minion by Keystone
Typesetting, Inc.
Library of Congress Cataloging-
in-Publication Data appear on
the last printed page of this book.

The distribution of this book is
supported by a generous grant
from the Gill Foundation.

CONTENTS

······································

ACKNOWLEDGMENTS

······································

We are indebted to the individuals and institutions that enabled the creation
of this project. First, we would like to thank the volume's contributors for
their patience during the compilation and publication process: their support
and commitment has made the journey a smooth one. Further, the following
scholars were presenters at the Black Queer Studies in the Millennium conference, and while their work does not appear in this volume their imprint is
on its final form: M. Jacqueline Alexander, Lindon Barrett, Jennifer DeVere
Brody, Cheryl Clarke, Jerome M. Culp Jr., Cheryl Dunye, Gerard Fergerson,
Shari Frilot, Thomas Glave, Thomas A. Harris, Alycee Lane, Wahneema
Lubiano, Darieck Scott, Jane Splawn, and Yvonne Welbon.

We would like to thank the centers, departments, organizations, and programs at the University of North Carolina at Chapel Hill that contributed
resources to the conference out of which this volume emerged, including
African and African American Studies, Carolina Alternative Meetings of Professional and Graduate Students (CAMP), Communication Studies, Comparative Literature, Curriculum in Women's Studies, the English Department, the Office of the Vice Provost for Graduate Studies and Research, the
Sonja Haynes Stone Black Cultural Center, the Student Finance Committee,
the University Program in Cultural Studies, and especially the Williamson
Committee to Promote Gay and Lesbian Studies. The following individuals
also contributed to making the conference a success: Renee Alexander, Kelly
Gallagher, Mark Pippen, Douglas McLachlan, Glenn Grossman, Tess Chak-
kalakal, Marie Nesnow, Robin Vander, Stephen Lewis, Travaughn Eubanks,
Curt Blackman, Christi Mayville, Daniel Lebold, Olateju Omolodun, Jamie
Lipschultz, Gladys Jasmine, Erica Smiley, Lucy Pearce, Elizabeth Blackwood,
Camille Simpson, Tiffany Foster, Kim Curtis, David Roberts, Karolyn Tyson,
Joanna Muster, Chandra Ford, Kelly Rowett, Jules Odendahl, Doug Taylor,
and Rachel Hall.

Many friends and colleagues gave their support at various stages of the project. Special thanks goes to Cedric Brown, Dwight Conquergood, Sandra Richards, and Cheryl Wall.

Special thanks to Darlene Clark Hine and the Department of African American Studies at Northwestern University who provided funding to publish this volume.

We are deeply indebted to Ken Wissoker, editor-in-chief at Duke University Press, for staying the course and supporting this project. We would also like to thank the production staff at the Press for their professionalism, helpfulness, and diligence.

Finally, we thank Stephen Lewis, who always manages to step in in the nick of time.

....

SHARON P. HOLLAND

....

FOREWORD:

"HOME" IS A FOUR-LETTER WORD

The editors of this volume deploy the term "interanimation" to describe the intellectual dynamic at play in the essays' various musings. I can think of no better word or way to describe both this collection and my experience of its genesis. In April 2000, I traveled to North Carolina to witness an unprecedented event: the field in which I had been laboring since my junior year at Princeton was now coming of age. I moved toward a space that attempted to define a connection between "black" and "queer" at a time when "queer" had its own controversial orbit. Would "queer" obfuscate the presence of lesbians in a movement that, although "grounded in social and political activism," according to the editors, had its own specific historical struggle over the "inclusion" of women in the story of itself? The academic market, at least its emerging "queer" constituency, seemed to be interpreting "identity politics" as the root of all evil—simply get rid of "race" (always a fiction?) and the category of "woman" (already a misnomer?) and we would have our rebirth on the other side of our problem(s).

While "queer" studies began to define its origins from the complex re-making of identity politics, those of us already working in the field of black feminism found this "new" trajectory unsettling—scholars like Hazel Carby and Hortense Spillers had already unseated the idea of "woman" as a universal category; Gloria Hull, Barbara Smith, and others had already questioned the myopic identity politics of civil rights and women's activist networks. The question hardly seemed "new" to us at all, but rather more of the same: remaking discourse in the image of its rightful owners—whitewashing the product so that it could and would be more palpable to a growing constituency. Been there, done that. The present tension in the fields of feminist, ethnic, and queer studies reminded me of a talk I once heard while I was an assistant professor at Stanford. During this talk, a renowned scholar of the history of academic institutions and forms of knowledge production tried to explain the pressures brought to bear on English departments in the last decade of the twentieth century in terms of capital and interdisciplinarity. When my colleague in African American studies challenged him by recalling the formation of African American and Women's studies programs and the kind of bodies that those disciplinary "homes" brought to the academy, he seemed puzzled and rather annoyed. He mistook her challenge as personal and emotional (identity politics) rather than as intellectual. It was a misunderstanding that taught me a valuable lesson about the way that "race" and "gender" really work in the academy. I still find that rather than listen to what I am actually saying, colleagues will often see me—black, woman, lesbian— and have very high expectations for the kind of narrative that I might employ. Often, they run that tape simultaneously with my voice, so that the din of the taped voice is louder than my own. We have a script that colleagues expect us to deliver, and when we do not the damage is twofold: "How dare you not live up to my expectations" couples with the kind of shame that colleagues manifest when they realize that in order to argue with you, they would have had to listen to you in the first place. Since the latter is an embarrassing moment for speaker and audience, the deadlock is dead space.

I traveled to Chapel Hill, North Carolina, knowing that I would share space—at least for three days—with scholars who know that moment, who've felt its force. I wasn't expecting "home" and as the weekend progressed, so many of us testified to the bittersweet affect of that remedy. For me in particular, it was more bitter than sweet because the conference would return me to my family seat, as nearby Durham was "home" for my mother's people. My estrangement from my biological family had endured for thirteen years, so that when my plane landed at Raleigh-Durham airport, I felt like a thief in the night. As I trespassed upon a place that was no longer "home" for me, I walked into an intellectual space that was also a fraught location for my own "identity politics." The queer pleasure was overwhelming—that weekend, I loved Durham with a vengeance.

What I found at the Black Queer Studies in the Millennium conference was a group of colleagues interested in the "messiness" of it all. Each panel presented questions and challenges for the discipline(s) and for "blackness." Moreover, it taught us how to talk to one another—how to disagree in public, even though the stakes of that disagreement were and are so high. For us, blackness had a limit and a shape, shortcomings and advantages. As E. Patrick Johnson and Mae G. Henderson note, "we want[ed] to *quare* queer, throw shade on its meanings." And throw shade we did—it was a beautiful thing.

With the memory of that particular moment in mind, the editors of this volume, wittingly or unwittingly, group the essays in each section around an important intellectual moment in the conference. In this sense, this collection is a gift, a re-memory, for those of us who witnessed its power: the good, the bad, and at times, the ugly. For scholars new to the field, it provides an invaluable chronicle of an emerging field of inquiry—one that has its shape as the new queer of color critique, pace José Muñoz and Roderick Ferguson, to name only two. As scholars move ever increasingly toward issues of globalization and U.S. imperialism, the essays collected here unabashedly focus on the Americas as a specific site—as a place where black peoples have and still experience the force of this country's perpetual attempt to increase its borders and its reach.

Because hindsight is always dangerous, I will not critique what is missing from this collection, but rather only describe its missed opportunities as a kind of melancholia—the symptom always in search of dis-ease. What the collection does not and cannot articulate is the tension that arose between those who produce "culture" and those who consider themselves the arbiters of its critical reception. While many of us have considered the line between critic and culture to be porous, we quickly learned that there are important and salient differences between the two. Ironically enough, this tension also helped to obfuscate another typical division—that is, it failed to reproduce a now-familiar conference scene where "activists" and "academics" square off like gangstas in a B movie. Instead, the friction between critics and film-makers, journalists and theorists, was focused on the intellectual endeavor before us—simultaneously demonstrating the importance of our efforts and the necessity for the conference itself. Black Queer Studies in the Millennium still remains one of the only conferences I have attended where activists and academics weren't encouraged to rip each other to shreds. It was obvious in the conference auditorium—at least for that weekend—that we needed one another to complete the discourse, to do the work.

E. Patrick Johnson's solo performance at the end of a long Saturday articulated the drama of that weekend and the necessity of cultural production. It brought many of us back to the beginning—at one point we were all little black boys and girls who knew that we were "quare" and that we couldn't hide it. Like Morrison's classic line "eruptions of funk"—our quareness exploded upon the ordinary life of childhood and made family and friendship all the more difficult, morphing them into the bittersweet tonic that many of us now refer to as "home"—a place of refuge and escape. Our quareness also brought many of us to the public library and ultimately to the university as we searched for reflections of ourselves and began to find them tucked away in the Harlem Renaissance, embedded in second-wave feminism, and nestled at the heart of the civil rights struggle. The more we saw, the more we understood ourselves as backbone rather than anomaly; as producing the very friction necessary for "culture" to survive. And somewhere in there we learned to be quare, black, and proud. The scholars in this collection and at the conference struggled with the impossibility of representing blackness while simultaneously critiquing its adequacy as a signifier of a people and their cultural productions. This collection reminds those of us still working in and around the boundaries of quare studies of the necessity for our work. Home *is* a four-letter word and the practice of black queer/quare studies embodies all of its double meanings.

On the way to the airport, I took a detour past my grandmother's house with its magical grove of pine trees on one side and its ornery crabapple tree in the backyard. The tree was both lookout post (from its branches we could see the Q-Dogs stepping on the field of the local high school) and menace, as over the course of a decade each cousin fell from it, ran into it, or punctured himself or herself on one of its tree house nails, put there by one of our parents in their youth, no doubt. I rode past North Carolina Central University, where my grandfather once was an English and Latin Professor, and then traveled toward the A.M.E. Zion Church and remembered the uncomfortable dresses and the itchy stockings, along with the black women with perfumed bodies and plenty of juicy fruit gum in their purses in case you started "acting up." Quare even then, I never got the spirit everyone around me so passionately possessed, and when I turned twelve I told my mother that I couldn't go to church any longer. After we struck some kind of bargain, she let me spend my Sunday mornings with Johnny Weissmuller, Maureen O'Hara, Abbott and Costello, Bette Davis, and Joan Crawford; she left me to my queer pleasures. As I continued my trek out of Durham I stopped downtown at the Mutual Life Insurance building, a company my grandfather had helped to "raise up." Although I had been a vegetarian for some years, I pulled into the Winn-Dixie parking lot and headed for the breakfast meat aisle. God, I missed liver pudding. I fingered the plastic wrapping and thought about my first lesson in how to cook the mystery meat.

I must have been in a trance, because a woman behind me said, "Are you going to buy that meat, sugar, or are you going to look at it all afternoon instead?" I turned around and we laughed together as she patted my arm sympathetically and reached for a package. On the plane I finally understood the last line of *Absalom, Absalom!,* and I muttered "I don't hate it, I don't hate it" as we cut through cumulus clouds climbing to twenty-six thousand feet.

E. PATRICK JOHNSON AND
MAE G. HENDERSON

INTRODUCTION:

QUEERING BLACK STUDIES/

"QUARING" QUEER STUDIES

Black Queer Studies serves as a critical intervention in the discourses of black studies and queer studies. In seeking to interanimate both black studies and queer studies, this volume stages a dialogic and dialectic encounter between these two liberatory and interrogatory discourses. Our objective here is to build a bridge and negotiate a space of inquiry between these two fields of study while sabotaging neither and enabling both. To this end, we have put into dialogue a group of critics, writers, scholars, and cultural producers whose work links the twentieth-century achievements of black studies—a field that came of age in the 1970s and 1980s—with that of the still-emergent field of queer studies. The essays collected here reflect the scholarship of a broad range of theorists and cultural workers who principally engage black lesbian, gay, bisexual, and transgender studies. Many of these essays were first presented at the Black Queer Studies in the Millennium conference held at the University of North Carolina, Chapel Hill on April 4–6, 2000. But for the sake of inclusiveness, some essays not presented at the conference but representing the work of the attendees have been incorporated; and still others have been added to broaden and complement the disciplinary and methodological range and scope of the collection.

Although these essays span diverse disciplines and deploy multiple methodologies, they only begin to mine the rich theoretical terrain of black studies as it intersects with queer studies. Notably, many of the authors included in this volume are in the humanities as opposed to the social sciences, a bias that is a reflection of the background of the editors rather than a deliberate omission. Our goal, however, is to make disciplinary boundaries more permeable and thereby encourage border crossings between the humanities and social sciences. As such, the focus of inquiry here tends to be less on the formal disciplinary training of our contributors and more on the interdisciplinary intellectual content of their scholarship. Nevertheless, while some authors write from paradigms reflecting a perspective and training in the social sciences and/or the humanities, others deploy social science methodologies despite their affiliation with the humanities. Moreover, much of the interventionist work in the areas of race and sexuality has come out of the humanities and not the social sciences. Indeed, social science fields such as sociology have often been antagonistic toward African American culture and nonnormative sexualities in ways that have, according to Roderick Ferguson, "excluded and disciplined those formations that deviate from the racial ideal of heteropatriarchy."[1]

This collection of essays, then, represents a diverse range of critical and theoretical postures as well as a cross-section of disciplinary and interdisciplinary perspectives, including English literature, film studies, black studies, sociology, history, political science, legal studies, cultural studies, performance studies, creative writing, and pedagogical studies. More specifically, this volume is intended to provide students, scholars, and teachers with critical insight into the various and multiple intersections of race, class, gender, and sexuality as each section addresses issues of institutional, disciplinary, and interdisciplinary formations, including public policy, performance studies, pedagogical praxis, literary studies, and cultural studies. In addition, we hope that these dialogues will provide insight into the category of "queer" in raced communities outside the academy.

In its current configuration, the volume's content is clearly centered within the regional context of the United States. Nonetheless, we are aware of the very important implications of diaspora and postcolonial studies relative to black American sexuality. We are also conscious of the sometimes narcissistic and insular theorizing of U.S.-based academics who do not thoroughly engage the impact of globalization and U.S. imperialism on the transnational flows of racialized sexuality. Indeed, in his essay in this volume Rinaldo Walcott advocates a "diaspora reading practice" that would push the black studies project beyond a " 'neat' national project" and suggests that black diaspora queers have already begun to push some of those boundaries. Mindful of Walcott's critique of black studies' nationalism, our focus here primarily on U.S. racialized sexual politics is not meant to be totalizing or polemic but rather strategic. Black queer studies is a nascent field and we feel compelled to prioritize a concomitant embryonic theoretical discussion within U.S. borders in order to make an intervention "at home," as it were. What follows, then, is a brief history aimed at exposing the ways in which black studies and queer studies have heretofore eclipsed each other. The ultimate goal here is to demonstrate how both might be pressed into the service of a larger project—one imbricating race, class, gender, and sexuality.

Variously named "black studies," "Afro-American studies," "Africana studies" and "African American studies," programs and departments demarcating this disciplinary formation emerged in the late 1960s and early 1970s, due largely to the efforts of black students and faculty who petitioned, sat in, protested, and otherwise brought pressure to bear on white administrators at predominately white institutions of higher learning around the United States. After marking over thirty years of academic institutionalization, many of these departments and programs now assume leading roles in shaping canons and intellectual currents, as well as the main corpus of research on race in the United States and the diaspora. Not coincidentally, the Civil Rights and Black Power movements of this period provided the historical backdrop and social street scene fueling the interventions staged on the manicured lawns of the ivory tower. Nor was it a coincidence that the political and rhetorical strategies of the larger race and rights movement were deployed by intellectual and cultural activists demanding institutional support for the formation of black studies. Unfortunately, it was precisely this discursive maneuvering—largely formulated by the dominant black male leadership—that provided the anchor for an exclusionary agenda that effectively cordoned off all identity categories that were not primarily based on race.

Most conspicuous in these race-based arrangements, perhaps, was the manifestation of a distinct gender-sex hierarchy. Black heterosexual male leadership in the black studies movement either ignored or relegated to secondary status the experiences and contributions of black women who most often were expected to "stand by their men" in the academic struggle for race rights. Such blatant sexism and, in some cases, downright misogyny in the academy occluded the specificity of black women's experiences and contributions to and within black studies, at the level of both departmental formations and programs of study. Black women's institutional work as well as intellectual interventions in black studies departments remained understudied, devalued, or marginalized by the reigning black male theorists who deemed "race" to be the proper sphere of study.

Black feminist theorists, including Alice Walker, Gloria T. Hull, Patricia Bell Scott, Barbara Smith, Cheryl Clarke, Audre Lorde, Toni Cade Bambara, and Angela Davis, among others, worked to fill in the lacunae created by the omission of black women from the historical narrative of black studies. Notably, more than a few of these early interventionists were lesbians who sought not only to combat the sexism and homophobia within the Civil Rights and black studies movements, but also the racism and sexism within emergent women's rights and feminist studies movements. Gloria T. Hull, Patricia Bell Scott, and Barbara Smith's anthology, *All the Women Are White, All the Blacks Are Men, But Some of Us Are Brave* (1982), captures the status of black women within black studies and women's studies in the early days of their disciplinary formations.

Given the status of women (and class not lagging too far behind) within black studies, it is not surprising that sexuality, and especially homosexuality, became not only a repressed site of study within the field, but also one with which the discourse was paradoxically preoccupied, if only to deny and disavow its place in the discursive sphere of black studies. On the one hand, the category of (homo)sexuality, like those of gender and class, remained necessarily subordinated to that of race in the discourse of black studies, due principally to an identitarian politics aimed at forging a unified front under racialized blackness. On the other hand, the privileging of a racialist discourse demanded the deployment of a sexist and homophobic rhetoric in order to mark, by contrast, the priority of race. While black (heterosexual) women's intellectual and community work were marginalized, if not erased, homosexuality was effectively "theorized" as a "white disease" that had "infected" the black community.[2] In fact, sexuality as an object of discourse circulated mainly by way of defensive disavowals of "sexual deviance," frequently framed by outspoken heterosexual black male intellectuals theorizing the "black male phallus" in relation to "the black (w)hole" and other priapic riffs sounding the legendary potency of the heterosexual black man or, alternatively, bewailing his historical emasculation at the hands of overbearing and domineering black women.[3] It would be some time, as Audre Lorde discovered in the bars of New York during her sexual awakening, before black studies would come "to realize that [its] place was the very house of difference rather than the security of any one particular difference."[4]

Codified as a disciplinary discourse some twenty years later than black studies, queer studies—like black studies and feminist studies—emerged in the academy as the intellectual counterpart and component of another activist movement, namely that of ACT-UP, an AIDS activist group, and its off-shoot group Queer Nation. The political strategies of Queer Nation were strikingly similar to those employed in the Civil Rights movement, in that in its aim to speak to and on behalf of the oppression of sexual dissidents, other identity markers remained subordinated, if not erased. And, like the essentially identitarian politics propelling its political counterpart, queer studies/theory tended toward totalization and homogenization as well. Again, however, interventions by feminist theorists like Eve Sedgwick, Sue-Ellen Case, Diana Fuss, Teresa de Lauretis, and Judith Butler, to name a few, sought to correct queer theory's myopia by broadening its analytic lens to include a focus on gender.[5] Whether queer theory "engenders" difference (gay vs. lesbian) or "ungenders" ("queers") difference, it is not assured, according to social theorist Scott Bravmann, "that we will see the multiple social differences which are always there right alongside of gender and which are themselves integral to sexual identities and the performativity of gender."[6] Further, as Lisa Duggan reminds us, "any gay politics based on the primacy of sexual identity defined as unitary and 'essential,' residing clearly, intelligibly and unalterably in the body or psyche, and fixing desire in a gendered direction, ultimately represents the view from the subject position '20th-century Western white gay male.' "[7] In other words, essentialist identity politics often reinforces hegemonic power structures rather than dismantling them.

Despite its theoretical and political shortcomings, queer studies, like black studies, disrupts dominant and hegemonic discourses by consistently destabilizing fixed notions of identity by deconstructing binaries such as heterosexual/homosexual, gay/lesbian, and masculine/feminine as well as the concept of heteronormativity in general. Given its currency in the academic marketplace, then, queer studies has the potential to transform how we theorize sexuality in conjunction with other identity formations.[8] Yet, as some theorists have noted, the deconstruction of binaries and the explicit "unmarking" of difference (e.g., gender, race, class, region, able-bodiedness, etc.) have serious implications for those for whom these other differences "matter."[9] Lesbians, gays, bisexuals, and transgendered people of color who are committed to the demise of oppression in its various forms, cannot afford to theorize their lives based on "single-variable" politics. As many of the essays in this volume demonstrate, to ignore the multiple subjectivities of the minoritarian subject within and without political movements and theoretical paradigms is not only theoretically and politically naive, but also potentially dangerous. In the context of an expansive American imperialism in which the separation of church and state (if they ever really were separate) remains so only by the most tenuous membrane and in which a sitting president homophobically refers to as "sinners" certain U.S. citizens seeking the protection of marriage, the so-called axis of evil is likely to cut across every identity category that is not marked white, Anglo-Saxon, Protestant, heterosexual, American, and male.

Thus, we hope that the interanimation of these two disciplines—black studies and queer studies—whose roots are similarly grounded in social and political activism, carries the potential to overcome the myopic theorizing that has too often sabotaged or subverted long-term and mutually liberatory goals. As a productive and progressive political and analytical paradigm, the intersectionality of black and queer studies marks not only a Kuhnian paradigm shift, but also a generational shift mandated by the complexity of contemporary subjectivities. Monolithic identity formations, like monologic perspectives, cannot survive the crisis of (post)modernity. In today's cultural marketplace, the imperatives of race and sexuality must give way to messier but more progressive stratagems of contestation and survival. Therefore, as we see it, our project here is fundamentally a liberatory one—in the sense that it is grounded in the assertion of individual rights balanced by communal accountability in the interest of ensuring social justice. And "social justice inclusive of sexuality," argues Mark Blasius, "can only be conceptualized or enacted from explicit recognition of the relationships between sexual oppression and the oppression of other disenfranchised groups and coalition with them on the basis of our intersecting identities of class, gender, age, sexual orientation, 'able'- (and desirable-) bodiedness, race, and ethnicity, among others."[10] Toward this aim, our collection seeks to enlist the strategies, methodologies, and insights of black studies into the service of queer studies and vice versa.

Further, we seek to animate this dialogic/dialectic "kinship" by mobilizing the tensions embedded in the conjunction of "black" and "queer" in the title of this volume. Some have suggested that the conjoining of the modifier "black" to the noun "queer" potentially subverts the governing concept organizing the notion of "queer." Michael Warner, for example, suggests that "queer" represents "an aggressive impulse of generalization; [that] it rejects a minoritizing logic of toleration or simple political interest-representation in favor of a more thorough resistance to regimes of the normal."[11] Arguably, then, the attachment of the modifier risks reinstalling boundaries of exclusion in a project that professes as its goal the notion of broad inclusivity.

Nonetheless—and at the risk of seeming to create divisiveness when unity and community are the overriding goals—we believe that the term "black queer" captures and, in effect, names the specificity of the historical and cultural differences that shape the experiences and expressions of "queerness." Just as Warner argues that "people want to make theory queer, not just have a theory about queers," we want to *quare* queer—to throw shade on its meaning in the spirit of extending its service to "blackness."[12] Further, we believe that there are compelling social and political reasons to lay claim to the modifier "black" in "black queer." Both terms, of course, are markers or signifiers of difference: just as "queer" challenges notions of heteronormativity and heterosexism, "black" resists notions of assimilation and absorption. And so we endorse the double cross of affirming the inclusivity mobilized under the sign of "queer" while claiming the racial, historical, and cultural specificity attached to the marker "black."

This volume is divided into four parts, each of which activates the tensions between "black" and "queer."In the first part, "Disciplinary Tensions: Black Studies/Queer Studies," the essays explore the ways in which black studies has historically elided issues of (homo)sexuality and/or how queer studies has elided issues of race. The authors address this topic from different perspectives, including the examination of specific historical moments in the formation of both disciplines; as well as the interrogation of the "value" lodged and embedded in the terms that "overdetermine" their signification or offer trajectories for what we designate as "black queer studies" or black "gay" studies, if it turns out that "queer" does not signal the inclusiveness it proposes. The authors also question the effectiveness of queer studies in addressing issues of public policy that have had a direct impact on gays, lesbians, bisexuals, and transgendered people of color. The authors address how race does or does not factor into queer political organizing, how issues of poverty, homelessness, and health care affect the black gay community, and how institutional social science disciplinary formations further veify racial and sexual exclusionary practices.

Part 1 opens with Cathy Cohen's "Punks, Bulldaggers, and Welfare Queens: The Radical Potential of Queer Politics?" which explores the ways that queer theorists and queer activists, in an effort to deconstruct and challenge seemingly stable and normalizing categories of sexuality, have at times reinforced an ineffective and deceptive dichotomy between heterosexual and "queer." Despite claims to complicate our understanding of sexuality in general, including the category "heterosexual," some queer theorists, in particular queer activists, write and act in ways that homogenize everything that is publicly identifiable as heterosexual and most things that are understood to be "queer." What is left unexamined, according to Cohen, is the true distribution of power and privilege within these categories and how access to dominant power and resources structures the politics and radical possibilities of subjects existing on both sides of this dichotomy. Ultimately, Cohen is interested in the process through which we construct a politics that is truly liberating and transformative, inclusive of all those who stand on the (out)side of the dominant normalized ideal of state-sanctioned, white, middle- and upper-class male heterosexuality. Thus, central to this new politics is an understanding of the ways in which, for instance, race, class, and/or gender interact with sexuality to destabilize a monolithic understanding of such labels/categories as gay, heterosexual, or queer.

Roderick A. Ferguson directs focus away from queer activist formations of power and, therefore, exclusionary practices, and toward disciplinary formations and acts of power. In his "Race-ing Homonormativity: Citizenship, Sociology, and Gay Identity," Ferguson provides a genealogical critique of sexuality as a social construction. Ferguson accepts the claim made by queer sociologists that the discipline of sociology preceded queer studies and cultural studies in articulating the notion of sexuality as a social construction, but he challenges this focus on sexuality as a milestone for the discipline. Instead, he argues, the idea of sexuality as a social construction was invented within the category of ethnicity, which, rather than providing an alternative to race, articulated racial privilege and advanced racial exclusion. Ethnicity, argues Ferguson, transformed previously nonwhite immigrants into white Americans who were eligible for intermarriage with native-born whites. Sexuality as social construction, then, meant that these new immigrants could attain normative sexual and racial status and, therefore, embody American citizenship. Such a genealogy is important if we are to understand contemporary sexual formations, especially among gays and lesbians. Even in this historical moment, sexuality as social construction becomes a way of announcing the assimilability—and thus normativity—of white middle- and upper-class homosexuals as well as a means of excluding working-class and nonwhite queers on the basis of their inability to conform to normative ideals of American citizenship.

Dwight A. McBride's essay, "Straight Black Studies: On African American Studies, James Baldwin, and Black Queer Studies," seeks to account for the heterosexist strain in African Americanist discourse by considering the hegemony of the institutional politics of respectability while, at the same time, attempting to understand this contested history as part of the unstable past for the emergent discourse of black queer studies. McBride first considers Essex Hemphill, which he follows with a discussion of the centrality of James Baldwin to the vision of a usable past for black queer studies. Finally, he considers some of the challenges this emergent discourse poses to dominant constructions of African American studies as an institutional formation.

Overlapping with McBride's call for a "usable past of black studies," Rinaldo Walcott's essay, "Outside in Black Studies: Reading from a Queer Place in the Diaspora," adds to the black studies/queer studies binary a third disciplinary configuration, diaspora studies, to form a theoretical triumvirate. More specifically, Walcott's essay addresses the question of "respectability" in black studies' encounter with the erotics of black queer studies. Walcott suggests that an erotics of pedagogy or the lack thereof is one of the central concerns for thinking through the politics and pedagogy of black queer studies. Walcott also promotes the potential for black queer studies, to rejuvenate the liberatory possibilities of the black studies project. Alternatively, Walcott suggests that the possibilities of queer studies, as encompassed within black studies, can only act to elaborate the terms of a potential liberation because queer studies disrupts the current agenda of the black studies project by inserting new and different positions. Indeed, Walcott argues that queer positions open up blind spots and offer other ways of seeing that are instructive to the larger questions of blackness. Similarly, black studies offers a corrective for queer studies. In fact, since it is fairly evident that queer studies takes many of its founding mandates from the model of the black studies movements of the 1960s—in particular the constitution of its subjects of study as a minority—it is important to emphasize that black studies can also work to preserve the pertinence of questions of racial difference and its various class formations to a project that has quickly become a "white queer studies project."

Phillip Brian Harper's "The Evidence of Felt Intuition: Minority Experience, Everyday Life, and Critical Speculative Knowledge" focuses on anecdotes of the author's personal experiences both within and outside the academy. In this essay, Harper argues that the social and political import of minority identity must inevitably be teased out from the minority subject's intuitive suspicion concerning his or her treatment during specific encounters with others. Indeed, Harper argues that the very existence of such suspicion itself is a function of the minority condition. Rather than rejecting this intuitive knowledge as unacceptably "subjective" for the purposes of critical analysis, however, Harper insists that this aspect of minority experience—which derives from nonnormative racial and sexual identities—is a crucial element within the body of "speculative critical knowledge" that arguably comprises all social, cultural, and political critique.

E. Patrick Johnson's essay, "'Quare' Studies, or (Almost) Everything I Know about Queer Studies I Learned from My Grandmother," shifts the focus from the internal occlusions of sexuality within black studies to the racial and class occlusions within queer studies. In the tradition of black feminist critic Barbara Smith, Johnson's essay is a manifesto advocating a reconceptualization of queer studies—one that explicitly takes into account suppressed racial and class knowledges. In redefining "queer" as "quare"—his grandmother's black-dialect inflected pronunciation of "queer"—Johnson seeks to broaden the paradigmatic, theoretical, and epistemological scope of queer studies to include issues facing queers of color who also belong to racialized and classed communities. Johnson argues for a return to a "body politic" that neither reduces identity to a monolithic whole based on an essentialist notion of race or gender, nor elides issues of materiality in which the body becomes the site of trauma (e.g., the site at which racist, sexist, and homophobic violence is enacted). In the course of redefining queer as a concept, the author invokes examples of how (white) queer critics have eluded the question of race in the name of queer theory and how their readings of black queer cultural production are designed, in fact, to fortify the hegemony of white queer subjectivity.

Part 2 of this volume, "Representing the 'Race': Blackness, Queers, and the Politics of Visibility" explores the ways in which the black queer body signifies within the American imaginary. The essays here focus specifically on the ways in which blackness and queerness intersect in relation to visual economies undergirded by a politics of visibility that sometimes does and sometimes does not accommodate cultural as well as material privilege both within and outside queer communities. The authors engage these issues by examining the theoretical and political implications of the closet, the politics of outing oneself as a privileged heterosexual, the strategies by which we read queer black bodies and the politics that such readings configure, and the occlusion of black (homo)sexuality in mainstream gay and lesbian film. Opening this discussion is Marlon B. Ross's essay, "Beyond the Closet as Raceless Paradigm," in which he considers the ways in which the image and concept of the closet, as it has been articulated instrumentally in queer history and theory, constructs a racially loaded paradigm of same-sex desire, sexuality, and community. The closet paradigm, argues Ross, locates homosexual identification because it enables a powerful narrative of progress in terms both of the psychosexual development of the individual and of the sociopolitical formation of a legitimate sexual minority group. The closet defines sexual identity as a threshold experience in which one side of the door harbors deprivation and dispossession, while the other side reveals the potential for psychosexual fulfillment and cultural belonging. To be "closeted," then, is to be silenced and invisible and thus disempowered; to come out of the closet, in contrast, is to assume voice and accountability as well as empowerment. Thus, Ross queries an ideology of the closet as a master paradigm for same-sexual identification and, more specifically, a racial ideology operating in our appeals to the closet. Next, Ross theorizes what happens when the closet is applied as though its operation has no dependence on racial difference or no stake in acts of racial discrimination. Exploring queer theory and queer historiography as it relates to this query, Ross examines Michel Foucault's historical reconstruction of the modern invention of the homosexual as an anatomical object of sexological investigation in order to understand the racial implications of his historical claims as locally—and thus racially—situated.

Devon Carbado's project in "Privilege" is to promote a shift in—or at least a broadening of—our conceptualization of discrimination. In general, Carbado aims to expand the notion of what it means to be a perpetrator of discrimination by focusing on those who unquestionably accept their own racial, gender, and heterosexual privileges as well as those who fail to acknowledge their own victimless status vis-à-vis racism, sexism, and homophobia. In arguing that male feminism should focus on challenging male (especially male heterosexual) privilege, Carbado sets forth a strategy by which men can identify and thereby resist privilege, offering tentative suggestions on how such strategies might be deployed.

Kara Keeling's " 'Joining the Lesbians': Cinematic Regimes of Black Lesbian Visibility" moves away from the theoretical and cultural politics of visibility to its representation in film. Keeling begins with an examination of how, historically, black queer filmmakers have engaged the project of "making visible" that which has been rendered invisible and silenced. By honing in specifically on the category of the "black lesbian" and her representation in "black lesbian film," Keeling theorizes the process by which film representations of black queer women unproblematically reify the category "black lesbian" as if it were a priori, often excluding elements of this same identity that might counter discourses that seek the black lesbian's demise. Through her reading of Cheryl Dunye's film *The Watermelon Woman*, Keeling demonstrates what must be made invisible for the "black lesbian" to become "visible," examining the politics of such a move. Ultimately, Keeling argues that the images that have been purged from "the visible" nevertheless retain the potential to unsettle the hegemonic scopic order and the "common sense" that maintains them intact, although they remain always already vulnerable within the dominant order.

Turning from the black lesbian body to the black gay male body, Charles I. Nero's "Why Are Gay Ghettoes White?" opens by postulating that one of the paradoxes of contemporary gay male life is that homosexuality is considered pancultural, multiclassed, and multiracial even while the overwhelming "whiteness" of the "gay ghettoes" contradicts this reality. Further, although critics and scholars comment continuously on this paradox, none, argues Nero, offers even a plausible explanation for it. This discourse of authenticity, as it were, contains the ubiquitous rhetorical figure of the black gay impostor, which Nero examines in films and dramas by white gay and straight filmmakers and dramatists. Nero speculates here that the figure of the black gay impostor conceals the gay ghettoes as sites where racial formation occurs by naturalizing and normalizing the exclusion of black gay men. In this sense, the black gay impostor serves a function similar to the "controlling images" of black women that Patricia Hill Collins identifies in the discourse of elite white males (and their spokespersons). As a controlling image of black gay men, the impostor, finally, mediates the paradoxical coexistence of universal homosexuality with homogeneous gay neighborhoods. The impostor signifies a black presence, while, simultaneously, deflecting attention away from the exclusionary practices of racial formation.

Part 3 of this book, "How to Teach the Unspeakable: Race, Queer Studies, and Pedagogy," engages the issue of how integrating the study of sexuality into the classroom complicates a space that is always already fraught with erotic tensions and negotiations of power. These studies, in different ways, ask what is at stake when black queer pedagogy is mobilized in the academy. The authors in this section engage issues including the politics of outing oneself (or not) to students; how race and sexuality converge and diverge in the classroom space; how to negotiate the erotic tension in the lesbian and gay studies classroom; and the politics of offering "queer" readings of presumably "straight" black texts. In "Embracing the Teachable Moment: The

Black Gay Body in the Classroom as Embodied Text," Bryant Keith Alexander explores the "tensive" negotiation between the subject positions defined by the black gay male as teacher and that of teaching through the issues of race, culture, and gender. Alexander's essay struggles with notions of representation, voice, and imperialism in the classroom through its figuration of the black gay body as a "performed"—and, indeed, "embodied" text—signifying in the space of the classroom in multiple and complex ways. And although Alexander offers anecdotal and theoretical evidence from his courses on performance in support of his position, he chooses to conclude with the question: How can one *not* not teach about race and sexuality when one's very presence signals a teachable moment?

Assuming an alternate stance on the politics of pedagogy, at least in terms of taking for granted the queer professor's openness about his sexuality, Keith Clark's essay, "Are We Family? Pedagogy and the Race for Queerness," addresses, head-on, the politics of "outing" oneself in the classroom. By narrating his discomfort at the prospect of revealing his own sexuality to students, Clark ponders the pedagogical value of treading the dangerous waters of what it means to attempt to personally authorize the narratives of gayness and thereby risk essentializing homo(sexuality) in troubling ways. While still committed to unearthing same-gender-loving, or homoerotic, subtexts in African American literature, Clark cautions against pedagogical policing whereby the instructor proscribes and censures students in an effort to foster a "hate-free" atmosphere. Instead, he suggests, such censorship precludes invaluable teaching moments. Ultimately, Clark urges that we not allow the "race for queerness," or an official, sanctioned queer pedagogical discourse mandating the prioritizing of one identity over another, to eclipse questions of racial/ethnic affiliation, class struggle, and gender by re-closeting the complexity of identity in order to secure an unencumbered queer authenticity.

Maurice O. Wallace's essay, "On Being a Witness: Passion, Pedagogy, and the Legacy of James Baldwin," begins where Keith Clark's leaves off by examining, through a close reading of Baldwin, the knotty relations among black queer texts and the lives of black queer students. Through his reading of selected characters from Baldwin's fiction, viewed in the context of the author's equivocation on matters pertaining to Baldwin's own sexuality, Wallace works through the unpredictable nuances between the pedagogical practices that construct black gay and lesbian studies as a body of knowledge (a field of intellectual inquiry and consumption) and the pedagogical assumption of responsibility for the black gay, lesbian, or bisexual student to protect their socio-intellectual freedom. Wallace concludes his essay with a call for a pedagogical praxis, albeit theoretically "queer," in the sense of the term's recent, although contested, signification of a plurality of dissident sexualities and sex acts. Indeed, the author argues for a pedagogical praxis that is dialogically creative, necessarily undisciplined, and "misbehavedly" liberatory.

The authors of the essays in part 4, "Black Queer Fiction: Who Is 'Reading' Us?," perform readings of black queer literature, focusing on contemporary and earlier texts by both acclaimed and less well-known authors. While affirming the existence of a long-standing black gay and lesbian literary impulse in African American literature, critics have argued that a recognition of this aspect of the tradition remains well overdue. In a call for the recognition of this neglected but ever-growing tradition, the critics in this section focus on texts that are currently deemed noncanonical. In "But Some of Us Are Lesbians: The Absence of Black Lesbian Fiction," black lesbian essayist and fiction writer Jewell Gomez argues that the current climate of conglomerate book publishing, distribution, and sales has contributed significantly to the inaudibility of the black lesbian voice that was so expressive in the 1970s and 1980s. According to Gomez, black lesbian literature, and fiction in particular, has been marginalized largely as a result of the increasing popularity of nonfiction in the academy, a shift in focus that has rendered black lesbian voices less accessible in the classroom curriculum. By tracing the historical roots of black lesbian fiction and by demonstrating, along the way, the important contributions of the genre of lesbian fiction to the black literary tradition in general, Gomez demands not only critical attention to, but also the proliferation of, black lesbian fiction through increased publication. The inevitable question that Gomez ponders is how will the readers of tomorrow recognize great black lesbian literature if it is only talked about and not published?

In "James Baldwin's *Giovanni's Room*: Expatriation, 'Racial Drag,' and Homosexual Panic," Mae G. Henderson explores the relation between geographical expatriation, racial "drag," the construction of American nationality and masculinity, and "homosexual panic." By assuming a posture of literary "whiteface," Henderson argues, Baldwin is able to launch a critique of dominant ideologies and constructions of nationality and masculinity, assuming—but not naming—whiteness as a category. Such a narrative strategy not only demonstrates the author's insight into the social and psychological spaces inhabited by whiteness, but also enables Baldwin to avoid provoking white anxieties around issues of race and race relations. Finally, concludes Henderson, Baldwin's strategy of "narrative passing" constitutes the formal counterpart to his thematic of "sexual passing," just as his strategy of authorial race-crossing has its counterpart in a narrative of cultural and national boundary-crossing. In reading Baldwin's 1950s novel *Giovanni's Room* against his 1940s essay "Preservation of Innocence," Henderson argues that the novel constitutes a fictional enactment and elaboration of the author's critique of the "hardboiled" masculinity depicted in American World War II noir fiction. While insisting on the cultural critique of dominant constructions of gender and gender ideology implicit in Baldwin's text, Henderson also renders a modernist reading recuperating the "literariness" of the text by locating it in intertextual and revisionary relation to F. Scott Fitzgerald's great modernist classic *The Great Gatsby* and the traditional thematics of Jamesian American "innocence."

Faedra Chatard Carpenter takes up the issues of race and sexuality as represented in Robert O'Hara's contemporary play *Insurrection: Holding History* (1999). In her essay, "Robert O'Hara's *Insurrection*: 'Que(e)rying History,'" Carpenter explores how O'Hara's play uses a queer theoretical paradigm to explore the inherent capaciousness of historical narratives and to dismantle the monolithic authority of "normalizing ideologies." In O'Hara's play, Ron, a gay African American graduate student, is transported back into time to Nat Turner's slave rebellion. His journey, and the paradigm it inscribes, allow O'Hara to critique the notion of a "real" or "authentic" history, offering instead a perception of history's inherent "queerness"—its varied interpretations, textuality, and multiplicity. By intersecting issues of time, place, space, and perspective, O'Hara contests traditional notions of both history and identity by challenging the compulsive heteronormative acceptance of "authentic" historical narratives and their assumptions regarding classifications of race, sex, and gender. Further, Carpenter argues that O'Hara's deployment of history, language, dramatic form, and character is punctuated with the aesthetic of "camp" to directly combat traditional perceptions of what is historically "real." In so doing, O'Hara simultaneously "queers" any singular, authoritative notion of racial and sexual identity. In her analysis of O'Hara's play, Carpenter demonstrates queer theory's potential to encompass—and thereby usurp—the critical modes utilized in the studies of other marginalized voices.

The essays collected here not only blur boundaries by queering and querying the foundational modes of knowledge production in the academy and beyond, but also seek to specify some of the borders framing black gay, lesbian, bisexual, and transgendered critical analysis. The creative and imaginative strategies with which black queers negotiate the two epistemological sites of queerness and blackness are matched only by the rigor and seriousness with which the scholars in this volume approach their objects of inquiry. The editors are aware that these essays and their authors owe much to the generations on whose work and lived experiences we build to construct a *quare* tradition. And while these essays honor those long since gone and those yet unborn—those who have and those who will dare to break with "traditions" that would constrain individual freedoms—the critics and theorists whose work is presented here caution us always to be wary of political, social, and cultural institutions and practices that maintain the status quo and that portend our marginalization and silence.

NOTES

1. Roderick A. Ferguson, *Aberrations in Black: Toward a Queer of Color Critique* (Minneapolis: University of Minnesota Press, 2003), 18.

2. See Eldridge Cleaver, *Soul on Ice* (New York: Laurel, 1968); George Jackson, *Soledad Brother: The Prison Letters of George Jackson* (New York: Bantam Books, 1970); and Haki Madhubuti, *Black Men: Obsolete, Single, Dangerous? The Afrikan American in Transition: Essays in Discovery, Solution, and Hope* (Chicago: Third World Press, 1990).

3. See Houston A. Baker Jr., *Blues, Ideology, and Afro-American Literature* (Chicago: University of Chicago Press, 1984), 113–99; Cleaver, *Soul on Ice*; Jackson, *Soledad Brother*; and Madhubuti, *Black Men*.

4. Audre Lorde, *Zami: A New Spelling of My Name* (Watertown, Mass.: Persephone Press, 1982), 226.

5. See Scott Bravmann, *Queer Fictions of the Past: History, Culture, and Difference* (Cambridge: Cambridge University Press, 1997), 16–19.

6. Ibid, 21.

7. Lisa Duggan, "Making It Perfectly Queer," *Socialist Review* (1992): 1.

8. In recent years there have been a number of critical anthologies published that focus on either gay and lesbian or "queer" studies, including Henry Abelove, Michelé Aina Barale, and David Halperin, *The Gay and Lesbian Reader* (New York: Routledge, 1993); Joseph Bristow and Angelia R. Wilson, *Activating Theory* (London: Lawrence and Wishart, 1993); Brett Beemyn and Mickey Eliason, *Queer Studies* (New York: New York University Press, 1996); Donald Morton, *The Material Queer* (Boulder: Westview, 1996); and Martin Duberman, *Queer Representations* (New York: New York University Press, 1997). While all of these volumes contain sections on "identity" or present a few token essays by and/or about queers of color, none includes race as an integral component of its analysis.

Other relevant works in the field include Andy Mudhurst and Sally R. Munt's *Lesbian and Gay Studies: A Critical Introduction* (London: Cassell, 1997), a guide defining literary and critical terms in queer studies; Larry Gross and James D. Wood's *The Columbia Reader on Lesbians and Gay Men in Media, Society, and Politics* (New York: Columbia University Press, 1999), an interesting, albeit eclectic, collection of essays that examines the status of lesbians and gays in the dominant culture and proposes strategies of popular and institutional resistance to this representation; Michael Warner's influential *Fear of a Queer Planet* (Minneapolis: University of Minnesota Press, 1993), a volume representing a diverse range of perspectives on the impact of gender and sexuality on politics, theory, and culture; Shane Phelan's *Playing with Fire* (New York: Routledge, 1997), an anthology exploring the intersection between progressive politics and political theory as it addresses issues of queer rights and identities in the context of nation and state; Corey K. Creekmur and Alexander Doty's *Out in Culture* (Durham: Duke University Press, 1995), which juxtaposes the voices of popular culture critics and producers alongside those of critics and theorists of popular culture; Gordon Brent Ingram, Anne-Marie Bouthillette, and Yolanda Retter's *Queers in Space* (Seattle: Bay Press, 1997), which theorizes the geopolitical places and spaces where queers live, work, and play; Thomas Foster, Carol Siegel, and Ellen E. Berry's *The Gay '90s: Disciplinary and Interdisciplinary Formations in Queer Studies* (New York: New York University Press, 1997), a volume that highlights the tensions between disciplinary and interdisciplinary approaches to queer studies and how they impact the formation of lesbian and gay studies in the academy; and, finally, Michael Lowenthal's *Gay Men at the Millennium* (New York: Penguin, 1997), which proposes a gender-specific approach to the study of queer theory and politics. Although these volumes contribute greatly to the discourses of queer theory, politics, and activism, they either omit race as a category of analysis or, in instances where race is represented, the treatment of it appears to be obligatory or at best perfunctory. And, as valuable as they are, even those volumes that address issues of race, class, and sexuality (e.g., Essex Hemphill's *Brother to Brother,* [Boston: Alyson, 1991] and Joseph Beam's *In the Life,* [Boston: Alyson, 1986]) run the risk of totalizing the black gay experience by privileging black gay men—to the exclusion of black lesbians.

9. See Bravmann, *Queer Fictions of the Past*; Mark Blasius, ed., *Sexual Identities, Queer Politics* (Princeton: Princeton University Press, 2001); and Steven Seidman, *Difference Troubles: Queering Social Theory and Sexual Politics* (Cambridge: Cambridge University Press, 1997).

10. Blasius, *Sexual Identities, Queer Politics*, 12.

11. Warner, *Fear of Queer Planet*, xxvi.

12. See Johnson's reconceptualization of "queer" as "quare" in his essay in this volume.

PART I

. . . .

DISCIPLINARY TENSIONS:

BLACK STUDIES/QUEER STUDIES

CATHY J. COHEN

PUNKS, BULLDAGGERS,

AND WELFARE QUEENS: THE RADICAL

POTENTIAL OF QUEER POLITICS?

On the eve of finishing this essay, my attention is focused not on how to rework the conclusion (as it should be) but instead on the news stories of alleged racism at Gay Men's Health Crisis (GMHC). It seems that three black board members of this largest and oldest AIDS organization in the world have resigned over their perceived subservient position on the GMHC board. Billy E. Jones, former head of the New York City Health and Hospitals Corporation and one of the board members who quit, was quoted in the *New York Times* as saying that "much work needs to be done at GMHC to make it truly inclusive and welcoming of diversity. . . . It is also clear that such work will be a great struggle. I am resigning because I do not choose to engage in such struggle at GMHC, but rather prefer to fight for the needs of those ravaged by H.I.V."[1]

This incident raises mixed emotions for me, for it points to the continuing practice of racism that many of us experience on a daily basis in lesbian and gay communities. But, just as disturbing, it also highlights the limits of a lesbian and gay political agenda based on a civil rights strategy, where assimilation into, and replication of, dominant institutions are the goals. Many of us continue to search for a new political direction and agenda, one that does not focus on integration into dominant structures but instead seeks to transform the basic fabric and hierarchies that allow systems of oppression to persist and operate efficiently. For some of us, such a challenge to traditional gay and lesbian politics was offered by the idea of queer politics. Here we had a potential movement of young antiassimilationist activists committed to challenging the very way that people understand and respond to sexuality.

These activists promised to engage in struggles that would disrupt dominant norms of sexuality, radically transforming politics in lesbian, gay, bisexual, and transgendered communities.

Despite the possibility invested in the idea of queerness and the practice of queer politics, I argue here that a truly radical or transformative politics has not resulted from queer activism. In many instances, instead of destabilizing the assumed categories and binaries of sexual identity, queer politics has served to reinforce simple dichotomies between the heterosexual and everything "queer." An understanding of the ways in which power informs and constitutes privileged and marginalized subjects on both sides of this dichotomy has been left unexamined.

I query in this essay whether there are lessons to be learned from queer activism that can help us construct a new politics. I envision a politics where one's relation to power, and not some homogenized identity, is privileged in determining one's political comrades. I am talking about a politics where the nonnormative and marginal position of punks, bulldaggers, and welfare queens, for example, is the basis for progressive transformative coalition work. Thus, if any truly radical potential is to be found in the idea of queerness and the practice of queer politics, it would seem to be located in its ability to create a space in opposition to dominant norms, a space where transformational political work can begin.

THE EMERGENCE OF QUEER POLITICS AND
A NEW POLITICS OF TRANSFORMATION

Theorists and activists alike generally agree that it was not until the early 1990s that the term "queer" began to be used with any regularity.[2] This term would come to denote not only an emerging politics but also a new cohort of academics working in programs primarily in the humanities centered around social and cultural criticism.[3] Individuals such as Judith Butler, Eve Sedgwick, Teresa de Lauretis, Diana Fuss, and Michael Warner produced what are now thought of as the first canonical works of "queer theory." Working from a variety of postmodernist and poststructuralist theoretical perspectives, these scholars focused on identifying and contesting the discursive and cultural markers found within both dominant and marginal identities and institutions that prescribe and reify "heterogendered" understandings and behavior.[4] These theorists presented a different conceptualization of sexuality, one that sought to replace socially named and presumably stable categories of sexual expression with a new fluid movement among and between forms of sexual behavior.[5]

Through its conception of a wide continuum of sexual possibilities, queer theory stands in direct contrast to the normalizing tendencies of hegemonic sexuality rooted in ideas of static, stable sexual identities and behaviors. In queer theorizing, the sexual subject is understood to be constructed and contained by multiple practices of categorization and regulation that systematically marginalize and oppress those subjects thereby defined as deviant and "other." And, at its best, queer theory focuses on and makes central not only the socially constructed nature of sexuality and sexual categories, but also the varying degrees and multiple sites of power distributed within all categories of sexuality, including the normative category of heterosexuality.

It was in the early 1990s, however, that the postmodern theory being produced in the academy (later to be recategorized as queer theory) found its most direct interaction with the real-life politics of lesbian, gay, bisexual, and transgendered activists. Frustrated with what was perceived to be the scientific "de-gaying" and assimilationist tendencies of AIDS activism, with their invisibility in the more traditional civil rights politics of lesbian and gay organizations, and with increasing legal and physical attacks against lesbian and gay community members, a new generation of activists began the process of building a more confrontational political formation, which they labeled "queer politics."[6] Queer politics, represented most notoriously in the actions of the group Queer Nation, is understood as an "in your face" politics of a younger generation. Through action and analysis these individuals seek to make "queer" function as more than just an abbreviation for lesbian, gay, bisexual, and transgendered. Similar to queer theory, the queer politics articulated and pursued by these activists first and foremost recognizes and encourages the fluidity and movement of people's sexual lives. In queer politics sexual expression is something that always entails the possibility of change, movement, redefinition, and subversive performance—from year to year, from partner to partner, from day to day, and even from act to act. In addition to highlighting the instability of sexual categories and sexual subjects, queer activists also directly challenge the multiple practices and vehicles of power that render them invisible and at risk. However, what seems to make queer activists unique, at this particular moment, is their willingness to confront normalizing power by emphasizing and exaggerating their own antinormative characteristics and nonstable behavior. Joshua Gamson, in "Must Identity Movements Self-Destruct? A Queer Dilemma," writes that queer activism and theory pose the challenge of a form of organizing in which, far from inhibiting accomplishments, the *destabilization* of collective identity is itself a goal and accomplishment of collective action. The assumption that stable collective identities are necessary for collective action is turned on its head by queerness, and the question becomes: When and how are stable collective identities necessary for social action and social change? Secure boundaries and stabilized identities are necessary not in general, but in the specific, a point social movement theory seems currently to miss.[7]

Thus queer politics, much like queer theory, is often perceived as standing in opposition, or in contrast, to the category-based identity politics of traditional lesbian and gay activism. And for those of us who find ourselves on the margins, operating through multiple identities and thus not fully served or recognized through traditional single-identity-based politics, theoretical conceptualizations of queerness hold great political promise. For many of us, the label "queer" symbolizes an acknowledgment that through our existence and everyday survival we embody sustained and multi-sited resistance to systems (based on dominant constructions of race and gender) that seek to normalize our sexuality, exploit our labor, and constrain our visibility. At the intersection of oppression and resistance lies the radical potential of queerness to challenge and bring together all those deemed marginal and all those committed to liberatory politics.

The problem, however, with such a conceptualization and expectation of queer identity and politics is that in its present form queer politics has not emerged as an encompassing challenge to systems of domination and oppression, especially those normalizing processes embedded in heteronormativity. By "heteronormativity" I mean both those localized practices and those centralized institutions that legitimize and privilege heterosexuality and heterosexual relationships as fundamental and "natural" within society. I raise the subject of heteronormativity because it is this normalizing practice/power that has most often been the focus of queer politics.[8]

The inability of queer politics to effectively challenge heteronormativity rests, in part, on the fact that despite a surrounding discourse that highlights the destabilization and even deconstruction of sexual categories, queer politics has often been built around a simple dichotomy between those deemed queer and those deemed heterosexual. Whether in the infamous "I Hate Straights" publication or in queer kiss-ins at malls and straight dance clubs, very near the surface in queer political action is an uncomplicated under-standing of power as it is encoded in sexual categories: all heterosexuals are represented as dominant and controlling and all queers are understood as marginalized and invisible. Thus, even in the name of destabilization, some queer activists have begun to prioritize sexuality as the primary frame through which they pursue their politics.[9] Undoubtedly, within different contexts various characteristics of our total being—for example, race, gender, class, sexuality—are highlighted or called on to make sense of a particular situation. However, my concern is centered on those individuals who consis-tently activate only one characteristic of their identity, or a single perspec-tive of consciousness, to organize their politics, rejecting any recognition of the multiple and intersecting systems of power that largely dictate our life chances.

The focus of this essay is the disjuncture, evident in queer politics, be-tween an articulated commitment to promoting an understanding of sexual-ity that rejects the idea of static, monolithic, bounded categories, on the one hand, and political practices structured around binary conceptions of sexual-ity and power, on the other. Specifically, I am concerned with those mani-festations of queer politics in which the capital and advantage invested in a range of sexual categories are disregarded and, as a result, narrow and ho-mogenized political identities are reproduced that inhibit the radical poten-tial of queer politics. It is my contention that queer activists who evoke a single-oppression framework misrepresent the distribution of power within and outside of gay, lesbian, bisexual, and transgendered communities, and therefore limit the comprehensive and transformational character of queer politics.

Recognizing the limits of current conceptions of queer identities and queer politics, I am interested in examining the concept of "queer" in order to think about how we might construct a new political identity that is truly liberating, transformative, and inclusive of all those who stand on the outside of the dominant constructed norm of state-sanctioned white middle- and upper-class heterosexuality.[10] Such a broadened understanding of queerness must be based on an intersectional analysis that recognizes how numerous systems of oppression interact to regulate and police the lives of most people. Black lesbian, bisexual, and heterosexual feminist authors such as Kimberle Crenshaw, Barbara Ransby, Angela Davis, Cheryl Clarke, and Audre Lorde have repeatedly emphasized in their writing the intersectional workings of oppression. And it is just such an understanding of the interlocking systems of domination that is noted in the opening paragraph of the now famous black feminist statement by the Combahee River Collective: "The most general statement of our politics at the present time would be that we are actively committed to struggling against racial, sexual, heterosexual, and class oppression and see as our particular task the development of *integrated* analysis and practice based upon the fact that the major systems of oppression are interlocking. The synthesis of these oppressions creates the conditions of our lives. As Black women we see Black feminism as the logical political movement to combat the manifold and simultaneous oppressions that all women of color face."[11] This analysis of an individual's place in the world, which focuses on the intersection of systems of oppression, is informed by a consciousness that undoubtedly grows from the lived experience of existing within and resisting multiple and connected practices of domination and normalization. Just such a lived experience and analysis have determined much of the progressive and expansive nature of the politics emanating from people of color—people who are both inside and outside of lesbian and gay communities.

However, beyond a mere recognition of the intersection of oppressions there must also be an understanding of the ways our multiple identities work to limit the entitlement and status that some receive from obeying a heterosexual imperative. For instance, how would queer activists understand politically the lives of women (particularly women of color) on welfare, who may fit into the category of heterosexual but whose sexual choices are not perceived as normal, moral, or worthy of state support? Further, how do queer activists understand and relate politically to those whose same-sex sexual identities position them within the category of queer, but who hold other identities based on class, race, and/or gender categories that provide them with membership in and the resources of dominant institutions and groups?

Thus, inherent in our new politics must be a commitment to Left analysis and politics. Black feminists as well as other marginalized and progressive scholars and activists have long argued that any political response to the multilayered oppression that most of us experience must be rooted in a Left understanding of our political, economic, social, and cultural institutions. Fundamentally, a Left framework makes central the interdependency among multiple systems of domination. Such a perspective also ensures that while activists should rightly be concerned with forms of discursive and cultural coercion, we also recognize and confront the more direct and concrete forms of exploitation and violence rooted in state-regulated institutions and economic systems. The "Statement of Purpose" from the first Dialogue on the Lesbian and Gay Left comments specifically on the role of interlocking systems of oppression in the lives of gays and lesbians: "By leftist we mean people who understand the struggle for lesbian and gay liberation to be integrally tied to struggles against class oppression, racism and sexism. While we might use different political labels, we share a commitment to a fundamental transformation of the economic, political and social structures of society."[12]

A Left framework of politics, unlike civil rights or liberal frameworks, brings into focus the systematic relationship among forms of domination, where the creation and maintenance of exploited, subservient, marginalized classes is a necessary part of, at the very least, the economic configuration. For example, Urvashi Vaid in *Virtual Equality* writes of the limits of civil rights strategies in confronting systemic homophobia: "Civil rights do not change the social order in dramatic ways; they change only the privileges of the group asserting those rights. Civil rights strategies do not challenge the moral and antisexual underpinnings of homophobia, because homophobia does not originate in our lack of full civil equality. Rather, homophobia arises from the nature and construction of the political, legal, economic, sexual, racial and family systems within which we live."[13] Proceeding from the starting point of a system-based Left analysis, strategies built on the possibility of incorporation and assimilation are exposed as simply expanding and making accessible the status quo for more privileged members of marginal groups, while the most vulnerable in our communities continue to be stigmatized and oppressed.

It is important to note, however, that while Left theorists tend to provide a more structural analysis of oppression and exploitation, many of these theorists and activists have also been homophobic and heterosexist in their approach to or avoidance of the topics of sexuality and heteronormativity. For example, Robin Podolsky, in "Sacrificing Queers and Other 'Proletarian' Artifacts," writes that quite often on the Left lesbian and gay sexuality and desire have been characterized as "more to do with personal happiness and sexual pleasure than with the 'material basis' of procreation—we were considered self-indulgent distractions from struggle . . . [an example of] 'bourgeois decadence.' "[14] This contradiction between a stated Left analysis and an adherence to heteronormativity has probably been most dramatically identified in the writing of several feminist authors. I need only refer to Adrienne Rich's well-known article "Compulsory Heterosexuality and Lesbian Existence" as a poignant critique of the white, middle-class heterosexual standard running through significant parts of feminist analysis and actions.[15] The same adherence to a heterosexual norm can be found in the writing of self-identified black Left intellectuals such as Cornel West and Michael Eric Dyson. Thus, while these writers have learned to make reference—sparingly—to lesbian, gay, bisexual, and transgendered segments of black communities, they continue to foreground black heterosexuality and masculinity as the central unit of analysis in their writing—and most recently in their politics: witness their participation in the Million Man March.

This history of Left organizing and the Left's visible absence from any serious and sustained response to the AIDS epidemic have provoked many lesbian, gay, bisexual, and transgendered people to question the relevance of this political configuration to the needs of our communities. Recognizing that reservations of this type are real and should be noted, I still hold that a left-rooted analysis that emphasizes economic exploitation and class structure, culture, and the systemic nature of power provides a framework of politics that is especially effective in representing and challenging the numerous sites and systems of oppression. Further, the Left-centered approach that I embrace is one that designates sexuality and struggles against sexual normalization as central to the politics of all marginal communities.

THE ROOT OF QUEER POLITICS: CHALLENGING HETERONORMATIVITY?

In his introduction to *Fear of a Queer Planet: Queer Politics and Social Theory*, Michael Warner asks the question, "What do queers want?" He suggests that the goals of queers and their politics extend beyond the sexual arena to the acknowledgment of their lives, struggles, and complete existence; that is, that queers want to be represented and included fully in Left political analysis and American culture. What queers want is thus to be a part of the social, economic, and political restructuring of this society; as Warner writes, queers want to have queer experience and politics "taken as starting points rather than as footnotes" in the social theories and political agendas of the left. He contends that it has been the absence or invisibility of lived queer experience that has marked or constrained much of left social and political theories and that has "posited and naturalized a heterosexual society" in such theories. The concerns and emerging politics of queer activists, as formulated by Warner and others interested in understanding the implications of the idea of queerness, are focused on highlighting queer presence and destroying heteronormativity not only in the larger dominant society but also in extant spaces, theories, and sites of resistance, presumably on the Left. He suggests that those embracing the label of "queer" understand the need to challenge the assumption of heteronormativity in every aspect of their existence: "Every person who comes to a queer self-understanding knows in one way or another that her stigmatization is connected with gender, the family, notions of individual freedom, the state, public speech, consumption and desire, nature and culture, maturation, reproductive politics, racial and national fantasy, class identity, truth and trust, censorship, intimate life and social display, terror and violence, health care, and deep cultural norms about the bearing of the body. Being queer means fighting about these issues all the time, locally and piecemeal but always with consequences."[16]

Independent of the fact that few of us could find ourselves in such a grandiose description of queer consciousness, I believe that Warner's description points to the fact that in the roots of a lived "queer" existence are experiences with domination, and in particular heteronormativity, that form the basis for genuine transformational politics. In using the term "transformational" I mean a politics that does not search for opportunities to integrate into dominant institutions and normative social relationships but instead pursues a political agenda that seeks to change values, definitions, and laws that make these institutions and relationships oppressive.

Queer activists experiencing displacement both within and outside of lesbian and gay communities rebuff what they deem the assimilationist practices and policies of more established lesbian and gay organizations. These organizers and activists reject cultural norms of acceptable sexual behavior and identification and instead embrace political strategies that promote self-definition and full expression. Members of the Chicago-based group Queers United Against Straight-Acting Homosexuals (QUASH) state just such a position in the article "Assimilation Is Killing Us: Fight for a Queer United Front" published in their newsletter, *Why I Hated the March on Washington:*

> Assimilation is killing us. We are falling into a trap. Some of us adopt an apologetic stance, stating "that's just the way I am" (read: "I'd be straight if I could."). Others pattern their behavior in such a way as to mimic heterosexual society so as to minimize the glaring differences between us and them. No matter how much [money] you make, fucking your lover is still illegal in nearly half of the states. Getting a corporate job, a fierce car and a condo does not protect you from dying of

AIDS or getting your head bashed in by neo-Nazis. The myth of assimilation must be shattered.

. . . Fuck the heterosexual, nuclear family. Let's make families which promote sexual choices and liberation rather than sexual oppression. We must learn from the legacy of resistance that is ours: a legacy which shows that empowerment comes through grassroots activism, not mainstream politics, a legacy which shows that real change occurs when we are inclusive, not exclusive.[17]

At the very heart of queer politics, at least as it is formulated by QUASH, is a fundamental challenge to the heteronormativity—the privilege, power, and normative status invested in heterosexuality—of the dominant society.

It is in their fundamental challenge to a systemic process of domination and exclusion, with a specific focus on heteronormativity, that queer activists and queer theorists are tied to and rooted in a tradition of political struggle most often identified with people of color and other marginal groups. For example, activists of color have, through many historical periods, questioned their formal and informal inclusion and power in prevailing social categories. Through just such a process of challenging their centrality to lesbian and gay politics in particular, and lesbian and gay communities more generally, lesbian, gay, bisexual, and transgendered people of color advanced debates over who and what would be represented as "truly gay." As Steven Seidman reminds us in "Identity and Politics in a 'Postmodern' Gay Culture: Some Historical and Conceptual Notes," beyond the general framing provided by postmodern queer theory, gay and lesbian (and now queer) politics owes much of its impetus to the politics of people of color and other marginalized members of lesbian and gay communities. "Specifically, I make the case that postmodern strains in gay thinking and politics have their immediate social origin in recent developments in the gay culture. In the reaction by people of color, third-world-identified gays, poor and working class gays, and sex rebels to the ethnic/essentialist model of identity and community that achieved dominance in the lesbian and gay cultures of the 1970s, I locate the social basis for a rethinking of identity and politics."[18] Through the demands of lesbian, gay, bisexual, and transgendered people of color as well as others who did not see themselves or their numerous communities in the more narrowly constructed politics of white gays and lesbians, the contestation took shape over who and what type of issues would be represented in lesbian and gay politics and in larger community discourse.

While a number of similarities and connections between the politics of lesbians, gay men, bisexuals, and transgendered people of color during the 1970s and 1980s and queer activists of today clearly exist, the present-day rendition of this politics has deviated significantly from its legacy. Specifically, while both political efforts include as a focus of their work the radicalization and/or expansion of traditional lesbian and gay politics, the politics of lesbian, gay, bisexual, and transgendered people of color have been and continue to be much broader in terms of its understanding of transformational politics.

The politics of lesbian, gay, bisexual, and transgendered people of color has often been guided by the type of radical intersectional Left analysis that I detailed earlier. Thus, while the politics of lesbian, gay, bisexual, and transgendered activists of color might recognize heteronormativity as a primary system of power structuring our lives, it understands that heteronormativity interacts with institutional racism, patriarchy, and class exploitation to define us in numerous ways as marginal and oppressed subjects.[19] And it is this constructed subservient position that allows our sisters and brothers to be used either as surplus labor in an advanced capitalist structure and/or seen as expendable, denied resources, and thus locked into correctional institutions across the country. While heterosexual privilege negatively impacts and constrains the lived experience of "queers" of color, so too do racism, classism, and sexism.

In contrast to the Left intersectional analysis that has structured much of the politics of "queers" of color, the basis of the politics of some white queer activists and organizations has come dangerously close to a single oppression model. In experiencing "deviant" sexuality as the prominent characteristic of their marginalization, these activists begin to envision the world in terms of a "hetero/queer" divide. Using the framework of queer theory in which heteronormativity is identified as a system of regulation and normalization, some queer activists map the power and entitlement of normative heterosexuality onto the bodies of all heterosexuals. Further, these activists naively characterize as powerless all of those who exist under the category of "queer." Thus, in the process of conceptualizing a decentered identity of queerness meant to embrace those who stand on the outside of heteronormativity, a monolithic understanding of heterosexuality and queerness has come to dominate the political imagination and actions of many queer activists.

This reconstruction of a binary divide between heterosexuals and queers, while discernible in many of the actions of Queer Nation, is probably most evident in the manifesto "I Hate Straights." Written by an anonymous group of queers and distributed at gay pride parades in New York and Chicago in 1990, the declaration begins:

> I have friends. Some of them are straight.
>
> Year after year, I see my straight friends. I want to see how they are doing, to add newness to our long and complicated histories, to experience some continuity.
>
> Year after year I continue to realize that the facts of my life are irrelevant to them and that I am only half listened to, that I am an appendage to the doings of a greater world, a world of power and privilege, of the laws of installation, a world of exclusion. "That's not true," argue my straight friends. There is the one certainty in the politics of power: those left out of it beg for inclusion, while the insiders claim that they already are. Men do it to women, whites do it to blacks, and everyone does it to queers.
>
> . . . *The main dividing line, both conscious and unconscious, is procreation . . . and that magic word—Family* [emphasis added].[20]

Screaming out from this manifesto is an analysis that places not heteronormativity but heterosexuality as the central "dividing line" between those who would be dominant and those who are oppressed. Nowhere in this essay is there recognition that "nonnormative" procreation patterns and family structures of people who are labeled heterosexual have also been used to regulate and exclude them. Instead, the authors declare, "Go tell them [straights] to go away until they have spent a month walking hand in hand in public with someone of the same sex. After they survive that, then you'll hear what they have to say about queer anger. Otherwise, tell them to shut up and listen." For these activists, the power of heterosexuality is the focus, and queer anger the means of queer politics. Missing from this equation is any attention to, or acknowledgment of, the ways in which identities of race, class, and/or gender either enhance or mute the marginalization of queers, on the one hand, and the power of heterosexuals, on the other.

The fact that this essay is written about and out of queer anger is undoubtedly part of the rationale for its defense.[21] But I question the degree to which we should read this piece as just an aberrational diatribe against straights motivated by intense queer anger. While anger is clearly a motivating factor for such writing, we should also understand this action to represent an analysis and politics structured around the simple dichotomy of straight and queer. We know, for instance, that similar positions have been put forth in other anonymously published, publicly distributed manifestos. For example, in the document *Queers Read This,* the authors write, "Don't be fooled, straight people own the world and the only reason you have been spared is you're smart, lucky or a fighter. Straight people have a privilege that allows them to do whatever they please and fuck without fear." They continue by stating, "Straight people are your enemy."

Even within this document, which seems to exemplify the narrowness of queer conceptions, there is a surprising glimpse at a more enlightened Left intersectional understanding of what queerness might mean. As the authors state, for instance, "being queer is not about a right to privacy; it is about the freedom to be public, to just be who we are. It means every day fighting oppression; homophobia, racism, misogyny, the bigotry of religious hypo-crites and our own self-hatred." Evident in this one document are the inher-ent tensions and dilemmas that many queer activists currently encounter: How does one implement in real political struggle a decentered political identity that is not constituted by a process of seemingly reductive "othering"?

The process of ignoring or at least downplaying queers' varying relation-ships to power is evident not only in the writings of queer activists, but also in the political actions pursued by queer organizations. I question the ability of political actions such as mall invasions (pursued by groups such as the Queer Shopping Network in New York and the Suburban Homosexual Outreach Program [SHOP] in San Francisco) to address the fact that queers exist in different social locations. Lauren Berlant and Elizabeth Freeman describe mall invasion projects as an attempt to take "the relatively bounded spectacle of the urban pride parade to the ambient pleasures of the shopping mall. 'Mall visibility actions' thus conjoin the spectacular lure of the parade with Hare Krishna–style conversion and proselytizing techniques. Stepping into malls in hair-gelled splendor, holding hands and handing out fliers, the queer auxiliaries produce an 'invasion' that conveys a different message. 'We're here, we're queer, you're going shopping.' "[22] The activity of entering or "invading" the shopping mall on the part of queer nationals is clearly one of attempted subversion. Intended by their visible presence in this clearly coded heterosex-ual family economic mecca is a disruption of the agreed-on segregation between the allowable spaces for queer "deviant" culture and the rest of the "naturalized" world. Left unchallenged in such an action, however, are the myriad ways, besides the enforcement of normative sexuality, in which some queers feel alienated and excluded from the space of the mall. Where does the mall as an institution of consumer culture and relative economic privilege play into this analysis? How does this action account for the varying economic relationships that queers have to consumer culture? If you are a poor or working-class queer the exclusion and alienation you experience when entering the mall may not be limited to the normative sexual codes associated with the mall but rather may also be centered on the assumed economic status of those shopping in suburban malls. If you are a queer of color your exclusion from the mall may, in part, be rooted in racial norms and stereotypes that construct you as a threatening subject every time you enter this economic institution. Queer activists must confront a question that haunts most political organizing: How do we put into politics a broad and inclusive Left analysis that can actually engage and mobilize individuals with intersecting identities?

Clearly, there will be those critics who will claim that I am asking too much from any political organization. Demands that every aspect of oppression and regulation be addressed in each political act seem and indeed are unreasonable. However, I make the critique of queer mall invasions neither to stop such events nor to suggest that each oppression be dealt with by this one political action. Instead, I raise these concerns to emphasize the ways in which varying relations to power exist not only among heterosexuals but also among those who label themselves queer.

In its current rendition, queer politics is coded with class, gender, and race privilege, and may have lost its potential to be a politically expedient organizing tool for addressing the needs—and mobilizing the bodies—of people of color. As some queer theorists and activists call for the destruction of stable sexual categories—for example, moving instead toward a more fluid understanding of sexual behavior—left unspoken is the class privilege that allows for such fluidity. Class or material privilege is a cornerstone of much of queer politics and theory as they exist today. Queer theorizing that calls for the elimination of fixed categories of sexual identity seems to ignore the ways in which some traditional social identities and communal ties can, in fact, be important to one's survival. Further, a queer politics that demonizes all heterosexuals discounts the relationships—especially those based on shared experiences of marginalization—that exist between gays and straights, particularly in communities of color.

Queers who operate out of a political culture of individualism assume a material independence that allows them to disregard historically or culturally recognized categories and communities or, at the very least, to move fluidly among them without ever establishing permanent relationships or identities within them. However, I and many other lesbian and gay people of color, as well as poor and working-class lesbians and gay men, do not have such material independence. Because of my multiple identities, which locate me and other "queer" people of color at the margins in this country, my material advancement, my physical protection, and my emotional well-being are constantly threatened. In those stable categories and named communities whose histories have been structured by shared resistance to oppression, I find relative degrees of safety and security.

Let me emphasize again that the safety I feel is relative to other threats and is clearly not static or constant. For in those named communities I also find versions of domination and normalization being replicated and employed as more privileged/assimilated marginal group members use their associations with dominant institutions and resources to regulate and police the activities of other marginal group members. Any lesbian, gay, bisexual, or transgendered person of color who has experienced exclusion from indigenous institutions, such as the exclusion many openly gay black men have encountered from some black churches responding to AIDS, recognizes that even within marginal groups there are normative rules determining community membership and power. However, in spite of the unequal power relationships located in marginal communities, I am still not interested in disassociating politically from those communities, for queerness, as it is currently constructed, offers no viable political alternative since it invites us to put forth a political agenda that makes invisible the prominence of race, class, and to varying degrees gender in determining the life chances of those on both sides of the hetero/queer divide.

So despite the roots of queer politics in the struggles of "queer" people of color, despite the calls for highlighting categories that have sought to regulate and control black bodies like my own, and despite the attempts at decentralized grassroots activism in some queer political organizations, there still exist—for some, like myself—great misgivings about current constructions of the term "queer." Personally speaking, I do not consider myself a "queer" activist or, for that matter, a "queer" anything. This is not because I do not consider myself an activist; in fact, I hold my political work to be one of the most important contributions I make to all of my communities. But like other lesbian, gay, bisexual, and transgendered activists of color, I find the label "queer" fraught with unspoken assumptions that inhibit the radical political potential of this category.

The alienation, or at least discomfort, that many activists and theorists of color have with current conceptions of queerness is evidenced, in part, by the minimal numbers of theorists of color who engage in the process of theorizing about the concept. Further, the sparse numbers of people of color who participate in "queer" political organizations might also be read as a sign of discomfort with the term. Most important, my confidence in making such a claim of distance and uneasiness with the term "queer" on the part of many people of color comes from my interactions with other lesbian, gay, bisexual, and transgendered people of color who repeatedly express their interpretation of "queer" as a term rooted in class, race, and gender privilege. For us, "queer" is a politics based on narrow sexual dichotomies that make no room either for the analysis of oppression of those we might categorize as heterosexual, or for the privilege of those who operate as "queer." As black lesbian activist and writer Barbara Smith argues in "Queer Politics: Where's the Revolution?": "Unlike the early lesbian and gay movement, which had both ideological and practical links to the left, black activism, and feminism, today's 'queer' politicos seem to operate in a historical and ideological vacuum. 'Queer' activists focus on 'queer' issues, and racism, sexual oppression and economic exploitation do not qualify, despite the fact that the majority of 'queers' are people of color, female or working class . . . Building unified, ongoing coalitions that challenge the system and ultimately prepare a way for revolutionary change simply isn't what 'queer' activists have in mind."[23] It is this narrow understanding of the idea of queer that negates its use in fundamentally reorienting the politics and privilege of lesbian and gay politics as well as more generally moving or transforming the politics of the Left. Despite its liberatory claim to stand in opposition to static categories of oppression, queer politics and much of queer theory seem in fact to be static in the understanding of race, class, and gender and their roles in how heteronormativity regulates sexual behavior and identities. Distinctions between the status and the acceptance of different individuals categorized under the label of "heterosexual" thus go unexplored.

I emphasize here the marginalized position of some who embrace heterosexual identities not because I want to lead any great crusade to understand more fully the plight of "the heterosexual." Rather, I recognize the potential for shared resistance with such individuals. This potential is especially relevant not only for coalitional work but for a shared analysis, from my vantage point, to "queer" people of color. Again, in my call for coalition work across sexual categories, I do not want to suggest that same-sex political struggles have not, independently, played an essential and distinct role in the liberatory politics and social movements of marginal people. My concern, instead, is

. . . .

with any political analysis or theory that collapses our understanding of power into a single continuum of evaluation.

Through a brief review of some of the ways in which nonnormative heterosexuality has been controlled and regulated through the state and systems of marginalization, we may be reminded that differentials in power exist within all socially named categories. And through such recognition we may begin to envision a new political formation in which one's relation to dominant power serves as the basis of unity for radical coalition work in the twenty-first century.

HETEROSEXUALS ON THE (OUT)SIDE OF HETERONORMATIVITY

In the text following I want to return to the question of a monolithic understanding of heterosexuality. I believe that through this issue we can begin to think critically about the components of a radical politics built not exclusively on identities but rather on identities as they are invested with varying degrees of normative power. Thus, fundamental to my concern about the current structure and future agenda of queer politics is the unchallenged assumption of a uniform heteronormativity from which all heterosexuals benefit. I want again to be clear that there are, in fact, some who identify themselves as queer activists who do acknowledge relative degrees of power, along with heterosexual access to that power, even evoking the term "straight queers": "Queer means to fuck with gender. There are straight queers, bi queers, tranny queers, lez queers, fag queers, SM queers, fisting queers in every single street in this apathetic country of ours."[24]

Despite such sporadic insight, much of the politics of queer activists has been structured around the dichotomy of straight versus everything else, assuming a monolithic experience of heterosexual privilege for all those identified publicly with heterosexuality. A similar reductive dichotomy between men and women has consistently reemerged in the writing and actions of some feminists. And only through the demands, the actions, and the writing of many "feminists" and/or lesbians of color have those women who stand outside the norm of white, middle-class, legalized heterosexuality begun to see their lives, needs, and bodies represented in feminist theory.[25] In a similar manner lesbian, gay, bisexual, and transgendered people of color have increasingly taken on the responsibility for at the very least complicating and most often challenging reductive notions of heteronormativity articulated by queer activists and scholars.[26]

If we follow such examples, complicating our understanding of both heteronormativity and queerness, we move one step closer to building the progressive coalition politics that many of us desire. Specifically, if we pay attention to both historical and current examples of heterosexual relationships that have been prohibited, stigmatized, and generally repressed, we may begin to identify those spaces of shared or similar oppression and resistance that provide a basis for radical coalition work. Further, we may begin to answer certain questions: In narrowly positing a dichotomy of heterosexual privilege and queer oppression under which we all exist, are we negating a basis of political unity that could serve to strengthen many communities and movements seeking justice and societal transformation? How do we use the relative degrees of ostracism that all sexual/cultural "deviants" experience to build a basis of unity for broader coalition and movement work?

A little history (as a political scientist a little history is all I can offer) might be helpful here in trying to sort out the various ways that heterosexuality, especially as it has intersected with race, has been defined and experienced by different groups of people. Such information should also help to underscore the fact that many of the roots of heteronormativity are in white-supremacist ideologies that sought (and continue) to use the state and its regulation of sexuality, in particular through the institution of heterosexual marriage, to designate which individuals were truly "fit" for the full rights and privileges of citizenship. For example, the prohibition of marriages between black women and men imprisoned in the slave system was a component of many slave codes enacted during the seventeenth and eighteenth centuries. M. G. Smith, in his article on the structure of slave economic systems, succinctly states: "As property slaves were prohibited from forming legal relationships or marriages which would interfere with and restrict their owner's property rights."[27] Herbert Gutman, in *The Black Family in Slavery and Freedom, 1750–1925,* elaborates on the ideology of slave societies that denied the legal sanctioning of marriages between slaves, and further reasoned that blacks had no conception of family.[28]

> The *Nation* identified sexual restraint, civil marriage, and family stability with civilization itself.
>
> Such mid-nineteenth-century class and sexual beliefs reinforced racial beliefs about Afro-Americans. As slaves, after all, their marriages had not been sanctioned by the civil laws and therefore "the sexual passion" went unrestrained. . . . Many white abolitionists denied the

slaves a family life or even, often, a family consciousness because for them [the whites] the family had its origins in and had to be upheld by the civil law.[29]

Thus it was not the promotion of marriage or heterosexuality per se that served as the standard or motivation of most slave societies. Instead, marriage and heterosexuality, as viewed through the lenses of profit and domination and the ideology of white supremacy, were reconfigured to justify the exploitation and regulation of black bodies, even those presumably engaged in heterosexual behavior. It was this system of state-sanctioned, white male, upper-class heterosexual domination that forced these presumably black heterosexual men and women to endure a history of rape, lynching, and other forms of physical and mental terrorism. In this way, marginal group members lacking power and privilege although engaged in heterosexual behavior have often found themselves defined as outside the norms and values of dominant society. This position has most often resulted in the suppression or negation of their legal, social, and physical relationships and rights.

In addition to the prohibition of marriage between slaves, A. Leon Higginbotham Jr., in *The Matter of Color: Race and the American Legal Process: The Colonial Period,* writes of the legal restrictions barring interracial marriages. He reminds us that the essential core of the American legal tradition was the preservation of the white race. The "mixing" of the races was to be strictly prohibited in early colonial laws. The regulation of interracial heterosexual relationships, however, should not be understood as exclusively relegated to the seventeenth, eighteenth, and nineteenth centuries. In fact, Higginbotham informs us that the final law prohibiting miscegenation (the "interbreeding" or marrying of individuals from different "races" that was actually meant to inhibit the "tainting" of the white race) was not repealed until 1967: "Colonial anxiety about interracial sexual activity cannot be attributed solely to seventeenth-century values, for it was not until 1967 that the United States Supreme Court finally declared unconstitutional those statutes prohibiting interracial marriages. The Supreme Court waited thirteen years after its *Brown* decision dealing with desegregation of schools before, in *Loving v. Virginia,* it agreed to consider the issue of interracial marriages."[30]

It is this pattern of regulating the behavior and denigrating the identities of those heterosexuals on the outside of heteronormative privilege—in particular those perceived as threatening systems of white supremacy, male domination, and capitalist advancement—that I want to highlight here. An understanding of the ways in which heteronormativity works to support and reinforce institutional racism, patriarchy, and class exploitation must therefore be a part of how we problematize current constructions of heterosexuality. As I stated previously, I am not suggesting that those involved in publicly identifiable heterosexual behavior do not receive political, economic, and social advantages, especially in comparison to the experiences of some lesbian, transgendered, gay, and bisexual individuals. But the equation linking identity and behavior to power is not as linear and clear as some queer theorists and activists would have us believe.

A more recent example of regulated nonnormative heterosexuality is located in the debates and rhetoric regarding the "underclass" and the destruction of the welfare system. The stigmatization and demonization of single mothers, teen mothers, and, primarily, poor women of color dependent on state assistance has had a long and suspicious presence in American "intellectual" and political history. It was in 1965 that Daniel Patrick Moynihan released his "study" titled *The Negro Family: The Case for National Action*, which would eventually come to be known simply as the Moynihan report. In this document the author points to the "pathologies" increasingly evident in so-called Negro families, notably the destructive nature of Negro family formations. Indeed, the introduction argues that "the fundamental problem in which this is most clearly the case is that of family structure. The evidence—not final, but powerfully persuasive—is that the Negro family in urban ghettos is crumbling. A middle-class group has managed to save itself, but for vast numbers of the unskilled, poorly educated, urban working-class the fabric of conventional social relationships has all but disintegrated." Later in the document Moynihan goes on to describe the crisis and pathologies facing the Negro family structure as being generated by the increasing number of households headed by single females, the increasing number of "illegitimate" births, and, of course, increasing welfare dependency: "In essence, the Negro community has been forced into a matriarchal structure, which because it is so out of line with the rest of the American society seriously retards the progress of the group as a whole and imposes a crushing burden on the Negro male and, in consequence, on a great many Negro women as well. . . . In a word, most Negro youth are in danger of being caught up in the tangle of pathology that affects their world, and probably a majority are so entrapped. . . . Obviously, not every instance of social pathology afflicting the Negro community can be traced to the weakness of family structure. . . . Nonetheless, at the center of the tangle of pathology is the weakness of the family structure."[31]

It is not the nonheterosexist behavior of these black men and women that is under fire but rather the perceived nonnormative sexual behavior and family structures of these individuals, whom many queer activists—without regard to the impact of race, class, or gender—would designate as part of the heterosexist establishment or those mighty "straights they hate." Over the last thirty years the demonization of poor women, engaged in nonnormative heterosexual relationships, has continued under the auspices of scholarship on the "underclass." Adolph L. Reed, in "The 'Underclass' as Myth and Symbol: The Poverty of Discourse about Poverty," discusses the gendered and racist nature of much of this literature, in which poor women, often black and Latina, are portrayed as unable to control their sexual impulses and eventual reproductive decisions; unable to raise their children with the right moral fiber; unable to find "gainful" employment to support themselves and their "illegitimate children"; and of course unable to manage "effectively" the minimal assistance provided by the state. Reed writes,

> The underclass notion may receive the greatest ideological boost from its gendered imagery and relation to gender politics. As I noted in a critique of Wilson's *The Truly Disadvantaged,* "family" is an intrinsically ideological category. The rhetoric of "disorganization," "disintegration," "deterioration" reifies one type of living arrangement—the ideal type of the bourgeois nuclear family—as outside history, nearly as though it were decreed by natural law. But—as I asked earlier—why exactly is out-of-wedlock birth pathological? Why is the female-headed household an indicator of disorganization and pathology? Does that stigma attach to *all* such households—even, say, a divorced executive who is a custodial mother? If not, what are the criteria for assigning it? The short answer is race and class bias inflected through a distinctively gendered view of the world.[32]

In this same discourse of the "underclass," young black men engaged in "reckless" heterosexual behavior are represented as irresponsible baby factories, unable to control or restrain their "sexual passion" (to borrow a term from the seventeenth century). And, unfortunately, often it has been the work of professed liberals like William Julius Wilson, in his book *The Truly Disadvantaged,* that, while not using the word "pathologies," has substantiated in its own tentative way the conservative dichotomy between the deserving working poor and the lazy, Cadillac-driving, steak-eating, welfare queens of Ronald Reagan's imagination.[33] Again, I raise this point to remind us of the numerous ways that sexuality and sexual deviance from a prescribed norm have been used to demonize and to oppress various segments of the population, even some classified under the label "heterosexual."

The policies of politicians and the actions of law enforcement officials have reinforced, in much more devastating ways, the distinctions between acceptable forms of heterosexual expression and those to be regulated— increasingly through incarceration. This move toward the disallowance of some forms of heterosexual expression and reproductive choice can be seen in the practice of prosecuting pregnant women suspected of using drugs— nearly 80 percent of all women prosecuted are women of color; through the forced sterilization of Puerto Rican and Native American women; and through the state-dictated use of Norplant by women answering to the criminal justice system and by women receiving state assistance.[34] Further, it is the "nonnormative" children of many of these nonnormative women that Newt Gingrich would place in orphanages. This is the same Newt Gingrich who, despite his clear disdain for gay and lesbian "lifestyles," has invited lesbians and gay men into the Republican Party but made no such offer to the women on welfare discussed above. Who, we might ask, is truly on the outside of heteronormative power? Maybe most of us?

CONCLUSION: DESTABILIZATION AND RADICAL COALITION WORK

While the points I make above may, in fact, seem interesting or troubling or both, we might ask what does it have to do with the question of the future of queer politics? It is my argument, as I stated earlier, that one of the great failings of queer theory and especially queer politics has been their inability to incorporate into analysis of the world and strategies for political mobilization the roles that race, class, and gender play in defining people's differing relations to dominant and normalizing power. I present this essay as the beginning of a much longer and protracted struggle to acknowledge and delineate the distribution of power within and outside of queer communities. This is a discussion of how to build a politics organized not merely by reductive categories of straight and queer, but organized instead around a more intersectional analysis of who and what the enemy is and where our potential allies can be found. This analysis seeks to make clear the privilege and power embedded in the categorizations of, on the one hand, an upstanding, "morally correct," white, state-authorized, middle-class male heterosexual, and on the other, a culturally deficient, materially bankrupt, state-dependent *heterosexual* woman of color, who is found most often in our urban centers (those that haven't been gentrified), on magazine covers, and on the evening news.

I contend, therefore, that the radical potential of queer politics, or any liberatory movement, rests on its ability to advance strategically oriented political identities arising from a more nuanced understanding of power. One of the most difficult tasks in such an endeavor (and there are many) is not to forsake the complexities of both how power is structured and how we might think about the coalitions we create. Far too often movements revert to a position in which membership and joint political work are based on a necessarily similar history of oppression—but this is too much like identity politics.[35] Instead, I am suggesting here that the process of movement building be rooted not in our shared history or identity but in our shared marginal relationship to dominant power that normalizes, legitimizes, and privileges.

We must, therefore, start our political work from the recognition that multiple systems of oppression are in operation and that these systems use institutionalized categories and identities to regulate and socialize. We must also understand that power and access to dominant resources are distributed across the boundaries of "het" and "queer" that we construct. A model of queer politics that simply pits the grand "heterosexuals" against all those oppressed "queers" is ineffectual as the basis for action in a political environment dominated by Newt Gingrich, the Christian Right, and the recurring ideology of white supremacy. As we stand on the verge of watching those in power dismantle the welfare system through a process of demonizing the poor and young—primarily poor and young women of color, many of whom have existed for their entire lives outside the white, middle-class heterosexual norm—we have to ask if these women do not fit into society's categories of marginal, deviant, and "queer." As we watch the explosion of prison construction and the disproportionate incarceration rates of young men and women of color, often as part of the economic development of poor white rural communities, we have to ask if these individuals do not fit society's definition of "queer" and expendable.

I am not proposing a political strategy that homogenizes and glorifies the experience of poor heterosexual people of color. In fact, in calling for a more expansive Left political identity and formation I do not seek to erase the specific historical relation between the stigma of "queer" and the sexual activity of gay men, lesbians, bisexuals, and transgendered individuals. And in no way do I intend or desire to equate the experiences of marginal heterosexual women and men to the lived experiences of queers. There is no doubt that heterosexuality, even for those heterosexuals who stand outside the norms of heteronormativity, results in some form of privilege and feelings of supremacy. I need only recount the times when other women of color, more economically vulnerable than myself, expressed superiority and some feelings of disgust when they realized that the nice young professor (me) was "that way."

However, in recognizing the distinct history of oppression that lesbian, gay, bisexual, and transgendered people have confronted and challenged, I am not willing to embrace every queer as my marginalized political ally. In the same way, I do not assume that shared racial, gender, and/or class position or identity guarantees or produces similar political commitments. Thus, identities and communities, while important to this strategy, must be complicated and destabilized through a recognition of the multiple social positions and relations to dominant power found within any one category or identity. Kimberlé Crenshaw, in "Mapping the Margins: Intersectionality, Identity Politics, and Violence against Women of Color," suggests that such a project use the idea of intersectionality to reconceptualize or problematize the identities and communities that are "home" to us. She demands that we challenge those identities that seem like home by acknowledging the other parts of our identities that are excluded: "With identity thus reconceptualized [through a recognition of intersectionality], it may be easier to understand the need to summon up the courage to challenge groups that are after all, in one sense, 'home' to us, in the name of the parts of us that are not made at home. . . . The most one could expect is that we will dare to speak against internal exclusions and marginalizations, that we might call attention to how the identity of 'the group' has been centered on the intersectional identities of a few. . . . Through an awareness of intersectionality, we can better acknowledge and ground the differences among us and negotiate the means by which these differences will find expression in constructing group politics."[36] In the same ways that we account for the varying privilege to be gained by a heterosexual identity, we must also pay attention to the privilege that some queers receive from being white, male, and upper class. Only through recognizing the many manifestations of power, across and within categories, can we truly begin to build a movement based on one's politics and not exclusively on one's identity.

I want to be clear here that what I am calling for is the destabilization and not the destruction or abandonment of identity categories.[37] We must reject a queer politics that seems to ignore in its analysis of the usefulness of traditionally named categories the roles of identity and community as paths to survival, using shared experiences of oppression and resistance to build indigenous resources, shape consciousness, and act collectively. Instead, I would suggest that it is the multiplicity and interconnectedness of our identities that provide the most promising avenue for the *destabilization and radical politicalization* of these same categories.

This is not an easy path to pursue because most often it requires building a political analysis and political strategies around the most marginal members of our society, some of whom look like us but many of whom do not. Most often, this will mean rooting our struggle in, and addressing the needs of, communities of color, and it will mean highlighting the intersectionality of one's race, class, gender, and sexuality and the relative power and privilege that one receives from being a man and/or being white and/or being middle class and/or being heterosexual. This challenge is a particularly daunting one because so much of our political consciousness has been built around simple dichotomies such as powerful/powerless; oppressor/victim; enemy/ comrade. It is difficult to feel safe and secure in those spaces where both one's relative privilege and experiences with marginalization are understood to shape a commitment to radical politics. However, as Bernice Johnson Reagon so aptly put it in her essay, "Coalition Politics: Turning the Century," "if you feel the strain, you may be doing some good work."[38]

And while this is a daunting challenge and an uncomfortable position, those who have taken it up have not only survived but succeeded in their efforts. For example, both the needle exchange and prison projects pursued through the auspices of ACT-UP New York point to the possibilities and difficulties involved in principled transformative coalition work. In each project individuals from numerous identities—heterosexual, gay, poor, wealthy, white, black, Latino—came together to challenge dominant constructions of who should be allowed care and who deserved it. No particular identity exclusively determined the shared political commitments of these activists; instead their similar positions, as marginalized subjects relative to the state— made clear through the government's lack of response to AIDS—formed the basis of this political unity.

In the prison project, it was the contention of activists that the government, which denied even wealthy gay men access to drugs to combat HIV and

AIDS, must be regarded as the same source of power that denied incarcerated men and women access to basic health care, including those drugs and conditions needed to combat these diseases. The coalition work that this group engaged in involved a range of people, from formerly incarcerated individuals to heterosexual men and women of color to those we might deem privileged white lesbians and gay men. And this same group of people who came together to protest the conditions of incarcerated people with AIDS also showed up at public events to challenge the homophobia that guided the government's and the biomedical industries' response to this epidemic. The political work of this group of individuals was undoubtedly informed by the public identities they embraced, but these were identities that they further acknowledged as complicated by intersectionality and placed within a political framework where their shared experience as marginal, nonnormative subjects could be foregrounded. Douglas Crimp, in his essay "Right On, Girlfriend!," suggests that through political work our identities become remade and must therefore be understood as relational. Describing such a transformation in the identities of queer activists engaged in, and prosecuted for, needle exchange work, Crimp writes: "But once engaged in the struggle to end the crisis, these queers' identities were no longer the same. It's not that 'queer' doesn't any longer encompass their sexual practices; it does, but it also entails a *relation* between those practices and other circumstances that make very different people vulnerable both to HIV infection and to the stigma, discrimination, and neglect that have characterized the societal and governmental response to the constituencies most affected by the AIDS epidemic."[39]

The radical potential of those of us on the outside of heteronormativity rests in our understanding that we need not base our politics in the dissolution of all categories and communities, but rather that we instead need to work toward the destabilization and remaking of our identities. Difference, in and of itself—even that difference designated through named categories—is not the problem. Instead it is the power invested in certain identity categories and the idea that bounded categories are not to be transgressed that serve as the basis of domination and control. The reconceptualization not only of the content of identity categories but of the intersectional nature of identities themselves, must become part of our political practice. We must thus begin to link our intersectional analysis of power with concrete coalitional work. In real terms this means identifying political struggles such as the needle exchange and prison projects of ACT-UP that transgress the boundaries of identity to highlight, in this case, both the repressive power of the state and the normalizing power evident within both dominant and marginal communities. This type of principled coalition work is also being pursued in a more modest fashion by the Policy Institute of the National Gay and Lesbian Task Force. Recently, the staff at the task force distributed position papers not only on the topics of gay marriages and gays in the military but also on right-wing attacks against welfare and affirmative action. Here we have political work based in the knowledge that the rhetoric and accusations of nonnormativity that Newt Gingrich and others on the Right launch against women on welfare closely resemble the attacks of nonnormativity mounted against gays, lesbians, bisexuals, and transgendered individuals. Again it is the marginalized relation to power, experienced by both of these groups—and I do not mean to suggest that the groups are mutually exclusive—that frames the possibility for transformative coalition work. This prospect diminishes when we do not recognize and deal with the reality that the intersecting identities that gay people embody—in terms of race, class, and gender privilege—put some of us on Gingrich's side of the welfare struggle (e.g., Log Cabin Republicans). And in a similar manner a woman's dependence on state financial assistance in no way secures her position as one supportive of gay rights and/or liberation. While a marginal identity undoubtedly increases the prospects of shared consciousness, only an articulation and commitment to mutual support can truly be the test of unity when pursuing transformational politics.

Finally, I realize here that I have been short on specifics when trying to describe how we move concretely toward a transformational coalition politics among marginalized subjects. The best I can do in response is to offer this discussion as a starting point for reassessing the shape of queer, lesbian, gay, bisexual, and transgendered politics as we begin the twenty-first century. A reconceptualization of the politics of marginal groups allows us not only to privilege the specific lived experience of distinct communities, but also to search for those interconnected sites of resistance from which we can wage broader political struggles. Only by recognizing the link between the ideological, social, political, and economic marginalization of punks, bulldaggers, and welfare queens can we begin to develop political analyses and political strategies effective in confronting the linked yet varied sites of power in this country. Such a project is important because it provides a framework from which the difficult work of coalition politics can begin. And it is in these complicated and contradictory spaces that the liberatory and Left politics that so many of us work for is located.

NOTES

I would like to thank Mark Blasius, Nan Boyd, Ed Cohen, Carolyn Dinshaw, Jeff Edwards, Licia Fiol-Matta, Joshua Gamson, Lynne Huffer, Tamara Jones, Carla Kaplan, Ntanya Lee, Ira Livingston, and Barbara Ransby for their comments on various versions of this essay.

1. David W. Dunlap, "Three Black Members Quit AIDS Organization Board," *New York Times,* January 11, 1996, B2.

2. The very general chronology of queer theory and queer politics referred to throughout this essay is not meant to indicate the definitive historical development of each phenomenon. Instead the dates are used to provide the reader with a general frame of reference. See Steven Epstein, "A Queer Encounter: Sociology and the Study of Sexuality," *Sociology Theory* 12.2 (1994): 188–202, for a similar genealogy of queer theory and queer politics.

3. Donald Morton, "The Politics of Queer Theory in the (Post)Modern Movement," *Genders* 17 (fall 1993): 121.

4. See Chrys Ingraham, "The Heterosexual Imaginary: Feminist Sociology and the Theories of Gender," *Sociological Theory* 12 (1994): 203–19, for a discussion of the heterogendered imaginary.

5. Arlene Stein and Kenneth Plummer, " 'I Can't Even Think Straight': 'Queer' Theory and the Missing Sexual Revolution in Sociology," *Sociological Theory* 12 (1994): 182.

6. Allan Bérubé and Jeffrey Escoffier, "Queer/Nation," *Out/look: National Lesbian and Gay Quarterly* 11 (winter 1991): 12.

7. Joshua Gamson, "Must Identity Movements Self-Destruct? A Queer Dilemma," *Social Problems* 42 (1995): 403.

8. See Mark Blasius, *Gay and Lesbian Politics: Sexuality and the Emergence of a New Ethic,* (Philadelphia: Temple University Press, 1994), 19–20; and Michael Warner, ed., *Fear of a Queer Planet: Queer Politics and Social Theory* (Minneapolis: University of Minnesota Press, 1993), xxi–xxv.

9. I want to be clear that in this essay I am including the destruction of sexual categories as part of the agenda of queer politics. While a substantial segment of queer activists and theorists call for the destabilization of sexual categories, there are also those self-avowed queers who embrace a politics built around the deconstruction and/or elimination of sexual categories. For example, a number of my self-identified queer students engage in sexual behavior that most people would interpret as transgressive of sexual identities and categories. However, these students have repeatedly articulated a different interpretation of their sexual behavior. They put forth an understanding that does not highlight their transgression of categories, but rather one that represents them as individuals who operate outside of categories and sexual identities altogether. They are sexual beings, given purely to desire, truly living sexual

fluidity, and not constrained by any form of sexual categorization or identification. This interpretation seems at least one step removed from that held by people who embrace the fluidity of sexuality while still recognizing the political usefulness of categories or labels for certain sexual behavior and communities. One example of such people might be those women who identify as lesbians and who also acknowledge that sometimes they choose to sleep with men. These individuals exemplify the process of destabilization that I try to articulate within this essay. Even further removed from the queers who would do away with all sexual categories are those who also transgress what many consider to be categories of sexual behaviors while they publicly embrace one stable sexual identity (for example, those self-identified heterosexual men who sleep with other men sporadically and secretly).

10. I want to thank Mark Blasius for raising the argument that standing on the outside of heteronormativity is a bit of a misnomer, since as a dominant normalizing process it is a practice of regulation in which we are all implicated. However, despite this insight I will on occasion continue to use this phrasing while understanding the limits of its meaning.

11. Combahee River Collective, "The Combahee River Collective Statement," in *Home Girls: A Black Feminist Anthology,* ed. Barbara Smith (New York: Kitchen Table: Women of Color Press, 1983), 272.

12. Dialogue on the Lesbian and Gay Left, "Statement of Purpose." Duncan Conference Center, Del Ray Beach, Florida, April 1993.

13. Urvashi Vaid, *Virtual Equality: The Mainstreaming of Gay and Lesbian Liberation* (New York: Anchor, 1995), 183.

14. Robin Podolsky, "Sacrificing Queers and Other 'Proletarian' Artifacts," *Radical America* 25.1 (January 1991): 54.

15. Adrienne Rich, "Compulsory Heterosexuality and Lesbian Existence," in *Powers of Desires: The Politics of Sexuality,* ed. Ann Snitow, Christine Stansell, and Sharon Thompson (New York: Monthly Review, 1983), 177–206.

16. Warner, *Fear of a Queer Planet,* vii, xiii.

17. Queers United Against Straight-Acting Homosexuals, "Assimilation Is Killing Us: Fight for a Queer United Front," *Why I Hated the March on Washington* (1993): 4.

18. Steven Seidman, "Identity and Politics in a 'Postmodern' Gay Culture," in Warner, ed., *Fear of a Queer Planet,* 106.

19. For a discussion of Left analysis and the limits of queer theory, see Rosemary Hennessy, "Queer Theory, Left Politics," *Rethinking Marxism* 17.3 [1994]: 85–111.

20. Queer Nation, "I Hate Straights" manifesto, New York, 1990.

21. Lauren Berlant and Elizabeth Freeman, "Queer Nationality," in Warner, ed., *Fear of a Queer Planet,* 200.

22. Berlant and Freeman, "Queer Nationality," 210.

23. Barbara Smith, "Queer Politics: Where's the Revolution?" *Nation* 257.1 (July 5, 1993): 13–14.

24. Anonymous, quoted in Mary McIntosh, "Queer Theory and the War of the Sexes," in Joseph Bistrow and Angelia R. Wilson, ed., *Activating Theory: Lesbian, Gay, Bisexual Politics* (London: Lawrence and Wishart, 1993), 31.

25. See Hazel Carby, *Reconstructing Womanhood: The Emergence of the Afro-American Woman Novelist* (New York: Oxford University Press, 1987); Patricia Hill Collins, *Black Feminist Thought: Knowledge, Consciousness, and the Politics of Social Empowerment* (Boston: Unwin Hyman, 1990); bell hooks, *Feminist Theory: From Margin to Center* (Boston: South End, 1984).

26. See Jacqui Alexander, "Redefining Morality: The Postcolonial State and the Sexual Offences Bill of Trinidad and Tobago," in Chandra Talpade Mohanty, Ann Russo, and Lourdes Torres, eds., *Third World Women and the Politics of Feminism* (Bloomington: Indiana University Press, 1991), 133–152; Elias Farajaje-Jones, "Ain't I a Queer?," paper presented at the Creating Change Conference, National Gay and Lesbian Task Force, November 1995, Detroit; Audre Lorde, *Sister Outsider* (New York: Crossing Press, 1984); Cherríe Moraga and Gloria Anzaldúa, eds., *This Bridge Called My Back: Writings by Radical Women of Color* (New York: Kitchen Table; Women of Color Press, 1983); and Barbara Smith, *Home Girls: A Black Feminist Anthology* (New York: Kitchen Table Women of Color Press, 1983).

27. M. G. Smith, "Social Structure in the British Caribbean about 1820," *Social and Economic Studies* 1.4 (August 1953): 71.

28. Herbert G. Gutman, *The Black Family in Slavery and Freedom, 1750–1925* (New York: Vintage, 1976).

29. Ibid., 295.

30. A. Leon Higginbotham Jr., *In the Matter of Color: Race and the American Legal Process: The Colonial Period* (New York: Oxford University Press, 1978), 41.

31. Daniel Patrick Moynihan, *The Negro Family: The Case for National Action* (Washington, D.C.: Office of Planning and Research, U.S. Department of Labor, 1965), 29–30.

32. Adolph L. Reed Jr., "The 'Underclass' as Myth and Symbol: The Poverty of Discourse about Poverty," *Radical America* 24.1 (January 1990): 33–34.

33. William Julius Wilson, *The Truly Disadvantaged: The Inner City, the Under-class, and Public Policy* (Chicago: University of Chicago Press, 1987).

34. For an insightful discussion of the numerous methods used to regulate and control the sexual and reproductive choices of women, see Suzanne Shende, "Fighting the Violence against Our Sisters: Prosecution of Pregnant Women and the Coercive Use of Norplant," in *Women Transforming Politics: An Alternative Reader*, ed. Cathy Cohen, Kathleen Jones, and Jones Tronto (New York: New York University Press, 1997), 123–35.

35. See Shane Phelan, *Identity Politics: Lesbian Feminism and the Limits of Community* (Philadelphia: Temple University Press, 1989).

36. Kimberlé Williams Crenshaw, "Mapping the Margins: Intersectionality, Iden-

tity Politics, and Violence against Women of Color." *Stanford Law Review* 43 (1991): 1299.

37. See Tamara Jones, "Inside the Kaleidoscope: How the Construction of Black Gay and Lesbian Identities Inform Political Strategies" (unpublished essay, 1995) for an articulation of differences between the destabilization and the destruction of identity categories.

38. Bernice Johnson Reagon, "Coalition Politics: Turning the Century," in Smith, ed., *Home Girls*, 362.

39. Douglas Crimp, "Right On, Girlfriend!" in Warner, ed., *Fear of a Queer Planet*, 317–18.

RODERICK A. FERGUSON

RACE-ING HOMONORMATIVITY:
CITIZENSHIP, SOCIOLOGY, AND
GAY IDENTITY

In "A Queer Encounter: Sociology and the Study of Sexuality" sociologist Steven Epstein correctly argues that queer studies was not the first discipline to confront sexuality as a social phenomenon. Indeed, before the publication of Foucault's *History of Sexuality: Volume 1* and before the rise of queer studies, sociology refuted presumptions about the biological foundations of sexuality and began to see the social as the proper location from which to explain sexual practices, meanings, and identities. As Epstein argues, without the work of sociologists like Ken Plummer, John Gagnon, William Simon, Mary McIntosh, and others, "neither queer theory nor lesbian and gay studies in general could be imagined in their present forms without the contributions of sociological theory."[1] For example, Epstein states that John Gagnon and William Simon in their 1973 text *Sexual Conduct: The Social Sources of Human Sexuality* addressed the naturalization of sexuality in general and of homosexuality in particular. In doing so, they confronted the construction of homosexuality as the horizon of the unnatural. Ken Plummer, in his 1982 essay "Symbolic Interactionism and Sexual Conduct: An Emergent Perspective," attempted to denaturalize sexuality by attending to the subjective meanings that constitute it. Even earlier, Mary McIntosh in "The Homosexual Role" (1968) applied labeling theory to homosexuality, illustrating the ways in which homosexuality is labeled a deviant practice so that the larger society can construct itself as heterosexual and pure.[2]

In this essay I do not discount Epstein's claim about sociology's distinction nor do I dismiss the innovations made by the sociologists mentioned above. Sociology did—because of the work of Gagnon, Simon, Plummer, and McIntosh—precede Foucault and queer studies in designating sexuality as a socially constructed category.[3] Instead of discounting Epstein, then, I attempt in this essay to frustrate a triumphant understanding of such a precedent. To do this, I connect sociology's designation of sexuality as a social phenomenon to past and present social formations that invest in practices of racial exclusion and racial privilege. More specifically, I argue that sociology's understanding of social construction in general and of sexuality in particular arises in the midst of white racial formations. In order to make this argument, I refocus sociology's interest in sexuality from the 1960s and 1970s and onto the 1980s, during a period formed in the wake of European migrations to the United States and in the midst of widespread anxiety about African American urban communities. A narrative about sociology's triumph over biological notions of sexuality risks subjugating the histories and practices of racial exclusion that occasion sociological renderings of sexuality.

Locating sociological arguments about sexuality within white racial formations taking place in the early decades of the twentieth century also begs the question of how contemporary arguments about the socially constructed nature of sexuality might point to such formations in our present period as well. In light of this I argue here that sociological arguments about the socially constructed nature of (homo)sexuality index the contemporary entrance of white gays and lesbians into the rights and privileges of American citizenship. As they extend such practices and access racial and class privileges by conforming to gender and sexual norms, white gay formations in particular become homonormative locations that comply with heteronormative protocols. This compliance compels polymorphous exclusions and regulations of subjects whose nonnormative gender and sexual differences are understood through the particularities of race and class. Indeed, homonormativity describes a new and emergent contradiction. For instance, white homonormative racial formations claim privileges to the detriment of those communities marginalized by normative regulations—regulations that are racialized, classed, and gendered.

In his critique of historiographies that inscribe homosexuality in terms of coherence, David Halperin suggests the ways in which those formations regulate the discontinuous and incoherent features that constitute modern homosexuality. In this essay I extend that argument by showing how white homonormative formations understand class and racial differences that suggest gender and sexual nonnormativity as incoherent and thereby worthy of regulation. I therefore attempt to disinter the subjugated histories of homosexuality's incoherence as the intertwining differences of gender, race, and class produce that incoherence. Moreover, I ask how that incoherence violates the illusory coherence of American citizenship and is therefore worthy of regulation. In the conclusion I offer a few words about how the epistemological denaturalization of forms of difference previously understood to be rooted in biology is situated within the varied history of citizen formations within the United States.

SOCIAL CONSTRUCTION AND THE GENEALOGY OF WHITE ETHNICITY

In the history of sociology, theories of social construction have been tied to the theorization and emergence of racial and ethnic formations. Indeed, we may locate the genealogy of sociology's interest in social construction in the 1930s with the Chicago school of sociology. These epistemological interventions arose within a dialectic of racial exclusion and ethnic inclusion. As U.S. capital promoted immigration and, later, African American migration for the purposes of surplus extraction, industrialization disrupted erotic and racial boundaries. Robert Park and others believed that this emerging economic mode encouraged social relations that disrupted traditional intimate arrangements. Of this period, Park wrote: "In the long run, however, peoples and races who live together, sharing the same economy, inevitably interbreed, and in this way, if no other, the relations which were merely co-operative and economic become social and cultural. When migration leads to conquest, either economic or political, assimilation is inevitable."[4] In the national imagination, anxieties about heteropatriarchal disruption were thoroughly racialized, marking immigrants and U.S.-born minorities as biological threats to the normative ideals that underwrote American citizenship. In an era in which race was associated with the normative attributes of national difference, miscegenation would symbolize the violation of racialized heteronormativity and its guarantee of American (i.e., "white") racial purity. The *Saturday Evening Post* extolled Madison Grant's 1916 text *The Passing of the Great Race*, which upheld "the purity of the 'Nordic,' the race of the white man par excellence against 'Alpine,' 'Mediterranean' and Semitic invaders." Moreover, native whites flooded their representatives in congress with letters advocating immigration restriction and the "preservation of a 'distinct American type.' "[5] Racial exclusion was thus designed to protect the heteronormative status of native-born whites.

As a category designed for the express purpose of assimilation, ethnicity worked to foster compliance and identifications with the normative properties of the American citizen-subject. That normativity constructed heteropatriarchy as the ideal mode of social relations for an industrializing United States. In the racial logic of the state, immigrants and native-born nonwhites were racialized as the antithesis of heteropatriarchal ideals. In this context, sociologists and political officials formulated a conception of ethnicity that would situate European immigrants within the heteronormative idealizations of the American state.

As ethnicity and social construction were invented in the midst of immigration and migration, racial exclusion and ethnic assimilation provided the genealogical context for sociology's inscriptions of race and sexuality as socially constructed. Such compliance and identification could only take place by debunking race as a biological determinant of social life and rendering it into an element of culture that could be reformulated for racial identification predicated on heteronormativity. Put simply, ethnic assimilation required European immigrants to comply with heteronormative protocols as newly racialized whites. While other Americans questioned the status of European immigrants as white, Theodore Roosevelt endorsed the naturalization of European immigrants on the basis that native whites could intermarry with European immigrants. According to Roosevelt, this "mixture of blood" through intermarriage could produce a "new ethnic type in this melting pot of nations."[6] The creation of this new ethnic type depended on heterosexual reproduction secured through common whiteness. When the federal government conflated citizenship with whiteness in the post–World War II era, it was asserting that European immigrants could attain both the ideals of whiteness and heteropatriarchy—that they could be candidates for racialized heteronormativity. In doing so, Roosevelt—like Park—was attempting to argue that southern and eastern European immigrants were corporeally similar to native whites and therefore eligible partners in heterosexual reproduction and marriage. While ethnically different, European immigrants enjoyed racial similarity to native whites.

In the United States, monogamous, dyadic, and normative heterosexuality invented not only the intelligibility of gender but citizenship and white immigration as well. As a formation that promoted such intelligibility, ethnicity suggested cultural conformity with heteronormativity at the same time that it implied corporeal similarity between native whites and European immigrants. Ethnicity, therefore, did not suggest the absence of racial difference but named the process by which European racial differences were rearticulated and managed to comply with the normative itineraries of heteropatriarchy. In doing so, ethnicity promoted identification with the racialized ideals of the American citizen-subject.

The invention of ethnicity was the context out of which social construction emerged. As such, social construction was invented according to the normative protocols of ethnicity in particular and of American citizenship in general. Social construction posited culture as both the index of difference and normativity. If culture was the measure of normative identifications, and if normativity was defined as a constitutive racializing logic of liberal capitalism, then culture was the target of regulation, exclusion, and discipline as well as the register of state identification.

THE NONNORMATIVE PROPERTIES OF RACIAL DIFFERENCE

As whiteness became a structure of identification and an institution of assimilation, sociology inscribed race in theories of culture rather than situating it within theories of fixed biological differences.[7] To reiterate, identifying with the racialized ideals of citizenship and becoming an "ethnic type" depended on the designation of culture as the socially constructed domain of difference. Ethnic identification as a sign of normative compliance made social construction into a technology of racial exclusion. Robert Park, in "Racial Assimilation in Secondary Groups," implied that ethnic assimilation was achieved at the expense of racial exclusion: "The fact that the Japanese bears in his features a distinctive racial hallmark, that he wears, so to speak, a racial uniform, classifies him. He cannot become a mere individual, indistinguishable in the cosmopolitan mass of the populations, as is true, for example, of the Irish and, to a lesser extent, of some of the other immigrant races. The Japanese like the Negro is condemned to remain among us an abstraction, a symbol, and a symbol not merely of his own race, but of the Orient and of that vague, ill-defined menace we sometimes refer to as the 'yellow peril.'"[8] As the Irish represent the achievement of ethnic assimilation—in part because of corporeal similarity—the Japanese American and the African American represent the inevitability of racial exclusion because of a corporeal difference that suggested cultural incongruity.

As racial difference became a sign of cultural incongruity, homosexuality ceased to be a sign of biological difference and was instead rearticulated as a sign of cultural difference. In 1938 Conrad Bentzen, a student of Chicago school sociologist Ernest Burgess, wrote an essay titled "Notes on the Homosexual in Chicago." In it he argues that "to explain the homosexual in the simple terms of biological variation or gland functioning is most confusing when a study is made in the field. We speak of variations in the primary sexual characteristics with hermaphrodites as living examples of this peculiar twist of human nature. Then we go a step further and explain the secondary sexual characteristics in much the same manner but here the student becomes involved in a complexity of possibilities. He quite willingly admits that the functioning of the genital glands is certain to affect the virility of a person. He realizes that there are a certain number of masculine as well as feminine characteristics in all of us. In other words that we are basically bisexual." As Bentzen presumes a general bisexual disposition, he is ultimately interested in how that disposition is regulated. As he states, the "normal" person "experiences this conflict [between his heterosexual and homosexual propensities] in some degree but the normal usually manages to suppress his homosexual desires and find complete satisfaction for his libido in one person." He continues, "But when you throw the student in with a group of homosexuals and they keep fluctuating between one role and another it becomes obvious that the analysis must have a broader basis."[9] As a student of sociology, Bentzen is interested in that broader basis.

Social space provided an explanation for that broader basis, that is, for the external influences on the variability of gender and sexuality. In discussing the function of social space in the racialization of Asian Americans, Henry Yu argues that Chicago school sociologists "used [spatial metaphors] to map space . . . The metaphorical linking of racial identity and physical location . . . gave rise on the one side to notions of place that were highly racialized, and . . . to notions of ethnic, racial, and cultural identity that adopted the tangible features of land. Cultures became self-contained objects with clear physical boundaries. Culture was bounded, with a borderline demarcating the difference between one culture and another."[10] This logic that understood space in terms of racial difference and identity led Bentzen to explain the broader basis for gender and sexual variation. As Bentzen notes: "In the city of Chicago there are several places where the homosexuals congregate in public. Here the social taboos of a conventional society have been raised and the repressed individual can find full expression for those smoldering desires burning within." African American neighborhoods, in particular, were social spaces that could potentially throw gender and sexual stability into confusion. Put simply, the communal and cultural difference of the South Side suggested a vulnerability to homosexuality.

Continuing this line of thought through an ethnography of a "black and tan party," Bentzen writes:

> Every night we will find the place crowded with both races, the black and the white, both types of lovers, the homo and the hetro [sic] . . . Before long the orchestra strikes up a tune and the master of ceremonies appears on the stage. This person is a *huge* mulatto with *wide* shoulders and narrow lips. *It* wears a white satin evening gown that reveal [sic] the unmistakable breasts of a woman. The lips are heavily painted and are *so full* that they make a red block against the *ghostly white countenance. It* is a *lascivious creature* that strikes the *normal* as extremely *repulsive.* With a deep husky voice it begins to sing a wild song and as the tempo increases the stage rapidly fills with a remarkable collection of sexual *indeterminants.* [The black and tan] does provide an outlet for these *unstable* people who are forced to repress their feelings in the normal group. But still we wonder if this process of conditioning and obvious approval doesn't encourage those on the borderline to *slip* into this role of uncertainty?[11]

As Kevin Mumford argues in his text *Interzones: Black/White Sex Districts in Chicago and New York in the Early Twentieth Century,* black and tan parties during this period were known for their inversion of racial hierarchies, for "race-mixing," and as sites from which same-sex relationships and identities could emerge.[12] At the heart of Bentzen's piece is an ambivalence about the socially constructed nature of sexuality. Bentzen is ready to acknowledge the arbitrariness of sexuality, but he is not at all ready to relinquish the normative underpinnings of sexuality. Those underpinnings for Bentzen are explicitly racial, defining themselves in an antagonism to the gendered and sexual transgressions that take place in the racialized nonwhite space of the South Side. As the terrain that exists as the antithesis of whiteness and normalized heterosexuality, the South Side represents that corporeal difference and cultural incongruity that obstructs assimilation. As ethnicity was the racialized mode of gender and sexual intelligibility, nonwhite racial difference was the racialized mode of gender and sexual confusion and "indeterminacy." While ethnicity functioned as a category of racial and heteronormative equivalence, racial difference operated as a sign of nonheteronormativity and exclusion. As sexuality was rendered into a social construction, it was turned into a technology of race, imagining African American culture as the antithesis of compliance, discipline, and normativity.

Through Park, we can see how racial exclusion and ethnic assimilation expressed a dialectic. That dialectic inscribed the normative imperatives of racial exclusion onto sociology's understanding of social construction. As the object of social construction, culture became the object that had to be regulated according to the normative protocols of ethnicity. More to the point, culture became the litmus for compliance and nonconformity with the normative ideals of citizenship. As a cultural form, the black and tan implied an outright nonconformity, an annihilation of gender and sexual convention typified in a transgendered mulatta who "strikes the normal as . . . repulsive."

HOMONORMATIVITY AND THE COHERENCE OF CITIZENSHIP

In contemporary sociology, the designation of sexuality as a social construction emerges with the assertion of homosexuality as a new category of normativity. In his 1987 article "Gay Politics, Ethnic Identity," Epstein points to the emergence of a gay ethnicity organized around heteronormative compliance: "The lifestyles of homosexuals and heterosexuals (at least among the white middle class) would seem in some ways to be moving closer together, even as the identity categories congeal . . . To the extent that there is some truth in the argument, it would seem that gays are becoming 'the same' as straights to the extent that they are 'different.'"[13] We can think of this last assertion as part of a genealogy in which minoritized subjects demand and aspire to recognition by the liberal capitalist state. As Epstein implies, the assertion of gay identity ceases to suggest an alienation from but rather an intersection with heterosexual normativity. To reiterate, "gays are becoming the 'same' as straights to the extent that they are 'different.'" Here Epstein evokes the classic function of ethnicity—that is, as a category that preserves and expresses difference by regulating it so that one can still claim the supposed universal properties of citizenship. In "On the Jewish Question," Marx addresses how the logic of the rights-based subject evokes difference under the regulations of citizenship. Marx begins his argument by engaging Bruno Bauer's claim that in order for the Jew to become a citizen, the Jew must renounce religious difference as part of the protocols of the secular state.

Marx corrects Bauer's assumption by arguing that Bauer confuses the nature of political emancipation and the state's relationship to difference:

> Man emancipates himself politically from religion by expelling it from the sphere of public law to that of private law. Religion is no longer the spirit of the state, in which man behaves, albeit in a specific and limited way and in a particular sphere, as a species-being in community with other men. It has become the spirit of civil society, of the sphere of egoism and of the bellum omnium contra omnes. It is no longer the essence of community, but the essence of differentiation . . . It is now only the abstract avowal of an individual folly, a private whim or caprice. The infinite fragmentation of religion in North America, for example, already gives it the external form of a strictly private affair. It has been relegated among the numerous private interests and exiled from the life of the community as such. But one should have no illusions about the scope of political emancipation. The division of man into the public person and the private person, the displacement of religion from the state to civil society—all this is not a stage in political emancipation but its consummation. Thus political emancipation does not abolish, and does not even strive to abolish, man's real religiosity.[14]

Marx sees religion as part of the particular secular elements of the state that must be confined to the private and regulated for the good of citizenship. Presently, homosexuality emerges as one of the secular elements of the contemporary state, an element from which the state struggles to emancipate itself, an element that must be regulated to facilitate the "coherence" of American citizenship. In doing so, homosexual difference can be preserved as a private particularity rather than abolished as a general threat. As the secularization of religion provides the conditions for participation and recognition of the Jew, the normalization of homosexuality outlines the requirements for homosexual participation and recognition. As the secularization of religion relegated religious differences to the private terrain, so did the normalization of homosexuality confine homosexual difference to the private sphere. As a category of the politically emancipated and of those who enter white racial formation through the regulation of particular differences, ethnicity is yet another name for the rights-based subject who claims difference through the regulatory regimes of citizenship. That subject requires a socially constructed notion of culture so that it may press difference to the needs of regulation.

Regulating homosexual difference in order to claim coherence as a public citizen is part of the homonormative subject's entrance into racial privilege. If rights-based action and an affiliation with the illusory and universal community of the state achieves coherence and emancipation for homosexuality, then homosexuality achieves coherence and emancipation by regulating gender and sexuality. That regulation is part of the racialized regimes of American citizenship. In other words, the appeal to gender and sexual normativity by gays and lesbians in this moment, inevitably, operates as a mode of state identification that promotes racial exclusion. Gay rights has become a site of racial exclusion and privilege defined by the rights to marriage, hate crime protection, and military inclusion.

In terms of gay marriage, legal scholar Daryl Hutchinson, in his article "Out Yet Unseen: A Racial Critique of Gay and Lesbian Legal Theory and Political Discourse," responds to arguments that gay marriage is the ultimate sign of homosexual emancipation. He writes, "Only those individuals buffered from racial, class, and gender oppression and who, but for their homosexual orientation are "virtually normal," could reasonably expect as narrow a reform as legal marriage to bring them almost complete ('ninety percent') equality and liberation. Women, men of color, and the economically disadvantaged (including many white gay men) need much broader and deeper social change to improve their lives. Thus, the disparate responses of white men, women, and gay men of color to the same-sex marriage movement [is] likely evidence that they are unequally affected by social power and, therefore, would benefit differently—if at all—from state recognition of their relationships."[15] As Hutchinson suggests, marriage is in keeping with the protocols of rights-based subjectivity, protocols that inspire identification with the normative ideals of citizenship. Presumably, marriage will make the virtually normal completely so. In addition to ignoring the particular concerns and needs of people of color and the poor, marriage as the sign of normativity extends racial discourses that understand women of color who head single-parent homes as the antitheses of citizenship and normativity.

In terms of hate crime protection, legal scholars Jane Spade and Craig Wilse, in "Confronting the Limits of Gay Hate Crimes Activism: A Radical Critique," outline the ways in which hate crime legislation is constituted in favor of homonormative identities and practices. The laws codify those identities and practices as they specifically leave out protections against transgender and nonwhite subjects. As they state: "The homosexual identity that hate crimes statutes write into law leaves out all sorts of sexual and gender deviants, only providing protections for those same privileged people who the mainstream gay and lesbian movement perpetually serves. Neutral constructions of gender and sexuality compromise people of color and poor people by refusing to acknowledge the interlocking forces of subordination at work in their lives."[16] Hate crime activism has shed light on individuals from subordinate groups who are victimized because of their marginality. As Spade and Wilse note, any critique of hate crimes must acknowledge the advances made by hate crime legislation. But they go on to state that hate crime legislation "reflects the weaknesses of, the overall assimilationist, inclusion-focused mainstream gay agenda."[17] One such weakness is the ways in which hate crime legislation understands violence targeted at social groups as a manifestation of individual prejudice. This formulation of violence as personal rather than social indexes how hate crime legislation intersects with white racial formations. As George Lipsitz notes in *The Possessive Investment in Whiteness*, white racial formations develop out of a disavowal of racism's institutional articulations.[18] Inasmuch as hate crime legislation individualizes violence, and inasmuch as it constitutes the core agenda of mainstream gay organizations, such legislation points to a homonormative racial formation consolidated through a disavowal of inequality's fundamentally structural nature.

Hate crime legislation also betrays a homonormative formation in relation to its understanding of homosexual identity. Spade and Wilse argue that "the legal discourse of hate crimes denies the multiple and shifting characteristics of identity in favor of a simplistic notion that, for example, homosexuality is the same in all people and is not produced in relation to other social variables like language and economic class."[19] Presuming that homosexuality is the same in all people opens it to white racial formation. As homonormative formations cite homosexuality as a category of equivalence, they work to regulate differences of race, gender, and class—differences that disrupt the coherence of homonormativity as an identity politics.

Another site of homonormative formation is homosexual access to the military. As M. Jacqui Alexander and Chandra Mohanty argue in their introduction to *Feminist Genealogies, Colonial Legacies, and Democratic Futures*:

> No understanding of these post–Cold War processes would be complete, however, without an analysis of the strategic function of militarized

masculinity in the reproduction of colonization . . . In "(de)militarized" contexts such as the United States, the figure of the hypermasculinized soldier, previously embodied in the image of whiteness, is diffused globally as the agent of U.S. might . . . New kinds of racial and sexual reconfigurations occur in this era of demilitarization and Cold War politics, when white masculinity can no longer figure itself around particular definitions of soldiering. Because of shifts in the U.S. economy, for instance, the job of state policing now draws disproportionately on the labor and bodies of people of color, both women and men.

One of the most dramatic examples of the crisis in heteromasculinity is the recent state-generated discourse in the United States on "gays" in the military. After months of contestation (including a predictable state lament over its own threatened identity in the context of a reduced military), heteromasculinity reasserted itself, rendered "gay" sexually present yet silent, and erased lesbian sexuality almost entirely. Further, this conclusion promised homosexuality in whiteness, making it possible for "invisible" lesbian and gay soldiers to intervene in the Third World and within communities of color at home.[20]

Homonormative formations arise out of a historic context in which U.S. hegemony enjoys locations within and outside the nation's borders. As with hate crime legislation, we see homonormative formations consolidating over the right to the military. As the nation-state loses coherence because of shifts in the U.S. economy, because of its need for a heterogeneous workforce, and because of the challenges to national authority in the wake of processes of globalization that have no respect for national boundaries, homonormative formations emerge to recuperate the national identity's coherence. As we situate homonormative formations within the genealogy of white ethnicity, we can see the ways in which participation in the public sphere and the recognition as citizen are purchased by regulation, in this case silence.

In this post–September 11th moment, the United States remilitarizes itself to assert hegemony over Arab and Muslim nations. In a *New York Times Magazine* article titled "This Is a Religious War," gay neoconservative Andrew Sullivan writes of the U.S. "war against terrorism." Occasioned by the attacks on the World Trade Center and commenting on the historic indignation that Muslims must have felt over the supremacy of the West (i.e., "the collapse of the Ottoman Empire," "the establishment of the state of Israel," "American bases in Saudi Arabia," etc.), he writes: "I cannot help thinking of this defensiveness [to Western culture by Muslims] when I read stories of the suicide bombers sitting poolside in Florida or racking up a $48 vodka tab in an American restaurant. We tend to think that this assimilation into the West might bring Islamic fundamentalists around somewhat, temper their zeal. But in fact, the opposite is the case. The temptation of American and Western culture—indeed, the very allure of such culture—may well require a repression all the more brutal if it is to be overcome . . . We are fighting for the universal principles of our Constitution, and the possibility of [the] free religious faith it guarantees."[21] We can think of Sullivan's article as paradigmatic of homonormative formations in this moment. Sullivan, as the virtually normal and authentic gay, helps situate the Muslim and the Arab within the colonial gaze of the state. Sullivan endorses the regulations of the state as the means to stability. Abroad, this means endorsing the brutal disciplinary measures of the U.S. government. Domestically, this means supporting fascist and panoptic techniques of discipline against Arab and Muslim immigrants as well as against Arab Americans. Gay rights, inasmuch as it pushes for military inclusion, is only about encouraging those techniques.

The regulations that are called for in the contemporary period count homonormative surveillance as part of their genealogy. In "The Shadows of Stonewall: Examining Gay Transnational Politics and the Diasporic Dilemma," Martin Manalansan designates the mainstream gay and lesbian emphasis on the act of coming out as one site that has served to regulate the racialized and gendered difference of immigrant queers of color. Manalansan points to the racial exclusions produced by homosexual conformity with the developmental narratives of liberal capitalism. He writes: "By privileging Western definitions of same-sex sexual practices, non-Western practices are marginalized and cast as 'premodern' or unliberated. Practices that do not conform with Western narratives of development of individual political subjects are dismissed as unliberated or coded as 'homophobic.' "[22] This logic presents coming out as the standard of liberation and modernity and racializes the closet as the symbol of premodern backwardness. Manalansan writes, "Like the straight modern political subject, the gay subject moves from the immature concealment of his or her sexuality to the mature visibility of political participation in the public sphere. The assumption that practices that are not organized around visibility are 'closeted' and the interpretation that lack of explicitly gay-identified people in the public arena signifies that a homophobic attitude is prevalent in the culture are not interrogated."[23] Extending Manalansan's critique, the racialization of the queer immigrant of color takes place alongside other forms of racialization as well. For instance, gays and lesbians engage homonormative formations at the expense of non-white and/or working-class single mothers who violate the protocols of nuclearity and heteropatriarchy. Homonormative formations emerge to the detriment of HIV-positive immigrants of color who cannot seize visibility as a means of addressing the state because of the threat of deportation. As figures of cultural illegitimacy and backwardness, the single mother and the positive immigrant represent the antithesis of the norms, rights, and privileges that a gay ethnic formation claims to represent. As ethnicity is drawn within normative parameters constituted by racialized privilege and heteronormative conformity, homonormative formations—as they express those parameters—base their practices of exclusion on the racialized logic of cultural difference and nonnormativity.

One way to understand this formulation is to explore the ways in which the formation of homonormative subjectivities and social relations names homosexuality's entrance into white supremacy. As formations excluded from and pathologized by U.S. nationalism in its many iterations, the economically and racially marginalized compel a critique of homonormative formations. As homonormative formations achieve cultural normativity by appealing to liberal capital's regimes of visibility, the immigrant, the poor, and the person of color suffer under the state's apparatuses—apparatuses that render them the cultural antitheses of a stable and healthy social order.

It should be clear by now that this essay is about more than sociology. Indeed, it addresses the complex and intertwined relationships between social formations, difference, and epistemological and national identities. The logic of canonical and homonormative formations intersect by representing the relationships outlined here as disconnected rather than mutually constitutive. Audre Lorde, in her essay "The Master's Tools Will Never Dismantle the Master's House," targets discrete formations as precisely the tools that antiracist queer work must never take up. She writes: "Within the interdependence of mutual (nondominant) differences lies that security which enables us to descend into the chaos of knowledge and return with true visions of our future, along with the concomitant power to effect those changes which can bring the future into being."[24] As we work against normativity, we work against it in all its iterations—political, social, cultural, and epistemological. Our security must come, then, through an engagement with the intersections that characterize our past, present, and future. In the intersections is where we fashion languages against coherence. Intersections are

necessarily messy, chaotic, and heterodox. Why necessarily so? Because intersections are not about identity.

NOTES

1. Steven Epstein, "A Queer Encounter: Sociology and the Study of Sexuality,"
Sociological Theory 12.2 (1994), 189.

2. Ibid., 189–95.

3. We should not take this to mean, however, that the articulation of sexuality by
various sociologists is identical to sexuality as it is understood by Foucault or by queer
theorists.

4. Robert Park, *Race and Culture: Essays in the Sociology of Contemporary Man*
(London: Free Press of Glencoe, 1950), 354.

5. David Roediger and James Barrett, "Inbetween Peoples: Race, Nationality, and
the 'New-Immigrant' Working Class," in *Colored White: Transcending the Racial Past*,
ed. David Roediger (Berkeley: University of California Press, 2002), 142–47.

6. Ibid., 141.

7. I thank Chandan Reddy for bringing this argument to the fore and for this very
helpful language.

8. Robert Park, "Racial Assimilation in Secondary Groups," *American Journal of
Sociology* 19 (1914): 610.

9. Conrad Bentzen, "Notes on the Homosexual in Chicago," March 14, 1938.
Ernest Burgess Collection. Box 145, folder 10. Chicago: University of Chicago Library.
Special Collections.

10. Henry Yu, *Thinking Orientals: Migration, Contact, and Exoticism in Modern
America* (New York: Oxford University Press, 2001), 54.

11. Bentzen, "Notes on the Homosexual in Chicago." Emphasis added.

12. Kevin Mumford, *Interzones: Black/White Sex Districts in Chicago and New York
in the Early Twentieth Century* (New York: Columbia University Press, 1997).

13. Epstein, "A Queer Encounter," 150.

14. Karl Marx, "On the Jewish Question," in *The Marx/Engels Reader*, ed. Robert
Tucker (New York: Norton, 1972), 35.

15. Daryl Hutchinson, "Out Yet Unseen: A Racial Critique of Gay and Lesbian
Legal Theory and Political Discourse," *Connecticut Law Review* (winter 1997): 11.

16. Jane Spade and Craig Wilse, "Confronting the Limits of Gay Hate Crimes
Activism: A Radical Critique," *Chicano-Latino Law Review* 21 (2000): 35.

17. Ibid., 45.

18. George Lipsitz, *The Possessive Investment in Whiteness: How White People Profit
from Identity Politics* (Philadelphia: Temple University Press, 1998).

19. Spade and Wilse, "Confronting the Limits of Gay Hate Crimes Activism," 46.

20. M. Jacqui Alexander and Chandra Talpade Mohanty, eds., *Feminist Genealogies, Colonial Legacies, Democratic Futures* (New York: Routledge, 1997), xxvi.

21. Andrew Sullivan, "This Is a Religious War." *New York Times Magazine,* October 7, 2001, 52.

22. Martin Manalansan, "In the Shadows of Stonewall: Examining Gay Transnational Politics and the Diasporic Dilemma," in *The Politics of Culture in the Shadow of Capital,* ed. Lisa Lowe and David Lloyd (Durham: Duke University Press, 1997), 486.

23. Ibid., 489–90.

24. Audre Lorde, "The Master's Tools Will Never Dismantle the Master's House," in *Sister Outsider* (Freedom, Calif.: Crossing Press, 1993), 111.

DWIGHT A. MCBRIDE

STRAIGHT BLACK STUDIES:
ON AFRICAN AMERICAN STUDIES,
JAMES BALDWIN, AND BLACK
QUEER STUDIES

> The sexual question and the racial question have always been
> entwined, you know. If Americans can mature on the level of
> racism, then they have to mature on the level of sexuality.
> —James Baldwin, in *Conversations with James Baldwin*

This essay is in large measure descriptive in its efforts to account for a
phenomenon that has been part of African Americanist discourse for as long
as the study of African Americans has been of any public and institutional
significance—that is, its heterosexist strain. This essay is also in part analytical
in that in its efforts to describe this phenomenon it attempts to provide a
usable past for black queer studies. I begin here by framing these concerns
with a brief interpretive gloss of remarks made by Essex Hemphill regarding
the situation of black homosexuals in dominant culture. From there, I move
to consider the motivations of the heterosexist strain inherent in much of
African Americanist discourse. This course then leads me to a brief reading
of James Baldwin's *Giovanni's Room* as a text that both provides a challenge to
traditional modes of analysis for African American literary production and
suggests a broadening of what African Americanist critique might mean.
This suggested broadening leads me to a consideration of the critical sensibility we have come to call black queer studies with some attention paid to
the challenges it poses to dominant constructions of African American studies as an institutional formation.

The following text is taken from Essex Hemphill's short but strident personal essay "Loyalty":

I speak for the thousands, perhaps hundreds of thousands of men who live and die in the shadows of secrets, unable to speak of the love that helps them endure and contribute to the race. Their ordinary kisses of sweet spit and loyalty are scrubbed away by the propaganda makers of the race, the "Talented Tenth" . . .

The Black homosexual is hard pressed to gain audience among his heterosexual brothers; even if he is more talented, he is inhibited by his silence or his admissions. This is what the race has depended on in being able to erase homosexuality from our recorded history. The "chosen" history. But the sacred constructions of silence are futile exercises in denial. We will not go away with our issues of sexuality. We are coming home.

It is not enough to tell us that one was a brilliant poet, scientist, educator, or rebel. Whom did he love? It makes a difference. I can't become a whole man simply on what is fed to me: watered-down versions of Black life in America. I need the ass-splitting truth to be told, so I will have something pure to emulate, a reason to remain loyal.[1]

Here Hemphill not only describes well the predicament of the black homosexual in dominant articulations of the African American community, but he also goes far toward metaphorically describing the relationship of black queer identity to dominant articulations of the proper object of the analysis that has congress under the rubric of African American studies—that is, as he states, a race-centered understanding of blackness "riddled with omissions."[2] Indeed, have I seldom witnessed elsewhere the fierce insistence on the impossibility of disarticulating race and sexuality that Hemphill offers in this essay. Journalistic in tone but laced with the poet's diction and phrasing, shockingly sexual, unapologetic about the centrality of sexual pleasure, politically strident (even bordering on sermonic), and all under the mockingly simple title "Loyalty"—Hemphill's essay is keen to demonstrate how the very models of intervention into racial discrimination at the heart of the analysis represented by African American studies are themselves committed to the flattening out (if not the evisceration) of queers or queer sexuality and the challenges they pose to the heterosexist construct that is "the African American community."

Consider for a moment the rhetoric of Hemphill's essay itself: "We will not go away with our issues of sexuality. We are coming home." This rhetorical construction depends on the separation of black gays and lesbians from the location of "home," which Hemphill posits they are "coming home to." This rendering of home as a site of contestation—as opposed to the "welcome table" or "comforting" characterization of home associated with the most dominant, public, and politically salient renderings of the African American community—signals the terms of the relationship of black queer subjectivity to African American identity for Hemphill. Indeed, "home" (a term to which I will return) is the very nexus that has to be rethought. For Hemphill, nothing less than the "ass-splitting truth" will give him something "pure to emulate, a reason to remain loyal." In this appeal for a reason to remain loyal, the writer simultaneously recognizes the political need for the grand unifying category of "the African American community" even as he presses (to the very threat of disloyalty) for a more inclusive version of it.

Also noteworthy in Hemphill's essay is the sarcasm with which he represents "the propaganda makers of the race, the 'Talented Tenth'": "Men emasculated in the complicity of not speaking out, rendered mute by the middle-class aspirations of a people trying hard to forget the shame and cruelties of slavery and ghettos. Through denials and abbreviated histories riddled with omissions, the middle class sets about whitewashing and fixing up the race to impress each other *and* the racists who don't give a damn."[3] In reading this essay, I feel not altogether unlike Farah Griffin who, in the course of her search for a usable past for black feminism, arrived at her critical investigation of the sexism of W. E. B. DuBois (a recognized early male proponent of black feminism).[4] For Hemphill, surely one of the great progenitors of black queer studies, is likewise not without his own limitations. Two features of Hemphill's complaint stand out in this regard: first, the exclusivity (or specificity) of his complaint is made on behalf of gay black men with no explicit recognition of black lesbians; and, second, the way in which he locates the black middle class as the bearers of the ideology or politics of black respectability fails to recognize the dissemination of such ideology beyond the boundaries of that construction. Still, black respectability can be said to be not only at the heart of Hemphill's critique of the African American community's conservatism but also at the heart of a usable past for black queer studies as one of the primary objects of its analysis.[5]

For our purposes, Kali Gross, following the work of Evelyn Brooks Higginbotham,[6] characterizes black respectability in the following manner:

> Historically, as a form of resistance to the negative stigmas and caricatures about their morality, African Americans adopted a "politics

of respectability." Claiming respectability through manners and morality furnished an avenue for African Americans to assert the will and agency to redefine themselves outside the prevailing racist discourses. Although many deployed the politics of respectability as a form of resistance, its ideological nature constituted a deliberate concession to mainstream societal values. The self-imposed adherence to respectability that permeated African American women's lives, as well as African American culture, also later impacted African American activism and the course of scholarship in African American Studies. This strict adherence to what is socially deemed "respectable" has resulted in African American scholars' confining their scholarship on African Americans to often the most "heroic," and the most successful attributes in African American culture; it has also resulted in the proliferation of analyses which can be characterized as culturally defensive, patriarchal, and heterosexist.[7]

Indeed, the politics of black respectability as understood in this way can be seen as laying the foundation for the necessary disavowal of black queers in dominant representations of the African American community, of African American history, and of African American studies.

This essay, then, represents a set of concerns about the related state of African American studies, the state of Baldwin scholarship, and the complicated relationship that Baldwin exhibits to identity politics and how that complexity presages the need for a critical sensibility I align with black queer studies. Indeed, we are in a moment now when this critical sensibility called black queer studies is self-consciously in search of a usable past to define and clarify the significance of its arrival on the scene in its current incarnation. This is evidenced by a proliferation of recent work produced at the margins of race and sexuality.[8]

In my treatment of Baldwin that follows, I do not want to suggest that there have not been other figures who might serve as models in our search for a usable past for black queer studies. Quite the contrary, this is more of a call for further work and further intervention in and interpretation of the past of black queer studies and of the object of its analysis. In fact, one colleague who responded to an earlier version of this essay usefully suggested that by moving my discussion beyond Baldwin to the generation of writers preceding him (Hughes, Locke, McKay), I might avoid essentializing black gay subjectivity.[9] My colleague's concern took me back to the process of conceptualizing

Black Like Us with my coeditors as we worked to construct a narrative for the tradition of queer African American literature (a term about which there will doubtless be much more dissent and drama—as experienced already in the process of obtaining permissions to reprint excerpts from certain living writers and from the estates of certain dead writers who have had problems with the book's subtitle).[10] We decided that in our narrative of this literary tradition the important distinction we wanted to make regarding Baldwin as a kind of transition figure from that earlier generation of writers was to mark him as the first "openly gay" black writer. That is, the fact that he was the first to talk publicly about his homosexuality and to purposefully make use of it in his fiction.

In an interview done in the later years of his life (captured in Karen Thorsen's 1989 documentary *James Baldwin: The Price of the Ticket*), when asked to reflect on why he chose so early on to write about his sexuality (in *Giovanni's Room*) given that he was dealing with the burden of being a black writer in America, Baldwin stated: "Well, one could say almost that I did not have an awful lot of choice. *Giovanni's Room* comes out of something that tormented and frightened me—the question of my own sexuality. It also simplified my life in another way because it meant that *I had no secrets*, nobody could blackmail me. You know . . . you didn't tell me, I told you" (emphasis added). This is not the same, of course, as saying that Baldwin embraced gay sexuality associated with the gay liberation movement, to which he had a rather complicated relationship. Still his public "outing" of himself we regard as significant not only in the development of this particularized tradition of queer African American fiction but also in posing a challenge to dominant, respectable, sanitized narratives of the African American literary tradition and what it can include.

My claim in this regard is, perhaps, finally a modest one: that the state of critical discourse that proceeds under the rubric of African American studies, with its limited embrace of a race-centered identity bias, does so at the expense of other critical forms of difference that are also rightly constitutive of any inclusive understanding of black subjectivity. Perhaps one of the clearest challenges to this kind of thinking that privileges "race" (specifically here racial blackness) as the logos of African American studies can be witnessed in the example of James Baldwin's life and work—and particularly in *Giovanni's Room*. Through a brief consideration of Baldwin's relationship to questions of identity (both his own and his representations of it) we will come to see that his logic is emblematic of long-silent but real complexities and challenges to dominant constructions of the field of African American studies itself.

Given the advent of cultural studies in the academy—with its focus on inter-disciplinarity or transdisciplinarity, critical theory, and an ever-broadening notion of "culture"—it seems more possible today than ever before to engage a prophetic Baldwin in all of the complexity he represents to critical inquiry by considering the various roles he has occupied. Baldwin was no more content to be simply a black writer, a gay writer, or an activist than he was to write exclusively in the genre of the novel, drama, poetry, or the essay. And the topoi of his work and the landscape of his critical and creative imagination are broad, to say the very least. To borrow a phrase from Walt Whitman (in another context): Baldwin is large; he contains multitudes!

Scholarship, however, has tended to relegate Baldwin to one or the other of his identities, rather than directing our thinking—not only of Baldwin but of African American studies generally—in a direction that speaks to the intricate social positions that African Americans occupy. This has much to do with the fact that the trend in scholarship itself—prior to the advent of cultural studies—was ostensibly to identify a particular theme, a category, or a political ideology at work in a text or across an oeuvre in order to fix that variable as part of the process of examining the work in question. Neither Baldwin's life nor his work is easily given over to such an approach. If we try to follow, for example, the deployment of a single idea like "home" or "nothingness" in the context of *Giovanni's Room* (as Kathleen Drowne does in her essay " 'An Irrevocable Condition': Constructions of Home and the Writing of Place in *Giovanni's Room*")[11] we begin immediately to perceive the difficulty of reading Baldwin. Ideas, even in the realm of his imaginative representations, are rarely static for him. Rather, they are drawn to reflect the complex experience of these ideas in our lives. This represents, perhaps, one of the reasons that the critical legacy regarding Baldwin's work has been relatively sparse when viewed in proportion to his voluminous contribution to African American letters.

This is not to say that Baldwin "the man" has not been of great interest or that he has not often appeared in aphoristic ways. Baldwin's words have been used in the work of film directors ranging from Marlon Riggs to Spike Lee; alluded to and cited in popular black gay fiction such as James Earl Hardy's

B-Boy Blues; and quoted by notable African American cultural critics, and race men, such as Henry Louis Gates Jr. and Cornel West. Still, what has gone missing is a sustained, critical engagement with Baldwin's content in the thoroughly active way that criticism has continued to engage with, for example, Richard Wright. This is a point that echoes with more than a little sense of deja vu given that a similar claim was forwarded by Trudier Harris in her groundbreaking 1985 study *Black Women in the Fiction of James Baldwin*:

> On occasion I was surprised to discover that a writer of Baldwin's reputation evoked such vague memories from individuals in the scholarly community, most of whom maintained that they had read one or more of his fictional works. When I began a thorough examination of Baldwin scholarship, however, some of that reaction became clearer. Baldwin seems to be read at times for the sensationalism readers anticipate in his work, but his treatment in scholarly circles is not commensurate to that claim to sensationalism or to his more solidly justified literary reputation. It was discouraging, therefore, to think that one of America's best-known writers, and certainly one of its best-known black writers, has not attained a more substantial place in the scholarship on Afro-American writers.[12]

It is interesting to observe that in 1985 Harris could still note with authority her supposition that many read Baldwin for the "sensationalism" he and his work represented. What I want to be more explicit about, however, is what Harris starts to recognize here implicitly. That is, that Baldwin was read in part because of his exceptionalism, aberrance, or difference from other black writers. Baldwin provided a generation of American and African American readers with characters who were racialized, sexualized, and class inflected in complex ways. Indeed, he does this in such a way that at times a Baldwin reader might yearn for an overdetermined, naturalistic protagonist like "Bigger Thomas" to hold on to. But perhaps this point only leads to the need for a larger project to address the question of the relationship between African American literary criticism and the state and progress of racialized discourse in America over time. I offer these ideas here simply to make the point that cultural studies work and black queer studies work has shown that it is possible to think critically about African Americans and African American culture without simply essentializing the category of racial blackness; appealing to outmoded and problematic notions of an authentic blackness; or fixing, reifying, and/or separating race, gender, and/or sexuality in the name of their political serviceability to racial blackness. With the advent of cultural studies, it seems finally possible to understand Baldwin's vision of and for humanity in its complexity, locating him not as exclusively gay, black, expatriate, activist, or the like, but rather as an intricately negotiated amalgam of all of those things—an amalgam that had to be constantly tailored to fit the circumstances in which he was compelled to articulate himself. The transdisciplinary quality of the intellectual work most closely associated with cultural studies has made it possible for those open to its lessons and trained in African American studies to arrive at a critical sensibility—the emergent black queer studies—that can begin the difficult process of thinking about the ways in which race and sexuality are so deeply imbricated.[13]

Here I want to suggest first that although Baldwin's work challenges static notions of racial identity, his awareness of the hegemony of the category of race in black antiracist discourse still limits the terms of his possible identifications with his gay sexuality. Second, I want briefly to sketch a reading of *Giovanni's Room* that suggests that it is Baldwin's understanding of these same identificatory limits that necessitate the whiteness of the characters in his novel for reasons having to do with its broad, forward-looking, prophetic project.

I begin with the following question: What happens discursively when a gay black man takes up the mantle of race discourse? Again in Thorsen's 1989 documentary of Baldwin's life, there are two moments to which I want to call attention by way of addressing this question. The first is a statement made by Amiri Baraka, and the second is a statement made by Baldwin himself from television interview footage. I turn to these less literally textual examples to demonstrate that in our more casual or less-scripted moments our subconscious understanding of the realities of race discourse is laid bare even more clearly.

Baraka's regard for Baldwin is well documented in the film; for example, he talks about how Baldwin was "in the tradition" and how his early writings, specifically *Notes of a Native Son,* spoke to a whole generation. In an attempt to describe or to account for Baldwin's homosexuality, however, Baraka falters in his efforts to unite the racially significant image of Baldwin that he clings to with the homosexual Baldwin. As Baraka states: "Jimmy Baldwin was neither in the closet about his homosexuality, nor was he running around proclaiming homosexuality. I mean, he was what he was. And you either had to buy that or, you know, *mea culpa,* go somewhere else." The poles of the rhetorical continuum that Baraka sets up here for his understanding of homosexuality are very telling. To Baraka's mind, one can either be in the closet or be "running around proclaiming homosexuality" (the image of the effete gay man and the gay activist collide here, it would seem). For Baraka what makes Baldwin acceptable to enter the pantheon of race men is the fact that his sexual identity is unlocatable. It is neither here nor there, or perhaps it is everywhere at once, leaving undecided and undecidable the entire question. And if Baldwin is undecided about his sexual identity, the one identity to which he seems firmly committed is his racial identity. The rhetorical ambiguity around his sexual identity, according to Baraka, is what makes it possible for Baldwin to be a race man who was "in the tradition."

Baldwin himself, it seems, was well aware of the dangers of (indeed, the "price of the ticket" for) trying to synthesize his racial and sexual identities. He understood that his efficacy as race man was—in part at least—a result of limiting his public activism to his racial politics. The frame of Thorsen's documentary certainly confirms this in the way it represents Baldwin's own response to his sexuality. As Baldwin states: "I think the trick is to say yes to life . . . It is only we of the twentieth century who are so obsessed with the particular details of anybody's sex life. I don't think those details make a difference. And I will never be able to deny a certain power that I have had to deal with, which has dealt with me, which is called love; and love comes in very strange packages. I've loved a few men; I've loved a few women; and a few people have loved me. That's . . . I suppose that's all that's saved my life." It is of interest here to note that while Baldwin is making this statement, the camera pans down to his hands, which are fidgeting with his cigarette and cigarette holder. This move on the part of the camera undercuts the veracity of Baldwin's statement and suggests that he himself does not quite believe all of what he is saying.[14]

If Baldwin's statement on sexuality raises the complications of speaking from a complex racial/sexual identity location, the following excerpt from a television interview on the *Dick Cavett Show* in 1973 illustrates this point all the more clearly:

> I don't know what most white people in this country feel, but I can only conclude what they feel from the state of their institutions. I don't know if white Christians hate Negroes or not, but I know that we have a Christian church which is white and a Christian church which is black . . . I don't know if the board of education hates black people, but I know the textbooks they give my children to read and the schools that we go to.

Now this is the evidence! You want me to make an act of faith risking myself, my wife, my woman, my sister, my children on some idealism which you assure me exists in America which I have never seen.

This passage is conspicuous for the manner in which Baldwin assumes the voice of the representative race man—a category that Hazel Carby complicates in her book on the topic.[15] In the very last sentence, when Baldwin affects the position of race man, part of the performance includes the masking of his specificity, his sexuality, and his difference. And in black antiracist discourse, when all difference is concealed what emerges is the heterosexual black man "risking [himself], [his] wife, [his] woman and [his] children." The image of the black man as protector, progenitor, and defender of the race is what Baldwin assumes here. The truth of this rhetorical transformation is that in order to be the representative race man, one must be both heterosexual and male.[16] Again, it is not my intention here to fault Baldwin for this move, but rather to say that even with his own recognition of the politics of his circumstances he does find ways to mount a counterdiscourse (usually through his fiction) to such exclusive racial identity constructions.

Now let me turn briefly to *Giovanni's Room* to elaborate further on the character of Baldwin's counterdiscourse in this regard. Baldwin makes plain a logic in 1957 that has come to be a received part of public discourse about homosexuality in America today. That is, one of the reasons that people fear queer sexuality so violently has to do with the fact that it threatens an ideology in America that is older and stronger even than baseball or apple pie—it threatens the idea of "home." This is what Baldwin understands and presages so well in *Giovanni's Room* through the representation of the complexity of the character of David, drawn as he is at the crossroads of nationality (Americanness), sexuality (or homosexuality or at least bisexuality), and home (or place and social responsibility/respectability). In order that the themes of this work might be (to use an ugly word for a moment) "universalized," Baldwin knew enough about how race worked in America (and continues to work) to know that it was impossible to use black characters. In a letter dated January 1954 to William Cole—the editor who first brought Baldwin and *Go Tell It on the Mountain* to the attention of Knopf—Baldwin wrote the following words about *Giovanni's Room* shortly after he had begun working on it:

It's a great departure for me; and it makes me rather nervous. It's not about Negroes first of all; its locale is the American colony in Paris. What is really delicate about it is that since I want to convey something about the kinds of American loneliness, I must use the most ordinary type of American I can find—the good, white Protestant is the kind of image I want to use. This is precisely the type of American about whose setting I know the least. Whether this will be enough to create a real human being, only time will tell. It's a love story—short, and wouldn't you know it, tragic. Our American boy comes to Europe, finds something, loses it, and in his acceptance of his loss becomes, to my mind, heroic.[17]

Here we see, among other things, that only whiteness is sufficient to represent large, broad, "universal" concerns. To Baldwin's mind, black characters—in their always overdrawn specificity—could only represent in the 1950s popular imagination the problems specific to blacks and are therefore easily dismissed as irrelevant beyond those confines. Marlon Ross puts the entire business of the whiteness of the characters in *Giovanni's Room* somewhat differently, though along similar lines of thought, when he writes: "If the characters had been black, the novel would have been read as being 'about' blackness, whatever else it happened actually to be about. The whiteness of the characters seems to make invisible the question of how race or color has, in fact, shaped the characters—at least as far as most readers have dealt with the novel." Ross continues:

> In other words, Baldwin revises W. E. B. Du Bois's question "How does it feel to be a problem?" For Baldwin, it is not "the strange meaning of being black" that is the "problem of the Twentieth Century," nor even "the problem of the color-line." Baldwin makes the central problem of the twentieth century the strange meaning of being white, as a structure of feeling within the self and within history—a structure of felt experience that motivates and is motivated by other denials. In *Giovanni's Room,* he posits the white man as a problem and then fantasizes what it might mean for a particular upperclass white man to become aware of the problematic nature of his desire—color not as "line" of demarcation but instead as a point of departure. Given the invisibility of whiteness as a racially constricted burden of desire, however, Baldwin also shows how even the most deeply taboo and widely outlawed desire can be cushioned by the privileged invisibility of whiteness.[18]

It is important to note that Ross's essay implies (albeit does not make explicit) that Baldwin's novel may be among the possible progenitors of the area of whiteness studies, a field of inquiry that has gained a lot of attention over the past decade or so.

Giovanni's Room is not a novel about gay sexuality as much as it is about the social and discursive forces that make a "problem" of gay sexuality. Even in this context, however, Baldwin does not sacrifice the complexity of the social and discursive forces involved in this process. Everywhere in *Giovanni's Room* national identity, for example, is sexualized. Consider the following scene from David's visit to the American Express Office in Paris and how he describes the Americans:

> *At home,* I could have distinguished patterns, habits, accents of speech— with no effort whatever: *now* everybody sounded, unless I listened hard, as though they had just arrived from Nebraska. *At home* I could have seen the clothes they were wearing, but *here* I only saw bags, cameras, belts, and hats, all clearly from the same department store. *At home* I would have had a sense of the individual womanhood of the woman I faced; here the most ferociously accomplished seemed to be involved in some ice-cold or sun-dried travesty of sex, and even grandmothers seemed to have no traffic with the flesh. And what distinguished the men was that they seemed incapable of age; they smelled of soap, which seemed indeed to be their preservative against the dangers and exigencies of any more intimate odor; the boy he had been shone, somehow, unsoiled, untouched, unchanged, through the eyes of the man of sixty, booking passage with a smiling wife, to Rome. [emphasis added][19]

David sees these Americans abroad in the new light of the foreigner's eye. The language he invokes to characterize them is not dissimilar in tone from the language that Giovanni will later use to describe David in the heat of their final argument in the novel. Especially noteworthy here is the claim that Americans preserve a kind of innocence that has "no traffic with the flesh."

Part of David's dilemma throughout the novel is that he views sexual identity as in need of domestication so that it can be turned into "home" (witness his despair about "wandering" [84],[20] his "sorrow," "shame," "panic," and "great bitterness" about the "beast Giovanni had awakened in him" [110–11]). This sense of home, fixity, stability—represented in the novel by America and his father—comes through most clearly in a letter from David's father to David where we learn of his (surely tongue-in-cheek) nickname, Butch. The father writes: "Dear Butch . . . aren't you ever coming home? Don't think I'm only being selfish but its true I'd like to see you. I think you have been away long enough, God knows I don't know what you're doing over there, and you don't write enough for me even to guess. But my guess is you're going to be sorry one of these fine days that you stayed over there, looking at your navel, and let the world pass you by. There's nothing over there for you. You're as American as pork and beans, though maybe you don't want to think so anymore" (119–120).

David's father's obsession is, in part, with time. Again, this is an obsession that Giovanni identifies as very American. To David's father's mind if David is not being a man of action (and in accordance with a rather predetermined heteronormative script, at that) then he is wasting time by wandering. Wandering is an important theme in *Giovanni's Room*: wandering, or lack of focus, is associated with wayward sexualities (Hella in Spain, David with Giovanni). It is dangerous. As David queries at one of the moments when he faces the fear of his sexuality: "The beast which Giovanni had awakened in me would never go to sleep again . . . would I then, like all the others, find myself turning and following all kinds of boys, down God knows what dark avenues, into what dark places?" (111). Gay sexuality in the novel points up desire's ability to be unfocused. This lack of focus is ultimately one of the biggest threats to heterosexuality (in a world where heterosexuality equals focus). Hearth, home, and heteronormative pairings are all impossible without the sexual focus they presuppose in the form of monogamous, heterosexual coupling.

David's desire for Hella itself represents his desire for the idea of "home." Consider the scene when they are reunited at the train station in Paris:

> I had hoped that when I saw her something instantaneous, definitive, would have happened in me, something to make me know where I should be and where I was. But nothing happened . . .
>
> Then I took her in my arms and something happened then. I was terribly glad to see her. It really seemed with Hella in the circle of my arms, that my arms were home and I was welcoming her back there. She fitted in my arms as she always had, and the shock of holding her caused me to feel that my arms had been empty since she had been away. (158–59)

If home equals heterosexuality equals nationhood, then it is David's desire to fulfill the heteronormative narrative laid out for him as his American birthright that he recognizes in Hella. Indeed, the lure of it is so strong in this moment that it has the force—even if only for the moment—of erasing any and all of David's prior wayward sexual exploits. He feels as if his "arms had been empty since she had been away." Again, I want to suggest that a rather complicated relationship between home, nation, and sexuality (which I do not sort out completely here) is represented in the text and bears further consideration.

From the time we begin to hear David's story he is, to the logic of his mind, already in trouble—an American in Paris, exiled, unfocused, wandering. David is plagued not simply by some nebulous ideology about gay sexuality but by the complex set of responses that arise when the young American man comes up against the overwhelming weight of what is expected of him in the world. This is the drama that drives David's psychological angst in the narrative. Giovanni names it in the final argument between the two of them in this exchange:

> [David] "All this love you talk about—isn't it just that you want to be made to feel strong? You want to go out and be the big laborer and bring home the money, and you want me to stay here and wash the dishes and cook the food and clean this miserable closet of a room and kiss you when you come in through that door and lie with you at night and be your little *girl* . . . that's all you mean when you say you love me. You say I want to kill *you*. What do you think you've been doing to me?"
>
> "I am not trying to make you a little girl. If I wanted a little girl, I would be *with* a little girl."
>
> "Why aren't you? Isn't it just that you're afraid? And you take *me* because you haven't got the guts to go after a woman, which is what you *really* want?"
>
> He was pale. "You are the one who keeps talking about *what* I want. But I have only been talking about *who* I want." (188–89)

The last word is Giovanni's here. David is still trying to explain his feelings, his sexuality in terms of a heteronormative cultural narrative, which is why he is consumed by the "what" (ideological forces). Giovanni, on the other hand is unhampered by such concerns and is focused on "who" he loves (David) and not on what it means.

This moment is reminiscent of one earlier in the same argument when Giovanni first ruminates on why David is leaving him:

> "Giovanni," I said, "you always knew that I would leave one day. You knew my fiancée was coming back to Paris."

"You are not leaving me for her," he said. . . . "You are not leaving me for a *woman*. If you were really in love with that little girl, you would not have to be so cruel to me."

"She's not a little girl," I said. "She's a woman and no matter what you think, I *do* love her—"

"You do not," cried Giovanni, sitting up, "love anyone! You have never loved anyone, I am sure you never will! You love your purity, you love your mirror—you are just like a little virgin, you walk around with your hands in front of you as though you had some precious metal, gold, silver, rubies, maybe diamonds down there between your legs! You will never let anybody touch it—man or woman. You want to be clean. You think you came here covered with soap and you think you will go out covered with soap—and you do not want to stink, not even for five minutes, in the meantime . . . You want to leave Giovanni because he makes you stink. You want to despise Giovanni because he is not afraid of the stink of love. You want to kill him in the name of all your lying little moralities." (186–87)

The very thing that Baldwin extols here in Giovanni in contrast to David (i.e., David's obsession with being pure and clean—rendered, by association, as a very American desire complicated by his nationality in the novel) is what characterizes the topoi of Baldwin's work and art. He did not care for purity. Rather, he wallowed in the dirt of the unclean places of the psyche, the cluttered rooms where life, for him, really happened. David—not unlike the representations of an institutionalized African American studies—represents the pitfalls and suffering of a life lived in observance of the rules about what we should be, how we should love, indeed, what we should feel. While the price exacted on Giovanni for the choice to live freely in defiance of social order is high, it seems to receive Baldwin's ultimate approbation. On the other hand, although David lives he is the one who represents a more profound death—indeed, an emotional death that he must live with.

As a novel with no African American characters yet written by an African American gay writer, *Giovanni's Room* itself challenges dominant understandings of what constitutes African American literature, the work that proceeds under the rubric of African American literary criticism, and the forms of analysis that would come to have congress under the institutional formation of African American studies. Given its unusual status, it seems to me somewhat prophetic in its call for a criticism, a way of thinking, a critical sensibility that would not arrive on the scene until many years after its publication in 1956. In this regard, Baldwin's novel perhaps represents one of the early direct calls for a more textured conceptualization of the kind of complex formulations necessary in artistic production, criticism, and discourse to truly address anything that approximates the richness and complexity of that most politically essential and politically irksome appellation "the African American community."

In an essay in a December 2000 issue of the *Chronicle of Higher Education*, historian Nell Irvin Painter had occasion to reflect on the state of African American studies:

> After more than a quarter-century in academe, including a couple of stints as the director of a program in African-American studies and countless conversations with colleagues around the country, I have reached some conclusions regarding black faculty members and black studies. First, black studies: The time is right for a reassessment of the field. Last year several prominent departments and programs in African-American/Afro-American/black studies celebrated their 30th anniversaries—including Cornell University, Harvard University, the University of California at Berkeley, and my own Princeton University. (The pioneering department at San Francisco State University was founded three years earlier than those others.) Second, black faculty members: Our numbers remain small, although not inconsequential. Finally, both black studies and black faculty members, often seen in countless academic minds as kindred phenomena, still face familiar frustrations. For the widespread American assumption that black people are not intellectual affects everyone in higher education who is black or who does black studies.[21]

It is not the particular claims that Painter makes in her essay that concern me here; indeed, her remarks are not only sound but ring very true as a description of black faculty and of black studies in the contemporary academy. Still, what fascinates me most about this piece for my purposes is the mode in which African American studies is presented by Painter, whose perspective is quite representative of the state of African Americanist discourse. Her article focuses entirely on the institutional problems that African American studies faced in its inception, and on how many of those problems continue to plague such departments and programs in the academy to this very day.

Painter's discourse represents African American studies as embattled institutionally and, once again, identifies the primacy of that crisis as one of race to the extent that the fundamental problem for her is still how "the widespread American assumption that black people are not intellectual affects everyone in higher education who is black or who does black studies." In setting up her examination of African American studies in this way, Painter's remarks necessarily center on how an embattled African American studies has to respond to the racist forces of institutions that resist its presence in a variety of ways. And indeed, in this regard Painter's rhetorical strategy is not unique but can be seen as rather representative. What this strategy does not allow, however, is space for an analysis or a critique of the internal structure and strictures of the race-based discourse of African American studies itself, which, of course, underlies and animates Painter's representation of the field. That is, Painter's reflections come short of addressing the limitations of the exclusionary race-based thinking necessitated when institutional location is the primary rhetorical concern for African American studies, but also such rhetoric often blinds us to such realities.

Admittedly, this has much to do with the discursive history of African American studies in white academic institutions—that is, in most contexts the question of racial representation (in terms of bodies on campuses and in terms of curricula) was primary to the institutional rise of African American studies. Still, this does not fully address the traditional discursive bias in African American studies for the analysis of black culture, history, life, and politics that centers on racial blackness to the exclusion of other important categories of analysis that rightfully belong to any comprehensive understanding of black people in all of our complexity.

In her essay "Nothing Fails Like Success," Barbara Johnson discusses the discursive impact of the rise of deconstructionism in the academy in relation to the rhetoric of "success." Her example is instructive to our case here as well. Part of how success is defined, in terms of the institutional success of an intellectual project in the academy, has to do with its successful integration into a system that may at first have resisted its presence. This could, Johnson maintains, entail a loss of the very radicality of the subject that created the institutional resistance to it to begin with. Johnson puts the matter in this way: "As soon as any radically innovative thought becomes an *ism*, its specific groundbreaking force diminishes, its historical notoriety increases, and its disciples tend to become more simplistic, more dogmatic, and ultimately more conservative, at which time its power becomes institutional rather than analytical."[22] Here we should recall Painter's institutional representation of African American studies from a little earlier, alongside the African American literary establishment's inability to adequately (until very recently) address Baldwin's *Giovanni's Room*, as I discussed above. Johnson's concerns about the institutionalization of deconstruction well illuminate our discussion of African American studies. Though African American studies is not precisely an "ism," it functions institutionally, in terms of its location and its history, much like one. And, more important, it is based in a fundamental "ism"—"racism"—that has its own troubled past within academia.[23]

Literary and cultural critic Wahneema Lubiano, in her incisive essay "Mapping the Interstices between Afro-American Cultural Discourse and Cultural Studies: A Prolegomenon," usefully defines African American studies as

> a name for the institutionalization of a set of imperatives, approaches, political engagements, and privileged "interdisciplinariness" as paradigms and sites for counter-hegemonic cultural work. Historically, intellectuals involved in Afro-American Studies have seen their work as explicit and implicit interruptions (or attempts to interrupt) the traditional academic strangleholds on knowledge categories. The object of their interventions is to change the world by means of demystifying the relationship of "knowledge" producers to "knowledge," as well as to foreground the connection between "culture" and Afro-American "everyday life."[24]

Again, as with Barbara Johnson, here with Lubiano there is the recognition of the problem inherent in African American studies' institutional rise. Though the specifics of my claim are not what Lubiano or Johnson had in mind, their work makes this present articulation possible. My claim, again, is that African American studies' institutional rise necessitated the primacy of race politics with regard to its embattled and contested institutional status. It is often the case that in institutional warfare, so to speak, institutions reduce and simplify the identities of the subjects they interpellate. The political privileging of race politics on the institutional level, in this context, had the effect of privileging the category of race in the intellectual identity of African American studies. This could not help but to limit in great measure the scope and possibility of the knowledge-corrective work that proceeded under the banner of African American studies. Seldom did such work allow for diversity in the very idea of, or representation of, black subjectivity. This often led to the collapsing of differences of gender, class, and sexuality into a more homogeneous, hegemonic black subjectivity.

The work that I am suggesting is underway in the emergent field of black queer studies, then, is not so much a return of the repressed as it is another phase in what Lubiano identifies as the "contestatory nature of Afro-American cultural discourse." In a reading of Alain Locke's "The Legacy of the Ancestral Arts," from his time-honored classic *The New Negro*, Lubiano offers the following words:

> Following the pattern of continual reconstitution of Afro-Americanness established from as varied a group as one could imagine . . . ex-slaves, craftspersons, laborers, intellectuals, political activists, preachers, and the critics of the Harlem Renaissance rewrote African American history in order to rewrite African American identity and to transform the material conditions of African American life. They were interested in scientizing, in specialized professional discourses—something about which some later manifestations of Black Studies (as [Sinclair] Drake, [Johnetta] Cole, and [Lucius] Outlaw above note) would be suspicious, a suspicion embodied in critiques of "objectivity" and other paradigms of Western knowledge.[25]

If Lubiano's assessment of the "pattern of continual reconstitution" is true, then the arrival on the scene of black queer studies should neither shock nor surprise. In fact, the work of Baldwin, in the context of such a rendering of the evolution of African American studies, would make his prophetic call for a black queer studies a near inevitability.

If Baldwin has only in more recent years come into a kind of critical vogue it is because of what I am suggesting is the insufficiency of a traditional African American studies—as shown by the arrival onto the scene, in turn and over time, of black feminist critique, black diaspora studies (which addresses the transatlantic or global context of African American studies), and more recently black queer studies, which has insisted on bringing home issues of sexuality in an African American studies context. Baldwin's early work like *Giovanni's Room* posed challenges, as I have discussed, not only for literary studies but for what would become black studies and queer studies. The specificity of the challenges posed are now being met by the specificity of the sensibility of what I am calling black queer studies—which is located at the porous limits of both African American studies and of queer studies.[26]

Baldwin's work not only reminds us again and again but, indeed, insists on the constant rearticulation of the "complexity of racial identities."[27] He reminds us that whenever we are speaking of race, we are always already speaking about gender, sexuality, and class.

NOTES

I wish to thank my colleagues in the University of Illinois, Chicago Queer Faculty Reading Group (especially Jennifer Brody, Sharon Holland, Jamie Hovey, John D'Emilio, and Gretchen Kenagy) for their comments on an early draft of this essay. For the opportunity to present this work, I also wish to thank the Program in Gender Studies and the Departments of African American Studies and English at Northwestern University; the Department of African American Studies at Yale University; the Center for the Study of Gender, the Center for the Study of Race, Politics, and Culture, and the Lesbian and Gay Studies Project at the University of Chicago; and the Master of Arts in Liberal Studies Program at Dartmouth College.

1. Essex Hemphill, *Ceremonies* (San Francisco: Cleis Press, 2000 [1992]), 70.

2. Ibid.

3. Ibid.

4. Farah Griffin, "Black Feminists and DuBois: Respectability, Protection, and Beyond," *Annals of the American Academy of Political and Social Science* 568 (March 2000): 28–40.

5. Devon Carbado, Donald Weise, and I make this argument in our coedited volume, *Black Like Us: A Century of Lesbian, Gay, and Bi-Sexual African American Fiction* (San Francisco: Cleis Press, 2002).

6. Evelyn Brooks Higginbotham, *Righteous Discontent: The Women's Movement in the Black Baptist Church, 1880–1920* (Cambridge, Mass.: Harvard University Press, 1994).

7. Kali N. Gross, "Examining the Politics of Respectability in African-American Studies," *University of Pennsylvania Almanac* 43.28 (April 1, 1997), online at http://www.upenn.edu/almanac/v43/n28/benchmrk.html.

8. Its most self-conscious manifestations to date, perhaps, come in the form of the extraordinary Black Queer Studies in the Millennium conference organized by E. Patrick Johnson and Mae G. Henderson (and hence this volume) as well as in a special issue of the journal *Callaloo*, coedited by Jennifer Brody and myself, titled "Plum Nelly: New Essays in Black Queer Studies," which was launched at the Black Queer Studies in the Millennium conference. After the Black Nations/Queer Nations conference held in New York City in 1995, the Black Queer Studies in the Millennium conference represents the single most significant gathering of its kind to take place in the country. At the time of this writing, an announcement of the confer-

ence listing the names of the participants could be found archived on the Web at http://www.unc.edu/~epjohnso/bqs.html.

9. I am thankful to Susan Manning at Northwestern University for engaging me in this very productive conversation.

10. The original subtitle was "A Century of Queer African American Literature." It was changed in response to concerns and discussion over the term "queer."

11. Kathleen Drowne, " 'An Irrevocable Condition': Constructions of Home and the Writing of Place in *Giovanni's Room*," in *Re-Viewing James Baldwin: Things Not Seen,* ed. D. Quentin Miller (Philadelphia: Temple University Press, 2000).

12. Trudier Harris, *Black Women in the Fiction of James Baldwin* (Knoxville: University of Tennessee Press, 1985), 3–4.

13. Some of the most visible exemplars of this kind of work, to name but a few, include literary and cultural critics Phillip Brian Harper, *Are We Not Men? Masculine Anxiety and the Problem of African-American Identity* (New York: Oxford University Press, 1996); Robert Reid-Pharr, *Black Gay Man* (New York: New York University Press, 2001); and Cathy Cohen, *The Boundaries of Blackness: AIDS and the Breakdown of Black Politics* (Chicago: University of Chicago Press, 1999).

14. As offered in the 1949 essay "The Preservation of Innocence," which he wrote and published in the small Moroccan journal *Zero,* Baldwin knows just how profoundly important sexuality is to discussions of race. But it is also important to recognize the desire registered here for sexuality not to make a difference. When we understand this statement as spoken in a prophetic mode, it imagines a world in which the details of a person's sex life can "matter" as part of a person's humanity but not have to "matter" in terms that usurp their authority or legitimacy to represent the race.

15. Hazel Carby, *Race Men* (Cambridge, Mass.: Harvard University Press, 1998).

16. Black women, in this regard, would in the confines of race discourse appear to be ever the passive players. They are rhetorically useful in that they lend legitimacy to the black male's responsibility for their care and protection, but they cannot speak any more than can the gay or lesbian brother or sister. See Dwight A. McBride, "Can the Queen Speak? Racial Essentialism, Sexuality and the Problem of Authority," *Callaloo* 21.2 (1998): 363–79. The gendered portion of this critique has been argued by black feminist critics since at least the early 1970s with the likes of Toni Cade Bambara, *The Black Woman: An Anthology* (New York: Mentor, 1970) and extending to more recent works such as Carby, *Race Men*; Valerie Smith, *Not Just Race, Not Just Gender: Black Feminist Readings* (New York: Routledge, 1998); E. Frances White, *Dark Continent of Our Bodies: Black Feminism and the Politics of Respectability* (Philadelphia: Temple University Press, 2001); Griffin, "Black Feminists and DuBois," and many others.

17. This letter is read aloud by Cole in the film *James Baldwin: The Price of the Ticket* (dir. Karen Thorsen, Nobody Knows Productions, 1989).

18. Marlon B. Ross, "White Fantasies of Desire: Baldwin and the Racial Identities

of Sexuality," *James Baldwin Now*, ed. Dwight A. McBride (New York: New York University Press, 1999), 25.

19. James Baldwin, *Giovanni's Room* (New York: Dell, 1988 [1956]), 118. Further references to this work are given as page numbers in the text.

20. A euphemism utilized by Gertrude Stein in *Melanctha* to signal wayward or promiscuous sexuality.

21. Nell Painter, "Black Studies, Black Professors, and the Struggles of Perception," *Chronicle of Higher Education*, December 15, 2000, B7.

22. Barbara Johnson, "Nothing Fails Like Success," in *A World of Difference* (Baltimore: Johns Hopkins University Press, 1987), 11.

23. The following is the OED entry for "racism": "1936 L. DENNIS Coming Amer. Fascism 109 If . . . it be assumed that one of our values should be a type of racism which excludes certain races from citizenship, then the plan of execution should provide for the annihilation, deportation, or sterilization of the excluded races. 1938 E. & C. PAUL tr. Hirschfeld's Racism xx. 260 The apostles and energumens of racism can in all good faith give free rein to impulses of which they would be ashamed did they realise their true nature. 1940 R. BENEDICT Race: Science & Politics i. 7 Racism is an ism to which everyone in the world today is exposed. 1952 M. BERGER Equality by Statute 236 Racism, tension in industrial, urban areas. 1952 Theology LV. 283 The idolatry of our time—its setting up of nationalism, racism, vulgar materialism. 1960 New Left Rev. Jan./Feb. 21/2 George Rogers saw fit to kow-tow to the incipient racism of his electorate by including a line about getting rid of 'undesirable elements.' "

24. Wahneema Lubiano, "Mapping the Interstices between Afro-American Cultural Discourse and Cultural Studies: A Prologue," *Callaloo* 19. 1 (1996): 68.

25. Ibid., 73–74.

26. Black queer studies has been defined by Jennifer DeVere Brody and myself in "Plum Nelly" as a critical sensibility that draws "its influences from sources such as identity politics, cultural studies, feminist and gender studies, race theory, gay and lesbian studies, masculinity studies and queer studies." Its primary goal is the push "for a greater degree of specificity in both the questions being formulated and on the conclusions being reached at the margins of American society" (286). See Jennifer DeVere Brody and Dwight A. McBride, introduction to "Plum Nelly: New Essays in Black Queer Studies," *Callaloo* 23.1 (2000): 286–88.

27. The very language of this phrase is caught up in the primacy of race in the discussion of racial identity. But for now it will have to suffice.

· ·

RINALDO WALCOTT

· ·

OUTSIDE IN BLACK STUDIES:

READING FROM A QUEER PLACE

IN THE DIASPORA

> Kissing my ass could bring you closer to god.
> —Dusty Dixon, in *Welcome to Africville*

Toward the end of the last millennium and the beginning of the new one, reassessments have been taking place of the black studies project and its emergent twin, black diaspora studies. Manning Marable's edited collection *Dispatches from the Ebony Tower;* Carole Boyce Davies's *Decolonizing the Academy: Diaspora Theory and African New-World Studies;* and several issues of the *Black Scholar* (vol. 30, no. 3–4; vol. 31, no.1) are exemplary texts in these reassessments. A bevy of conferences have also taken place, for example Black Queer Studies in the Millennium (University of North Carolina, Chapel Hill, April 2000); African, Afro-American and African Diaspora Studies in the Twenty-First Century (University of Pennsylvania, Philadelphia, April 2000); as well as the conference that led to the edited collection by Davies. These reassessments of the black studies project place on the table, at least for me, what might be at stake in our readings of what constitute the terms, codes, and conditions of the project. And, to this end, much of these conversations concerning the black studies project return us to its very recent past and clearly to memories of trauma, pain, injury, and what is recognized as a precarious triumph in its institutionalization. In this essay I investigate what might be at stake when the black studies project, diaspora studies, and queer studies collide in our reading practices. I argue for what I call a diaspora reading practice, which can disrupt the centrality of nationalist discourses within the black studies project and thereby also allow for an elaboration of a black queer diaspora project.[1]

I initially wanted to title this essay "Why Black Studies Won't Go Down, But I Keep Blowing Wid It," but I did not want to give the impression that I am only interested in oral or verbal forms of communicating. However, when Dusty Dixon tells us in Dana C. Inkster's film *Welcome to Africville* (1999) that kissing her ass could bring you closer to god, she places a premium on the relationship between the practice of the erotic and the erotics of pedagogy. It is the erotics of pedagogy or the lack thereof that I want to hint at (among other things) in relation to the black studies project. I want to comment on what I see as the potential of a black queer diaspora studies to rejuvenate the liberatory moments of the black studies project. Let me state here that I think the possibilities of black queer studies within the black studies project can only act to elaborate the terms of a potential liberation, because queer studies interrupts the black studies project as it stands by putting on the agenda new and different positions and conditions for thinking. Let me be clear, I am not constituting black queer studies as the vanguard of a liberatory project but rather as the unthought of what might be thinkable within the confines of the black studies project proper and what might be the constitutive knowledge of a renewed black studies project proper. Is black queer studies the improper subject of the black studies project? Or can black queer studies even reside within the confines of the black studies project proper? These are important questions and are not meant to be immediately resolved but rather continually evoked as the basis for an ethicality to the black studies project. Further, I want to evoke a more troubling side of the black studies project—its inability to continue to render complex and shifting notions of community and, for my purpose, diaspora.[2] And yet community as a discourse and a practice remains the fetish of the black studies project. Why is this? My intervention is concerned with the thought of thinking and with the thought and practice of thinking queerly. I am primarily interested in issues of conceptualization as opposed to the empirical foundationality of the black studies project per se. In this regard I will conclude my comments by returning to and discussing the film *Welcome to Africville* as an example of what the exploration of a queer unthought can bring to questions of community, nation, diaspora, and therefore the black studies project.

The black studies project tends to produce community in two overlapping registers: first, community as homogenous, despite much noises to the contrary; and, second, black community as largely based in the United States and therefore relegated to the "national thing."[3] There are variations on these themes but they tend to largely remain steady. The 1980s witnessed the crashing of the community as one in the black studies project by the black British cultural studies invasion. In many senses this was a celebratory return of the repressed and therefore the diaspora, to the black studies project. The various continual returns to the continental space of Africa complicates my reduction. However, these interventions into the black studies project tend to turn on how U.S. blackness is implicated and positioned and often the debate or the limit of analysis tends to get stuck there, even when the diaspora is at issue.[4] The Caribbean, Latin America, and Canada (the latter being the most queer of diaspora places) are hardly taken up within the black studies project.[5] Again, there are always some exceptions; but why is it that the black studies project has hung its hat so lovingly on U.S. blackness and therefore a "neat" national project? And how does a renewed interest in questions of the diaspora seem to only be able to tolerate U.S. blackness and British blackness? Finally, how does imperialism figure in national subaltern studies? Let me say that this is not an argument for inclusion—such arguments do not take seriously diaspora circuits and the identifications, disidentifications, and cultural sharing and borrowing that occur in that symbolic and political space. The brief point that I want to make here is that black diaspora queers have actually pushed the boundaries of transnational identification much further than we sometimes recognize.[6] Black diaspora queers live in a borderless, large world of shared identifications and imagined historical relations produced through a range of fluid cultural artifacts like film, music, clothing, gesture, and signs or symbols, not to mention sex and its dangerously pleasurable fluids. In fact, black diaspora queers have been interrupting and arresting the black studies project to produce a bevy of identifications, which confound and complicate local, national, and transnational desires, hopes, and disappointments of the post–Civil Rights and post–Black Power era.

I want to bring to bear the sensibilities of the diaspora to read the black studies project, but I also want to signal some difficult moments concerning conceptions of community and diaspora in the black studies project when queers cruise in that zone. In particular, I want to exorcise the repressed relationship between the black studies project as a national issue and therefore its limit—a limit that places it in disjunct time with diaspora desires and identifications. To exorcize this repression I need briefly to outline what I think is at stake in calling out the nation-centered heteronormativity of the black studies project. It is only too obvious to say that by and large the black studies project has in its thought produced black community as assumed and essentially heterosexual. Despite the evidence of difference, and even sometimes its celebration, the black studies project has not adequately incorporated nor engaged the thought of thinking blackness differently, especially when it encounters black queers. I think this lack has much to do with the pedagogical nature of the black studies project—its careful desire for "epistemological respectability"[7] and its continued ambiguous and ambivalent institutionalization. The historical precariousness of the black studies project in the U.S. academy means that its pedagogical impulse has been fashioned by an attempt to correct current and historical wrongs and to produce a relation to knowledge production that is irreducible to the so-called lived experiences of a homogenized blackness or black community. In this sense the black studies project is too narrowly fashioned as a corrective for wounds and/or injuries, and in a larger sense for African American dislocations from a Euro-normative nation-making project.[8] In short, the black studies project in its institutionalization has come to stand in for one kind of black respectable community through which its relation to its imagined community is a one-on-one match. Black queers mess with that desired respectability by bringing their shameful and funky sexual practices to it.[9] As we all know, it is exactly this attempt to have a one-on-one match that constitutes the major crises of the black studies project and projects for the making of community everywhere—even in queer studies proper. What is demanded is a rethinking of community that might allow for different ways of cohering into some form of recognizable political entity. Put another way, we must confront singularities without the willed effort to make them cohere into a oneness; we must struggle to make a community of singularities of which the unworking of the present ruling regime, a regime that trades on the myths of homogeneity, must be central. In short, a different sociality is required—a sociality of mutual recognitions.[10]

It is the wounds and injuries of African American positionality, and black peoples more generally, that have conditioned the monolingual voice of the black studies project. The wound of always seeming to be on the outside has worked to produce the black studies project as a constant corrective to the elisions of normative national narratives. Nonetheless, I want to augment and amend a question that William Haver asked of queer studies and research: What if black studies [queer studies] were to refuse epistemological respectability, to refuse to constitute that wounded identity as an epistemological object such as would define, institute, and thus institutionalize a disciplinary field?[11] Haver is insistent that subaltern studies and research might refuse, in his words, the "intellectual hegemony, to provide a better explanation of the world"[12] in favor of articulating a world in which we act politically. That is, a political theory of acts that concerns itself with "an active intervention, a provocation: an interruption rather than a reproduction."[13] What would such a practice of black studies do to our relation to knowledge? Would this queer black studies produce a kind of knowledge that would allow "for something queer to happen" to all of us in the black studies project, as Deborah Britzman has asked of the discipline of education? Can the black studies project "stop being straight"?[14] I would like to suggest that it could.

Haver further argues that research is an "unworking without destination, thinking as departure, 'research' is essentially nomadic, something that happens."[15] Haver calls for a queer research that does more than reproduce recognizable social and cultural wounds of queer identity. He is neither dismissing nor undermining the evidence of the punishing nature within which proclaiming such identities occurs, but rather he would have us think the thought of thinking identity when those thoughts result in something queer happening to all of us in the contexts of the institutional sites of "research," pedagogy, and importantly disciplinarity. But his comments are important to me for other reasons as well, in particular his suggestion that "research" as a departure accords with conceptualizations of the diaspora, which has as one of its tenants the problematics of departure. In fact, I am suggesting that the interruption of the black studies project by black diaspora queers is in part a departure from the project only to return to it in ways that elaborate it by extending its discourse and potential as a liberatory project reaching beyond the institutional site and location.

I want to ask what queer positions might mean for the remaking of the black studies project as a multidisciplinary and cross-disciplinary configuration. I want to ask why the "difficult knowledge" of the black queer diaspora remains on the edges. In particular I want to use Deborah Britzman's notion of "difficult knowledge"[16] to ask what is difficult about black queer positions in the black studies project and what might be at stake when black queer positions continue to occupy the edges of the black studies project. To draw on Marlon Riggs, I want to ask some questions along with him that speak to the problematic utterances of community within current black diaspora discourses. As Riggs suggests concerning community: "All terms denoting an ideological frame of reference that enforces a rigorous exclusion of certain kinds of difference, that erects stifling enclosures around a whole range of necessary debates, or, alternately, confines them within an easily recognisable—and controllable—psychosocial arena should be suspect and questioned."[17] On the agenda here is to think simultaneously a number of overlapping concerns—community, black queer positions, and what I call the "whatever" of black studies. In terms of the "whatever" of black studies, I draw on and develop Giorgio Agamben's formulation of the "whatever" to suggest one way in which the uncertainties and commonalties of blacknesses might be formulated in the face of some room for surprise, disappointment, and pleasure without recourse to disciplinary and punishing measures.[18] This is a whatever that can tolerate the whatever of blackness without knowing meaning—black meaning, that is—in advance of its various utterances.

By making use of the whatever in conjunction with (black) queer theory and the recognition of the difficult knowledge it brings to bear on the black studies project I mean to ask tough questions concerning the nature of black diasporic communities and the disciplinary weakness of the black studies project as a community building and making exercise. In this sense I am attempting to grapple with the thorny question of the making of black community via the routes of academic disciplinarity and what might be at stake in the making of this community. I am particularly driven to these questions by the challenge, and may I say limit, of Charles H. Rowell's afterword to *Shade: An Anthology of Fiction by Black Gay Men of African Descent*. In "Signing Yourself: An Afterword" Rowell argues against both racism and heteronormativity by both white and black Americans, gay and straight alike. I am exercised by Rowell's claims in his afterword for a number of reasons, and I share both a solidarity and an antagonism with his argument. He is particularly interested in charting one specific aspect of the black diaspora— its queer twists and turns. I stand in solidarity with that aspect of the project, but in concentrating on this one element Rowell takes a rather punishing twist when he calls the "Third World" into question for prohibiting gay men from "signing themselves gay."[19] It is not the evidence of this inability that I take issue with concerning Rowell's indictment of some parts of the black diaspora and Africa, but rather what I read as the "ideological frame" from which he utters his critique. His inability to account for the contradictions within his argument is surprising. For as he calls the Third World into question he must simultaneously also call the First World into question. And yet he leaves us with the bitter taste that somehow the possibility for queer life in the Great Free North is so much better than it is in the so-called Third World. What I find troubling about his speech acts in his afterword is that they takes quite an imperialist U.S. stance, particularly reading from my queer place in the diaspora (Canada). This imperialist stance is of the kind that does not adequately (or does only in nuanced ways) account for the disjunctures of desire, political utterances, and disappointment in various spaces and places, even nations. In some respects Rowell fails to see when the sexual is not intellectual, to paraphrase one of my favourite songs from the queer party circuit. Instead, his argument suggests that even if things are bad in the United States then elsewhere the situation is dire, and that folks elsewhere have a long developmental path to take, almost along the lines of UNESCO. Such utterances are rampant in the "new" sexiness of diaspora discourse in the contemporary black studies project. It is Rowell's attempt to make African American and therefore U.S. exceptionality singular that I contest. But what Rowell does not consider are all the ways in which men in the Third World might sign themselves queer in ways that might not constitute an intelligible speech act for him. I am exercised by Rowell because he is both pushing and elaborating the limits of the black studies project at the same time that his push contracts for what it cannot adequately account for elsewhere. His diaspora desire is ultimately, despite its claim otherwise, a national thing.

I contest Rowell's assertions because I think that politically the invocation of the diaspora requires us to think in ways that simultaneously recognize the national spaces from which we speak and gesture to more than those spaces. In fact, sometimes it might require a subversion or at the least an undermining of the national space. In the contemporary black studies project the sexy trendiness of the diaspora is continuously being appropriated to speak to a singular context of African American concerns. On the one hand, it seems impossible for Rowell to really traverse the space of the black diaspora and in particular of crossing the forty-ninth parallel and heading north to another moment of blackness, much less than heading to the Third World to liberate it; yet, on the other hand, black Canadian Courtnay McFarlane makes the journey south in his poem "Gill's Paradise."

> Crown Heights
> Paradise found/Brooklyn black/crumbles
> Through gypsy cab/Classon and Pacific streets
> a hell/to eyes not seein' home/
> On this neglect paved/urban artery
> apathy's pothole/open hydrant/piss stained wall
> street corners/"the Dream"

Burned-out shell/stands/three-stories
three sets of eyes/concrete sealed
willful/blind/remembers better days
Next door Gill's Paradise/is overpainted 'ho
gaudy yellow façade/single palm/Rastaman
and lion of Judah/testify to longings/distant/unfilled
romance defiant/in decay
Gill's beckons

Or, in McFarlane's "Craig":

was jumping/in Tracks/
capital T/D/C/Washington
carryin' on/makin' noise/being loud
in black and white/polka dotted pantihose
tight white tank top/matching canvas Keds/the slip on kind
dancin'/and cruising/in disco drag[20]

What is at stake here are the ways in which some black diaspora queers find African American queers, yet the reverse always seems impossible. This sexual/textual economy of unequal exchange is important in how we conceptualize the limits of contemporary discourses of the diaspora and questions of community within the black studies project. The inability within some versions of the black studies project to think of the nation alongside the outernational is in some senses also a queer diaspora position, at least in its inconsistency. But as we know, the diaspora by its very nature, its circumstances, is queer. What do I mean by this? I mean that the territories and perambulations of diaspora circuits, identifications, and desires are queer in their making and their expressions. Reginald Shepherd's *Some Are Drowning,* a collection of poetry, charts the sexual desiring racialized territories of the New World by highlighting the (homo)erotics of the conquest of the Americas and transatlantic slavery.[21] In a different way, which is even more troubling and disturbing, Gary Fisher takes us deeper into uncharted, at least textually, territories of racialized sex acts, fantasies, and desires.[22] These black queer territorial claims rewrite blackness in ways that require us to examine blackness beyond the singularity of victim or resistor so that a more nuanced rendering is at least approached.

Drawing on Arjun Appadurai's notion of "scapes" of various sorts, we might understand Fisher's, Shepherd's, and McFarlane's poetics as those of sexscapes.[23] These sexscapes chart the difficult territories of "streets and residences" and "peaks of nipples" as Shepherd puts it in one of his poems. Even more concretely, however, these sexscapes chart the politics of the black queer diaspora in both its ephemera and its varying political acts. What is at stake here is an understanding of a black queer diaspora across and within, in which artifact, desire, pleasure, and disappointment can sometimes be the basis of the struggle over and the making of imaginary community. Isaac Julien's film art, Joseph Beam's anthology *In the Life*, Pat Parker's poetry, Audre Lorde's oeuvre, and Samuel Delany's memoir are just examples of artifacts used in the making of this black queer diaspora.[24] The more difficult and intangible moments of interiority, sensibility, and political utterance play out in localized and transnational political alliances, desires, pleasures, and disappointments.

My investment in questioning the boundaries of a heteronormative black studies project, in particular its diaspora perambulations, have much to do with my own investment in the black studies project as a liberatory project. But I want to qualify this project by suggesting that some of the questions that made the black studies project the site of radicality at one particular historical moment might now require that we seek new questions.[25] I am grandly suggesting, then, that black queer studies is both the edge and the cutting edge of a reinvigorated black studies project. In this aspect, a black queer studies might go a long way in producing formulations of community and the rethinking of community conceptually that might be more useful for our postmodern, outernational times. This, in essence, is why I find Charles Rowell's afterword troubling and limiting in its conception of the black queer diaspora. His inability to really go down—that is, to really go south—is ultimately a queer political disappointment. His argument, despite the material object of the anthology, still fits the frame of a black studies project discourse that Kobena Mercer identifies as disappointment. Mercer argues, and I agree, "that questions of sexuality have come to mark the interior limits of decolonisation, where the utopian project of liberation has come to grief."[26]

I want to make clear that I still understand the black studies project as marginal within the contemporary North American academy. But the marginality of the black studies project and its resistance through the reproduction of a minoritarian discourse of assertiveness is particularly important historically and politically for black queer studies. A black queer studies partakes of this assertive tradition and extends it into new and politically troubling territories. In this sense, black queer studies is attempting to reclaim the ground that Mercer marks as disappointment in the black studies project. Mercer attends to this by charting territories for thinking about blackness that are reflective of national political positions and events but also, importantly, far exceed the demands of the national. This is the demand of a "postconceptual" black studies project that can do more than tolerate sexual difference and that can take the diaspora seriously enough to peek outside national concerns and narratives.

The tensions and relations between the black studies project and diaspora sensibilities sorely require revisiting in this era of renewed interests in invoking the term diaspora. Such a study could begin with the debates between DuBois and Garvey and DuBois and McKay. The debate between Gilroy and Chandler, Gilroy and Dyson, and a plethora of nation/diaspora skirmishes would then be important to flesh out the significance of the tensions of diasporic discourses within the black studies project. In addition, the ways in which different intellectuals and scholars within the black studies project are positioned in terms of both their political utterances and the nuances of their politics is crucial: for example, the political difference between Harold Cruse and Larry Neal; or, in more general terms, the difference between nation-centered approaches as opposed to more diasporic orientations—that is, pan-African or outernational. What is important here is to signal the distinction between different inflections of the black studies project. One component of the distinction is how different individual intellectuals and scholars see themselves in relation to the desires of national narrations and narratives. The black studies project has never been a singular project, despite contemporary attempts to rewrite its history into a singular, nation-centered one. So while an argument can be made for the continuing marginalization of the black studies project in the North American academy, it is also important to point out that within the black studies project its own self-generating discourses have produced what can be described as "official positions." These positions provide particular confines and directives of what might and might not count as a part of the black studies project. One of the first incursions into "official black studies" was that of feminism. Others, like queer theory, have since arrived. Therefore, by the "official black studies" moniker I mean to signal the terms on which the originary project conceptualized a singular blackness, thereby foreclosing other moments that could only then return as the unruly, or the whatever, of a fabricated homogeneity and offer a different perspective and reading.

William Haver, in "Of Mad Men Who Practice Invention to the Brink of

Intelligibility," an essay on Samuel Delany's *Mad Men,* argues that "queer theory is queer only to the extent that it sustains an erotic relation/non-relation to the extremity that interrupts it: queer theory is queer precisely in its incompleteness."[27] Haver's insistence on the possibilities of queer theory lying in its incompleteness is also where I see the possibilities of the unfinished project of black studies in its encounters with black queer theory and/or queer positions. The pedagogy of the black studies project in its suggestion of possible liberation and its insistence on narratives of liberation bares a historiography that requires a continual reassessment of the politics of dispossession among its imagined community. The thing that must be thought as the content and politics of the black studies project is definitely a queer thing—community. I am suggesting here that it is because queer communities reside at various assorted edges that the queering of the black studies project in a sustained way holds the potential for the continual attempt to think about the difficult politics of liberation at its limits.

For example, Houston Baker's now-notorious claim at the Black Popular Culture conference in 1992 that he is not gay is a case in point. Such an utterance (and I am referring only to what is printed in the book *Black Popular Culture* that resulted from the conference) is the expressed place where some versions of the black studies project encounter the difficult terrain of community or, put another way, the tensions and antagonisms of family, which underwrite the black studies project, come to the fore. Baker's claim is a moment, which I think is pedagogical in many ways for the black studies project. Particularly crucial is the edge that black queer bodies occupy in our concerns within the field as histories of the field are being written. Here I think of Baynard Rustin and Lorraine Hansberry, both of whom are cutting edge and also currently occupying the edge of the black studies project.

But let me express a provocation not of my making but rather in the words of another black gay guy. In "Making Ourselves from Scratch," Joseph Beam writes: "As African-Americans, we do not bequeath financial portfolios. We pass from generation to generation our tenacity. So I ask you: What is it that we are passing along to our cousin from North Carolina, the boy down the block, our nephew who is a year old, or our sons who may follow us in the life? What is it that we leave them beyond this shadow play: the search for a candlelit romance in a poorly lit bar, the rhythm and the beat, the furtive sex in the back street? What is it that we pass along to them or do they, too, need to start from scratch?"[28] In response, Dana Inkster's film *Welcome to Africville* takes up the challenge made by Beam. With this in mind I turn to a reading of Inkster's film as an example of a diaspora reading practice to demonstrate what might be at stake when we risk reading for and creating works that think the unthought of blackness.

Welcome to Africville is a fifteen-minute film that recalls the thirtieth anniversary (in 1999) of the destruction of one of black Canada's oldest communities, which was founded in the 1800s by ex-African Americans. The narrative of the destruction, or rather the interruption in the narrative of the destruction and dispersal, is told through three generations of women from the Dixon family, and also through a bartender. These actors do not tell the why of the destruction—they refuse to do so—but rather they tell the why of their sexual practices, desires, disappointments, pleasures, and adventures as well as their loss. The grandmother (Anna Dixon) tells of a strong desire to have what she calls a "numb love," being too old for anything else. Her daughter (Mary Dixon) tells of her sexual adventures in the big city and her fantasies. And the granddaughter (Mary Dixon) tells of the possibility of finding love. The bartender (Julius Johnson) details the possibility of finding love, with a commentary on masculinity. Some of the images in the film, such as the archival footage of the demolition of the community, tell the story of the Canadian state's racist action. The actors' stories arrive through an off-screen interviewer's attempt to gather responses to the impending demolition. The film opens with these lines: "Yes they making us move . . . but I don't want to talk about that . . . history will tell the story." Instead, these characters tell the story of a black history of erotics often demolished in heterosexist acts parallel to those of racist acts. These characters tell of love, loss, and desire defying what kind of history and what history can tell as a necessary part of black community and queer community.

What makes this film useful for my purpose here is not only its complex layering of writing history but also the way in which Inkster queers the history of Africville by making something queer happen to viewers. She tells the story of Africville through the voices of at least two generations of black women who love other women. Anna Dixon (played by Kathy Imre of *Shaft's Big Score*) is the grandmother. Me'shell Ndegeocello composed and performed the original blusey, soulful score. The film brings together a cast of diasporic players to tell a national story of pain and loss, which not only gestures to the historical dispersal across U.S. borders—before and after Africville—but has echoes across the black diaspora. The film participates in a rather large project—a project of diaspora desires and connections—yet it is still able to productively engage its local context. It is a product that through fiction is able to complicate the historical record of blackness. By telling the now-sacred story of Africville through the eyes of black lesbians, Inkster creates the opportunity for reflecting differently on historical context and memory and not only what is remembered but who is allowed to remember and how. Inkster tells the sex of memory; hers is a queer memory with much significance for interrupting disciplinarity.

Welcome to Africville takes its immediate influences from Isaac Julien's and Marlon Riggs's meditations on history and black queerness. Inkster is, however, closer to Julien than to Riggs in the subtlety of her cinematic styling—her shots are posed like photographs. But, importantly, she is among a group of black lesbian filmmakers returning to the archives and opening them up in challenging ways; the black queer living-dead is placed to rest with cinematic love and care. These queer cinematic returns and departures force new kinds of questions concerning what the black studies project has often only whispered about and might not be publicly ready for yet. At the same time, these returns make something queer happen to all of us in the black studies project. In many ways, then, *Welcome to Africville* is in conversation with Cheryl Dunye's *Watermelon Woman* (1997) and Julie Dash's *Daughters of the Dust* (1991). At the same time, it engages the many documentaries chronicling Africville's demolition[29] and also moves away from them to bring a different or a queer look to black Canadian historiography. In addition, Inkster's film fixes a black lesbian feminist gaze on critical cinematic diasporic representations, in particular the chronicling of black queer histories that have been overwhelmingly male in cinematic presentation.

It was reported that when Inkster's film was screened in Halifax, Nova Scotia (Africville was located just outside Halifax's city's limits) it came as a shock to the local black audience. Apparently the audience was aghast that the sacred story of Africville might be fictionalized and told through the eyes of at least two lesbians. This response is similar, I think, to the institutional positioning of the black studies project. Because Inkster refuses epistemological respectability by refusing to represent the wound as only the loss of property—a representation that potentially might elicit the collective respect of black folks by white folks and therefore serve as evidence of black victimization—her film was a shock to some. Instead, Inkster's erotics of loss can provoke a different possibility of encountering the demolition of Africville. The site thus becomes symbolic of all that is loss/lost when history forecloses certain kinds of knowledge, especially queer queries and feminist queries concerning the past and what David Scott calls the "changing pres-ent."[30] These queries do not only return, recover, and correct but they tell a cautionary tale opening up new "problem-spaces"[31] that can act to effectively allow for a more politically inflected changing present that is in accord with the continued ambivalent and ambiguous nature of the institutionalization of the black studies project. But what queer black studies requires the black studies project to risk is its wounded "specialism," so that a queer peda-gogy of erotics might allow something queer to happen to all who enter the disciplinary zone of the black studies project. But if only the black stud-ies project could do more than think the unthought of queer conditionality and encounter the sensuality of—to paraphrase Dusty Dixon—kissing some queer ass, the possibility of the continuation of this audacious project for lib-eration might proceed unabated until liberation is a condition of our being.

NOTES

1. An elaboration of diaspora reading practice can be found in my essay "Beyond the 'Nation Thing': Black Studies, Cultural Studies, and Diaspora Discourse (or the Post-Black Studies Moment)," in *Decolonizing the Academy: African Diaspora Studies,* ed. Carole Boyce Davies et al. (New York: African World Press, 2003).

2. For exemplary critiques of family as community and the inherent conceptual problem in that kind of theorizing, see Hazel Carby, *Race Men* (Boston: Harvard University Press, 1998); Paul Gilroy, *There Ain't No Black in the Union Jack: The Cultural Politics of Race and Nation* (London: Hutchinson, 1987); Stuart Hall, "Cultural Identity and Diaspora" in *Identity: Community, Culture, Difference,* ed. Jonathan Rutherford (London: Lawrence and Wishart, 1990), 222-37.

3. Slavoj Žižek, *Looking Awry: An Introduction to Jacques Lacan through Popular Culture* (Cambridge, Mass.: MIT Press, 1991).

4. See Paul Gilroy, *The Black Atlantic: Modernity and Double Consciousness* (Cambridge, Mass: Harvard University Press, 1993) and Michael Hanchard, *Orpheus and Power: The Movimento Negro of Rio de Janeiro* (Princeton, N.J.: Princeton University Press, 1994).

5. See Jane Rhodes on Mary Ann Shadd and her attempt to make her United States black again in *Mary Ann Shadd Cary: The Black Press and Protest in the Nineteenth Century* (Bloomington: Indiana University Press, 1998). See also my reply to Rhodes's book: "'Who Is She and What Is She to You?': Mary Ann Shadd Cary and the (Im)possibility of Black Canadian Studies," in *Rude: Contemporary Black Canadian Cultural Criticism,* ed. Rinaldo Walcott (Toronto: Insomniac Press, 2000), 27–48.

6. An example of this is the popularity of Isaac Julien and Marlon Riggs, which

extends across the black diaspora. Other examples include the invitation of Pomo Afro Homos to Toronto or the popularity of Bill T. Jones among black gay men who are otherwise not interested in dance.

7. William Haver, "Queer Research; or, How to Practice Invention to the Brink of Intelligibility," in *The Eight Technologies of Otherness,* ed. Sue Golding (London: Routledge, 1997), 280.

8. For a discussion of the injury and rights discourse that informs my argument in this essay, see Wendy Brown's *States of Injury* (Princeton: Princeton University Press, 1995).

9. See Cornel West, *Race Matters* (Boston: Beacon Press, 1993).

10. See Jean-Luc Nancy, *The Inoperative Community* (Minneapolis: University of Minnesota Press, 1991); Giorgio Agamben, *The Coming Community* (Minneapolis: University of Minnesota Press, 1993); William Haver, *The Body of This Death: Historicity and Sociality in the Time of AIDS* (Stanford: Stanford University Press, 1996); Sylvia Wynter, "On Disenchanting Discourse: 'Minority' Literary Criticism and Beyond," in *The Nature and Context of Minority Discourse,* ed. Abdul Janmohamed and David Lloyd (New York: Oxford University Press, 1990): and Sylvia Wynter, "1492: A New World View," in *Race, Discourse, and the Origin of the Americas: A New World View,* ed. Vera Hyatt and Rex Nettleford (Washington, D.C.: Smithsonian Institution Press, 1995).

11. Haver, "Queer Research," 280.

12. Ibid., 282.

13. Ibid., 283.

14. Deborah Britzman, "Is There a Queer Pedagogy? or, Stop Being Straight" *Educational Theory* 45 (spring 1995): 151–66.

15. Haver, "Queer Research," 283.

16. Deborah Britzman, *Lost Subjects, Contested Objects* (Albany: State University of New York Press, 1998).

17. Marlon Riggs, "Unleash the Queen," in *Black Popular Culture,* ed. Gina Dent (Seattle: Bay Press, 1992), 101.

18. Agamben, *The Coming Community.*

19. Charles Rowell, "Signing Yourself: An Afterword," in *Shade: An Anthology of Fiction by Black Gay Men of African Descent* (New York: Avon, 1996).

20. Lynn Crosbie and Michael Holmes, eds., *Plush: Selected Poems of Sky Gilbert, Courtnay McFarlane, Jeffery Conway, R. M. Vaughan, and David Trinidad* (Toronto: Coach House Press, 1995), 46–49.

21. Reginald Shepherd, *Some Are Drowning* (Pittsburgh: University of Pittsburgh Press, 1994).

22. Gary Fisher, *Gary in Your Pocket: Stories and Notebooks of Gary Fisher,* ed. Eve Sedgwick (Durham: Duke University Press, 1996); for a reading of Fisher, see Robert

Reid-Pharr, "The Shock of Gary Fisher," in *Dangerous Liaisons: Blacks, Gays, and the Struggle for Equality,* ed. Eric Brandt (New York: New Press, 1996), 243–56.

23. Arjun Appadurai, "Disjuncture and Difference in the Global Cultural Economy," in *Colonial Discourse and Postcolonial Theory: A Reader,* ed. Patrick Williams and Laura Chrisman (New York: Columbia University Press, 1994), 324–339.

24. For a sample of some of these artifacts, see Joseph Beam, ed., *In The Life: A Black Gay Anthology* (Boston: Alyson, 1996); Audre Lorde, *Sister Outsider* (Freedom, CA: The Crossing Press, 1984) and *Zami: A New Spelling of My Name,* (Freedom, Calif.: Crossing Press, 1982); Samuel Delany, *The Motion of Light in Water: Sex and Science Fiction Writing in the East Village, 1957–1965* (New York: Plume, 1988); Essex Hemphill, ed., *Brother to Brother: New Writings by Black Gay Men* (Boston: Alyson, 1991); and Essex Hemphill, *Ceremonies* (New York: Plume, 1992). Also see the films of Isaac Julien, Marlon Riggs, and the oeuvre of James Baldwin, as well as house music and disco.

25. See David Scott, *Refashioning Futures: Criticism after Postcoloniality* (Princeton: Princeton University Press, 1999).

26. Kobena Mercer, "Decolonization and Disappointment: Reading Fanon's Sexual Politics," in *The Fact of Blackness: Frantz Fanon and Visual Representation,* ed. Alan Reed (Seattle: Bay Press, 1999), 116.

27. Joseph Beam, "Making Ourselves from Scratch," in *Brother to Brother: New Writings by Black Gay Men,* ed. Essex Hemphill (Boston: Alyson, 1991), 262.

28. For example, see *Remember Africville,* 1992, dir. Shelagh Mackenzie, National Film Board of Canada.

29. Scott, *Refashioning Futures,* 110.

30. Ibid.

31. Gayatri Chakravorty Spivak, *Outside in the Teaching Machine* (New York: Routledge, 1993).

PHILLIP BRIAN HARPER

THE EVIDENCE OF FELT INTUITION:

MINORITY EXPERIENCE, EVERYDAY LIFE,

AND CRITICAL SPECULATIVE

KNOWLEDGE

I don't travel much, but as my acquaintances all know, I like to make much of my travels. Lately in particular, I've tried to mine my relatively meager experience along these lines for possible critical insight into the meanings of identity, citizenship, and U.S. nationality.[1] These efforts represent an undertaking that is only just beginning; and yet, in some ways, it has also been going on for a long time. For instance, I remember a journey I took during the 1985–86 academic year (needless to say, that's the way I measure time—in academic years), a journey from Madison, Wisconsin, where I had gone to visit my boyfriend, Thom Freedman, back to Ithaca, New York, where I was finishing my graduate coursework. To be precise, the leg of the journey that concerns me here took me only from Madison to Syracuse because it entailed travel by rail, and at that time (and I believe still) Ithaca did not have a train station.

On the train to Syracuse, as I occupied myself by alternately reading and napping, I was approached by a fellow passenger—a trim and nattily dressed middle-aged white man—who indicated to me that he had won a deck of cards through some contest on the train from Los Angeles, and he and a few other passengers were going to get up a game back in the dining car; did I want to join them? No, I did not, but this fact did not at all diminish the man's friendliness or his interest, as he continued to pursue small talk with me, being absorbed in particular by the question of where I might be from. Could it be Sri Lanka? For I looked very much like a good friend of his who was from Sri Lanka, though I very remarkably spoke perfect English with no accent at all. I assured him that, to the extent to which this was so, it was because I was not from Sri Lanka but from Detroit, Michigan, where I had been born and reared.

His quite notable surprise on learning this fact would not, I imagine, have seemed unfamiliar to any number of black people from across the country. It certainly did not seem unfamiliar to me. I had encountered it before, and so I felt quite sure about what it meant, what bemused and paradoxical message it conveyed despite all of the bearer's efforts to dissemble it, which, to be perfectly frank, were not especially extensive. It said, in effect: "How can this be so? There is not, to my knowledge at least, any sizable population of Sri Lankans living in Detroit, and in any event, this fellow has not indicated that he is of Sri Lankan extraction, as might well be the case even if he were born and reared in Detroit. On the other hand, there are, as I know all too well, an overwhelmingly large number of black people living in Detroit—so large a percentage, in fact, that the chances are very good that any Detroiter picked at random from the municipal phone book will actually turn out to be black. Come to think of it, this young man's skin tone now appears to me rather different than on first glance—more mundane, somehow, though I can't quite explain why; and, indeed, ungratefully so, as I had been entirely willing to give it the benefit of the doubt, to offer it the excuse of deriving from Sri Lanka, as quite clearly would be the preferable instance, and as it quite clearly must, if not from some other, similarly distant, locale, since indeed the person bearing it speaks perfect English with no accent at all, which is to say that, all contrary evidence notwithstanding, he most certainly cannot be black, which he nevertheless seems to be implying that he is. In which case, how can this be so?"

If, as I have suggested, such surprise would not strike a large number of black people as at all unfamiliar, this is because it is the function of a continuing social process that is so widespread and ordinary as to be humdrum;[2] moreover, this process has a name, and we know that name so well that it sounds to us quaint, not to say theoretically unsophisticated, as it most likely figures to those of us working in professional-academic social and cultural critique. But of course, the precondition of banality is an element of truth so widely accepted that it doesn't bear repeating, or else why would it register as simplistic and commonplace to begin with? And so it is with the concept of the stereotype, especially given our awareness of how much is disallowed by this relatively crude analytic tool, the extent to which it belies the great complexity of cultural representation. Yet its continuing operation in our society is a fact that cannot be denied, just as it cannot be denied that the man on the train was himself engaging in the process of stereotype: the projection of an idea in his mind—or, to be more precise, the subscription to an idea in circulation throughout the culture—with such abiding force and intensity that it took on a phantom solidity and thus superseded the reality comprised in the actual personage whose existence it had been marshaled to explain. Which is why he could not hear me when I said—as I effectively *was* saying, though I did not actually mouth the words—that I was black, for the entity that would have been connoted for him by that term did not, evidently, speak standard English, or read the books I was reading, or sit blandly staring out Amtrak train windows in a manner whose effect must have been rather fetching—which I surmised it to be, because I had surmised in the first place that the man was sexually attracted to me and that this was the reason for his initial approach. Given this, his surprise at the probability of my being black said something more than I have already suggested; it additionally said: "How can this be so? For you are attractive and interesting to me, neither of which, as a rule, I find black people to be"—a claim he substantiated after registering his surprise by lumbering awkwardly away. Needless to say, we did not speak again.

Most of what I have related here I do not know to be fact. The train trip occurred; the man did approach me; we had the exchange I narrated above. What it all *meant*, though, I can't rightly determine, which is perhaps why the episode haunts me today. The man's thoughts, in particular, are inaccessible to me, as he never once told me what ran through his mind. Yet, rather than thwart my assessment of the event, this fact seems only to have intensified my recourse to guesswork and conjecture, as is shown by the firmness of the conclusions I have drawn. This is not unique; indeed, I would argue that minority existence itself induces such speculative rumination, because it continually renders even the most routine instances of social activity and personal interaction as possible cases of invidious social distinction or discriminatory treatment. As one lesbian-identified U.S. woman recently put it while discussing for *Newsweek* magazine her day-to-day experiences with her partner and their two children: "One of our neighbors has never spoken to us. . . . When we go out, he goes in. But we don't know if that's just the way he is or if it's because we're lesbians."[3]

Personally, I find this abiding uncertainty and the speculation it engenders exceedingly exhausting, which may account for the fact that I *don't* travel much, for in my estimation travel only increases the likelihood of one's finding oneself amid such indeterminacy, incessantly encountering new unknown persons whose reactions to one cannot be predicted and very likely will throw one yet again into a state of confusion that, because it cannot be resolved, feels profoundly debilitating. I am convinced that this experience is what Virginia Woolf had in mind when she wrote of Clarissa Dalloway that "she always had the feeling that it was very, very dangerous to live even one day";[4] and if that experience constitutes the generic state of individual consciousness in the context of modernity, then how much more emphatically must it constitute the consciousness of the minority subject, whose definitionally nongeneric character itself entails repeated exposure to indeterminable events? I shall return shortly to this matter of indeterminacy, and to what I will insist is the hard work of speculation that it necessitates. But first let me consider the business of being *misperceived*, as I have suggested I was by the man on the train, for it seems to me to bear on the question of how we all pursue work in the field of queer studies.

Before I go too far in a direction that so clearly could lead to tiresome complaint, I should explicitly acknowledge that I have been extremely fortunate—not only in the results of my queer studies work but in my overall professional-academic positioning—and I am very grateful for my indisputable good luck. For a long time, however, I used to joke to friends that the basis for my success lay in a combination of tokenism and hackwork, forwarded through a sort of intellectual and professional promiscuity whereby I simply never said no to a particular type of proposition—a proposition that generally sounded something like this, as it came to my ear from the far end of a phone line: "Hi, we've never met, but I got your name from X, who met you through Y when you were at a conference with Z and who suggested I give you a call because I'm editing a book volume [or special journal issue] on queer sexuality [or racial politics] that's almost ready to go to press except for the fact that we don't yet have in it any pieces addressing racial politics [or queer sexuality], and X said you'd be the perfect person to contribute something, which I hope you can do because it would really round out the collection, and since all the other authors are already finished with their pieces because they were solicited well over a year ago we really need to have received this essay by our deadline of last Tuesday, but if you absolutely have to have more time then I can probably negotiate with the press editor for an extra two weeks, but no more, and can you do it, are you interested, aren't you grateful that I called?" And yes, I always said, yes, oh yes, like some pathetically obsequious version of Molly Bloom, and then cleared my schedule for the next two weeks, and installed myself in front of my keyboard, and hammered out an essay at such a furious pace that I didn't have time to worry that it was bad or to double-check the argument or to have second thoughts about submitting it to a press—and so on and so on, until the next thing I knew, voilà! I had a cv, I had a publication record, I seemed to have what could be called a *career,* and that career, moreover, seemed to implicate a profile in what we've all learned to refer to as the field of queer studies.

This was not necessarily a bad development, mind you, especially with respect to my material well-being. It's just that I didn't quite realize that it was happening—or, to be more precise about it, I didn't quite realize what it actually meant, since I didn't feel at all certain what queer studies—or, as it was generally and much more problematically called at that relatively early date, queer theory—was. But then, who did? We are, after all, talking about an extremely new framework for cultural criticism and social analysis, one that was only just emerging and consolidating—if, indeed, it has consolidated, itself a questionable proposition at the time when I first began working in the area in 1988, a mere twelve years ago. In fact, within the few years after that date, the very definition of the enterprise began to be publicly discussed and debated, with no certain outcome except contestation itself. This unsettled state of affairs has since been assimilated as a signal constituent within queer critique, which during the last five to seven years or so has been characterized by numerous commentators as fundamentally provisional, anticipatory, and incomplete—and thus properly irreducible to a coherent singular project.[5] I actually feel no reason whatsoever to protest on this score, since it seems to me—as to many others—that it is precisely the indeterminate character of queer critique that predicates its analytic force. On the other hand, while that indeterminacy—and here I am using the word in its most literal sense—is frequently cited as a positive attribute of queer analysis, it is much more rarely manifested in the actual critical work that aspires to the rubric, or—and this latter fact constitutes a primary reason for the former—in the contexts in which that work emerges and circulates.

This claim itself is by now a commonplace, and yet this doesn't mean that its full significance has been adequately elaborated. That significance extends far beyond the objection—as valid and urgent as it is—that what is currently recognized as queer studies is, for instance, unacceptably Euro-American in orientation, its purview effectively determined by the practically invisible—because putatively nonexistent—bounds of racial whiteness.[6] It encompasses as well (to continue for the moment with the topic of whiteness) the abiding failure of most supposed queer critique to subject whiteness itself to sustained interrogation and thus to delineate its import in sexual terms, whether conceived in normative or nonnormative modes. In other words, to speak personally, it bothers me less that white practitioners of queer critique tend not to address the significance of racial nonwhiteness in the phenomena of sex and sexuality they explore (though one often wishes they would, and, indeed, some do) than that they tend not to address the effect of racial *whiteness* on the very manifestations of those phenomena and on their understanding of them; for the upshot of this failure—somewhat paradoxically, given the interest of queer criticism in definitional fluidity—is an implicit acquiescence to received notions of what constitutes *sex and sexuality,* however nonnormative, as though the current hegemony in this regard were not thoroughly imbricated with the ongoing maintenance of white supremacist culture.[7]

At the same time (for as I have indicated, I am positing this critical shortcoming as only one example of the practical limitations that queer studies has both expressed and suffered), it is just as easy—and just as valid—to note that the vast majority of work in black studies (and I'm confining my observations to that field both because it's the one I know best and because such a focus is demanded by the occasion) has similarly failed to interrogate how conventional ideas of racial blackness—however variously they may be valued—are themselves conditioned by disparate factors of sex and sexuality, mobilized in myriad ways that may or may not be recognizable as "proper," the consideration of which is crucial to fully understanding the social and cultural significances of blackness itself.

There was a point—and it perhaps hasn't yet ended; I can't be entirely sure—when this latter issue was of primary concern for me in my own critical work, when it constituted the problem that I felt most urgently compelled to address and, in my small way, to help redress. This point served as the context in which in 1988 I began drafting my first professional-critical foray onto the overlapping terrains of gender, sexuality, and African American identity, which resulted in an essay, "Eloquence and Epitaph," on responses to the AIDS-related death of television news anchor Max Robinson.[8] First published—finally—in *Social Text* in 1991, the piece was relatively quickly assimilated into a burgeoning critical enterprise that was by then already negotiating the theoretical distinctions and methodological differences that might obtain between "lesbian and gay studies," on the one hand, and "queer theory," on the other; come to think of it, the essay's occupation of the contested overlap of these two conceptual fields might be symbolized by the fact that, in 1993, it was reprinted in two different anthologies whose actual sharing of key theoretical concerns was belied by the notable difference between their two titles: *The Lesbian and Gay Studies Reader,* edited by Henry Abelove, Michèle Aina Barale, and David M. Halperin, and *Fear of a Queer Planet: Queer Politics and Social Theory,* edited by Michael Warner.[9] Indeed, it might be interesting to explore the tensions regarding both the name and the practice of queer critique—and the latter's relationship to other modes of critical inquiry—that were evident in the very introduction to *The Lesbian and Gay Studies Reader,* with the aim of discovering what they could have signified in what now appears to be the watershed year of 1993[10]—but to follow up on either of these propositions would actually take me far afield from my primary point, for the fact is that, while I obviously did not eschew the attention the essay was gaining among exponents of either queer theory or lesbian and gay studies, nor did I gainsay its being apprehended in terms of those fields, I had actually conceived of "Eloquence and Epitaph" as an intervention into the field of black studies and, to be more precise about it, *African American* studies, which seemed to me sorely in need of remediation as far as discussion of sexuality, let alone AIDS, was concerned—and only slightly more so at the end of the 1980s, alas, than it does today, at the dawn of the twenty-first century.

This doesn't mean that I was completely uninterested in contributing to the conversation about the direction of either queer politics or queer critique, and in fact I made an attempt in this regard in a footnote to the essay, in which I explained my repeated use throughout the article of the word *homosexual* by emphasizing the limited degree to which African American men who have sex with other men might identify with the terms *gay* or *queer.*[11] To the extent that my work in that essay was understood exclusively or primarily as an instance of sexuality studies per se, however, it was radically—and perhaps willfully—*misperceived,* inasmuch as its accomplishment in this vein could not in any way be separated from its function as an instance of *African Americanist* critical analysis.

This probably wouldn't have been clear, however, until yet a few years later—in 1996, to be exact—when the essay's incorporation into my book on black masculinity effectively forced readers to recognize its argument as part of a larger engagement with the very definition of African American identity and thus to face the potentially uncomfortable question of how homosexual activity might itself be implicated in the latter.[12] After all, while by 1996 the

....

essay had been anthologized in three books devoted to queer sexuality—or to examinations of AIDS conceived in relation to queer sexuality[13]—it had not, as far as I could tell from my admittedly unsystematic but nonetheless sustained review, made the slightest impact in the field of African American studies broadly understood, where it seemed to meet with a nearly deafening official silence. In fact, it occurs to me now that only once in my career did the conversation I parodied earlier actually center on my possibly contributing to a volume on *race* as distinct from sexuality, and that was in the case of the catalogue for the Whitney Museum's infamous 1995 *Black Male* exhibition, which itself clearly entailed a focus on questions of gender (with sexuality thus understood as an ancillary effect) and which quite notably, I think, did *not* originate in a properly academic context. Within the latter realm, in the field of African American studies, a profound silence about sexuality has generally continued to be the order of the day.

Now, please, don't get me wrong. Not only am I not complaining about some perceived personal slight (I am very lucky; I acknowledge it again), but I also don't mean that individual scholars and critics in African American studies didn't read the essay in its original *Social Text* venue and personally indicate to me their sense of its worth. In 1999 I was introduced to an audience at the University of Pennsylvania by Michael Awkward, who pointedly and graciously cited the essay's value for him. More illustrative, perhaps, at the 1993 American Studies Association convention in Boston I ran into Michael Eric Dyson in a crowded hotel lobby, and he told me how much he had liked the piece; he sounded very sincere, his voice so understated and muted that it approximated a whisper. Rather, the silence to which I allude consisted in the field's general failure to meet the challenge thrown down at the end of the essay, which specifically charged that nothing less than the very lives of black people depend on our radically changing the discourses that shape them—*including* the discourse loosely comprised in the academic field of African American studies, where all too frequently lip service is mistaken for such substantive transformation, with the result that the field's profoundly heteronormative character has yet to be dislodged to any noticeable degree.

Now, the silence on this score that I perceived within the precincts of African American studies would not, I imagine, have seemed unfamiliar to any number of black people who identify even slightly with any of the subject positions potentially connoted by the term *queer sexuality*. It certainly did not seem unfamiliar to this particular black faggot. I had encountered it before, and so I felt quite sure about what it meant, what tense and admonitory message was conveyed in the very form of implacable muteness. It said: "Now this cannot be, for while all sorts of interpersonal activity might be forwarded by individuals bearing to differing degrees the phenotypical signs of racial blackness and indeed consciously and explicitly subscribing to the identity, the significance of the deed—which may even be pleasurable in its power—must not in all cases be rendered as word—which is undeniably powerful in its punch, which affords us the terms of our life and our death, and by which we have strived to wrest our survival from the teeth of a world that would have us forlorn. Because propriety is requisite for success in this vein, we simply cannot acknowledge what you would have us acknowledge, as upon consideration you surely must see."

As a matter of fact, however, I *don't* at all see, which, as it happens, is very much to the point, since the majority of what occupies me here concerns the status of that which is not readily perceptible by conventional means. After all, one of the most intractable and infuriating problems encountered by the would-be commentator on dissident sexual practices is the charge that the evidence for our arguments is not solid—which, indeed, it often is not, in literal terms. But what does this mean, really? It means (for instance) that sex and sexuality are by definition evanescent experiences, made even more so in our sociocultural context by the peculiar ways that we negotiate them verbally. It isn't exactly that we don't talk about them, as Foucault famously demonstrated in *The History of Sexuality, Volume 1*, but rather that the *modes* through which we talk about them displace them ever further from easy referential access:[14] we exaggerate; we obfuscate; we tease and we hint; we mislead by indirection; and in fact we outright *lie*—and I don't mean merely with respect to our own personal practices, though I do indeed mean that in part. More than this, though, I mean that we, as a social collectivity, routinely deceive ourselves about the character and the extent of the sexual activity engaged in by human beings in general, and most especially by those in our own extended cultural context. In other words, we most certainly do not "see" dissident sexuality—queer sexuality—evidenced in the ways conventionally called for by the more positivist-minded folk whom we encounter in our professional activity; and it is precisely for this reason that I do not at all "see" that we should refrain from discussing it—as a thankfully growing number of us are proceeding to do—for we have to take our objects of analysis on the terms that define them, if we hope to make any headway whatever toward the increased understanding we supposedly seek.

What this means, it seems to me, for black queer studies, is that we must necessarily take recourse—for the umpteenth time in the history of our extended endeavor—to the evidence of things not seen and, further, to a particular subcategory within this genre, what I call in the title of this lecture the evidence of felt intuition. Before I elaborate on the character of this latter phenomenon, it is probably worth spelling out explicitly exactly *why* we are compelled to proceed in this way, and I can easily do that, because the answer has been so incisively indicated in an exceptionally valuable instance of the all-too-rare work that has been done in this regard. I am thinking of Deborah McDowell's groundbreaking analysis of Nella Larsen's fiction, which itself offers the key to our query that McDowell perspicaciously seizes upon; for the "nameless . . . shameful impulse" to which Larsen refers in her novel *Quicksand*—and which McDowell suggests she explores even more fully, if just as tacitly, in the later novel *Passing*—is *nameless* precisely because it is *shameful*.[15] Indeed, inasmuch as, in any given moral negotiation—which is to say, in any human activity or personal interaction whatsoever—the name recedes to precisely the same extent that shame waxes, we will necessarily be forced to attend to the relative *absence* of the name—the relative lack of positive evidence, if you will—*whenever* we seek to reckon with the significances of queer sexuality—of *homosexuality,* to speak the name bluntly—which it would be foolish to think does not still engender a *profound* sense of shame in U.S. culture and society and, Lord knows, in a large number of more or less overlapping African American communities comprised therein.

So, then, how to proceed? (For not to proceed is not an option, unless one actually approves of the status quo, and given that we are all human and not yet dead, I assume that none of us does.) How to consider the meaning of an experience no concrete evidence of which exists, and of which we can therefore claim no positive knowledge? I tried to address this question in my essay on responses to the death of Max Robinson, in which I admitted flat out that "I have no idea whether Max Robinson's sex partners were male or female or both," explaining that "I acknowledge explicitly my ignorance on this matter because to do so . . . is to reopen sex in all its manifestations as a primary category for [critical] consideration"—particularly in the study of African American culture and society.[16] This was an effective gesture as far as that article was concerned, partly because it came toward the end of the piece and thus comported perfectly with the essay's larger call to action; and partly because what obtained in the case of Max Robinson was not sheer unbounded uncertainty but rather uncertainty regarding a fairly clearly delimited arena of human endeavor—namely, sexual activity—coupled with an emphatic *dead certainty*—the fact of Robinson's AIDS-related demise—that made the uncertainty all the more urgent and compelling an object of interrogation, largely because it inevitably propelled critical inquiry in a highly provocative and controversial direction.

One might well worry, however, that we won't always have the benefit—as dubious as that benefit was in the instance at hand—of such a definitive counterphenomenon against which we can gauge the possible meanings of a sexuality that remains almost entirely unarticulated, and what then? Well, to be quite frank, I don't think that we are at risk of ever facing that scenario, for reasons that I will elucidate shortly. Leaving that point aside for the moment, though, let us simply consider what might happen in the instances (whose number and frequency will certainly increase the more we pursue critical consideration of black queer sexuality) where the objects of our analysis are so ethereal that they appear to offer us no hard evidence at all. Well, in those cases, we will doubtless have to take recourse in a direction to which I have already alluded and rely on the evidence of felt intuition. Immediately upon invoking it, of course, I realize that this phrase may strike some as worrisome, for it seems conventionally to refer to mere instinctive emotion, rather than to the engagement with external factors that is understood to be the rightful province of critical thought. On consulting the dictionary in order to settle my own fears on this score, however, I discovered that intuition is exactly the word I want, etymologically speaking, since in its root meaning it connotes precisely such outward engagement, signifying contemplation, or the practice of looking (Latin *tuērī*, to look [at]) *upon* (Latin *in*, on) some entity or another—and, by extension, coming to some speculative conclusion about it.

This process seems to me to characterize a significant portion of our lives, and most assuredly a large percentage of minority experience, given the uncertainty that I have already suggested defines the latter. In fact, I remember a train trip from Madison to Syracuse during which I rebuffed a white man who approached me. He'd asked if I'd join him in a game of cards, but I surmised that he was sexually attracted to me. Now, for a long time, from the late 1970s through the early 1990s, I used to lead educational workshops on "lesbian and gay lifestyles" in various institutional settings—schools, social service centers, halfway houses for young offenders. Like many people, members of these audiences often wanted to know whether gay men could identify others of our kind by the way they looked; I generally said that I could, but not by the way they looked to me so much as the way they looked at me, and this is what I noticed about the man on the train—the way he looked at me as he stood over my seat, asking me whether I'd like to play cards. I don't know for a fact that he was attracted to me; I only know that look and the sensation in my face when I'm giving the same look to somebody else.

Does this look—and the knowledge of it that I have accumulated over the years—constitute sex? It well might. Does it constitute *sexuality?* I have no doubt that it does. Am I ineluctably compelled to speculate about it, so as to arrive at some judgment that has its own consequences? I believe that I am, or else how would I get through the day, as fraught as it is with the possibility of danger? The man might just as easily have been an ax murderer, which would certainly have put a damper on things had I decided to follow through on what seemed to me his flirtatious inquiries. Or he might even have been a rather more run-of-the-mill homophobe, out to victimize gay men by queer-baiting them first. In any case, we necessarily adjudicate such situations on the fly every single day of our natural lives, and some of us much more frequently than others. Precisely because minority experience is character-ized by the uncertainty I have already referenced, we basically stake our lives and we take our chances, hoping that we haven't miscalculated the risk. Things could go deadly wrong, as I am frequently reminded; after all, judging from photographs I've seen in the news, I probably would have gone home with Jeffrey Dahmer if he'd asked me, and we all know what the result of that gamble would have been. The point, however, is not the peril, but rather the fact that we cannot not test it, for not to proceed speculatively is, to speak plainly, not to live. And it certainly is not to perform critical analysis, which incontrovertibly depends on speculative logic for the force of its arguments, as we all know deep down.

This is true, moreover, not only in the case of our actual scholarly work but also in our metacritical understanding of its effects. Take my account of responses to my essay, "Eloquence and Epitaph." Much of what I have related here I do not know to be fact. I did write that essay; it was published as indicated; it was taken up or not in the ways I have sketched. What it all *means,* though, I can't say for certain, and so I inevitably recur to speculative habit. Indeed, the whole metaphorics of "seeing" that I elaborated above is the product entirely of my own surmisings, however much it helps me in plotting my next analytic move amid the critical context that I want to help transform. One hopes my conclusions are not wholly off the mark, for a great deal of what I propose here is predicated on them. And, of course, that would be the objection to speculative knowledge—that it potentially leads us astray from known data, from the concrete reality of worldly existence (as if entire disciplines weren't based on speculation; as if we didn't credit those disciplines with the discovery of truth), and indeed it might do so, but then what's wrong with that?

God knows I, for one, feel the need for a break, a relief from the stressful uncertainty entailed by the recurrent exigencies of daily life. As I stated at the outset, I find it exhausting, so much so that lately I've been rethinking my position and pondering the prospect of a little travel, which might be just the thing to ease my anxiety. How potentially invigorating, after all, to leave behind the quotidian contexts in which uncertainty is debilitating, in favor of brand-new situations where it might serve as a tonic. I imagine myself ensconced in the luxury of first class, languidly attending to the scenery about me. A fellow passenger approaches me and invites me to cards, but I surmise that he is sexually attracted to me, a young man from Sri Lanka all alone in the world, with perhaps not too firm a command of the language. I look at him looking; I contemplate him; I stake my life and I take my chances and I do not rebuff him, for who knows what may happen if I follow it through? I have the feeling that it is very, very exciting to live even one day. I could go anywhere, I could meet anyone, anything of great interest could transpire between us, and wouldn't it be just a bit well deserved? I am tired, after all; I work far too hard. And yes, I said, yes, I would like that, yes, and why shouldn't I have it? And so just last month I took a concrete step to make it quite feasible for the first time in my life: I bit the bullet and took the plunge and I applied for a passport so I could travel abroad.

A bothersome procedure, this passport application, requiring documents that I have stored too safely away. But I proceed on my mission, and I rifle through my belongings, because if I succeed in this endeavor I might actually escape. And that is my objective, now—an escape from my "real" life, since I've decided that there really is nothing wrong with that, nothing wrong with evading the brute facts of routine existence. So, yellowed and brittle and torn as it is, I retrieve my birth certificate from the box where I've hidden it—not the "abstracted" certificate of birth *registration* that I desperately had Thom FedEx to me in Toronto when I was worried that I wouldn't be allowed to recross the border into the United States after the 1997 Modern Language Association convention; and not the *original* document, either, passed directly from the Michigan Department of Health to my parents to me; but still, a properly stamped copy of that record, issued on the relatively distant date of August 1975, and so emanating an aura of antique officialdom that is substantiated by the information it actually bears. For what appears on this form, in two noteworthy places—first in the all-important section devoted to information about the father (of primary significance, one presumes, for the establishment of legitimacy, patronym, and lineal propriety, no doubt accounting for its preeminent position), and second in the rather less-prominent section given over to the mother (smaller than that for the father, of course, since there is no need for the box which in the father's case is inscribed with the parent's "usual occupation," the very existence of the certificate of live birth itself evidently attesting to what the mother's occupation must be)—but confirmation of the "color or race" of the parents, which in each instance is neatly recorded, in crisp typescript form and with an initial capital letter, as "Negro." And that, my friends, was that, by which I mean not that I forwent the passport application or the plans for travel (God knows I deserve it; God knows I am tired) but that I dispensed with any illusions about being able to escape the hard facts of my day-to-day material life.

For even if I left, I would have to return, would have to recross the borders of the United States, where the significance of the "Negro" designation is so thoroughly sedimented that it conditions even my attempt to forget what it means. And what led me to that realization but the very trajectory of my fantastic speculation, by means of which I had thought to leave such facts behind? I personally don't believe that we can ever go very far down the path of speculative rumination without encountering the material realities to which the realm of speculation is conventionally opposed, if only because they shape the very terms by which we forward our speculation in the first place, whether we recognize it or not.

In other words, if speculative reasoning often appears as the only tool we have by which to forward the type of critical analysis our situation demands, such reasoning itself is necessarily conditioned by the material factors in which it is undertaken, and those material factors without exception all have histories that themselves can serve to guide us in our critical work. To what history (among others) does my birth certificate attest, for instance, but the highly complex one regarding the very possibility—let alone the meaning—of precisely that African American family in rich and tense relation to which black queerness now incontrovertibly stands? What does it signify in its registration of my father's occupation, in 1961, as a self-employed attorney but the highly vexed history of the African American professional classes?—a vexedness further attested by the fact that my mother, who was *also* a self-employed attorney at the time that I was born, has no official occupation listed on my birth certificate at all. What do my parents' disparate places of birth—rural Alabama in my father's case, Detroit in my mother's—which are also indicated on the document, suggest but the profoundly consequential history of twentieth-century black migration from the South to the urban North, with all of the complexities we know are elided in the too simple characterization of the phenomenon I have just provided? What does the form's presumption of my parents' officially sanctioned marital status (indicated in its stipulation that the mother of the new infant provide her full "maiden" name) connote but the long history of the black family's officially *contested* character? And what is the fate of these various histories but that they are borne by and signified in the person whose birth is certified by this document, who in turn carries them into any situation in which he speculatively makes his way, for better or worse—*including* such situations as the tantalizingly sexualized one that occurred during my train trip, where those histories were condensed and effectively activated (whether my interlocutor knew it or not) in the very instant that my racial identity came to the fore as a point of consternation in my exchange with my fellow passenger.

The speculation in which I engaged during that encounter, then, was thoroughly bound up with the material factors that constituted my subjectivity within it, and it is in relation to those factors that my speculative rumination derives its ultimate meaning, however abstractly theoretical it may appear at first blush. This, I guess, explains why I harbor no reservations about theory, because I don't see it as ever being "merely" theoretical. Moreover, as far as queer studies is concerned, theory may in some respects be all that we have, if by theory we mean (to be etymological again) *a way of seeing* that allows us to apprehend our world in different and potentially productive ways.

To the extent that this meaning of the term does not imply coherence or exclusionary unity, we can likely even admit it as a way of characterizing queer critical work, which itself should enable us to see the fissures and inconsistencies in what conventionally appears as the wholly coherent infrastructure of normative culture. And the engine most capable of driving our novel perceptions in this vein is the very social materiality that, on first consideration, might seem to obscure our view: my own blackness, for instance (or anyone else's), which both predicated and thwarted my encounter on the train and then propelled my rumination on it along queer critical lines.

I am hoping that such practice will define the direction of black queer studies in the new millennium, for I am convinced that its explanatory and transformative potential hasn't even begun to be tapped. Not that I naively believe that we will ever resolve *all* the problems that confront us, by this or any other means, but I remain fully determined that the task must continually be pursued, for the sake of the partial progressive change that we indisputably must make. And it's funny, but suddenly that determination, too, seems to be a function of my blackness itself—or at least of the blackness that has historically been constituted in U.S. society. For I was reminded of that logic when I examined my birth certificate, which, after all, registers my blackness—my "Negro-ness"—not as an attribute of my own person (for the "color or race" of the actual child whose birth is attested is nowhere recorded on the document) but only as a trait of the persons who engendered me, from whom I simply inherit it as a tacit matter of course. Pondering this fact, I couldn't help but note how it seems to extend and recapitulate the old antebellum rule that a child born in the context of slavery would necessarily follow the condition of the mother. Reflecting on this, I was unable to suppress an overwhelming sense of perverse pleasure, even as I considered the difficult critical and political work that confronts us, in the face of which we might understandably be tempted to leave well enough alone. But no, I thought, as I worried over this possibility, that sad state of affairs will never materialize. For in a way that nineteenth-century lawmakers could never have either predicted or appreciated, we really *are* just like our mothers: we are *never* satisfied.

This essay is for Jeff Nunokawa.

NOTES

My thanks to the participants in the conference Black Queer Studies in the Millennium, and to Mae G. Henderson and, especially, E. Patrick Johnson for organizing that remarkable event; to Carlos Decena for his consistently invaluable research assistance; and to Carolyn Dinshaw and David M. Halperin for the encouragement and earlier opportunity to publish this essay.

1. See my essay " 'Take Me Home': Location, Identity, Transnational Exchange," in *Private Affairs: Critical Ventures in the Culture of Social Relations* (New York: New York University Press, 1999), 125–54 (reprinted in expanded form in *Callaloo* 23 [2000]: 461–78).

2. Indeed, my sense that many black people would find my interlocutor's reaction relatively unremarkable is validated by the fact that a parody of such response found its way into an early-1990s solo presentation by the African American performer Alva

Rogers. In her 1991 one-woman show, *Alva,* Rogers hilariously lampooned white people's typically incredulous insistences that the dark-skinned person with whom they have had any degree of engaging intellectual or social interaction cannot possibly "really" be black. *Alva* was presented on February 8–9, 1991, at the Institute of Contemporary Art in Boston.

3. Quoted in Pat Wingert and Barbara Kantrowitz, "Gay Today: The Family: Two Kids and Two Moms," in John Leland, "Shades of Gay," *Newsweek,* March 20, 2000, 50.

4. Virginia Woolf, *Mrs. Dalloway* (San Diego: Harcourt Brace Jovanovich, 1990), 8.

5. In a volume whose objective of providing an "introduction" to "queer theory" may strike us as somewhat paradoxical, given the putative incoherence of the field, Annamarie Jagose, in *Queer Theory: An Introduction* (New York: New York University Press, 1996; esp. "Queer," 72–100), actually offers a highly nuanced and helpful account of these various assessments. Of particular value among the works Jagose cites are Lauren Berlant and Michael Warner, "What Does Queer Theory Teach Us about X?" *PMLA* 110 (1995): 343–49; Alexander Doty, "What Makes Queerness Most?" in *Making Things Perfectly Queer: Interpreting Mass Culture* (Minneapolis: University of Minnesota Press, 1993), xi–xix, esp. xiii–xix; Lisa Duggan, "Making It Perfectly Queer," *Socialist Review,* no. 22 (1992): 11–31; Lee Edelman, "Queer Theory: Unstating Desire," *GLQ* 2 (1995): 343–48; David M. Halperin, *Saint Foucault: Towards a Gay Hagiography* (New York: Oxford University Press, 1995), esp. 62–67; and Eve Kosofsky Sedgwick, *Tendencies* (Durham: Duke University Press, 1993), esp. "Queer and Now," 1–20.

6. See, for example, the trenchant critique along these lines made by Cathy Cohen, "Punks, Bulldaggers, and Welfare Queens: The Radical Potential of Queer Politics?" in this volume.

7. In characterizing the U.S. sociocultural context as a site of white supremacist hegemony, I am following the lead taken by bell hooks in *Killing Rage: Ending Racism* (New York: Holt, 1995).

8. Phillip Brian Harper, "Eloquence and Epitaph: Black Nationalism and the Homophobic Impulse in Responses to the Death of Max Robinson," *Social Text,* no. 28 (1991): 68–86.

9. Henry Abelove, Michèle Aina Barale, and David M. Halperin, eds., *The Lesbian and Gay Studies Reader* (New York: Routledge, 1993); Michael Warner, ed., *Fear of a Queer Planet: Queer Politics and Social Theory* (Minneapolis: University of Minnesota Press, 1993).

10. The passage from *The Lesbian and Gay Studies Reader* that I refer to here incorporates the editors' note that "we have reluctantly chosen not to speak here and in our title of 'queer studies,' despite our own attachment to the term," along with their reasons for that decision (xvii). Jagose glosses what she sees as the passage's "defensive" tone (*Queer Theory,* 4). Regarding the significance of 1993, I have in mind not only the release during that year of the aforementioned anthologies but also the

contemporaneous publication of Sedgwick's *Tendencies* and Judith Butler's *Bodies That Matter: On the Discursive Limits of "Sex"* (New York: Routledge, 1993), as well as the appearance on the critical scene of *GLQ,* the defining periodical in the field.

11. See Harper, "Eloquence and Epitaph," 85–86 n.19.

12. Phillip Brian Harper, *Are We Not Men? Masculine Anxiety and the Problem of African-American Identity* (New York: Oxford University Press, 1996), 3–38.

13. See Timothy E. Murphy and Suzanne Poirier, eds., *Writing* AIDS: Gay Literature, Language, and Analysis (New York: Columbia University Press, 1993), 117–39.

14. Michel Foucault, *The History of Sexuality, Volume 1,* trans. Robert Hurley (New York: Vintage, 1990).

15. See Deborah E. McDowell, "The 'Nameless . . . Shameful Impulse': Sexuality in Larsen's *Quicksand* and *Passing*" (1986), in *The Changing Same: Black Women's Literature, Criticism, and Theory,* ed. Cheryl Wall (Bloomington: Indiana University Press, 1995), 78–97. The referenced passage from Nella Larsen's fiction appears in the novel *Quicksand* (1928), in *"Quicksand" and "Passing,"* ed. Deborah E. McDowell (New Brunswick: Rutgers University Press, 1986), 95.

16. Harper, "Eloquence and Epitaph," 81.

E. PATRICK JOHNSON

"QUARE" STUDIES, OR

(ALMOST) EVERYTHING I KNOW

ABOUT QUEER STUDIES I LEARNED

FROM MY GRANDMOTHER

I love queer. Queer is a homosexual of either sex. It's more convenient than saying "gays" which has to be qualified, or "lesbians and gay men." It's an extremely useful polemic term because
it is who we say we are, which is, "Fuck You."—Spike Pittsberg,
in Cherry Smith, "What Is This Thing Called Queer?"

I use queer to describe my particular brand of lesbian feminism, which has much to do with the radical feminism I was
involved with in the early 80's. I also use it externally to describe
a political inclusivity—a new move toward a celebration of
difference across sexualities, across genders, across sexual preference and across object choice. The two link.—Linda Semple,
in Smith, "What Is This Thing Called Queer?"

I'm more inclined to use the words "black lesbian," because
when I hear the word queer I think of white, gay men.—Isling
Mack-Nataf, in Smith, "What Is This Thing Called Queer?"

I define myself as gay mostly. I will not use queer because it
is not part of my vernacular—but I have nothing against its
use. The same debates around naming occur in the "black
community." Naming is powerful. Black people and gay people
constantly renaming ourselves is a way to shift power from
whites and hets respectively.—Inge Blackman, in Smith, "What
Is This Thing Called Queer?"

Personally speaking, I do not consider myself a "queer" activist or, for that matter, a "queer" anything. This is not because I do not consider myself an activist; in fact I hold my political work to be one of my most important contributions to all of my communities. But like other lesbian, gay, bisexual, and transgendered activists of color, I find the label "queer" fraught with unspoken assumptions which inhibit the radical political potential of this category.—Cathy Cohen, "Punks, Bulldaggers, and Welfare Queens"

Quare Etymology (with apologies to Alice Walker)[1]

Quare (Kwâr), *n*. **1.** meaning *queer;* also, opp. of *straight;* odd or slightly off kilter; from the African American vernacular for queer; sometimes homophobic in usage, but always denotes excess incapable of being contained within conventional categories of *being;* curiously equivalent to the Anglo-Irish (and sometimes "Black" Irish) variant of queer, as in Brendan Behan's famous play *The Quare Fellow*.

—*adj*. **2.** a lesbian, gay, bisexual, or transgendered person of color who loves other men or women, sexually and/or nonsexually, and appreciates black culture and community.

—*n*. **3.** one who *thinks* and *feels* and *acts* (and, sometimes, "acts up"); committed to struggle against all forms of oppression—racial, sexual, gender, class, religious, etc.

—*n*. **4.** one for whom sexual and gender identities always already intersect with racial subjectivity.

5. quare is to queer as "reading" is to "throwing shade."

I am going out on a limb. This is a precarious position, but the stakes are high enough to warrant risky business. The business to which I refer is reconceptualizing the still-incubating discipline called "queer" studies. Now, what's in a name? This is an important question when, as James Baldwin proclaims, I have "no name in the street" or, worse still, "nobody *knows* my name."[2] I used to answer to "queer," but when I was hailed by that naming, interpellated in that moment, I felt as if I was being called "out of my name." I needed something with more "soul," more "bang," something closer to "home." It is my name after all!

Then I remembered how "queer" is used in my family. My grandmother, for example, used it often when I was a child and still uses it today.[3] When she says the word, she does so in a thick, black, southern dialect: "That sho'll is a 'quare' chile." Her use of "queer" is almost always nuanced. Still, one might wonder, what, if anything, could a poor, black, eighty-something, southern, homophobic woman teach her educated, middle-class, thirty-something, gay grandson about queer studies? Everything. Or *almost* everything. On the one hand, my grandmother uses "quare" to denote something or someone who is odd, irregular, or slightly off-kilter—definitions in keeping with traditional understandings and uses of "queer." On the other hand, she also deploys "quare" to connote something excessive—something that might philosophically translate into an excess of discursive and epistemological meanings grounded in African American cultural rituals and lived experience. Her knowing or not knowing vis-à-vis "quare" is predicated on her own "multiple and complex social, historical, and cultural positionality."[4] It is this culture-specific positionality that I find absent from the dominant and more conventional usage of "queer," particularly in its most recent theoretical reappropriation in the academy.

I knew there was something to the term "quare," that its implications reached far beyond my grandmother's front porch. Little did I know, however, that it would extend from her porch across the Atlantic. Then, I found "quare" in Ireland.[5] In his *Quare Joyce*, Joseph Valente writes, "I have elected to use the Anglo-Irish epithet *quare* in the title as a kind of transnational/ transidiomatic pun. *Quare*, meaning odd or strange, as in Brendan Behan's famous play, *The Quare Fellow*, has lately been appropriated as a distinctively Irish variant of *queer*, as in the recent prose collection *Quare Fellas*, whose editor, Brian Finnegan, reinterprets Behan's own usage of the term as having 'covertly alluded to his own sexuality.' "[6] Valente's appropriation of the Irish epithet "quare" to "queerly" read James Joyce establishes a connection between race and ethnicity in relation to queer identity. Indeed, Valente's "quare" reading of Joyce, when conjoined with my grandmother's "quare" reading of those who are "slightly off-kilter," provides a strategy for reading racial and ethnic sexuality. Where the two uses of "quare" diverge is in their deployment. Valente deploys "quare" to devise a queer literary exegesis of Joyce. Rather than drawing on "quare" as a *literary* mode of reading/theorizing, however, I draw on the *vernacular* roots implicit in my grandmother's use of the word to devise a strategy for theorizing racialized sexuality.

Because much of queer theory critically interrogates notions of selfhood, agency, and experience, it is often unable to accommodate the issues faced by gays and lesbians of color who come from "raced" communities. Gloria Anzaldúa explicitly addresses this limitation when she warns that "queer is used as a false unifying umbrella which all 'queers' of all races, ethnicities and classes are shored under." While acknowledging that "at times we need this umbrella to solidify our ranks against outsiders," Anzaldúa nevertheless urges that "even when we seek shelter under it ["queer"], we must not forget that it homogenizes, erases our differences."[7]

"Quare," on the other hand, not only speaks across identities, it *articulates* identities as well. "Quare" offers a way to critique stable notions of identity and, at the same time, to locate racialized and class knowledges. My project is one of recapitulation and recuperation. I want to maintain the inclusivity and playful spirit of "queer" that animates much of queer theory, but I also want to jettison its homogenizing tendencies. As a disciplinary expansion, then, I wish to "quare" "queer" such that ways of knowing are viewed both as discursively mediated and as historically situated and materially conditioned. This reconceptualization foregrounds the ways in which lesbians, bisexuals, gays, and transgendered people of color come to sexual and racial knowledge. Moreover, quare studies acknowledges the different "standpoints" found among lesbian, bisexual, gay, and transgendered people of color differences—differences that are also conditioned by class and gender.[8]

Quare studies is a theory of and for gays and lesbians of color. Thus, I acknowledge that in my attempt to advance "quare" studies, I run the risk of advancing another version of identity politics. Despite this, I find it necessary to traverse this political minefield in order to illuminate the ways in which some strands of queer theory fail to incorporate racialized sexuality. The theory that I advance is a "theory in the flesh."[9] Theories in the flesh emphasize the diversity within and among gays, bisexuals, lesbians, and transgendered people of color while simultaneously accounting for how racism and classism affect how we experience and theorize the world. Theories in the flesh also conjoin theory and practice through an embodied politic of resistance. This politics of resistance is manifest in vernacular traditions such as performance, folklore, literature, and verbal art.

This essay offers an extended meditation on and an intervention in queer theory and practice. I begin by mapping out a general history of queer theory's deployment in contemporary academic discourse, focusing on the lack of discourse on race and class within the queer theoretical paradigm. Following this, I offer an analysis of one queer theorist's (mis)reading of two black gay performances. Next, I propose an intervention in queer theory by outlining the components of quare theory, a theory that incorporates race and class as categories of analysis in the study of sexuality. Quare theory is then operationalized in the following section, where I offer a quare reading of Marlon Riggs's film *Black Is . . . Black Ain't*. The final section calls for a conjoining of academic praxis with political praxis.

"RACE TROUBLE": QUEER STUDIES OR THE STUDY OF WHITE QUEERS

At the moment when queer studies has gained momentum in the academy and forged a space as a legitimate disciplinary subject, much of the scholarship produced in its name elides issues of race and class. While the epigraphs that open this essay suggest that "queer" sometimes speaks across (homo)sexualities, they also suggest that "queer" is not necessarily embraced by gays, bisexuals, lesbians, and transgendered people of color. Indeed, the statements of Mack-Nataf, Blackman, and Cohen reflect a general suspicion of the term "queer," that the term often displaces and rarely addresses their concerns.[10]

Some queer theorists have argued that their use of "queer" is more than just a reappropriation of an offensive term. Cherry Smith, for example, maintains that the term entails a "radical questioning of social and cultural norms, notions of gender, reproductive sexuality and the family."[11] Others underscore the playfulness and inclusivity of the term, arguing that it opens up rather than fixes identities. According to Eve Sedgwick, "What it takes—all it takes—to make the description 'queer' a true one is the impulsion to use it in the first person."[12] Indeed, Sedgwick suggests, it may refer to "pushy femmes, radical faeries, fantasists, drags, clones, leatherfolk, ladies in tuxedos, feminist women or feminist men, masturbators, bulldaggers, divas, Snap! queens, butch bottoms, storytellers, transsexuals, aunties, wannabes, lesbian-identified men or lesbians who sleep with men, or . . . people able to relish, learn from, or identify with such."[13] For Sedgwick, then, it would appear that queer is a catch-all not bound to any particular "identity," a notion that moves us away from binaries such as "homosexual/heterosexual" and "gay/lesbian." Micheal Warner offers an even more politicized and polemical view: "The preference for 'queer' represents, among other things, an aggressive impulse of generalization; it rejects a minoritizing logic of toleration or simple political interest-representation in favor of a more thorough resistance to regimes of the normal. For academics, being interested in Queer theory is a way to mess up the desexualized spaces of the academy, exude some rut, reimagine the public from and for which academic intellectuals write, dress, and perform."[14] The foregoing theorists identify "queer" as a site of indeterminate possibility, a site where sexual practice does not necessarily determine one's status as queer. Indeed, Lauren Berlant and Michael Warner argue that queer is "more a matter of aspiration than it is the expression of an identity or a history."[15] Accordingly, straight-identified critic Calvin Thomas appropriates Judith Butler's notion of "critical queerness" to suggest that "just as there is more than one way to be 'critical,' there may be more than one (or two or three) to be 'queer.' "[16]

Some critics have applied Butler's theory of gender to identity formation more generally. Butler calls into question the notion of the "self" as distinct from discursive cultural fields. That is, like gender, there is no independent or pure "self" or agent that stands outside socially and culturally mediated discursive systems. Thus, any move toward identification is, in Butler's view, to be hoodwinked into believing that identities are discourse free and capable of existing outside the systems that those identity formations seek to critique. Even when identity is contextualized and qualified, Butler still insists that theories of identity "invariably close with an embarrassed 'etc.' "[17] Butler's emphasis on gender and sex as "performative" would seem to undergird a progressive, forward-facing theory of sexuality. In fact, some theorists have made the theoretical leap from the gender performative to the racial performative, thereby demonstrating the potential of her theory for understanding the ontology of race.[18]

But, to riff off of the now-popular phrase "gender trouble," *there is some "race" trouble here with queer theory.* More particularly, in its "race for theory,"[19] queer theory has often failed to address the material realities of gays and lesbians of color. As black British activist Helen (charles) asks, "What happens to the definition of 'queer' when you're washing up or having a wank? When you're aware of misplacement or displacement in your colour, gender, identity? Do they get subsumed . . . into a homogeneous category, where class and other things that make up a cultural identity are ignored?"[20] What, for example, are the ethical and material implications of queer theory if its project is to dismantle all notions of identity and agency? The deconstructive turn in queer theory highlights the ways in which ideology functions to oppress and to proscribe ways of knowing, but what is the utility of queer theory on the front lines, in the trenches, on the street, or anyplace where the racialized and sexualized body is beaten, starved, fired, cursed—indeed, when the body is the site of trauma?[21]

Beyond queer theory's failure to focus on materiality, it also has failed to acknowledge consistently and critically the intellectual, aesthetic, and political contributions of nonwhite, non-middle-class gays, bisexuals, lesbians, and transgendered people in the struggle against homophobia and oppression. Moreover, even when white queer theorists acknowledge these contributions, rarely do they self-consciously and overtly reflect on the ways in which their own whiteness informs their own critical queer position, and this is occurring at a time when naming one's positionality has become almost standard protocol in other areas of scholarship. Although there are exceptions, most often white queer theorists fail to acknowledge and address racial privilege.[22]

Because transgendered people, lesbians, gays, and bisexuals of color often ground their theorizing in a politics of identity, they frequently fall prey to accusations of "essentialism" or "anti-intellectualism." Galvanizing around identity, however, is not always an unintentional "essentialist" move. Many times, it is an intentional strategic choice.[23] Cathy Cohen, for example, suggests that "queer theorizing which calls for the elimination of fixed categories seems to ignore the ways in which some traditional social identities and communal ties can, in fact, be important to one's survival."[24] The "communal ties" to which Cohen refers are those that exist in communities of color across boundaries of sexuality. For example, my grandmother, who is homophobic, nonetheless must be included in the struggle against oppression in spite of her bigotry. While her homophobia must be critiqued, her feminist and race struggles over the course of her life have enabled me and others in my family to enact strategies of resistance against a number of oppressions, including homophobia. Some queer activists groups, however, have argued fervently for the disavowal of any alliance with heterosexuals, a disavowal that those of us who belong to communities of color cannot necessarily afford to make.[25] Therefore, while offering a progressive and sometimes transgressive politics of sexuality, the seams of queer theory become exposed when that theory is applied to identities around which sexuality may pivot, such as race and class.

As a counter to this myopia and in an attempt to close the gap between theory and practice, self and Other, Audre Lorde proclaims:

> Without community there is no liberation, only the most vulnerable and temporary armistice between an individual and her oppression. But community must not mean a shedding of our differences, nor the pathetic pretense that these differences do not exist. . . .

*I urge each one of us here to reach down into that deep place of
knowledge inside herself and touch the terror and loathing of any difference that lives there. See whose face it wears. Then the personal as the
political can begin to illuminate all our choices.*[26]

For Lorde, a theory that dissolves the communal identity—in all of its difference—around which the marginalized can politically organize is not a
progressive one. Nor is it one that gays, bisexuals, transgendered people, and
lesbians of color can afford to adopt, for to do so would be to foreclose
possibilities of change.

"YOUR BLUES AIN'T LIKE MINE": THE INVALIDATION OF "EXPERIENCE"

As a specific example of how some queer theorists (mis)read or minimize the
work, lives, and cultural production of gays, lesbians, bisexuals, and transgendered people of color, and to lay the groundwork for a return to a focus
on embodied performance as a critical praxis, I offer an analysis of one queer
theorist's reading of two black gay performances. In *The Ethics of Marginality*,
for example, queer theorist John Champagne uses black gay theorists' objections to the photographs of Robert Mapplethorpe to call attention to the
trouble with deploying "experience" as evidentiary.[27] Specifically, Champagne focuses on a speech delivered by Essex Hemphill, a black gay writer
and activist, at the 1990 OUTWRITE conference of gay and lesbian writers. In
his speech, Hemphill critiqued Mapplethorpe's photographs of black men.[28]
Champagne takes exception to Hemphill's critique, arguing that Hemphill's
reading is "monolithic" and bespeaks "a largely untheorized relation between
desire, representation, and the political."[29] What I wish to interrogate, however, is Champagne's reading of Hemphill's apparent "emotionality" during
the speech.

In Champagne's account, Hemphill began to cry during his speech, to
which there were two responses: one of sympathy/empathy and one of protest. Commenting on an overheard conversation between two whites in the
audience, Champagne writes, "Although I agreed with much of the substance
of this person's comments concerning race relations in the gay and lesbian
community, I was suspicious of the almost masochistic pleasure released in
and through this public declaration of white culpability."[30] Here I find it
surprising that Champagne would characterize what appears to be white
reflexivity about racial and class privilege as "masochistic," given how rare

such self-reflexivity is in the academy and elsewhere. After characterizing as masochistic the two whites who sympathetically align themselves with Hemphill, Champagne aligns himself with the one person who displayed vocal disapproval by booing at Hemphill's speech:

> I have to admit that I admired the bravura of the lone booer. I disagreed with Hemphill's readings of the photographs, and felt that his tears were an attempt to shame the audience into refusing to interrogate the terms of his address. If, as Gayatri Spivak has suggested, we might term the politics of an explanation the means by which it secures its particular mode of being in the world, the politics of Hemphill's reading of Mapplethorpe might be described as the politics of tears, a politics that assures the validity of its produced explanation by appealing to some kind of "authentic," universal, and (thus) uninterrogated "human" emotion of experience.[31]

Champagne's own "bravura" in *his* reading of Hemphill's tears illuminates the ways in which many queer theorists, in their quest to move beyond the body, ground their critique in the discursive rather than the corporeal. I suggest that the two terrains are not mutually exclusive, but rather stand in a dialogical/dialectical relationship to one another. What about the authenticity of pain, for example, that may supercede the cognitive and emerges from the heart—not *for* display but *despite* display? What is the significance of a black *man* crying in public? We must grant each other time and space not only to talk *of* the body, but through it as well.[32] In Champagne's formulation however, bodily "experience" is anti-intellectual and Hemphill's "black" bodily experience is manipulative. This seems to be an un–self-reflexive, if not unfair, assumption to make when, for the most part, white bodies are discursively and corporeally naturalized as universal. Historically, white bodies have not been trafficked, violated, burned, and dragged behind trucks because they embody racialized identities. In Champagne's analysis of "blackness," bodily "whiteness" goes uninterrogated.[33]

In order to posit an alternative reading of Hemphill's tears, I turn to bell hooks's insights regarding the ways in which whites often misread emotionality elicited through black cultural aesthetics. "In the context of white institutions, particularly universities," hooks writes, "that mode of address is questionable precisely because it moves people. Style is equated in such a setting with a lack of substance." It is hooks's belief that this transformation of cultural space requires an "audience [to] shift . . . paradigms" and, in that way, "a marginal aspect of black cultural identity [is] centralized."[34] Unlike Champagne's own diminution of the "subversive powers [and politics] of style,"[35] hooks affirms the transgressive and transformative potential of style, citing it as "one example of counter-hegemonic cultural practice" as well as "an insertion of radical black subjectivity."[36] Despite Champagne's statements to the contrary, his own reading of Hemphill constitutes himself as a "sovereign subject" within his theory of antisubjectivity, a positionality that renders him "overseer" of black cultural practices and discourse. On the other hand, Hemphill's tears, as a performance of black style that draws on emotionality, may be read as more than simply a willful act of manipulation to substantiate the black gay "experience" of subjugation and objectification. More complexly, it may be read as a "confrontation with difference which takes place on new ground, in that counter-hegemonic marginal space where radical black subjectivity is *seen*, not overseen by any authoritative Other claiming to know us better than we know ourselves."[37] In his "reading" of Hemphill, Champagne positions himself as "authoritative Other," assuming, as he does, the motivation behind Hemphill's tears.[38]

Champagne also devotes an entire chapter to *Tongues Untied*, a work by black gay filmmaker Marlon Riggs. Once again critiquing what he sees as the film's problematic reliance on "experience" as evidentiary, Champagne offers a queer reading of Riggs's film to call into question the filmic representation of blackness and class:

> In *Tongues Untied*, one of the consequences of failing to dis-articulate, in one's reading, the hybrid weave of discursive practices deployed by the film might be the erasure of what I would term certain discontinuities of class, race, and imperialism as they might interweave with the necessarily inadequate nominations "Black" and "gay." For example, much of the film seems to employ a set of discursive practices historically familiar to a middle-class audience, Black and non-Black alike. The film tends to privilege the (discursive) "experience" of middle-class Black gay men, and is largely articulated from that position. The film privileges poetry, and in particular, a poetry that seems to owe as much historically to Walt Whitman and William Carlos Williams as to Langston Hughes or Countee Cullen; moreover, the film's more overtly political rhetoric seems culled from organized urban struggles in the gay as well as Black communities, struggles often headed by largely middle-class people. Another moment in the film that suggests a certain

middle-class position is arguably one of the central images of the film, a series of documentary style shots of what appears to be a Gay Pride Day march in Manhattan. A group of black gay men carry a banner that reads "Black Men Loving Black Men Is a Revolutionary Act," apparently echoing the rhetoric of early middle-class feminism. Furthermore, the men who carry this banner are arguably marked as middle-class, their bodies sculpted into the bulging, muscular style so prominent in the gay ghettos of San Francisco and New York.[39]

Champagne's critique is problematic in several ways. First, it is based on the premise that *Tongues Untied* elides the issue of class in its focus on race and homosexuality. Champagne then goes on to demonstrate the ways in which the film speaks to a middle-class sensibility. What is missing here is an explanation as to why black middle-class status precludes one from socially and politically engaging issues of race and sexuality. Because Champagne does not provide such an explanation, the reader is left to assume that the black middle-class subject position, as Valerie Smith has suggested, "is a space of pure compromise and capitulation, from which all autonomy disappears once it encounters hegemonic power."[40] Second, in his class-based analysis Champagne reads literary selections, material goods, and clothing aesthetics as "evidence" of the film's middle-class leanings. However, he fails to recognize that the *appearance* of belonging to a particular class does not always reflect one's actual class status. In the black community, for instance, middle-class status is often performed—what is referred to in the vernacular as acting "boojee" (bourgeois). The way a black person adorns herself or publicly displays his material possessions may not necessarily reflect his or her economic status. Put another way, one might *live* in the projects but not necessarily *appear* to.[41] Champagne, however, misreads signs of class in the film in order to support his thesis that middle-class status in the film is symptomatic of deeply rooted sexual conservatism and homophobia. Incredibly, he links this conservatism not only to that of antiporn feminists but also to political bigots like Jesse Helms.[42]

I am perplexed as to why the film cannot privilege black, middle-class gay experience. Is *Tongues Untied* a red herring of black gay representation because it does not do the discursive work that Champagne wishes it to do? Is it *The Cosby Show* in "gay face" because it portrays black middle-class life (and I'm not sure that it does)? Positioning the film in such a light seems to bespeak just the kind of essentialism that Champagne so adamantly argues against. That is, he links class and epistemology to serve the purpose of his critique, yet dismisses race-based ways of knowing. Why is class privileged epistemologically while "raced" ways of knowing are dismissed? Champagne states that "to point out that Riggs's film seems to privilege the (discursive) experience of largely middle-class urban Black gay men and to employ conventions of filmmaking familiar to a middle-class audience is not, in and of itself, a criticism of the video."[43] This disclaimer notwithstanding, Champagne goes on to do a close (mis)reading of various moments and aesthetics of the film—from specific scenes to what he argues is the film's "experimental documentary" style—to substantiate his class critique.

Unlike Champagne's deployment of queer theory, the model of quare studies that I propose would not only critique the concept of "race" as historically contingent and socially and culturally constructed/performed, it would also address the material effects of race in a white supremacist society. Quare studies requires an acknowledgment by the critic of her or his position within an oppressive system. To fail to do so would, as Ruth Goldman argues, "[leave] the burden of dealing with difference on the people who are themselves different, while simultaneously allowing white academics to construct a discourse of silence around race and other queer perspectives."[44] One's "experience" within that system, however discursively mediated, is also materially conditioned. A critic cannot ethically and responsibly speak from a privileged place, as Champagne does, and not own up to that privilege. To do so is to maintain the force of hegemonic whiteness, which, until very recently, has gone uninterrogated.[45]

"QUARING" THE QUEER: TROPING THE TROPE

Queer studies has rightfully problematized identity politics by elaborating on the processes by which agents and subjects come into being; however, there is a critical gap in queer studies between theory and practice, performance and performativity. Quare studies can narrow that gap to the extent that it pursues an epistemology rooted in the body. As a "theory in the flesh," quare necessarily engenders a kind of identity politics, one that acknowledges difference within and between particular groups. Thus, identity politics does not necessarily mean the reduction of multiple identities into a monolithic identity or narrow cultural nationalism. Rather, quare studies moves beyond simply theorizing subjectivity and agency as discursively mediated to theorizing how that mediation may propel material bodies into action. As Shane

Phelan reminds us, the maintenance of a progressive identity politics asks "not whether we share a given position but whether we share a commitment to improve it, and whether we can commit to the pain of embarrassment and confrontation as we disagree."[46]

Quare studies would reinstate the subject and the identity around which the subject circulates that queer theory so easily dismisses. By refocusing our attention on the racialized bodies, experiences, and knowledges of transgendered people, lesbians, gays, and bisexuals of color, quare studies grounds the discursive process of mediated identification and subjectivity in a political praxis that speaks to the material existence of "colored" bodies. While strategically galvanized around identity, quare studies should be committed to interrogating identity claims that exclude rather than include. I am thinking here of black nationalist claims of "black authenticity" that exclude, categorically, homosexual identities. Blind allegiance to "isms" of any kind is one of the fears of queer theorists who critique identity politics. Cognizant of that risk, quare studies must not deploy a totalizing and/or homogeneous formulation of identity, but rather a contingent, fragile coalition in the struggle against common oppressive forms.

A number of queer theorists have proposed potential strategies (albeit limited ones) that may be deployed in the service of dismantling oppressive systems. Most significantly, Judith Butler's formulation of performativity has had an important impact not only on gender and sexuality studies, but on queer studies as well. While I am swayed by Butler's formulation of gender performativity, I am disturbed by her theory's failure to articulate a meatier politics of resistance. For example, what are the implications of dismantling subjectivity and social will to ground zero within oppressive regimes? Does an overemphasis on the free play of signifiers propel us beyond a state of quietism to address the very real injustices in the world? The body, I believe, has to be theorized in ways that not only describe the ways in which it is brought into being but also what it *does* once it *is* constituted and the relationship between it and the other bodies around it. In other words, I desire a rejoinder to performativity that allows a space for subjectivity, for agency (however momentary and discursively fraught), and, ultimately, for change.

Therefore, to complement notions of performativity, quare studies also deploys theories of performance. Performance theory not only highlights the discursive effects of acts, it also points to how these acts are historically situated. Butler herself acknowledges that the conflation of "performativity to performance would be a mistake."[47] Indeed, the focus on performativity

....

alone may problematically reduce performativity and performance to one interpretative frame to theorize human experience. On the other hand, focusing on both may bring together two interpretative frames whose relationship is more dialogical and dialectical.

In her introduction to *Performance and Cultural Politics*, Elin Diamond proposes such a relationship between performance and performativity:

> When being is de-essentialized, when gender and even race are understood as fictional ontologies, modes of expression without true substance, the idea of performance comes to the fore. But performance both affirms and denies this evacuation of substance. In the sense that the "I" has no interior secure ego or core identity, "I" must always enunciate itself: there is only performance of a self, not an external representation of an interior truth. But in the sense that I do my performance in public, for spectators who are interpreting and/or performing with me, there are real effects, meanings solicited or imposed that produce relations in the real. Can performance make a difference? A performance, whether it inspires love or loathing, often consolidates cultural or subcultural affiliations, and these affiliations, might be as regressive as they are progressive. The point is, as soon as performativity comes to rest on *a* performance, questions of embodiment and political effects, all become discussible.
>
> Performance . . . is precisely the site in which concealed or dissimulated conventions might be investigated. When performativity materializes as performance in that risky and dangerous negotiation between doing (a reiteration of norms) and a thing done (discursive conventions that frame our interpretations), between somebody's body and the conventions of embodiment, we have access to cultural meanings and critique. Performativity . . . must be rooted in the materiality and historical density of performance.[48]

I quote Diamond at length here because of the implications that her construal of performance and performativity have for reinstating subjectivity and agency through the performance of identity. Although fleeting and ephemeral, these performances may activate a politics of subjectivity.

The performance of self is not only a performance or construction of identity for or toward an "out there," or even merely an attachment or "taking up"[49] of a predetermined, discursively contingent identity. It is also a performance of self for the self in a moment of self-reflexivity that has the potential to transform one's view of self in relation to the world. People have a need to exercise control over the production of their images so that they feel empowered. For the disenfranchised, the recognition, construction, and maintenance of self-image and cultural identity function to sustain, even when social systems and codes fail to do so. Granted, formations or performances of identity may simply reify oppressive systems, but they may also contest and subvert dominant meaning systems. When gays, lesbians, bisexuals, and transgendered people "talk back," whether using the "tools of the master"[50] or the vernacular on the street, their voices, singularly or collectively, do not exist in some vacuous wasteland of discursivity. As symbolic anthropologist Victor Turner suggests, their performances

> are not simple reflectors or expressions of culture or even of changing culture but may themselves be active *agencies* of change, representing the eye by which culture sees itself and the drawing board on which creative actors sketch out what they believe to be more apt or interesting "designs for living." . . . Performative reflexivity is a condition in which a sociocultural group, or its most perceptive members acting representatively, turn, bend, or reflect back upon themselves, upon the relations, actions, symbols, meanings, codes, roles, statuses, social structures, ethical and legal rules, and other sociocultural components which make up their public selves.[51]

Turner's theory of performative cultural reflexivity suggests a transgressive aspect of performative identity that neither dissolves identity into a fixed "I" nor presumes a monolithic "we." Rather, Turner's assertions suggest that social beings "look back" and "look forward" in a manner that wrestles with the ways in which that community of folk exists in the world and theorizes that existence. As Cindy Patton warns, not everyone who claims an identity does so in the ways that critics of essentialist identity claim they do.[52]

Theories of performance, as opposed to theories of performativity, also take into account the context and historical moment of performance.[53] We need to account for the temporal and spatial specificity of performance not only to frame its existence, but also to name the ways in which it signifies. Such an analysis would acknowledge the discursivity of subjects and it would also "unfix" the discursively constituted subject as always already a pawn of power. Although many queer theorists appropriate Foucault to substantiate the imperialism of power, Foucault himself acknowledges that discourse has the potential to disrupt power: "Discourses are not once and for all subser-

. . . .

vient to power or raised up against it, any more than silences are. We must make allowances for the complex and unstable process whereby discourse can be both an instrument and an effect of power, but also a hindrance, a stumbling-block, a point of resistance and a starting point for an opposing strategy. Discourse transmits and produces power; it reinforces it, *but also undermines and exposes it, renders it fragile and makes it possible to thwart it.*"[54] Although people of color, myself included, may not have theorized our lives in Foucault's terms, we have used discourse in subversive ways because it was necessary for our survival. Failure to ground discourse in materiality is to privilege the position of those whose subjectivity and agency, outside the realm of gender and sexuality, have never been subjugated. The tendency of many lesbians, bisexuals, gays, and transgendered people of color is to unite around a racial identity at a moment when their subjectivity is already under erasure.

Elaborating more extensively on the notion of performance as a site of agency for lesbian, gay, bisexual, and transgendered people of color, Latino performance theorist José Muñoz proposes a theory of "disidentification" whereby queers of color work within and against dominant ideology to effect change: "Disidentification is [a] mode of dealing with dominant ideology, one that neither opts to assimilate within such a structure nor strictly opposes it; rather, disidentification is a strategy that works on and against dominant ideology. Instead of buckling under the pressures of dominant ideology (identification, assimilation) or attempting to break free of its inescapable sphere (counteridentification, utopianism), this 'working on and against' is a strategy that tries to transform a cultural logic from within, always laboring to enact permanent structural change while at the same time valuing the importance of local and everyday struggles of resistance."[55] Muñoz's concept of "disidentification" reflects the process through which people of color have always managed to survive in a white supremacist society: by "working on and against" oppressive institutional structures.

The performance strategies of African Americans who labored and struggled under human bondage exemplify this disidentificatory practice. For instance, vernacular traditions that emerged among enslaved Africans—including folktales, spirituals, and the blues—provided the foundation for social and political empowerment. These discursively mediated forms, spoken and filtered through "black" bodies, enabled survival. The point here is that the inheritance of hegemonic discourses does not preclude one from "disidentifying," from putting those discourses in the service of resistance. Although they had no institutional power, enslaved blacks refused to become helpless victims and instead enacted their agency by cultivating discursive weapons based on an identity as oppressed people. The result was the creation of folktales about the "bottom rail becoming the top riser" (i.e., the slave rising out of slavery) or spirituals that called folks to "Gather at the River"(i.e., to plan an escape).

These resistant vernacular performances did not disappear with slavery. Gays, lesbians, bisexuals, and transgendered people of color continued to enact performative agency to work on and against oppressive systems. Quare singers like Bessie Smith and Ma Rainey, for instance, used the blues to challenge the notion of inferior black female subjectivity and covertly brought the image of the black lesbian into the American imaginary.[56] Later, through his flamboyant style and campy costumes, Little Richard not only fashioned himself as the "emancipator" and "originator" of rock-n-roll, he also offered a critique of hegemonic black and white masculinity in the music industry. Later still, the black transgendered singer Sylvester transformed disco with his high, soaring falsetto voice and gospel riffs. Indeed, Sylvester's music transcended the boundary drawn between the church and the world, between the sacred and profane, creating a space for other quare singers, like Blackberri, who would come after him. Even RuPaul's drag of many flavors demonstrates the resourcefulness of quares of color to reinvent themselves in ways that transform their material conditions. Quare vernacular tools operate outside the realm of musical and theatrical performance as well. Performance practices such as vogueing, snapping, "throwing shade," and "reading" attest to the ways in which black gays, lesbians, bisexuals, and transgendered people demonstrate the ways of devising technologies of self-assertion and summoning the agency to resist.[57]

Taken together, performance and quare theories alert us to the ways in which these disidentificatory performances serve material ends, and they do this work by accounting for the context in which these performances occur. The stage, for instance, is not confined solely to the theater, the dance club, or the concert hall. Streets, social services lines, picket lines, loan offices, and emergency rooms, among others, may also serve as useful staging grounds for disidentificatory performances. Theorizing the social context of performance sutures the gap between discourse and lived experience by examining how quares use performance as a strategy of survival in their day-to-day experiences. Such an analysis requires that we, like Robin Kelley, reconceptualize "play" (performance) as "work."[58] Moreover, quare theory focuses attention on the social consequences of those performances. It is one thing to do drag on the club stage, yet quite another to embody a drag queen identity on the street. Bodies are sites of discursive effects, but they are sites of social ones as well.

I do not wish to suggest that quare vernacular performances do not, at times, ideologically collude with sexist, misogynist, racist, and even homophobic constructions of the Other. Lesbian, bisexual, gay, and transgendered people of color must always realize that we cannot transgress for transgression's sake lest our work end up romanticizing and prolonging our state of struggle and that of others. In other words, while we may all occasionally enjoy the pleasures of "transgressive" performance, we must transgress responsibly or run the risk of creating and sustaining representations of ourselves that are anti-gay, anti-woman, anti-transgender, anti-working class, and anti-black. Despite this risk, we must not retreat to the position that changes within the system are impossible. The social movements of the past century are testament that change is possible.

Ultimately, quare studies offers a more utilitarian theory of identity politics, focusing not just on performers and effects, but also on contexts and historical situatedness. It does not, as bell hooks warns, separate the "politics of difference from the politics of racism."[59] Quare studies grants space for marginalized individuals to enact "radical black subjectivity,"[60] by adopting the both/and posture of "disidentification." Quare studies proposes a theory grounded in a critique of essentialism and an enactment of political praxis. Thus, such theorizing may *strategically* embrace identity politics while also acknowledging the contingency of identity, a double move that Angelia Wilson adroitly describes as "politically necessary and politically dangerous."[61]

SEEING THROUGH QUARE EYES: READING
MARLON RIGGS'S *BLACK IS . . . BLACK AIN'T*

In Marlon Riggs's documentary, *Black Is . . . Black Ain't*, we find an example of quare theory operationalized, and hence a demonstration of the possibilities of quare. Completed after Riggs's death in 1994, this documentary chronicles his battle with AIDS and also serves as a meditation on the embattled status of black identity. *Black Is . . . Black Ain't* "quares" "queer" by suggesting that identity, although highly contested, manifests itself in the flesh and, therefore, has social and political consequences for those who live in that flesh. Further "quaring" queer, the film also allows for agency and authority by visually privileging Riggs's AIDS experience narrative. Indeed, the film's documentation of Riggs's declining health suggests an identity and a body in the process of *being* and *becoming*. Quare theory elucidates the mechanics of this both/and identity formation, and, in so doing, it challenges a static reading of identity as only performativity or only performance.

In examining this issue I will first focus on how the film engages performativity, focusing as it does on problematizing notions of essential blackness. One of the ways in which the film engages this critique is by pointing out how, at the very least, gender, class, sexuality, and region all impact the construction of blackness. Indeed, even the title of the film points to the ways in which race defines, as well as confines, African Americans. The recurrent trope used by Riggs to illuminate the multiplicity of blackness is that of gumbo, a dish that consists of whatever ingredients the cook wishes to use. It has, Riggs remarks, "everything you can imagine in it."[62] This trope also underscores the multiplicity of blackness insofar as gumbo is a dish associated with New Orleans, a city confounded by its mixed-raced progeny and the identity politics that mixing creates. The gumbo trope is apropos because, like "blackness," gumbo is a site of possibilities. The film argues that when African Americans attempt to define what it means to be black, they delimit the possibilities of what blackness can be. But Riggs's film does more than just stir things up. In many ways it reduces the heat of the pot, allowing everything in the gumbo to mix and mesh, yet maintain its own distinct flavor. Chicken is distinct from andouille sausage, rice from peas, bay leaves from thyme, cayenne from paprika. Thus, Riggs's film suggests that African Americans cannot begin to ask dominant culture to accept either their difference as "others" or their humanity until African Americans accept the differences that exist among themselves.

Class represents a significant axis and divisiveness within black communities. As Martin Favor persuasively argues, "authentic" blackness is most often associated with the "folk," or working-class blacks.[63] Moreover, art forms such as the blues and folklore that are associated with the black working class are also viewed as more genuinely black. This association of the folk with black authenticity necessarily renders the black middle class as inauthentic and apolitical. In *Black Is . . . Black Ain't,* Riggs intervenes in this construction of the black middle class as "less black" by featuring a potpourri of blacks from various backgrounds. Importantly, those who might be considered a part of the "folk" questionably offer some of the most anti-black sentiments, while those black figures most celebrated in the film—Angela

. . . .

Davis, Barbara Smith, Michele Wallace, and Cornel West—are of the baby boomer generation. Riggs undermines the idea that "authentic" blackness belongs to the black working class by prominently displaying interviews with Davis, Wallace, and Smith. While ostracized for attending integrated schools and speaking Standard English or another language altogether, these women deny that their blackness was ever compromised. The film critiques hegemonic notions of blackness based on class status by locating the founding moment of black pride and radical black activism within black middle-class communities in the 1960s, thereby reminding us that "middle class" is also an ideological construct as contingently constituted as other social and subject positionalities.

Riggs also unhinges the link between hegemonic masculinity and authentic blackness. By excerpting misogynist speeches by Louis Farrakhan, a southern black preacher, and the leader of an "African" village located in South Carolina and then juxtaposing them with the personal narratives of bell hooks and Angela Davis, Riggs undermines the historical equation of "real" blackness with black masculinity. The narrative that hooks relates regarding her mother's spousal abuse is intercut with and undercuts Farrakhan's sexist and misogynist justification of Mike Tyson's sexual advances that eventually led to his being accused of and convicted for raping Desiree Washington. The narrative set forth by hooks's story also brackets the sexism inherent in the black preacher's and African leader's justification of the subjugation of women based on biblical and African mythology. Musically framing this montage of narratives is rap artist Queen Latifah's performance of "U-N-I-T-Y," a song that urges black women to "let black men know you ain't a bitch or a 'ho."[64] Riggs's decision to use Latifah's song to administer this critique is interesting on a number of levels, the most notable of which is that Latifah's own public persona, as well as her television and motion picture roles, embody a highly masculinized femininity or, alternatively, what Judith Halberstam might call "female masculinity."[65] Riggs uses Latifah's song and the invocation of her persona in the service of further disrupting hegemonic constructions of black masculinity, as well as illuminating the sexism found within the black community.

While I find the film's critique of essentialized blackness persuasive, I find even more compelling its critique of homophobia in the black community and its demand for a space for homosexual identity within constructions of blackness. As a rhetorical strategy, Riggs first points to those signifiers of blackness that build community (e.g., language, music, food, and religion).

Indeed, the opening of the film with the chantlike call and response of black folk preaching references a communal cultural site instantly recognizable to many African Americans. But just as the black church has been a political and social force in the struggle for the racial freedom of its constituents, it has also, to a large extent, occluded sexual freedom for many of its practitioners, namely gays and lesbians. Thus, in those opening scenes, Riggs calls attention to the double standard found within the black church by exemplifying how blackness can "build you up, or bring you down," hold you in high esteem or hold you in contempt. Riggs not only calls attention to the racism of whites; he also calls attention to homophobia in the black community, particularly in the black church. Throughout the film, however, Riggs challenges the traditional construction of the black church by featuring a black gay and lesbian church service. Given the black church's typical stance on homosexuality, some might view this avowal of Christianity as an instance of false consciousness. I argue, however, that these black gay and lesbians are employing disidentification insofar as they value the cultural rituals of the black worship service yet resist the fundamentalism of its message. In the end, the film intervenes in the construction of black homosexuality as anti-black by propagating gay Christianity as a legitimate signifier of blackness.

Riggs's film implicitly employs performativity to suggest that we dismantle hierarchies that privilege particular black positionalities at the expense of others, that we recognize that a darker hue does not give us any more cultural capital or claim to blackness than does a dashiki, braids, or a southern accent. Masculinity is no more a signifier of blackness than femininity; heterosexuality is no blacker than homosexuality; and living in the projects makes you no more authentically black than owning a house in the suburbs. Indeed, what Riggs suggests is that we move beyond these categories and these hierarchies that define and confine in order to realize that, depending on where you are from and where you are going, black is and black ain't.

While the film critically interrogates cleavages among blacks, it also exposes the social, political, economic, and psychological effects of racism, and the role racism has played in defining blackness. By adopting this dual focus rather than exclusively interrogating black discursivity, Riggs offers a perspective that is decidedly quare. He calls attention to differences among blacks and between blacks and their "others";[66] he grounds blackness in lived experience; and he calls attention to the consequences of embodied blackness. The montage of footage from the riots in Los Angeles and the interviews with young black men who characterize themselves as "gangbangers" bring into clear focus the material reality of black America and how the black body has historically been the site of violence and trauma.

Nowhere in the film is a black body historicized more pointedly and more powerfully, however, than in the scenes where Riggs is featured walking through the forest naked or narrating from his hospital bed from which his t-cell count is constantly announced. According to Riggs, these scenes are important because he wants to make the point that not until we expose ourselves to one another will we be able to communicate effectively across our differences. Riggs's intentions notwithstanding, his naked black body serves another function within the context of the film. It is simultaneously in a state of being *and* becoming. I intend here to disrupt both of these terms by refusing to privilege identity as either solely performance or solely performativity and by demonstrating the dialogic/dialectic relationship of these two tropes.

Paul Gilroy's theory of diaspora is useful in clarifying the difference between being and becoming. According to Gilroy, "Diaspora accentuates *becoming* rather than *being* and identity conceived diasporically, along these lines, resists reification."[67] Here, Gilroy associates "being" with the transhistorical and transcendental subject and "becoming" with historical situatedness and contingency. In what follows, I supplement Gilroy's use of both terms by suggesting that "being" and "becoming" are sites of performance *and* performativity. I construe "being" as a site of infinite signification as well as bodily and material presence. "Being" calls the viewer's attention not only to "blackness" as discourse, but also to embodied blackness in that moment where discourse and flesh conjoin in performance. If we look beyond Riggs's intent to "expose" himself to encourage cross-difference communication, we find that his nakedness in the woods functions ideologically in ways that he may not wish. For example, his nakedness may conjure up the racist stereotype of the lurking, bestial, and virile black male that became popular in the eighteenth- and nineteenth-century American imaginary. On the other hand, his embodied blackness in the woods and in his hospital bed also indicate a diseased body that is fragile, vulnerable, and a site of trauma, a site that grounds black discursivity materially in the flesh. At the literal level, Riggs's black male body is exposed as fragile and vulnerable, but it also synecdochically stands in for a larger body of racist discourse on the black male body in motion. This trope of black bodily kinesthetics is manifest in various forms (e.g., the vernacular expression, "keep the nigger running"; the image of the fugitive slave; and contemporary, hypermasculinized images of black athletes). Racist readings of Riggs's black male body are made possible by the context in which Riggs's body appears—that is, the woods. Within this setting, blackness becomes problematically aligned with nature, reinscribing the black body as bestial and primal. This imagery works against Riggs's intentions—namely, running naked in the woods as a way to work through the tangled and knotty web that is identity. Indeed, the images of Riggs running naked through the woods signify in multiple troubling ways that, once let loose, cannot be contained by either Riggs's authorial intentions or the viewer's gaze. The beauty of *being*, however, is that where it crumbles under the weight of deconstruction, it reemerges in all its bodily facticity. Although Riggs's body signifies in ways that constrain his agency, his embodied blackness also enlivens a discussion of a "fleshy" nature. Whatever his body signifies, the viewer cannot escape its material presence.

Riggs's body is also a site of becoming: he dies before the film is completed. Riggs's body physically "fades away," but its phantom is reconstituted in our current discourse on AIDS, race, gender, class, and sexuality. Thus, Riggs's body discursively rematerializes and intervenes in hegemonic formulations of blackness, homosexuality, and the HIV-infected person. As a filmic performance, *Black Is . . . Black Ain't* resurrects Riggs's body such that when the film is screened at universities, shown to health care providers, viewed in black communities, or rebroadcast on PBS where it debuted, the terms and the stakes for how we think about identity and its relation to HIV/AIDS are altered. Like Toni Morrison's character Sula, Riggs dreams of water carrying him over that liminal threshold where the water "would envelop [him], carry [him], and wash [his] tired flesh always."[68] After her death, Sula promises to tell her best friend Nel that death did not hurt, ironically announcing her physical death alongside her spiritual rebirthing. Her rebirthing is symbolized by her assuming a fetal position and traveling "over and down the tunnels, just missing the dark walls, down, down until she met a rain scent and would know the water was near."[69] Riggs dreams of a similar journey through water. In his dream, Harriet Tubman serves as a midwife cradling his head at the tunnel's opening and helps him make the journey. Once on the other side, Riggs, like Sula, lives on and also makes good on his promise to return through his living spirit captured in the film. The residual traces of Riggs's body become embedded in the ideological battle over identity claims and the discourse surrounding the disproportionate number of AIDS-infected people of color. His becoming, then, belies our being.

Ultimately, *Black Is . . . Black Ain't* performs what its title announces: the simultaneity of bodily presence and absence, being and becoming. Although Riggs offers his own gumbo recipe that stands in for blackness, he does so only to demonstrate that, like blackness, the recipe can be altered, expanded, reduced, watered down. At the same time, Riggs also asks that we not forget that the gumbo (blackness) is contained within a sturdy pot (the body) that has weathered abuse; that has been scorched, scoured, and scraped; a pot/body that is in the process of becoming, but nonetheless *is*.

Unlike queer theory, quare theory fixes our attention on the discursive constitution of the recipe even as it celebrates the improvisational aspects of the gumbo and the materiality of the pot. While queer theory has opened up new possibilities for theorizing gender and sexuality, like a pot of gumbo cooked too quickly it has failed to live up to its critical potential by refusing *all* the queer ingredients contained inside its theoretical pot. Quare theory, on the other hand, promises to reduce the spillage, allowing the various and multiple flavors to coexist—those different flavors that make it spicy, hot, unique, and sumptuously brown.

BRINGIN' IT ON "HOME": QUARE STUDIES ON THE BACK PORCH

Thus far, I have canvassed the trajectory for quare studies inside the academy, focusing necessarily on the intellectual work that needs to be done to advance specific disciplinary goals. While there is intellectual work to be done inside the academy—what one might call "academic praxis"—there is also political praxis outside the academy.[70] If social change is to occur, gays, bisexuals, transgendered people, and lesbians of color cannot afford to be armchair theorists. Some us need to be in the streets, in the trenches, enacting the quare theories that we construct in the "safety" of the academy. While keeping in mind that political theory and political action are not necessarily mutually exclusive, quare theorists must make theory work for its constituency. Although we share with our white queer peers sexual oppression, gays, lesbians, bisexuals, and transgendered people of color also share racial oppression with other members of our community. We cannot afford to abandon them simply because they are heterosexual. "Although engaged in heterosexual behavior," Cathy Cohen writes, straight African Americans "have often found themselves outside the norms and values of dominant society. This position has most often resulted in the suppression or negation of their legal, social, and physical relationships and rights."[71] Quare studies must encourage strategic coalition building around laws and policies that have the potential to affect us all across racial, sexual, and class divides. Quare studies must incorporate under its rubric a praxis related to the sites of public policy, family, church, and community. Therefore, in the tradition of radical black feminist critic Barbara Smith,[72] I offer a manifesto that aligns black quare academic theory with political praxis.

We can do more in the realm of public policy. As Cathy Cohen so cogently argues in her groundbreaking book *The Boundaries of Blackness,* we must intervene in the failure of the conservative black leadership to respond to the HIV/AIDS epidemic ravishing African American communities.[73] Due to the growing number of African Americans infected with and contracting HIV, quare theorists must aid in the education and prevention of the spread of HIV as well as care for those who are suffering. This means more than engaging in volunteer work and participating in fund-raising. It also means using our training as academics to deconstruct the way HIV/AIDS is discussed in the academy and in the medical profession. We must continue to do the important work of physically helping our brothers and sisters who are living with HIV and AIDS through outreach services and fund-raising events, but we must also use our scholarly talents to combat the racist and homophobic discourse that circulates in white as well as black communities. Ron Simmons, a black gay photographer and media critic who left academia to commit his life to those suffering with AIDS by forming the organization US Helping US, remains an important role model for how we can use both our academic credentials and our political praxis in the service of social change.

The goal of quare studies is to be specific and intentional in the dissemination and praxis of quare theory, committed to communicating and translating its political potentiality. Indeed, quare theory is "bi"-directional: it theorizes from bottom to top and top to bottom. This dialogical/dialectical relationship between theory and practice, the lettered and unlettered, ivory tower and front porch, is crucial to a joint and sustained critique of hegemonic systems of oppression.

Given the relationship between the academy and the community, quare theorists must value and speak from what bell hooks refers to as "homeplace." According to hooks, homeplace "[is] the one site where one [can] freely confront the issue of humanization, where one [can] resist."[74] It is from homeplace that we people of color live out the contradictions of our lives. Cutting across the lines of class and gender, homeplace provides a place from which to critique oppression. I do not wish to romanticize this site by dismissing the homophobia that circulates within homeplace or the contempt that some of us (of all sexual orientations) have for "home."[75] I am suggesting, rather, that in spite of these contradictions, homeplace is that site that first gave us the "equipment for living"[76] in a racist society, particularly since we, in all of our diversity, have always been a part of this homeplace: housekeepers, lawyers, seamstresses, hairdressers, activists, choir directors, professors, doctors, preachers, mill workers, mayors, nurses, truck drivers, delivery people, nosey neighbors, and (an embarrassed?) "etc." SNAP!

Homeplace is also a site that quare praxis must critique. That is, we may seek refuge in homeplace as a marginally safe place to critique oppression outside its confines, but we must also deploy quare theory to address oppression within homeplace itself. One might begin, for instance, with the black church, which remains for some gays and lesbians a sustaining site of spiritual affirmation, comfort, and an artistic outlet. Quare studies cannot afford to dismiss, cavalierly, the role of the black church in quare lives. However, it must never fail to critique the black church's continual denial of gay and lesbian subjectivity. Our role within the black church is an important one. Those in the pulpit and those in the congregation should be challenged whenever they hide behind Romans and Leviticus to justify their homophobia. We must force the black church to name us and claim us if we are to obtain any liberation within our own communities.[77]

Regarding ideological and political conflicts in gay, lesbian, and transgendered communities of color, quare praxis must interrogate and negotiate the difference among our differences, including our political strategies for dealing with oppression and our politics of life choice and maintenance. Consequently, quare studies must also focus on interracial dating and the identity politics that such couplings invoke. Writer Darieck Scott has courageously addressed this issue, but we need to continue to explore our own inner conflicts around our and our peers' choice of sexual partners across racial lines.[78] Additionally, quare studies should interrogate another contested area of identity politics: relations between "out" and "closeted" members of our community. Much of this work must be done not in the academy but in our communities, in our churches, and in our homes.

Because I am not convinced that queer studies, theory, and activism are soon to change, I summon quare studies as an interventionist disciplinary project. Quare studies addresses the concerns and needs of gay, lesbian, bisexual, and transgendered people across issues of race, gender, and class as well as other identities and subject positions. While attending to discursive fields of knowledge, quare studies is also committed to theorizing the practice of everyday life. Because we exist in discursive as well as material bodies, we need a theory that speaks to that reality. Indeed, quare studies may breathe new life into our "dead" (or deadly) stratagems of survival.

CODA

Because I credit my grandmother for passing on to me the little bit of commonsense I still have, I conclude this essay with a story about her employment of "gaydar,"[79] a story that speaks to how black folk use "motherwit" as a "reading" strategy, as well as a way to "forget all those things they don't want to remember, and remember everything they don't want to forget."[80]

My grandmother lives in western North Carolina. When I went to live with her to collect her oral history for my dissertation, she spent a considerable amount of time catching me up on all of the new residents who had moved into her senior citizens' community. Dressed in her customary polyester cutoff shorts and cotton makeshift blouse, loosely tied sheer scarf draped around her dyed, jet black hair, legs crossed and head cocked to the side, my grandmother described to me, one by one, each of the new residents. She detailed, among other things, their medical histories and conditions, the number of children they had, their marital status, and perhaps most important, whether they were "pickles" or not. She used the term euphemistically to describe people who she believes are "not quite right in the head."

There was one resident, David, in whom my grandmother had a particular interest. I soon learned that David was a seventy-four-year-old white man who had to walk with the support of a walker and who had moved to my grandmother's community from across town. But these facts were not the most important things about David, but rather another fact that my grandmother revealed to me one day: "Well, you know we got one of them 'homalsexuals' living down here," she said, dryly. Not quite sure I had heard her correctly but also afraid that I had, I responded, "A what?" She replied, again just as dryly, "you know, one of them 'homalsexuals.'" This time, however, her voice was tinged with impatience and annoyance. Curious, yet a bit anxious about the turn the conversation was taking (I was not "out" to my grandmother), I pursued the issue further: "Well, how do you know the man's a homosexual, Grandmama?" She paused, rubbed her leg, narrowed her eyes, and responded, "Well, he gardens, bakes pies, and keeps a clean house." (She might not have gone to school, but she could most definitely *read*!) Like a moth to the flame, I opened the door to my own closet for her to walk in, and said, "Well, I cook and keep my apartment clean." Then, after a brief pause, I added, "But I don't like gardening. I don't like getting my hands dirty." As soon as the words "came out" of my mouth, I realized what I had done. My grandmother said nothing. She simply folded her arms and began to rock as if in church. The question she dare not ask sat behind her averted eyes: "You ain't quare are you, Pat?" Yes, Grandmama, quare, indeed.

NOTES

1. In the opening pages of *In Search of Our Mothers' Gardens*, Alice Walker coins and defines the term "womanist" in contrast to "feminist," to mark the specificity of womens of color's experiences of sexism and racism. I perform a similar critique in the move from "queer" to "quare" in order to include race and class analyses in queer theory. See Alice Walker, *In Search of Our Mothers' Gardens: Womanist Prose* (San Diego: Harcourt Brace Jovanovich, 1983), xi-xii.

2. See James Baldwin, *Nobody Knows My Name: More Notes of a Native Son* (New York: Vintage, 1993) and *No Name in the Street* (New York: Dial, 1972).

3. My grandmother made her transition on July 12, 2004, before the reprinting of this essay in this volume. I dedicate this contribution in her memory.

4. Mae G. Henderson, "Speaking in Tongues," in *Feminists Theorize the Political*, ed. Judith Butler and Joan W. Scott (New York: Routledge, 1992), 147.

5. I have long known about the connection between African Americans and the Irish. As noted in the film *The Commitments*, "The Irish are the blacks of Europe." The connection is there—that is, at least until the Irish became "white." For a sustained discussion of how Irish emigrants obtained "white" racial privilege, see Noel Ignatiev, *How the Irish Became White* (New York: Routledge, 1995).

6. Joseph Valente, "Joyce's (Sexual) Choices: A Historical Overview," in *Quare Joyce*, ed. Joseph Valente (Ann Arbor: University of Michigan Press, 1998), 4; emphasis added.

7. Gloria Anzaldúa, "To(o) Queer the Writer: *Loca, escrita y chicana,*" in *Inversions: Writing by Dykes and Lesbians,* ed. Betsy Warland (Vancouver: Press Gang, 1991), 250.

8. For more on "standpoint" theory, see Patricia Hill Collins, "The Social Construction of Black Feminist Thought," in *Words of Fire: An Anthology of African-American Feminist Thought,* ed. Beverly Guy-Sheftall (New York: New Press, 1995), 338–57.

9. Cherríe Moraga and Gloria Anzaldúa, eds., *This Bridge Called My Back: Writings by Radical Women of Color* (New York: Kitchen Table; Women of Color Press, 1983), 23.

10. Judith Butler, in *Bodies That Matter: On the Discursive Limits of "Sex"* (New

York: Routledge, 1993), anticipates the contestability of "queer," noting that it excludes as much as it includes but that such a contested term may energize a new kind of political activism. She proposes that "it may be that the critique of the term [queer] will initiate a resurgence of both feminist and anti-racist mobilization within lesbian and gay politics or open up new possibilities for coalitional alliances that do not presume that these constituencies are radically distinct from one another. The term will be revised, dispelled, rendered obsolete to the extent that it yields to the demands which resist the term precisely because of the exclusions by which it is mobilized" (228–29). Moreover, there are gay, bisexual, lesbian, and transgendered people of color who embrace "queer." In my experience, however, those who embrace the term represent a small minority. At the Black Queer Studies in the Millennium conference, for example, many of the attendees were disturbed by the organizers' choice of "queer" for the title of a conference on black sexuality. So ardent was their disapproval that it became a subject of debate during one of the panels.

11. Cherry Smith, "What Is This Thing Called Queer?" in *Material Queer: A LesBiGay Cultural Studies* Reader, ed. Donald Morton (Boulder: Westview, 1996), 280.

12. Eve Kosofsky Sedgwick, "Queer and Now," in *Tendencies* (Durham: Duke University Press, 1993), 9.

13. Ibid., 8.

14. Michael Warner, "Introduction," *Fear of a Queer Planet: Queer Politics and Social Theory,* ed. Michael Warner (Minneapolis: University of Minnesota Press, 1993), xxvi.

15. Lauren Berlant and Michael Warner, "What Does Queer Theory Teach Us about X?" *PMLA* 110 (May 1995): 344.

16. Calvin Thomas, "Straight with a Twist: Queer Theory and the Subject of Heterosexuality," in *The Gay '90s: Disciplinary and Interdisciplinary Formations in Queer Studies,* ed. Thomas Foster, Carol Siegel, and Ellen E. Berry (New York: New York University Press, 1997), 83.

17. Judith Butler, *Gender Trouble: Feminism and the Subversion of Identity* (New York: Routledge, 1990), 143.

18. See, for example, Stuart Hall, "Subjects in History: Making Diasporic Identities," in *The House That Race Built,* ed. Wahneema Lubiano (New York: Pantheon, 1997), 289–99; and Paul Gilroy, " 'Race,' Class, and Agency," in *There Ain't No Black in the Union Jack: The Cultural Politics of Race and Nation* (London: Hutchinson, 1987), 15–42.

19. Barbara Christian, "The Race for Theory," *Cultural Critique* 6 (1985): 51–63.

20. Helen (charles), " 'Queer Nigger': Theorizing 'White' Activism," in *Activating Theory: Lesbian, Gay, Bisexual Politics,* ed. Joseph Bristow and Angelia R. Wilson (London: Lawrence and Wishart, 1993), 101–2.

21. I thank Michèle Barale for this insight.

22. While it is true that many white queer theorists are self-reflexive about their

own privilege and indeed incorporate the works and experiences of gays, bisexuals, lesbians, and transgendered people of color into their work, this is not the norm. Paula Moya calls attention to how the theorizing of women of color is appropriated by postmodernist theorists: "[Judith] Butler extracts one sentence from [Cherríe] Moraga, buries it in a footnote, and then misreads it in order to justify her own inability to account for the complex interrelations that structure various forms of human identity." David Bergman also offers a problematic reading of black gay fiction when he reads James Baldwin through the homophobic rhetoric of Eldridge Cleaver and theorizes that black communities are more homophobic than whites ones. See Paula Moya, "Postmodernism, 'Realism,' and the Politics of Identity: Cherríe Moraga and Chicano Feminism," in *Feminist Genealogies, Colonial Legacies, Democratic Futures*, ed. M. Jacqui Alexander and Chandra Talpade Mohanty (New York: Routledge, 1997), 133; and David Bergman, *Gaiety Transfigured: Gay Self-Representation in American Literature* (Madison: University of Wisconsin Press, 1991), 163–87. For other critiques of simplistic or dismissive readings of the works of gays, bisexuals, lesbians, and transgendered people of color, see Helen (charles), "'Queer Nigger'"; Ki Namaste, "'Tragic Misreadings': Queer Theory's Erasure of Transgender Identity," in *Queer Studies: A Lesbian, Gay, Bisexual and Transgender Anthology*, ed. Brett Beemyn and Mickey Eliason (New York: New York University Press, 1996), 183–203; and Vivien Ng, "Race Matters," in *Lesbian and Gay Studies: A Critical Introduction*, ed. Andy Medhurst and Sally R. Munt (London: Cassell, 1997), 215–31. One notable exception is Ruth Goldman's "Who is That *Queer* Queer," in which she, as a white bisexual, calls to task other white queer theorists for their failure to theorize their whiteness: "Those of us who are white tend not to dwell on our race, perhaps because this would only serve to normalize us—reduce our queerness, if you will" (Goldman, "Who Is That *Queer* Queer?" in *Queer Studies: A Lesbian, Gay, Bisexual and Transgender Anthology*, ed. Brett Beemyn and Mickey Eliason [New York: New York University Press, 1996], 169–82).

23. For more on "strategic" essentialism, see Sue-Ellen Case, *The Domain Matrix: Performing Lesbian at the End of Print Culture* (Bloomington: Indiana University Press, 1996), 1–12; Teresa de Lauretis, "The Essence of the Triangle, or Taking the Risk of Essentialism Seriously: Feminist Theory in Italy, the U.S. and Britain," *differences* 1.2 (1989): 3–37; and Fuss, *Essentially Speaking*, 1–21.

24. Cathy Cohen, "Punks, Bulldaggers, and Welfare Queens: The Radical Potential of Queer Politics?" in this volume, 34.

25. For a sustained discussion of queer activists' disavowal of heterosexual political alliances, see Cohen, "Punks, Bulldaggers, and Welfare Queens," 28–37.

26. Audre Lorde, *Sister Outsider* (Freedom, Calif.: Crossing, 1984), 112–13; emphasis in original.

27. Champagne draws from Joan Scott's important essay, "The Evidence of Experience" (in *Feminists Theorize the Political*, ed. Judith Butler and Joan W. Scott [New

York: Routledge, 1992], 22–40), where Scott argues that "experience" is discursively constituted, mediated by and through linguistic systems and embedded in ideology. Like all discursive terrains, the ground on which "experience" moves is turbulent and supple, quickly disrupting the foothold we think we might have on history and the "evidentiary." Scott writes: "Experience is at once always already an interpretation *and* is in need of interpretation. What counts as experience is neither self-evident nor straightforward; it is always contested, always therefore political. The study of experience, therefore, must call into question its originary status in historical explanation. This will happen when historians take as their project *not* the reproduction and transmission of knowledge said to be arrived at through experience, but the analysis of the production of that knowledge itself" (37; emphasis in original). Scott is particularly concerned here with historiographies that draw on experience as evidentiary, especially in the name of historicizing difference. "By remaining within the epistemological frame of orthodox history," Scott argues, "these studies lose the possibility of examining those assumptions and practices that excluded considerations of difference in the first place" (24–25).

28. Robert Mapplethorpe's photographs of black gay men have been and continue to be the source of great controversy in the black gay community. The reactions to the photos range from outrage to ambivalence to appreciation. I believe the most complex reading of Mapplethorpe is found in Isaac Julien and Kobena Mercer's essay "True Confessions: A Discourse on Images of Black Male Sexuality" (in *Brother to Brother: New Writings on Black Gay Men*, ed. Essex Hemphill [Boston: Alyson, 1991]). They write: "While we recognize the oppressive dimension of these images of black men as Other, we are also attracted: We want to look but don't always find the images we want to see. This ambivalent mixture of attraction and repulsion goes for images of black gay men in porn generally, but the inscribed or preferred meanings of these images are not fixed; they can at times, be pried apart into alternative readings when different experiences are brought to bear on their interpretation" (170).

29. John Champagne, *The Ethics of Marginality: A New Approach to Gay Studies* (Minneapolis: University of Minnesota Press, 1995), 59.

30. Ibid., 58.

31. Ibid., 58–59.

32. I thank D. Soyini Madison for raising this issue.

33. I am speaking specifically about the historical devaluing of black bodies. In no way do I mean to deny that white gay, lesbian, bisexual, and transgendered people have been emotionally, psychologically, and physically harmed. The recent murder of Matthew Shepard is a sad testament to this fact. Indeed, given the ways in which his attackers killed him (i.e., tying him to a post, beating him and leaving him for dead), there is a way in which we may read Shepard's murder through a racial lens. What I am suggesting, however, is that racial violence (or the threat of it) is enacted on "black" bodies in different ways and for different reasons than it is on "white" bodies.

34. bell hooks, *Yearning* (Boston: South End, 1990), 21, 22.

35. Champagne, *The Ethics of Marginality,* 127–28.

36. hooks, *Yearning,* 22.

37. Ibid.

38. "Emotionality" as manipulative or putatively repugnant may also be read through the lens of gender. Generally understood as a weak (read feminine) gender performance, emotional display among men of any race or sexual orientation represents a threat to heteronormativity and therefore is usually met with disapproval.

39. Champagne, *The Ethics of Marginality*, 68–69.

40. Valerie Smith, *Not Just Race, Not Just Gender: Making Feminist Readings* (New York: Routledge, 1998), 67.

41. I do not wish to suggest that the appearance of poverty or wealth never reflects that one is actually poor or wealthy. What I am suggesting, however, is that in many African American communities, style figures more substantively than some might imagine. Accordingly, there exists a politics of taste among African Americans that is performed so as to dislodge fixed perceptions about who one is or where one is from. In many instances, for example, performing a certain middle-class style has enabled African Americans to "pass" in various and strategically savvy ways. For more on the performance of style in African American communities, see Barbara Smith, "Home," in *Home Girls: A Black Feminist Anthology,* (New York: Kitchen Table; Women of Color Press, 1983), 64–72; and Joseph Beam, "Introduction: Leaving the Shadows Behind," in *In the Life.* ed. Joseph Beam (Boston: Alyson, 1986), 13–18. For a theoretical perspective on the politics of taste, see Pierre Bourdieu, *Distinction: A Social Critique of the Judgment of Taste,* trans. Richard Nice (Cambridge: Harvard University Press, 1984).

42. Champagne writes: "Like the white antiporn feminists whose rhetoric they sometimes share, intellectuals like Riggs and Hemphill may in fact be expressing in *Tongues Untied* a (middle-) class-inflected sense of disgust related to sexuality—obviously, not related to all sexuality, but to a particularly culturally problematic kind. It is perhaps thus not a coincidence at all that the rhetoric deployed by Hemphill in his reading of Mapplethorpe should be so similar to that of Dworkin, Stoltenberg, and even Jesse Helms" (*The Ethics of Marginality*, 79).

43. Ibid., 69.

44. Goldman, "Who Is That *Queer* Queer?" 173.

45. For examples of white critics who interrogate "whiteness" as an obligatory and universalizing trope, see Ruth Frankenberg, ed., *Displacing Whiteness: Essays in Social and Cultural Criticism* (Durham: Duke University Press, 1997); Mike Hill, ed., *Whiteness: A Critical Reader* (New York: New York University Press, 1997); and David Roediger, *Towards the Abolition of Whiteness* (London: Verso, 1994).

46. Shane Phelan, *Getting Specific* (Minneapolis: University of Minnesota Press, 1994), 156.

47. Judith Butler, *Bodies That Matter*, 234.

48. Elin Diamond, ed., "Introduction," in *Performance and Cultural Politics* (New York: Routledge, 1996), 5; emphasis in original.

49. Butler, *Gender Trouble*, 145.

50. Lorde, *Sister Outsider*, 110.

51. Victor Turner, *The Anthropology of Performance*, (New York: Performing Arts Journal, 1986), 24; emphasis added.

52. Cindy Patton, "Performativity and Social Distinction: The End of AIDS Epidemiology." *Performativity and Performance*, ed. Andrew Parker and Eve Kosofsky Sedgwick (New York: Routledge, 1995), 181.

53. Mary Strine, "Articulating Performance/Performativity: Disciplinary Tasks and the Contingencies of Practice," paper presented at the National Speech Communication Association conference, San Diego, November 1996, 7.

54. Michel Foucault, *The History of Sexuality, Volume 1*, trans. Robert Hurley (New York: Random House, 1990), 100–1; emphasis added.

55. José Esteban Muñoz, *Disidentifications: Queers of Color and the Performance of Politics* (Minneapolis: University of Minnesota Press, 1999), 11–12.

56. For an analysis of Bessie Smith's explicitly lesbian blues songs, see Daphne Duval Harrison, *Black Pearls: Blues Queens of the 1920s* (New Brunswick: Rutgers University Press, 1998), 103–4.

57. See Marlon Riggs, "Black Macho Revisited: Reflections of a SNAP! Queen," in *Brother to Brother: New Writings by Black Gay Men*, ed. Essex Hemphill (Boston: Alyson, 1991), 253–57; E. Patrick Johnson, "SNAP! Culture: A Different Kind of 'Reading,'" *Text and Performance Quarterly* 15.3 (1995): 121–42; and E. Patrick Johnson, "Feeling the Spirit in the Dark: Expanding Notions of the Sacred in the African American Gay Community," 21 *Callaloo* (1998): 399–418.

58. Robin D. G. Kelley, "Looking to Get Paid: How Some Black Youth Put Culture to Work," in *Yo Mama's Disfunktional!: Fighting the Culture Wars in Urban America* (Boston: Beacon, 1997), 43–77.

59. hooks, *Yearning*, 26.

60. Ibid.

61. Angelia R. Wilson, "Somewhere over the Rainbow: Queer Translating," in *Playing with Fire: Queer Politics, Queer Theories*, ed. Shane Phelan (New York: Routledge, 1997), 107.

62. *Black Is . . . Black Ain't*, dir. Marlon Riggs (Independent Film Series, 1995).

63. See Martin Favor, *Authentic Blackness: The Folk in the New Negro Renaissance* (Durham: Duke University Press, 1999).

64. Queen Latifah, "U.N.I.T.Y." from *Black Reign* (Motown, 1993).

65. Judith Halberstam, *Female Masculinity* (Durham: Duke University Press, 1998), 1–42.

66. Paul Gilroy's construction of the "Diaspora" functions similarly to what I mean

here in that he propagates that "Diaspora" "allows for a complex conception of sameness and an idea of solidarity that does not repress the differences within in order to maximize the differences between one 'essential' community and others." See Paul Gilroy, " '. . . to be real': The Dissident Forms of Black Expressive Culture," in *Let's Get It On: The Politics of Black Performance,* ed. Catherine Ugwu (Seattle: Bay Press, 1995), 24.

67. Ibid.

68. Toni Morrison, *Sula* (New York: Knopf, 1973), 149.

69. Ibid.

70. I do not wish to suggest that the academy is not always already a politicized site. Rather, I only mean to suggest that the ways in which it is politicized are, in many instances, different from the ways in which "nonacademic" communities are politicized.

71. Cohen, "Punks, Bulldaggers, and Welfare Queens," in this volume, 39.

72. See Barbara Smith, "Toward a Black Feminist Criticism," in *All the Women Are White, All the Blacks Are Men, But Some of Us Are Brave,* ed. Gloria T. Hull, Patricia Bell Scott, and Barbara Smith (Old Westbury, N.Y.: Feminist Press, 1982), 157–75.

73. Cathy Cohen, *The Boundaries of Blackness: AIDS and the Breakdown of Black Politics* (Chicago: University of Chicago Press, 1999).

74. hooks, *Yearning,* 42.

75. For a critique of the notion of "home" in the African American community vis-à-vis homophobia and sexism, see Joseph Beam, "Brother to Brother: Words from the Heart," in *In the Life: A Black Gay Anthology,* ed. Joseph Beam (Boston: Alyson, 1986); Cheryl Clarke, "The Failure to Transform: Homophobia in the Black Community" in *Home Girls: A Black Feminist Anthology,* ed. Barbara Smith (New York: Kitchen Table Women of Color Press, 1983), 197–208; Kimberlé Williams Crenshaw, "Mapping the Margins: Intersectionality, Identity Politics, and Violence against Women of Color," *Stanford Law Review* 43 (1991): 1241–99; bell hooks, *Yearning* (Boston: South End, 1990); and Ron Simmons, "Some Thoughts on the Issues Facing Black Gay Intellectuals" in *Brother to Brother: New Writings by Black Gay Men,* ed. Essex Hemphill (Boston: Alyson, 1991), 211–28.

76. Kenneth Burke, *Philosophy of Literary Form* (Baton Rouge: Louisiana State University Press, 1967), 293.

77. For a sustained critique of homophobia in the black church, see Michael Eric Dyson, "The Black Church and Sex," in *Race Rules: Navigating the Color Line* (Reading, Mass.: Addison-Wesley, 1996), 77–108.

78. See Darieck Scott, "Jungle Fever? Black Gay Identity Politics, White Dick, and the Utopian Bedroom," *GLQ* 3 (1994): 299–32.

79. "Gaydar," a pun on "radar," is a term some gays and lesbians use to signal their ability to determine whether or not someone is gay.

80. Zora Neale Hurston, *Their Eyes Were Watching God* (New York: Harper and Row, 1990), 1.

PART II

REPRESENTING THE "RACE":
BLACKNESS, QUEERS, AND THE POLITICS
OF VISIBILITY

....

MARLON B. ROSS

....

BEYOND THE CLOSET

AS RACELESS PARADIGM

> If les/bi/gay people have some reason to take a long view of
> their situation, we know also that, in our current modes, we
> are a recent and ongoing creation. For we did not *come out,* in
> the wake of the Stonewall Riot of 1969, in the sense of emerg-
> ing, already formed, as if from behind a curtain. Rather, we
> have been making our history and hence our selves—though
> not, of course, in conditions of our own choosing.
> —Alan Sinfield, *Gay and After*

"Out of the closet and into the streets" is more than just a slogan of protest
politics. The phrase indicates to what extent the political strategy and agenda
of gay/lesbian rights have been deeply structured ideologically through the
closet paradigm. Similarly, in what academics call "queer theory" the closet
has become ground zero in the project of articulating an "epistemology" of
sexuality. Beyond political strategy and polemical tactics, the closet has become a philosophical concept grounding both lesbian-gay history and queer
theory by joining them at the hips as a legitimate academic discipline. Significantly, historians and theorists of queerness stake their claim to academic
centrality largely through the concept of the closet, as they argue with great
rigor and sophistication that the binary between closeted and uncloseted
sexual desire is a primary determinant of modernity and modernism. Occasionally, queer theorists like Neil Bartlett and Douglas Crimp have commented on the limitations of the closet concept for narrating queer history
and for mounting a viable queer politics, yet even they, in the end, leave the
concept itself intact as the sole basis for queer subjectivity and agency.[1] More
recently, Maurice Wallace has helped to vex the theory tying the closet to

modern same-sexuality by showing how African American writers, even as early as the antebellum period, used the closet to code the unspeakable secrets that shelter and expose the sexed racial subjectivity of black men. Finding the closet function littering black male discourse across the nineteeth century, Wallace concludes that "the singularly gay character of the closet no longer holds."[2]

I would like to vex the closet paradigm in the converse direction from Wallace by asking whether there is an *ideology* of the closet as master paradigm for intragender attraction and identification. More specifically, I want to explore how *racial* ideology functions in our appeals to the closet as the definitive articulation of modern sexuality and progressive homosexuality. Ultimately what I want to suggest here is that (white)queer theory and history are beset by what I call "claustrophilia," a fixation on the closet function as the grounding principle for sexual experience, knowledge, and politics, and that this claustrophilic fixation effectively diminishes and disables the full engagement with potential insights from race theory and class analysis.[3]

In his now classic history *Coming Out,* Jeffrey Weeks exemplifies the more typically authoritative and axiomatic reliance on the closet as the essential vehicle for narrating homosexuality as a necessary progress from dark secrecy to open consciousness. Speaking of the response to Oscar Wilde's trial, Weeks writes, "It was an *essential* step in the evolution of a modern homosexual consciousness."[4] In reading such a sentence, we take for granted the naturalness of words like "evolution" and "modern" as naming a historical development that measures the general progress of homosexual-identified people from a state of oppression to a state of openness, autonomy, and freedom. At the same time, these words are intended to call forth specific modes of intragender sexuality identified with North America and Western Europe, and, in fact, identified especially with the urban upper and middle classes (predominately whites) in the West.[5] Referring to evidence for "homosexual groupings" such as Molly houses in eighteenth-century England, Weeks makes explicit the equation between European premodernity as a past beyond which modern homosexuals have progressed and contemporary non-Western practices of intragender sexuality: "This embryonic sub-culture [in eighteenth-century England] was closely associated with transvestism and stereotyped effeminate behaviour, in a mode which *still* characterizes the *relatively undeveloped* sub-cultures of areas outside the major cities of western Europe and North America."[6] British Molly houses are seen as "embryonic" sites because they are the seed beds destined to spawn in Europe the first grown-up consciousness of a liberated homosexuality.

The word "undeveloped" is conventionally used to measure the extent to which a non-Western economy has progressed toward industrial capitalism. The slippage in Weeks's usage of the word here is common, whereby non-Western *culture* itself becomes "undeveloped"—in effect, historically stunted—in relation to the culture of the West. An undeveloped economy easily slides into an undeveloped culture, and, as we see in Weeks's logic, an undeveloped culture betokens analogously an undeveloped (homo)sexual subculture. One might ask, what does it mean for a sexual subculture to be "relatively undeveloped"? Relative to what? Failing to develop toward what? Such implicit judgments have political ramifications and ideological consequences for the attempt to understand intragender sexuality cross-culturally, as well as for the attempt to theorize and historicize the particular experience of homosexuality within the West. This sort of evolutionary logic is not peculiar to Weeks but instead has been intrinsic to the project of queer history and theory as it has been formulated in both academic and popular European-American thought across the political spectrum. The "coming out" or closet paradigm has been such a compelling way of fixing homosexual identification exactly because it enables this powerful narrative of progress, not only in terms of the psychosexual development of an individual and the sociopolitical birth and growth of a legitimate sexual minority group, but also more fundamentally as a doorway marking the threshold between up-to-date fashions of sexuality and all the outmoded, anachronistic others. This narrative of progress carries the residue, and occasionally the outright intention, borne within evolutionary notions of the uneven development of the races from primitive darkness to civilized enlightenment.[7]

BEYOND THE BODY HOMOSEXUAL: AN EPISTEMOLOGY OF RACIAL CLAUSTROPHILIA

In a touchstone passage in the *History of Sexuality,* Michel Foucault offers a sophisticated and now-influential way of understanding the formation of homosexuality as the scientific attempt to disclose or uncloset the secrets of perverse sexual attraction presumably hidden not only in the mentality and behavior of the pervert but also in the body parts. He writes: "The nineteenth-century homosexual became a personage, a past, a case history, and a childhood, in addition to being a type of life, a life form, and a morphology, with an indiscreet anatomy and possibly a mysterious physiology. Nothing that went into his total composition was unaffected by his sexuality. It was everywhere present in him: at the root of all his actions because it was their insidious and indefinitely active principle; written immodestly on his face and body because it was a secret that always gave itself away.... The homosexual was now a species."[8] Foucault points to the ways in which the homosexual person becomes visible both as an embodied locale and as a local phenomenon. Pinpointing the locale, Foucault theorizes it as a sort of transparent closet—"a secret that always gave itself away"—ironically marked *on* the living body, even though invisible *in* the dissected anatomy of the sexual deviant. (In other words, the homosexual's body itself becomes the "closet" that must be pried open to discover its secret homosexual motivations.) Pinpointing the local phenomenon, he instructively rethinks the closet paradigm as a discursive invention occurring in nineteenth-century Germany and England through the emerging sciences of sexology, psychoanalysis, and criminology. If the modern homosexual's body as a transparent closet is made visible by the peculiar discursive conditions of Anglo-Saxon science, what happens when this discourse targets bodies beyond this locality, bodies already made visible as an altogether other "type" "with an indiscreet anatomy and possibly a mysterious physiology"?

If we substitute "enslaved African" for Foucault's "nineteenth-century homosexual" and "race" for "sexuality" in the above quotation, his theory could be taken as explaining the invention of race, rather than sexuality, as a total composition and thus as a species identity. Of course, Foucault-influenced theorists interested in race, like Mary Louise Pratt and Ann Stoler, have done exactly this.[9] Robyn Wiegman, for instance, calibrates Foucault's theory to understand "how the 'logic' of race in U.S. culture anchors whiteness in the visible epistemology of black skin."[10] Borrowing from Foucault's own timeline, Wiegman pinpoints this visible epistemology of race in seventeenth-century Europe, using language similar to Foucault's in his identification of the homosexual formation. "By the late seventeenth century," Wiegman writes, "color had become *the primary* organizing principle around which the natural historian classified human differences, and a century later, it functioned as the visible precondition for anatomical investigations into the newly emergent object of knowledge, 'man.'"[11] Wiegman's focus on race as "the primary" organizing principle brings attention to Foucault's charting of sexuality as a "total composition" and the homosexual "species" as the axis of a secret anatomical difference. If we take seriously both Foucault's argument that the identity of modern homosexuality tends to be totalized as a singular species, and Wiegman's argument that race becomes the primary organizing principle of modernity at least a century earlier, then we arrive at a theoretical-historical impasse. If by the eighteenth century, race is already marked on "the body" as a totalizing sign of invisible anatomical species difference, then what happens in the nineteenth century, when, as Foucault argues, homosexuality is marked on "the body" as a totalizing sign of invisible anatomical species difference? Are Wiegman and Foucault talking about two totally different bodies?

Actually, they are and are not at the same time. For the concept of "the body" in both Foucault and Wiegman erects an abstraction that dissembles at those signal originary moments when, according to their theories, an emergent discourse of race or sexuality is formatively being graphed onto the actual bodies of particular groups of individuals. The phrase "the body," in other words, is shorthand for those bodies enlisted into an identity group, but the question is exactly how specific bodies, each of which is different from and similar to every other, get lumped together into different groups such that an abstract phrase like "the body" can meaningfully refer to everybody and *every body* supposedly belonging to that group. Foucault's abstract homosexual body refers to specific bodies belonging presumably to the Anglo-Saxon race, but unmarked by the gazes of the nineteenth-century scientists as such, and thus not remarked on by Foucault himself. In providing a corrective to Foucault by attempting to index how bodies become *racially* demarcated within historical discourses, Wiegman charts a narrative in which groups of bodies (different bodies? the same bodies?) become racialized, gendered, and sexualized at different moments. In other words, she composes a single narrative of the uneven development of racial and sexual discourses, and it is exactly the uneven timing of this development that allows her narrative to cohere.[12] Wiegman imagines and images this theoretical-historical impasse not as a matter of how originally interrelated identity discourses can be mapped onto a single specific body in an instant or at a glance but instead as a matter of how disparate ("seemingly unconnected") discourses distributed across different bodies can be drawn together over long stretches of time. While leaving the former (identities mapped onto a single body at a glance) ambiguous, she solves the latter (disparate discourses mapped across different bodies across time) by pointing to the role of analogy in the uneven emergence of these discourses:

Cultural practices of representation and signification were themselves altered, and it is in this process that analogy surfaced as a definitive mechanism for positing relations between things that were, from the level of appearances, seemingly unconnected. In the context of the nineteenth century's production of racial discourse, the privilege accorded to analogy enabled a host of other cultural determinants to be linked to and organically defined within the sphere of the body. Through the crafting of analogic relations, the deployment of race was multiplied, radiating outward to constitute new identities of bodies as sexual, gendered, and criminal excesses.[13]

The "sphere of the body" defined by race becomes over time (moments, days, weeks, decades, centuries?) the model for other "new identities of bodies" defined by something other than race: gender, sexuality, class, criminality, etc. The abstraction of "the body" into a further abstraction of its "sphere"— currently a customary and necessary way of talking about these problems in academe—has the effect of covering over how a *single person's body* could, from the outset (that is, at the originary moment within the nineteenth century or whenever), be seen as carrying both visible and invisible markers of more than one identity discourse already interfused and *embodied* in that single person. Furthermore, Wiegman's own insightful critical practices rely on a form of analogy borne out of this tendency for "grafting" onto heterogeneously marked bodies the same "analogic relations" among race, gender, and sexuality. That is, her readings consistently examine white men's bodies (white bodies already mapped as male) in relation to black men's bodies (male bodies already mapped as black) or straight men's in relation to women's or to homosexuals', etc. (in her readings of the 1980s buddy films, for instance). Because the discourses stand in analogic relation to one another, and because an identity discourse and "the body" it discourses on become almost interchangeable in Wiegman, how any one body gets composed, all at once, as male and also colored, or male and colored and feminine, or male and colored and white and feminine and homosexual, etc., remains in the shadows of her theory.

Wiegman's theory of uneven development poses other, more vexing, questions for us insofar as she herself leaves unanswered some larger questions about this uneven discursive development of race, gender, and sexuality. What does it mean for a racialized body to be named before a gendered or homosexualized one? How can we specify in theoretical terms a homosexualized body marked by racial difference? Can one body withstand the pressure of belonging to two species? Given the formative and ongoing role of the "definitive mechanism" of analogy, does the placement of a body in a species category work the same way in racial and sexual identification? Or do race, sex, sexuality, and criminality become visible differently because different discourses are at play, even when a single body is the anatomical object?[14] That Wiegman must recalibrate Foucault's history with race at its center indicates to what extent Foucault in fact needed to erase the question of racialized bodies in order to theorize the invention of the body homosexual as a unified—that is, unmarked and implicitly ubiquitous—Anglo-Saxon subject. Foucault's scientists can script their human subjects as total homosexual compositions only because those bodies are *not* already marked as Negroid or Oriental; that is, in other words, because they are silently, invisibly already marked as unspecified Anglo-Saxons. Likewise, Foucault himself can script the formation of homosexuality as a totalized identity only by leaving unremarked the racial ideology undergirding these emerging sciences.[15]

As Anglo-Saxon racial identification silently mediates between the putatively heterosexual scientists and their homosexual subjects, each quietly mirroring the racial normativity of the other's body by spotlighting their difference in sexual orientation, the scientists are able to foreground *sexual* deviance, rather than *racial* deviation, as the secret motivation closed up in the bodies of their homosexual subjects. In other words, the assumed racial sameness of the Anglo-Saxon sexologist and his Anglo-Saxon sexual subject not only makes their racial identity invisible but also makes possible the sexual difference between them. The sexologist seems to ask: What makes this other man's body sexually different from my own, given that we both seem to have the same sex organs? This may lead the scientist to examine the homosexual's sex organs more closely—to find a smaller cock, for instance, as explanation for his deviance. Or observing no measurable difference between his own sex organs (a normal heterosexual male's) and the homosexual's, the sexologist may produce an explanation for sexual difference between men based in other, more hidden, physiological deviations, such as the operation of the glands or hormones. Or, moving unobtrusively from physiology to epistemology, the sexologist might find an answer in the homosexual subject's consciousness as a sexed self, rather than in his physical body, by attributing homosexual difference to psychological attributes that leave no observable mark on or in the body itself. Beneath this neatly compartmentalized scientific inquiry, however, is a more muddled racial assumption unconsciously asked by the sexologist in this way: given that the homosexual subject is a racially normal Anglo-Saxon male with sex organs like my own, what is it that makes him sexually different from me? While the perceived racial difference of an African or Asian male could be used to explain any putatively observed sexual deviance, racial sameness becomes ground zero for the observed split between heterosexual and homosexual Anglo-Saxon men.

Although scientists from the seventeenth century until today have relied similarly on a variety of compartments to explain racial difference (including the physical, physiology, environment, and psychology), the evidence of such racial difference could explain beforehand any perceived observation of sexual difference. An African man is sexually deviant because of his racial difference, whether owing to a larger cock or diminished brain size that prevents sexual self-discipline or a primitive jungle environment that fosters exaggerated sexual passions. Even if the African male's sexual difference is *not* physically marked, his racial deviance is, such that racial difference necessarily overdetermines the capacity for sexual deviance as a bodily affair.

By ignoring the assumption of racial sameness as the crucial hidden motive that enables the white sexologist to observe sexual deviance as a difference in kind separating homosexuals from otherwise normal white men, Foucault also ignores the hidden function of uneven racial development in his own discourse. What makes the racialized body totally absent in Foucault's discovery of an origin for modern homosexual consciousness is a residual narrative of uneven racial development in the sciences: Anglo-Saxons discovered homosexual consciousness because the Anglo-Saxon race got there first. One has to ask why Anglo-Saxon scientists, in their fascination with investigating black bodies and body parts, did not decide to see an analogous relation between African and homosexual bodies, which, given Wiegman's theory, should have been the logical outcome. In a sense, they did, as they tended to view the homosexual subject (that is, the Anglo-Saxon male body marked by sexual difference) as racially retarded. Perverting the procreative purpose of the healthy Anglo-Saxon male, the homosexual necessarily also carried within his body a latent racial perversion, implicitly fostering the threat of racial reversion by failing to do his part to propagate the Anglo Saxon race.[16] How is it that Foucault could miss the contribution that racial identity must make to the Anglo-Saxon invention of a total homosexual body? As a result of such oversight, race, not homosexuality, becomes in Foucault's discourse the transparent closet, the secret identity that always gives itself away because it is dis/closed within the anatomy itself.

Does it make a racial difference that the closet paradigm, according to Foucault, has nineteenth-century Anglo-Saxon origins? From the viewpoint of the highly original and influential work of Eve Kosofsky Sedgwick, I think that we'd have to answer, absolutely. Taking seriously Foucault's notion that the (Anglo-Saxon) homosexual becomes a "total composition" sometime in the nineteenth century, Sedgwick ponders the "rather amazing fact that, of the very many dimensions along which the genital activity of one person can be differentiated from that of another . . . precisely one, the gender of object choice, emerged from the turn of the century, and has remained, as *the* dimension denoted by the now ubiquitous category of 'sexual orientation.'"[17] Sedgwick develops an epistemological theory of the closet not so much to answer this question, as to ask how the closet binary itself serves to construct and construe not just the binds of homosexual desire but also modern sexuality more generally. In some ways, the first question of why gender of object choice came to dominate sexual-orientation identity is more intriguing, especially as it might lead us to consider how within *European-American* ideology, gender of object choice becomes so wedded to the closet paradigm. We can say with some confidence that gender of object choice and the closet paradigm arise as the "ubiquitous"—that is, the global—definition of sexual orientation simply because of the political, economic, and cultural dominance of the West globally. Nonetheless, even within the West, and even under the discursive dominance of the closet paradigm, other ways of identifying persons engaged in intragender attractions beyond the closet binary have thrived from the turn of the nineteenth century to the present.

Instructively, Sedgwick picks up on the contradictory ways in which the larger homosexuality/heterosexuality binary has been theorized and historicized through both a "universalizing" and a "minoritizing" logic: "The contradictions that seem most active are the ones internal to all the important twentieth-century understandings of homo/heterosexual definition, both heterosexist and anti-homophobic. . . . The first is the contradiction between seeing homo/heterosexual definition on the one hand as an issue of active importance primarily for a small, distinct, relatively fixed homosexual minority (what I refer to as a minoritizing view), and seeing it on the other hand as an issue of continuing, determinative importance in the lives of people across the spectrum of sexualities (what I refer to as a universalizing view)."[18] Although it is difficult to understand either minoritizing or universalizing logic without studied attention to racial ideology, from which the minority/universal binary borrows, Sedgwick seeks to deconstruct this binary through sustained close readings of several texts by elite European-American males while bracketing the matter of racial ideology. In suggesting that she is making a critique of the canon from the inside, Sedgwick is able to make a case that within these writers can be found an epistemology of sexuality central "to the important knowledges and understandings of twentieth-century Western culture as a whole."[19] On the one hand, Sedgwick defines "Western culture as a whole" as this closed set of elite white men's works obsessed with un/closeted desire. In other words, the "knowledges and understandings of twentieth-century Western culture as a whole" become the property of a clique, a tiny minority. On the other hand, she takes the closet binary in these racially select texts as exemplary of *the* epistemology of *the* closet—in other words, as a universal phenomenon, at the least for everyone touched by modernity. Is "twentieth-century Western culture as a whole" meant to include the working classes, women, and people of color living in the West, and their particular processes of sexual identification? Does it include those in Africa and Asia whose subject identities have been crucially formed by, and in resistance to, European imperialism and colonialism? Or does her theory exclude these groups from "twentieth-century Western culture as a whole" and from the closet epistemology that she elaborates in Oscar Wilde, Henry James, Herman Melville, Friedrich Nietzsche, and Marcel Proust? When she speaks more precisely of Wilde as "the most formative individual influence on turn-of-the-century *Anglo-European* homosexual definition and identity," she seems to rely on a minoritizing logic. However, a few sentences later when she speaks of Proust as offering "what seems to have been the definitive performance of the presiding incoherences of *modern* gay (and hence nongay) sexual specification and gay (and hence nongay) gender," she seems to rely on a universalizing logic.[20] Are racialized and classed groups like African Americans included in this expansive gesture of "modern" gay and nongay sexuality and gender? Or are such groups marginal to the sexually modernizing closet binary, and thus outside the modernity that it performs? This is not simply a matter of the kind of critique that lesbian theorists like Terry Castle have lodged against Sedgwick for her exclusion of (white) lesbian subjects, although such a critique is in and of itself crucial.[21] It is not merely a matter, that is, of including a wider range of texts or subjects representing other racial and class cultures, but more fundamentally a question of whether Sedgwick's closet theory of modernity—and so her method of analysis—can account for these others. Is this theory itself shaped by racial assumptions? How would her closet theory need rethinking for it to account for the racial ideology operating within the closet binary itself?

Implicitly, Sedgwick's closet theory depends on a notion of the uneven development of the races, such that a miniscule, easily identifiable clique of elite white men (Wilde, Melville, James, Nietzsche, Proust) ambiguously do or do not determine the processes of sexual identification for everyone touched by modernity, regardless of race, class, gender, geography, degree of cultural "advancement" into modernity, etc. The closet theory seems very productive in ferreting out a particular kind of ambivalent (homo)sexual desire hidden in high, dense literary texts whose aesthetic practices are *already* shaped by the established European literary culture of readers and critics cultivated to read in such a manner by the texts themselves. This closet theory relies, then, on a paradoxically closed dialectic: the *close* reading method is already implicit in the method of the literary texts, whose aesthetic encourages the search for *closeted* meaning, and the literary texts themselves are produced in response to a literary establishment that values "deep" hidden meanings as a sign of "high" intellectual labor.[22] Sedgwick's preference for the method of *close* readings, in other words, is intimately related to the *closed* set of male European texts that exemplify the *closet* binary as formative to a *closed-off* modernity and modernism. The claustrophilia lurking in this method—that is, the fascination with the closet as the primary epistemological device defining sexual modernity—results in a sort of racial claustrophobia, the tendency to bind both intragender desire and modernity within a small but deep closet containing elite European men maneuvering to find a way out. Beyond the claustrophobic closet, these men's discourses—and the closet that functions in them—are shaped by cultures whose deeply embedded and thus invisible racial identifications play a large unanalyzed role in the conceptualization of desire and sexuality, knowledge and normativity.[23]

Likewise, the penchant for "epistemology" itself derives from a universalizing project that covers up the racial ideology at work in constructing the psychological depth of certain individual subjects (the minority of elite European males) constantly frustrated by their ideal objects of desire. Primitives, savages, the poor, and those uneducated in the long history of epistemology are not normally represented as epistemological subjects, partly because they do not have the luxury of composing the kind of voluminous texts that bear the weight of such deeply buried—and thus closed/closeted up—intellectual dilemmas begging for painstakingly close readings. People from these groups are conventionally seen neither as imprinting "the most formative individual influence" on history nor as enacting "the definitive performance of the presiding incoherences of" modernity. People from such groups are presumed to lead more collective (that is, *mass*) lives—that is, they are seen as shaped by the group identities formulated by the genius of great men. Unlike those who constitute the mass, whose individuality is so enmeshed by collective identity that we have no historical sense of their individualism, wordy geniuses like Melville and Proust transcend their racial and sexual group identities not by escaping them but by illustratively representing them self-consciously in their words. Sedgwick's epistemological logic runs something like this: Proust may be shaped by his identity as a homosexual European living at the turn of the century, but more crucially he shapes inordinately and disproportionately the historical consciousness of what it means not only to be such a body but also to be modern in any body. Because Proust belonged to a group that got there first (elite European homosexual men), his closet consciousness *is* modernity. Wherever else all the other identities may lag in this progress toward modern closet consciousness, without Proust the experience of others becomes incoherent. We can say, therefore, that the search for the epistemology of modern sexuality itself is a discourse shaped by racial identifications, for the cultural assumptions embedded in the search for epistemology are necessarily related to the long history of European metaphysics, aestheticism, ethnology, and ethnography, in which to know the procedure out of which knowledge is grounded and produced (the closet binary, for instance) is to know the essence of the object (the closet, for instance) desired or avoided by the subject (the white elite male homosexual, for instance). Like Foucault's and Wiegman's necessary reliance on "the sphere of the body," Sedgwick's desire for an epistemology of sexuality necessarily draws her attention to certain subjects (elite European men) and their objects (un/closeted desires) as constitutive of all modern culture from the outset.

How might a more racially aware investigation of "modern" sexuality reshape Sedgwick's theory, method, subjectivity, and topics? I'm not sure, but it might begin to take us beyond the closet itself, if not beyond modernity as a closed circuit of deeply buried ambivalent desire. Generalizations that ambiguously apply to all modern experience would have to be interrogated. For instance, Sedgwick discusses a transformation that she believes occurs at the turn of the nineteenth century: moving from the notion of sexual inversion (a female psyche in a male body or vice versa) to the notion of homosexuality as the choice of a same-gender object. Sedgwick claims that anal sex becomes definitive to the hetero/homosexual binary because of "the relative difficulty with which oral sex, as opposed to anal, can be schematized in the bipolar terms of active/passive or analogically male/female."[24] It has frequently been suggested that in the cultures of some male Latinos, some urban African Americans, and the imprisoned, oral sex *does* get highly polarized into active/passive and masculine/feminine, so much so that there is no ambiguity about the passivity/femininity of the sissy or punk who receives the penis into his mouth and the activeness/masculinity of the man who inserts the penis. The distinction between oral and anal intercourse in such instances is utterly irrelevant, whatever other anxieties and taboos may adhere to these particular sexual practices in these communities. The clarity of gender roles in these intragender sexual practices, whatever deep internal confusions and ambivalences might be invisibly at stake, attests to a potentially variant way of thinking about what is hidden and what exposed in such relationships. The masculine man cannot be in the closet if he is not considered a faggot for engaging in such behavior, just as the desire of the feminine faggot must be constantly and generally exposed within the community for him to be accessible for sex with "straight" men.[25] Because Sedgwick seems to be making a claim about the central role of anal sex—and the marginal role of oral sex—in all modern sexual and gender identity, the sexual-identity experiences of these populations would seem to contradict Sedgwick's generalization about the irrelevance of oral sex in the formation of modern sexuality. When her generalizations seem to contradict large populations defined by racial-class difference—Latinos, African Americans, and male prisoners, for instance—does this mean that the sexual identities of these populations are *not* modern? If these populations are outside of modern sexuality, in what cultural-temporal zone does their sexual identity reside? In a premodern or primitive condition? Or is it that the sexual identity of these populations is shaped by some alternative sense of modernity about which Sedgwick is not concerned? If there *are* alternative sexual modernities, however, wouldn't it be crucial for Sedgwick to explore at least one of them to test her giant claims about the axiomatic and ubiquitous influence of particular turn-of-the-century European homosexual men on all modern sexuality?

Not surprisingly, there is an implicit narrative of modern progress involved in Sedgwick's thinking. In premodern sexuality the concept of anal intercourse predominates such that the male sexual partners are gendered differently, the passive partner conceived as a gender invert whose true feminine self is hidden in a male body. Modernity is occasioned by the emergence of oral sex between men, a practice that Sedgwick sees as gender equivalence, thus producing "the *homo*-trope of gender sameness" between two men whose *homo*sexual (that is, *same*-gender) identity enables the "signifying visibility" of coming out as men who desire other men. For Sedgwick, then, it is perfect *equivalence,* represented by her notion of oral sex, that enables the two men to become *partners,* to recognize their *common* identity as men desiring men and thus to recognize the benefit of bringing this identity into the open. If modern homosexuality requires gender parity between sexual partners, what happens if there is racial disparity between them? Do the two partners have to be racially symmetrical as well as sexually so? Would a sexual relation between a man of African descent and a (homo)sexually self-conscious European constitute an emergence of modern homosexuality? If the European views his object of desire as racially other, can he still be seen as engaging in a sexually equivalent relationship? Do we bracket the structural effect of imperialism and race on the nature of the relationship? Must the African's native sexual practices be transformed to embrace the European's more "modern" sense of what it means to engage in intragender sex, whatever that might be? Or must the African's sense of sexuality be, by default, premodern, given the chances that his traditions of sexuality would neither conform to the European's sense of himself as more sexually modern nor to Sedgwick's notion of "signifying visibility" as a key to sexual modernity? We could ask similar questions closer to home, both geographically and temporally. For instance, are Carl Van Vechten's trysts with poor Negro boys in the 1920s instances of modern homosexuality, even if these boys conceive of intragender sexuality in "premodern" terms of gendered sexual roles, as frequently was (and sometimes remains) the case among black hustlers?[26] In the narrative of an emerging sense of equivalent partnership as the origin point of modern homosexuality, what role should we give to colonialist fantasies of conquest and to unequal racial-class standing involving monetary exchange? In the logistics of Sedgwick's evolutionary narrative, the presumption seems to be that both partners are necessarily white in the invention of modern homosexuality. Otherwise, race would have to be totally subsumed by sexual identity and thus be seen as an irrelevant feature of the same-sexual relationship.[27] We know, according to Sedgwick, that such consciousness is developed by white middle-class men like Wilde and Proust. We also know that others lag behind in premodernity where anal intercourse and its implicit gender-role disparity predominate. I would suggest that these implicit others in Sedgwick's discourse are necessarily racial and class others, those against whom Sedgwick's white middle-class homosexual pioneers are tacitly contrasted. A relation between a white modern homosexual and an African immersed in his traditional culture would be something other than modern homosexuality. To become a homosexual, the African would have to leave behind any traditional notions of intragender sexuality. In other words, he would have to become like his European counterpart. The unarticulated contrast between European sexual consciousness and the experiences of racialized others enables Sedgwick's narrative to cohere. Exactly because she does not analyze the experiences of such racial-class others, the epistemology that Sedgwick attributes to modernity and to sexuality can seem cogent, total, systematic. It could be that modernity emerges not only from the sense of sexual parity within Europe but also crucially in the racial disequilibrium implied in and operating through the notion of colonialist cross-racial sexual relations between men. Or we could also point out that any European sense of homosexual partnership based in an equivalence of oral sex cannot be understood without the backdrop of unequal sexual relations between upper-class men and their social inferiors—a significant aspect of the homosexual imaginary at the turn of the nineteenth century and later. In other words, homosexual modernity is constructed not only in relation to a premodern European past before sexual parity gave rise to the uncloseting of a common identity. It is also constructed over and against the premodern present of traditional (that is, *primitive*) sexual practices being engaged in by those not privy to Europe's progress toward homosexual identity.

At the beginning of *The Epistemology of the Closet,* Sedgwick says "that homo/heterosexual definition has been a presiding master term of the past century [the twentieth], one that has the same, primary importance for all modern Western identity and social organization (and not merely for homosexual identity and culture) as do the more traditionally visible cruxes of gender, class, and race."[28] If race and class hold "the same, primary importance for all modern Western identity and social organization," then we must ask how it is possible to understand the cultural history of sexual identity, even among a select group of elite white men, without bringing to bear these "more traditionally visible cruxes." In fact, race and class become traditionally *invisible* when the putative origins of modern homosexuality are disclosed, and therefore it seems all the more crucial for a theory attuned to the politics of in/visibility to take into account these cruxes that otherwise remain so exposed to view. Even as Sedgwick acknowledges "race" and other variables as possessing "the same, primary importance," her work, like Foucault's, achieves its masterful coherence partly as a consequence of ignoring the construction of racial ideology as integral to the invention of homosexual identity. This is not to suggest that Sedgwick's work is irrelevant to a project of theorizing the racial identity of same-sexual identifications. In fact, Sedgwick's influence within (white)queer theory necessitates a continued engagement with her theory and its racial, as well as sexual, consequences.

In absenting and bracketing race, Foucault and Sedgwick respectively are able to erect a coherent epistemology of the closet as a ground for modern identity. It is probably a more common practice in (white)queer theory and history to tokenize race, class, and other identity formations in the process of centering the closet as the paradigm of modern progress in which white middle-class gay men must necessarily play the starring roles. In most (white)queer theory, race and class make a cameo appearance—on stage just long enough to make sensational impact—only to disappear after they have served to foreground uncloseted desire as definitive of modern sexual identity. Such offhanded use of race or class to narrate experiences of (white) coming out can reveal much about the racial ideology of the closet paradigm in dominant queer discourses. In David Halperin's book *Saint Foucault*, for instance, he exploits race to draw an object lesson concerning "the kind of moral panic that can be unleashed in the public mind by the presence of socially recognized authority figures who are openly, visibly gay and who work to promote lesbian/gay political causes."[29] Describing his experience of becoming the object of media sensationalism as a result of a sexual harassment suit, Halperin writes, "Meanwhile, I had become, for fifteen minutes at least, the Willie Horton of lesbian/gay studies." In rhetorical terms, this equation works similarly to Clarence Thomas's quip that he was made a victim of a "high-tech lynching" motivated by Anita Hill's sexual harassment charges. As Deborah McDowell and others have argued, poststructuralist theories of sexuality frequently build a case for the instability of sexual identities by using black bodies as their stable foundation, as the deep well of empirical experience on and beyond which their own fluid identities can be playfully manipulated and differentiated.[30] Racial ideology, through Willie Horton's cameo appearance, provides Halperin's formal structure as metaphor, his tone as hyperbole, his subtext as the spectacle of racial injustice and suffering, and his context as the legitimacy afforded by racial minority status. Race becomes, in fact, the surplus value of Halperin's queer identity discourse, as we can see by what he says directly after narrating his fifteen minutes of being Willie Horton: "That turned out not to be quite so much fun as it sounds, but I don't want to exaggerate my sufferings. No one I really

....

cared about disowned me. I continued to get grants. My lecture invitations did not diminish; in fact, my lecture fee increased. My students defended me in person and in print."[31] Exactly what binds a middle-class gay white man's decision to come out and promote homosexuality to one African American man whose image is broadcast internationally against his will and whose identity—not to mention his person—is reduced to that of a vicious convict undeserving of parole? The lesson that Halperin draws from this returns us safely to his own refreshed identification with other (white, middle-class) "queers" beyond the closet: "Ultimately what the . . . affair brought home to me is the very real vulnerability which, until that moment, I hadn't realized I shared with all other lesbian and gay people in our society, a vulnerability I foolishly thought I had managed to escape *by coming out.*"[32] Though this is indeed valuable, the initial lesson that I draw is quite different. It is exactly the *material* condition of black skin—the material fact of not being able to move back and forth across a racial threshold—that distinguishes Horton's case from Halperin's. Crossing the closet threshold is, in this instance, not like crossing the color line to discover the vulnerability shared between a middle-class white queer and a presumably straight black male convict, both of whose names have been spectacularly maligned. In fact, Halperin's reaffirmed sense of queer community is achieved, ironically, through the mediation of Willie Horton's racial marginality. Halperin does not say that he gains a stronger sense of the vulnerability that he shares with outcast African American men and the criminally marginalized. That would be something indeed, for it would begin to interrogate the relation between sodomy as a historically criminalized practice and those who have been criminalized through racial and class ideology. Instead, in Halperin's drama, the black man is called up only to be left out of this experience of shared identity. Just as Willie Horton's image serves to legitimate and consolidate Halperin's claim to a marginal identity, so leaving Horton out of the network of shared identification serves to indicate how Halperin has progressed from the margins where Horton remains to a distinct minority community of out queers. It is not hyperbole to suggest that Halperin's sense of a tightly knit queerness grounded in an uncloseted sexual identity rests on the implicit racial and class sameness of his newfound identity. Or, more precisely, it rests on the banishment of the problem of racial-class difference, which would unravel this fantasy of a homosexual identity consolidated into total community solely through its subject's *identical* experiences of coming out. It is not really coming out but the marginalization of a racial and class other that grounds

Halperin's totalizing sense of a consolidated queer community. Exactly because race and class are made to be extraneous identities that can be dismissed with the symbolic purging of Willie Horton, it is exactly the closeting of these other categories that creates the fantasy of an uncloseted homosexual community whose singular identity can be wholly defined by and thus reduced to the compulsory experience of coming out. If to be part of this new community requires coming out exactly in this way, one wonders about men-loving men and women-loving women who do *not* experience or conceptualize their intragender attractions through this sort of coming out narrative.

In queer historiography, we see a similar dynamic at work, especially related to the narrative of progress afforded by the closet paradigm. Most histories of U.S. gay and lesbian people narrate the formation of modern homosexuality as a collective coming out story whereby isolated, alienated, closeted individuals are able to migrate to the largest urban centers in mass numbers as a result of the disruptions of World War II. Eventually effecting a collective uncloseting of identity, these individuals together form the new visible, militant gay, and to a lesser extent, lesbian ghettos awaiting them in the urban centers. How does this migration narrative signify in relation to that other one—the Great Migration, as it is called—of African Americans from just before World War I to just after World War II? I don't have time to investigate this here, but I want to suggest that silent oppositions are put into play against that othered racial narrative. Did black men-loving men and women-loving women migrate to urban areas in the same way under similar consequences and to the same effect? We can see such a silent opposition at work in George Chauncey's brilliantly revisionary book *Gay New York,* which admirably struggles to cross race and class lines to tell a more complicated uncloseting narrative of queer identities. About gay men's migration, Chauncey writes: "The city was a logical destination for men intent on freeing themselves from the constraint of the family, because of its relatively cheap accommodations and the availability of commercial domestic services for which men traditionally would have depended on the unpaid household labor of women."[33] As we know, most African Americans, whatever their sexual identity, in this period migrated with their families or with the intention to stay with members of "extended" family from back home. In any case, what they found was the opposite of "relatively cheap accommodations." African American migrants—of whatever sexual persuasion—were crowded together in exorbitantly overpriced tenements in largely segregated sectors of major cities. Many African American women, on arriving, found themselves employed in underpaid "household labor," perhaps some of them laboring for the very gay men whom Chauncey describes. As Chauncey himself points out, during the Great Migration, sometimes whole communities "re-created themselves on the blocks of Harlem and Chicago's South Side."[34] Whatever the resonances between the gay and the Great Migration narratives, the African American story implies a different tenor to the migration narrative from that of a simple unclaseting by leaving behind the constraints of the normative family in small-town America. Even for those occasional African Americans who may have migrated alone to unfamiliar cities in search of sexual freedom, we cannot assume that their experience of homosexual iden- tification would fit the gay migration narrative. However much an African American of the time may have desired to break with family as a way of claiming homosexual community, the reality of racial segregation would have intervened to reinforce the notion of belonging to a racial family whose kinship was compelled at first glance by skin color and other superficial features. Finally, we have to ask to what extent the migration narrative of gay white male identity especially reproduces the mythology of the urban pi- oneer, the white men who return to the "inner cities" to reclaim those territo- ries languishing amidst low property values in the hands of racial minor- ities.[35] The disparateness of these migration histories, and the role that the men-loving black men and women-loving black women play in each, has yet to be written. Such histories cannot be written, however, until we unpack the closet paradigm further and seek to move beyond it to other modes of analysis congenial to racial and class critique of sexual identity formation.

BLACK FAGGOTRY BEYOND THE CLOSET NARRATIVE

In the following quotation, the white anthropologist William G. Hawkes- wood suggests, after an ethnographic study of black men-loving men in Har- lem, that "coming out" may not play the pivotal role that it is given in dominant discourses on gay identity formation, both historical and personal: "For many gay men in Harlem, coming out was not a major concern, because their homosexuality, and later their gay identity, had always been assumed by family and friends. There was no need to 'come out.' Folks in their social networks had gradually taken for granted their sexual orientation."[36] Al- though this finding constitutes a surprising discovery for Hawkeswood, at- tention to African American history, literature, religion, and social experience indicates that intragender love has been constructed along axes not simply reducible to or easily characterized or explained by the closet paradigm and its attendant narrative of sexual evolution.[37] One of Hawkeswood's native informants, for instance, voices his non-coming-out experience this way:

> You know, they could tell I was gay. Even before I knew it. But I didn't think it was bad. You know like anything was wrong or anything. I just was like that. . . . I think because I thought it was natural then they all thought it was natural. No one ever caused any trouble. Sometimes the kids will call out "sissy" or "faggot," but I'd just say, "So what?" . . . I'm just myself. I carry on like this all the time. My brothers and sisters know. I think they probably heard the kids at school or on the block, you know, talkin' about me. So, they just knew. I didn't have to tell nobody. Everybody just kinda knew.[38]

Another informant says, "So I didn't have to come out. All the family knew. So it was no big deal."[39] In such statements, the emphasis is not on a binary of secrecy versus revelation but instead on a continuum of knowing that persists at various levels according to the kin and friendship relations within the community. Although sometimes imprecisely referred to as an "open secret," such attitudes express instead a strong sense that it is impossible *not* to know something so obvious among those who know you well enough. In such a context, to announce one's attraction by "coming out" would not necessarily indicate a progress in sexual identity, and it would not necessarily change one's identity from closeted to liberated as conceptualized in the dominant closet narrative. When the question of telling loved ones what they already know does become an issue, it can be judged a superfluous or perhaps even a distracting act, one subsidiary to the more important identifications of family, community, and race within which one's sexual attractions are already interwoven and understood.

Given the racialized assumptions of uneven development tacitly operating in both anthropology and gay/lesbian studies, we should expect Hawkeswood to "discover" the racial difference that sets African American homosexuals apart from modern homosexual progress. At the same time, given how "modern" homosexuality has been tacitly universalized and explicitly theorized as being grounded in the closet notion, we should also expect Hawkeswood's surprise at "discovering" an alternative expression of intragender sexuality existing within one of the world's most "advanced" cities.

In other words, the element of ethnographic surprise results from the white gay anthropologist's contradictory assumptions: on the one hand, expecting blacks to be culturally lagging in some form; on the other hand, expecting all expressions of homosexuality to be essentially defined through the closet binary. We must begin to investigate how intragender attraction can take on culturally variant implications within African American communities without necessarily being alien to dominant U.S. attitudes toward same-sexuality. It is an understatement to suggest that African American communities and discourses have been deeply influenced by these dominant attitudes because African Americans have helped to shape these attitudes. At the same time, given the messiness of cultural identification, we should not be surprised to discover—like Columbus stumbling again and again on the New World—that the black natives have different attitudes toward same-sexuality.

In the hard work now awaiting us we must rethink theories and histories of sexual identity by resisting the penchant for a narrative of unequal sexual development. We must be able to articulate the cultural differences in modes of sexual expression represented in various populations without falling—as a reflex reaction—into the closet paradigm as an easy common denominator for same-sexual identity. Such work requires us to examine all sorts of things that others have tended to avoid in queer theory and history. Richard Wright, for instance, is rarely mentioned as a writer who might lend insight into these matters. Unlike James Baldwin, who can easily become a token within gay/ lesbian studies, Wright presents a much more difficult case.[40] In examining homosexuality in African American discourse, commentators have focused either on texts written by authors identified as homosexual or on texts by authors considered homophobic. Whereas James Baldwin has been canonized in gay/lesbian scholarship, Richard Wright has either been placed in the homophobic camp or ignored even though Wright writes explicitly about homosexuality from various approaches.[41] In Wright's last published novel, *The Long Dream* (1958), for instance, he uses the character of a black sissy, Aggie, to bring the terrifying reality of lynching into the critical consciousness of the hero.

When Fish, as the hero is called, and his pals realize that their unprovoked attack on the sissy in their midst is similar to the lynching exploits by whites, they engage in a self-edifying dialogue that positions homosexuality and blackness in a more complicated relation than what we find in most (white)queer theory:

"We treat 'im like the white folks treat us," Zeke mumbled with a self-accusative laugh.

"Never thought of that," Sam admitted, frowning.

"Why you reckon he acts like a girl?" Fishbelly asked.

"Beats me," Tony said. "They say he can't help it."

"He could if he really *tried*," Zeke said.

"Mebbe he can't. . . . Mebbe it's like being black," Sam said.

"Aw naw! It ain't the same thing," Zeke said.

"But he ought to stay 'way from us," Fishbelly said.

"That's just what the white folks say about us," Sam told him.[42]

I do not have time here to analyze the theoretical import of such a passage for interrogating the claustrophilic assumptions of (white)queer theory. I must point out, however, that Wright is not interested in the closet paradigm in representing Aggie and his relation to the other boys in the rural South. He is instead interested in how the color line operates in tandem with a sexual line separating the normal and dominant from the abnormal and oppressed. What Fish and his friends learn, however, is that they cannot segregate Aggie without in effect killing him. When they retreat from beating him to death, they also begin to recognize that, as part of their human condition, they are capable of committing the same sort of atrocities that whites practice routinely against them. Even as they see Aggie as sexually different (and this has absolutely nothing to do with whether he's in or out of a closet), they also see him as intimately intertwined with their own sense of what constitutes their identity as blacks subject to lynching. Wright is *not* simply comparing same-sexuality and blackness (Aggie is both black and a sissy), and he is certainly *not* equating lynching and fag bashing. He is instead examining how the psychology of a people routinely lynched might interact with someone also considered inferior by dominant culture and routinely ostracized as a result. To think through the complications of this passage would be to think beyond racial-sexual analogizing. It would be to take race seriously as a complication of sexual identification, and sexuality seriously as a complication of racial identity. It would be to think beyond the closet without necessarily thinking that the closet has no bearing on such texts.

The question is not whether or not the closet can be made to apply to African Americans and other racialized and classed groups. Obviously, it can and does. The question, instead, concerns what happens when the closet *is* applied *as though* its operation has no dependence on racial-class thinking or no stake in acts of racial-class discrimination and exploitation. Conversely, we must ask how the trope of sexual closeting operates in racialized discourses like those about and especially by African Americans, both before and after the Stonewall uprisings, which are so frequently taken as the originary moment of global coming out politics. In other words, we have to consider how the gay/lesbian rights movement, with its out-of-the-closet paradigm, comes to dominate both discursively and politically the terms of intragender attraction and identification in U.S. society and, consequently, around the globe. The dominance of the closet paradigm within U.S. gay/lesbian civil rights politics, as well as the dominance of that kind of politics over global discussions of intragender eroticism, normalizes one mode of same-sexual identity by marginalizing other experiences and representations of intragender affiliation.

Given such a dynamic, it can be easy to forget that drag queens, effeminate men, butch women, prison punks, and racialized groups necessarily possess a different relation to normative institutions from that identified with white elite metropolitan gay men, and also may possess a different historical relation to Stonewall as the supposed originary moment of militant homosexual political organization. For instance, racialized minorities may operate under different social protocols concerning what it means to be visible and invisible within normative sites like the family, the classroom, the workplace, the church, the street, and the community more generally. We could ask, what does it mean for a drag queen to be in the closet—or to come out of it—wearing a dress rather than a suit and tie? Similarly, we must ask, what does it mean for African Americans to uncloset their sexuality *within* the context of a racial status already marked as an abnormal site over and against white bourgeois identity and its various signifiers of *racial* normativity? Is the closet notion a constitutive aspect of intragender attraction and affiliation within African American culture under the conditions of racial segregation, whose ideology still reigns de facto, if not de jure, at the outbreak of Stonewall? If not, then how is intragender passion bounded, scripted, identified, and practiced under these specific racial circumstances? If yes, then is the closet notion negotiated differently as a result of racial identification? Would an "open secret" of intragender affiliation signify in the same manner for African Americans, Native Americans, Latinos, Asian Americans, poor white people, and European Americans? How does the emergence of an uncloseting gay white male urban ghetto influence, and get influenced by, African American practices of same-sexuality?

Such questions can be answered only through serious long-term research under the aegis of a sexual-identity theory attuned to the realities and representations of racialized cultures, a theory that we are only now beginning to formulate, but that the current (white)queer theory seems not fully capable of handling. Necessarily, we must intervene to begin to figure out exactly where and how the current (white)queer theory may be of some help, and those places where it is merely a claustrophilic distraction.

NOTES

1. See Neil Bartlett, *Who Was That Man? A Present for Mr. Oscar Wilde* (London: Serpent's Tail, 1988): "Everything I knew focused too neatly on one central event, apparently reflecting our own contemporary situation, in which everything can be described as being before or after 'coming out.'" (29). Douglas Crimp, "Right On, Girlfriend!" in *Fear of a Queer Planet: Queer Politics and Social Theory*, ed. Michael Warner (Minneapolis: University of Minnesota Press, 1993): "Our outing fantasy— that the revelation of homosexuality would have a transformative effect on homophobic discourse—was only a fantasy after all, and a dangerous one at that . . . not to 'out' supposedly closeted gay men and lesbians, but to 'out' enforcers of the closet, not to reveal the 'secret' of homosexuality, but to reveal the 'secret' of homophobia" (308).

2. Maurice O. Wallace, *Constructing the Black Masculine: Identity and Ideality in African American Men's Literature and Culture* (Durham: Duke University Press, 2002), 115.

3. By the term "(white)queer" I do not mean to suggest that only people who identify as being of middle-class European descent exemplify these attitudes, nor that everyone identifying as such must necessarily espouse them. While I intend to expose a particular ideology grounding and legitimating mainstream gay/lesbian politics and queer academic theory broadly practiced by many individuals across race, class, gender, region, and sexuality, it is also the case, for circumstantial reasons, that the tendency to think in such terms may be more seductive—may be harder to resist—for someone identified as white and middle class.

4. Weeks focuses mainly on the history of homosexuality in Great Britain in *Coming Out: Homosexual Politics in Britain, from the Nineteenth Century to the Present* (London: Quartet, 1983), 22. For a succinct but helpful summary of "coming out" as a political act motivating and motivated by the Stonewall uprisings of 1969, see John D'Emilio, *Sexual Politics, Sexual Communities: The Making of a Homosexual Minority in the United States, 1940–1970* (Chicago: University of Chicago Press, 1983), 237–39.

5. Among the causes for the turn against homosexuality in the late nineteenth century, Weeks names "the developing working class culture" (19). Although I do not have space to attend to it here, the notion that "blue collar" culture is more

homophobic than the upper and middle classes is widespread. In the United States, the stereotype of the "red neck" encourages such an idea.

6. Weeks, *Coming Out*, 36; emphasis added.

7. The concept of "uneven development" is most identified with Marxist theory as a way of explaining which nations are most prone to achieve a communist condition based on how far and how quickly the bourgeois class of a nation has or has not advanced into industrial capitalism. As theorists have noted in tracing a radical take on the term through Marx, Engels, and Trotsky, it derives from Enlightenment notions of cultural, national, and racial progress and backwardness. A reactionary take on "uneven development," however, could also be traced from these same Enlightenment roots through racial supremacist thinkers from the eighteenth century to the present. On the general theory of "uneven development," see James Chandler, *England in 1819: The Politics of Literary Culture and the Case of Romantic Historicism* (Chicago: University of Chicago Press, 1998), 127–135. Neil Smith, *Uneven Development: Nature Capital and the Production of Space* (Oxford: Basil Blackwell, 1984, 1990), 95–105. On how such a theory gets racialized, see Winthrop Jordan, *White over Black: American Attitudes Toward the Negro, 1550–1812* (New York: Norton, 1968), especially 216–65; George M. Fredrickson, *The Black Image in the White Mind: The Debate on Afro-American Character and Destiny, 1817–1914* (1971; Hanover, N.H.: Wesleyan University Press, 1987), especially 71–96 and 228–55; and Lee D. Baker, *From Savage to Negro: Anthropology and the Construction of Race, 1896–1954* (Berkeley: University of California Press, 1998).

8. Michel Foucault, *History of Sexuality, Volume 1: An Introduction* (New York: Vintage, 1990), 43.

9. Actually, Pratt relies more on Foucault's *Order of Things* than on *History of Sexuality*; see Pratt, *Imperial Eyes: Travel Writing and Transculturation* (New York: Routledge, 1992), 28–31. Ann Stoler, *Race and the Education of Desire: Foucault's "History of Sexuality" and the Colonial Order of Things* (Durham: Duke University Press, 1995), especially 38 and 53.

10. Robyn Wiegman, *American Anatomies: Theorizing Race and Gender* (Durham: Duke University Press, 1995), 21.

11. Ibid., 24; emphasis added.

12. Given the messiness of such identity categories, it is perhaps intellectually dangerous to claim the temporal precedence of any one in order to historicize them all.

13. Wiegman, *American Anatomies*, 32.

14. Wiegman illuminates how difficult the negotiation of multiple identity categories can be in her superb discussion of Leslie Fiedler's *Love and Death in the American Novel* (New York: Anchor, 1992 [1960]); as well as in the important criticism of Robert K. Martin (*Hero, Captain, and Stranger: Male Friendship, Social Critique, and Literary*

Form in the Sea Novels of Herman Melville [Chapel Hill: University of North Carolina Press, 1986]); and Joseph Boone (*Tradition Counter Tradition: Love and the Form of Fiction* [Chicago: University of Chicago Press, 1987], 226–59), both of whom have outed the homosexual aspect repressed in Fiedler's reading of canonical U.S. fiction. Wiegman argues that the homosexual becomes a "phantasmatic" (that is, closeted) presence haunting his book "long after Fiedler's attempt to make him disappear." In uncloseting the homosexual, Martin and Boone do not pay "much attention to the interracial aspect of the bonding configuration and, in this elision, they tend to repeat the asymmetries of race through which Fiedler reads the bond" (152). Wiegman's use of analogy is thus an instructive attempt to juggle race, gender, and sexuality without letting any one drop from sight. Thanks to Wiegman's work, we can see how Martin and Boone provide other instances when the use of the closet paradigm tends unintentionally to background race. I would suggest that this is not just a matter of the difficulty inherent in trying to juggle race, gender, and sexuality, but more a challenge posed by how the closet paradigm at the heart of their queer practice serves to equate same-sexuality with particular kinds of white maleness.

15. In a crucial essay, "Scientific Racism and the Emergence of the Homosexual Body" (*Journal of the History of Sexuality* 5.2 [1994]: 264–65), Siobhan Somerville details "the various ways that late nineteenth- and early twentieth-century scientific discourses around race became available to sexologists and physicians as a way to articulate emerging models of homosexuality." Somerville's work represents an excellent example of thinking beyond racial-sexual analogy in linking these discourses. The essay goes far toward making "questions of race . . . inextricable from the study of sexuality, rather than a part of our peripheral vision" (266).

16. See, for instance, Weeks's discussion of the confusion existing in the work of Havelock Ellis, where an acquired homosexual predilection, as opposed to congenital "inversion," is seen as corrupting, and "it was the task of a sound social hygiene to make it difficult to acquire 'homosexual perversity'" (*Coming* Out, 62).

17. Eve Kosofsky Sedgwick, *The Epistemology of the Closet* (Berkeley: University of California Press, 1990), 8.

18. Ibid., 1.

19. Sedgwick writes: "The purpose of this book is not to adjudicate between the two poles of either of these contradictions, for, if its argument is right, no epistemological grounding now exists from which to do so. Instead, I am trying to make the strongest possible introductory case for a hypothesis about the centrality of this nominally marginal, conceptually intractable set of definitional issues to the important knowledges and understandings of twentieth-century Western culture as a whole" (2). On her defense of readings limited to the canon, see 48–59.

20. Ibid., 213; emphasis added.

21. See, for instance, Terry Castle, *The Apparitional Lesbian: Female Homosexuality and Modern Culture* (New York: Columbia University Press, 1993), 66–74. Ironi-

. . . .

cally, Castle's own theory of modernity as a phenomenon defined by its lesbian hauntings excludes nonwhite women. In one sentence, she alludes to some noted black women who were bisexual or lesbian as a way of gesturing toward whatever else exists outside "the realm of so-called high culture," which is her true concern: "Nor is the lesbian influence only to be found in the realm of so-called high culture. It is impossible to appreciate the blues, I would maintain, or the history of American jazz and popular song, without taking into account the unforgettable contributions of Bessie Smith, Ma Rainey, Gladys Bentley, Ethel Waters, Mabel Mercer, Alberta Hunter, or Janis Joplin" (18). Evidently, it is possible to appreciate lesbians' apparitional centrality to "modern culture" more generally without taking into account the experiences of nonwhite lesbians, or more fundamentally without accounting for the ways in which racial ideology operates in the representation of white lesbianism. Also see Biddy Martin's critique of Sedgwick in *Femininity Played Straight: The Significance of Being Lesbian* (New York: Routledge, 1996), 71–79. Martin points out "a tendency among some lesbian, bisexual, and gay theorists and activists to construct 'queerness' as a vanguard position that announces its newness and advance over against an apparently superceded and now anachronistic feminism with its emphasis on gender" (71).

22. Sedgwick's penchant for incredibly close(d) readings may partly stem from her academic training in eighteenth- and nineteenth-century British literature during the reign of new criticism, structuralism, and deconstruction—all of which overly value close(d) readings.

23. As Toni Morrison and others following her have pointed out, it is impossible to imagine the literary production of Melville, for instance, or modernism, as another instance, without the defining role that race plays in the constitution of them; see Morrison, *Playing in the Dark: Whiteness and the Literary Imagination* (New York: Vintage, 1992). Melville, among Sedgwick's closet writers, is the most obvious choice, but the question needs to be asked about all of them in less obvious ways.

24. Sedgwick, *Epistemology of the Closet*, 237.

25. For one influential discussion of such sexual patterns among Chicano men, see Tomas Almaguer, "Chicano Men: A Cartography of Homosexual Identity and Behavior," *differences* 3.2 (1991): 75–100. For another, see Robert McKee Irwin, *Mexican Masculinities* (Minneapolis: University of Minnesota Press, 2003).

26. On Van Vechten's sexual escapades with Negro boys in Harlem, see Bruce Kellner, "Carl Van Vechten's Black Renaissance," in *The Harlem Renaissance: Revaluations*, ed. Amiritjit Singh, William S. Shiver, and Stanley Brodwin (New York: Garland Publishing, 1989), 27.

27. All these hypothetical cases also hinge on an assumption operating in Sedgwick's notion of the essential partnering equivalence of oral sex and inequivalence of anal sex. We should not assume that oral sex necessitates or even suggests reciprocation on the part of the two partners. One person could desire always to be "active"

(that is, the inserter), and another to be passive. Racialized homosexual fantasies frequently involve such inequivalent scenarios, whereby, for instance, a white man desires to be sucked by a darker man or desires to suck a darker man without any desire for reciprocation. It's curious why Sedgwick would think that oral sex is any more reciprocal than anal sex. Perhaps she makes this assumption because oral sex can be engaged in simultaneously by both men ("69"), whereas anal sex cannot, but this explanation seems too literal-minded for Sedgwick's poststructuralist understandings.

28. Sedgwick, *Epistemology of the Closet*, 11.

29. Halperin, *Saint Foucault: Towards a Gay Hagiography* (New York: Oxford University Press, 1995), 12–13.

30. See, for instance, Deborah McDowell, *"The Changing Same": Black Women's Literature, Criticism, and Theory* (Bloomington: Indiana University Press, 1995), 156–75.

31. Halperin, *Saint Foucault*, 11.

32. Ibid.

33. George Chauncey, *Gay New York: Gender, Urban Culture, and the Making of the Gay Male World, 1890–1940* (New York: Basic Books, 1994), 135. It seems unjust to place Chauncey's thorough and complex treatment of race in his history of New York homosexuality next to Halperin's offhand exploitation of race in *Saint Foucault*. However, I do so to emphasize the continuity of their discourses. Both Chauncey and Halperin, in different ways, are strongly influenced by Foucault and Sedgwick.

34. Chauncey, *Gay New York*, 244.

35. On this notion of the white gay male as urban pioneer, see my essay, "Some Glances at the Black Fag: Race, Same-Sex Desire, and Cultural Belonging," in *African American Literary Theory: A Reader*, ed. Winston Napier (New York: New York University Press, 2000), 498–522. The idea of white gay men as "urban pioneers" was popular in the 1970s and 1980s, as represented in the Castro chapter of Frances Fitzgerald's *Cities on a Hill: A Journey through Contemporary American Cultures* (New York: Simon and Schuster, 1986), 58–60. Dennis Altman offers a critique of one aspect of this dynamic in *The Homosexualization of America, The Americanization of the Homosexual* (New York: St. Martin's Press, 1982), especially 32. The economic role of white middle-class gay males as new engines of urban entrepreneurship was the first stage in their reclaiming a mainstream identity that would eventually lead them back to their racial normativity awaiting them in the white suburbs.

36. William G. Hawkeswood, *One of the Children: Gay Black Men in Harlem* (Berkeley: University of California Press, 1996), 138.

37. As a matter of fact, if we started looking for it, we'd find other manifestations of same-sexual identity formation beyond the closet paradigm in Euro-American discourse and history as well, especially if we were to consider regional and class variations within the white population.

38. Hawkeswood, *One of the Children*, 138.

39. Ibid.

40. Baldwin, who resisted being called "gay," isn't so easy either, as a matter of fact. It has been convenient, however, to focus on Baldwin and Audre Lorde as the two preeminent cases representing black same-sexuality in gay/lesbian studies.

41. On the bilateral reception of Baldwin in queer and African American studies, see my essay "White Fantasies of Desire: Baldwin and the Racial Identities of Sexuality," in *James Baldwin Now*, ed. Dwight A. McBride (New York: New York University Press, 1999), 13–55.

42. Richard Wright, *The Long Dream* (New York: Harper, 1987 [1958]), 37.

DEVON W. CARBADO

PRIVILEGE

> It may be . . . that a damaging bias toward heterosocial or heterosexist assumptions inheres unavoidably in the very concept of gender. . . . The ultimate definitional appeal in any gender-based analysis must necessarily be to the diacritical frontier between different genders. This gives heterosocial and heterosexual relationships a conceptual privilege of incalculable consequence.—Eve Kosofsky Sedgwick, *Epistemology of the Closet*

This essay is part of a larger intellectual project to encourage a shift in—or at least a broadening of—our conceptualization of discrimination. My aim is to expand our notion of what it means to be a perpetrator of discrimination. Typically, we define a perpetrator of discrimination as someone who acts intentionally to bring about some discriminatory result.[1] This is a narrow and politically palatable conception; it applies to very few of us. In this essay I suggest that those of us who unquestionably accept the racial, gender, and heterosexual privileges we have—those of us who fail to acknowledge our victimless status with respect to racism, sexism, and homophobia—are also perpetrators of discrimination.[2]

Informing this privileged-centered understanding of discrimination is the notion that taking identity privileges for granted helps to legitimize problematic assumptions about identity and entitlement, assumptions that make it difficult for us to challenge the starting points of many of our most controversial conversations about equality. We simply assume, for example, that men should be able to fight for their country (the question is whether women should be entitled to this privilege); that heterosexuals should be able to get married (the question is whether the privilege should be extended to gays and lesbians); that white men should be able to compete for all the slots in a university's entering class (the question is whether people of color should be entitled to the privilege of "preferential treatment").

While a privileged-centered conception of discrimination usefully reveals the bi-directional effects of discrimination—namely, that discrimination allocates both burdens and benefits—the conception may prove entirely too much. After all, all of us enjoy some degree of privilege. Are all of us perpetrators of discrimination? The answer may depend on what we do with, and to, the privileges we have. Each of us makes personal and private choices with our privileges that entrench a variety of social practices, institutional arrangements, and laws that disadvantage other(ed) people.

For example, many of us get married and/or attend weddings, while lesbian and gay marriages are, in most parts of the United States (and the world), not legally recognized. Others of us have racially monolithic social encounters, live in de facto white only (or predominantly white) neighborhoods, or send our kids to white only (or predominantly white) schools. Still others of us have "straight only" associations—that is, our friends are all heterosexuals and our children's friends all have mommies and daddies. These choices are not just personal; they are political. And their cumulative effect is to entrench the very social practices—racism, sexism, classism, and homophobia—we profess to abhor.[3]

In other words, there is a link between identity privileges, and our negotiation of them, on the one hand, and discrimination, on the other.[4] Our identities are reflective and constitutive of systems of oppression. Racism requires white privilege. Sexism requires male privilege. Homophobia requires heterosexual privilege. The very intelligibility of our identities is their association, or lack thereof, with privilege. This creates an obligation on the part of those of us with privileged identities to expose and to challenge them.[5]

Significantly, this obligation exists not only as a matter of morality and responsibility. The obligation exists for a pragmatic reason as well. We cannot change the macro-effects of discrimination without ameliorating the power effects of our identities. Nor can our political commitments have traction unless we apply them to the seemingly "just personal" privileged aspects of our lives. Resistance to identity privileges may be futile, we cannot know for sure. However, to the extent that we do nothing, this much is clear: we perpetuate the systems of discrimination out of which our identities are forged.

But precisely what constitutes an identity privilege? Further, how do we identify them? And, finally, what acts are necessary to deprivilege our identities and to disrupt their association with power. These questions drive this essay. I begin here with a discussion of male privileges and then engage the privileges of heterosexuality.

MALE PRIVILEGES

Ever since Simone de Beauvior articulated the idea that women are not born women but rather become women, feminists have been grappling with ways to strip the category "women" of its patriarchal trappings. The hope is to locate the pre-patriarchal woman—the woman whose personal identity has not been over-determined by her gender.

The search for the pre-patriarchal woman is not based on the notion that, in the absence of patriarchy, there is some true female essence. (Indeed, it might not even be meaningful to refer to a person whose identity has not been over-determined by female gender norms as a woman.) The point is that people who are body-coded female cannot experience their personhood outside of the social construction of their gender, and the social construction of gender is both agency-denying and subordinating.

Of course, gender for men is also socially constructed and agency denying. One must learn to be a man in this society because manhood is a socially produced category. Manhood is a performance.[6] A script.[7] It is accomplished and re-enacted in everyday social relationships. Yet, men have not been inclined to examine the sex/gender category we inhabit, reproduce, and legitimize. Nor have men developed a practice of exposing the contingency and false necessity of manhood.[8] There is little effort within male communities to locate, or even imagine, the pre-patriarchal man, the man whose personal identity has not been over-determined by his gender. We (men) sometimes discuss gender inequality, but rarely do we discuss gender privilege. The assumption is that our privileges as men are not politically contingent, but social givens—inevitable and unchangeable.

Part of the reason men, especially white heterosexual men, do not conceive of themselves as en-gendered, and part of the reason men do not recognize their privileges, relates to negative identity signification. A white heterosexual man lives on the white side of race, the male side of gender, and the straight side of sexual orientation. He is, in this sense, the norm. Mankind. The baseline. He is our reference. We are all defined with him in mind. We are the same as or different from him.

Those of us on the "other" side of race, gender, or sexual orientation have to contend with and respond to negative identity signification. That is, we simultaneously live with and contest our nonnormativity. We are "different," and our identities have negative social meanings. For example, when I enter a department store, my "different" identity signifies not only that I am black and male but also that I am a potential criminal. My individual identity is lost in the social construction of black manhood. I can try to adopt race-negating strategies to challenge this dignity-destroying social meaning. I can work my identity (to attempt) to repudiate the stereotype.[9] I might, for example, dress "respectable" when I go shopping. There is, after all, something to the politics of dress, particularly in social contexts in which race matters—that is, in every American social context. I can appear less "black" in a social meaning sense via my sartorial practices.

Purchasing an item, especially something expensive, immediately on entering the store is another strategy I can employ to disabuse people of my "blackness." This sort of signaling strategy will reveal to the department store's security personnel what might not otherwise be apparent because of my race and gender: that I am a shopper. If I am not in the mood to dress up and I do not want to spend any money, there is a third strategy I can employ: solicit the assistance of a white sales associate. This, too, must be done early in the shopping experience. A white salesperson would not be suspected of facilitating or contributing to black shoplifting and can be trusted to keep an eye on me. Finally, I might simply whistle Vivaldi as I move among the merchandise: only a good (safe, respectable) black man would know Vivaldi or whistle classical music.[10]

White people do not have to worry about employing these strategies. White people do not have to work their identities to respond to these racial concerns.[11] Nor should they have to—no one should. However, white people should recognize and grapple with the fact that they do not have to employ or think about employing these strategies. White people should recognize that they do not have to perform this work.[12] This is a necessary first step for white people to come to terms with white privilege. Barbara Flagg and Peggy McIntosh[13] —two white women—make similar arguments. Their self-referential examination of whiteness is the analytical analogue to the examination of male identity and heterosexuality that this essay performs.

According to Barbara Flagg, "There is a profound cognitive dimension to the material and social privilege that attaches to whiteness in this society, in that the white person has an everyday option not to think of herself in racial terms at all." This, reasons Flagg, is indeed what defines whiteness: "To be white is not to think about it." Flagg refers to the propensity of whites not to think in racial terms as the "transparency phenomenon."[14]

Importantly, Flagg does not suggest that white people are unmindful of the racial identities of other whites or the racial "difference" of nonwhites: "Race is undeniably a powerful determinant of social status and so is always noticed, in a way that eye color, for example, may not be." Rather, her point is that because whiteness operates as the racial norm, whites are able "to relegate their own racial specificity to the realm of the subconscious."[15] As a result, racial distinctiveness is black, is Asian, is Latina/o, is Native American, but it is not white. To address transparency, Flagg suggests the "[reconceptualization of] white race consciousness . . . [to develop] a positive white racial identity, one neither founded on the implicit acceptance of white racial domination nor productive of distributive effects that systematically advantage whites."[16]

Peggy McIntosh's work provides a specific indication of some of the every-day "distributive effects" of white racial privilege. To illustrate the extent to which white privilege structures are implicated in day-to-day social encounters, McIntosh exposes the "unearned" advantages that she accrues on a daily basis because she is white. For example, precisely because she is white, McIntosh did not have to educate her children to be aware of systemic racism for their own daily physical protection.[17] Nor, observes McIntosh, does she have to worry about whether negative encounters with certain governmental entities (e.g., the IRS, the police) reflect racial harassment.[18]

McIntosh is careful to point out that the term "privilege" is something of a misnomer: "We usually think of privilege as being a favored state, whether earned, or conferred by birth or luck. . . . The word 'privilege' carries the connotation of being something everyone must want. Yet some of the conditions I have described here work to systematically over-empower certain groups." Accordingly, McIntosh distinguishes between "positive advantages that we can work to spread . . . and negative types of advantage that unless rejected will always reinforce our present hierarchies."[19]

Flagg's and McIntosh's interrogation of whiteness provides a methodology for men to interrogate gender. Their analysis suggests that men should challenge the social construction of gender employing *their* privileged gendered experiences as starting points. More particularly, men should detail and problematize the specific ways in which patriarchy materially advantages them. This experiential information should not displace or replace victim-centered or bottom-up accounts of sexism. That is, men's articulation of the ways in which they are the beneficiaries of patriarchy should not be a substitute for women's articulations of the ways in which they are the victims of patriarchy. Both narratives are valuable and illuminating. The telling of both helps to make clear that patriarchy is bi-directional. The patriarchal disempowerment of women is achieved through the empowerment of men.[20] The patriarchal construction of women as the second sex requires the construction of men as the first.[21] Patriarchy effectuates and maintains these relational differences.[22] It gives to men what it takes away from women.

The relational constitution of gender identities and experiences suggests that gender equality cannot be achieved unless gender privileges are relinquished. As Andrea Dworkin and Catherine Mackinnon put it: "Equality means someone loses power. . . . The mathematics are simple: taking power from the exploiters extends and multiplies the rights of those they have been exploiting."[23]

Broadly speaking, there are two categories of male privileges about which men should develop a consciousness. The first can be described as "an invisible package of unearned assets that [men] can count on cashing in each day."[24] The second category includes a series of disadvantages that men do not experience precisely because they are men. The following list presents examples from both.

1. I can walk in public, alone, without fear of being sexually violated.
2. Prospective employers will never ask me if I plan on having children.
3. I can be confident that my career path will never be tainted by accusations that I "slept my way to the top" (though it might be "tainted" by the perception that I am a beneficiary of affirmative action).
4. I don't have to worry about whether I am being paid less than my female colleagues (though I might worry about whether I'm being paid less than my white male colleagues).
5. When I get dressed in the morning, I do not worry about whether my clothing "invites" sexual harassment.
6. I can be moody, irritable, or brusque without it being attributed to my sex, to biological changes in my life, or to menstruating or experiencing "PMS" (though it might be attributable to my "preoccupation" with race).
7. My career opportunities are not dependent on the extent to which I am perceived to be "as good as a man" (though they may be depen-

dent on the extent to which I am perceived to be "a good black"—i.e., racially assimilable).

8. I do not have to choose between having a family or having a career.

9. I do not have to worry about being called selfish for having a career instead of having a family.

10. It will almost always be the case that my supervisor will be a man (though rarely will my supervisor be black).

11. I can express outrage without being perceived as irrational, emotional, or too "sensitive" (except if I am expressing outrage about race).

12. I can fight for my country without controversy.

13. No one will qualify my intellectual or technical ability with the phrase "for a man" (though they may qualify my ability with the phrase "for a black man").

14. I can be outspoken without being called a "bitch" (though I might be referred to as uppity).

15. I do not have to concern myself with finding the line between being assertive and aggressive (except with respect to conversations about race).

16. I do not have to think about whether my race comes before my gender, about whether I am black first and a man second.

17. The politics of dress—to wear or not to wear make-up, high heels, or trousers, to straighten or not to straighten, to braid or not to braid my hair—affect me less than they do women.

18. More is known about "male" diseases and how medicine affects male bodies than about "female" diseases and female bodies (though diseases that disproportionately affect black people continue to be understudied).

19. I was not expected to change my name upon getting married.

20. I am rewarded for vigorously and aggressively pursuing my career.

21. I do not have to worry about opposite-sex strangers or close acquaintances committing gender violence against me (though I do have to worry about racial violence).

22. I am not less manly because I play sports (though I may be considered less black and less manly if I do not play sports).

23. My reputation does not diminish with each additional person with whom I have sexual relations.

24. There is no societal pressure for me to marry before the age of thirty.
25. I can dominate a conversation without being perceived as domineering (unless the discussion is about race).
26. I am praised for spending time with my children, cooking, cleaning, or doing other household chores.
27. I will rarely have to worry whether compliments from my boss contain a sexual subtext (though I will worry that they may contain a racial subtext).
28. I am not expected to have a small appetite.
29. The responsibility for birth control is not placed on men's shoulders and men are not accused of getting pregnant.
30. There is a presumption that a person of my gender can run the country (though there is uncertainty about whether a person of my race can run the country).
31. White men don't have to worry about whether their gender will interfere with their ability effectively to bargain for a house, car, etc.
32. If I kiss someone on a first date, I do not have to worry about whether I have provided that person with a defense to rape.
33. Men I know do not consistently address me by pet names such as "baby" or "sweetheart," nor do strangers employ such terms to refer to or greet me.
34. I do not have to worry about resisting chivalry—refusing to go through the door first, paying for myself, etc. in order to maintain my independence.
35. I do not have to think about the "female gaze" (though I do have to think about the racial gaze).
36. I do not have to worry about being heckled or harassed by strangers because of my gender (though I do have to worry about "drive by" racial harassment).
37. I do not have to worry about leaving particular events early—such as a sporting event—to avoid a ridiculous wait at the bathroom.
38. I do not have to worry about varicose veins, spinal malalignment, or disk injury from wearing high heels.
39. To the extent that I dry-clean my clothes, I do not have to worry about the gender surcharge.
40. Every month is (White) Men's History Month.

This list does not reflect the male privileges of all men. It is both under and over inclusive. Class, race, and sexual orientation impact male identities, shaping the various dimensions of male privilege. For example, the list does not include as a privilege the fact that men are automatically perceived as authority figures. While this may be true of white men, it has not been my experience as a black man. Moreover, my list clearly reveals my class privilege. My relationship to patriarchy is thus not the same as that of a working-class black male. In constructing a list of male privilege, then, one has to be careful not to universalize manhood, not to present it as a "cohesive identity"[25] in ways that deny, obscure, or threaten the recognition of male multiplicity.

However, even taking male multiplicity into account, the preceding list of male advantages does not go far enough. The foregoing items do not directly address what one might call "male patriarchal agency"—the extent to which men make choices that entrench men's advantages and women's disadvantages. Some of the privileges I have identified are the products of the cumulative choices that men make every day in their personal and professional lives. The identification of privileges, then, is not enough. Resistance is also necessary, an issue I engage in the conclusion to this essay.

HETEROSEXUAL PRIVILEGES

Like maleness, heterosexuality should be critically examined. Like maleness, heterosexuality operates as an identity norm, the "what is" or "what is supposed to be" of sexuality. This is illustrated, for example, by the nature versus nurture debate. The question about the cause of sexuality is almost always formulated in terms of whether homosexuality is or is not biologically determined rather than whether sexual orientation, which includes heterosexuality, is or is not biologically determined. Scientists are searching for a gay, not a heterosexual or sexual orientation, gene. Like female identity, then, homosexuality signifies "difference"—more specifically, sexual identity distinctiveness. The normativity of heterosexuality requires that homosexuality be specified, pointed out. Heterosexuality is always already presumed.

Heterosexuals should challenge the normativity and normalization of heterosexuality. They should challenge the heterosexual presumption. But heterosexuals might be reluctant to do so to the extent that they perceive such challenges to call into question their (hetero)sexual orientation. As Lee Edelman observes in a related context, there "is a deeply rooted concern on the part of . . . heterosexual males about the possible meanings of [men subverting gender roles]."[26] According to Edelman, heterosexual men consider certain gender role inversions to be potentially dangerous because they portend not only a "[male] feminization that would destabilize or question gender" but also a "feminization that would challenge one's (hetero)sexuality."[27] Edelman's observations suggest that straight men may want to preserve what I am calling the "heterosexual presumption." Their investment in this presumption is less a function of what heterosexuality signifies in a positive sense and more a function of what it signifies in the negative—*not* being homosexual.

And there are racial dimensions to male investment in heterosexuality. For example, straight black male strategies to avoid homosexual suspicion could relate to the racial aspects of male privileges: heterosexual privilege is one of the few privileges that some black men have. These black men may want to take comfort in the fact that whatever else is going on in their lives, they are not, finally, "sissies," "punks," "faggots." By this I do not mean to suggest that black male heterosexuality has the normative standing of white male heterosexuality. It does not. Straight black men continue to be perceived as heterosexually deviant (overly sexual; potential rapists) and heterosexually irresponsible (jobless fathers of children out of wedlock). Still, black male heterosexuality is closer to white male heterosexual normalcy and normativity than is black gay sexuality. Consequently, some straight (or closeted) black men will want to avoid the "black gay [male] . . . triple negation" to which Marlon Riggs refers in the following quote: "Because of my sexuality I cannot be Black. A strong, proud, 'Afrocentric' black man is resolutely heterosexual, not even bisexual. . . . Hence I remain a sissy, punk, faggot. I cannot be a black gay man because, by the tenets of black macho, a black gay man is a triple negation."[28]

Assuming away the heterosexual presumption problem, assuming, in other words, that heterosexuals are willing to destabilize heterosexual normalcy by exposing their heterosexual privileges—that is, "coming out" as heterosexuals—do we want them to do so? Do heterosexuals reinforce heterosexual normativity when they come out? At first blush, the answer seems obvious: no. The notion would be that the more heterosexuals explicitly invoke their heterosexuality and "come out" as heterosexuals, the less it operates as an unstated norm. Yet, there are reasons to be concerned about heterosexuals "coming out."

These reasons are unrelated to concerns about whether individual acts of heterosexual signification undermine political efforts to establish a privacy norm around (homo)sexuality. The privacy norm argument would go something like the following: to the extent that heterosexuals are "closeted" (i.e., private) about their (hetero)sexuality, they help to send a message that (homo)sexuality is a private matter and should be irrelevant to social and political decision-making.

I am not persuaded by this sexual identity privacy argument. It is analogous to race-neutrality arguments: not invoking race, ignoring race, keeping race "private," helps to delegitimize the invidious employment of race as a relevant social category. However, keeping race private, removing race from public discourses, further entrenches racism. The social realities of race derive in part from the fact that race is always already public—a status marker of difference. Race continues to matter. Therefore, we ought to talk about it—and publicly. Avoiding public discussions about sexuality is not a sensible way to address the social realities of homophobia. Sexuality matters. Thus, we ought to have public discussions about why and how it matters. We have to deal publicly with sexuality before we can get beyond it.

My concerns about heterosexuals "coming out" relate to the social meaning of that act. Individual acts of heterosexual signification contribute to the growing tendency on the part of people who are not gay or lesbian to employ the term "coming out" to reveal some usually uncontroversial or safe aspect of their personhood. Nowadays, people are "coming out" as chocolate addicts, as yuppies, as soap opera viewers, and even as Trekkies. Sometimes the "outing" is more political: "I 'out' myself as a conservative," I heard someone say recently. This appropriation and redeployment of the term is problematic to the extent that it obscures the economic, psychological, and physical harms that potentially attend the gay and lesbian coming out (or outing) process. Although context would clearly matter, there is usually little, if any, vulnerability to "coming out" as a conservative, as a yuppie, as a Trekkie, etc. Nor is there usually any vulnerability to "coming out" as a heterosexual. The assertion of heterosexuality, without something more, merely reauthenticates heterosexual normalcy.[29]

Yet, more and more heterosexuals are "coming out," and often with good intentions. This "coming out" is performed explicitly and implicitly—affirmatively and by negation. Consider, for example, the way Houston Baker comes out in a panel discussion about gender, sexuality, and black images: "I am not gay, but I have many gay friends."[30] When asked about his decision to reveal his sexual identity in the negative (Baker did not say, " 'I am a heterosexual,' but 'I am not gay' "), Baker responds that in thinking about our identities, "You decide what you are not, rather than leaping out of the womb saying, 'I am this.' "[31]

....

The questions about whether Baker should have "come out" as a heterosexual in the affirmative or the negative obscures the fact that it is the "coming out" itself that is potentially problematic. As Bruce Ryder points out, "heterosexual men taking gay or lesbian positions must continually deal with the question of whether or not to reveal their heterosexuality." On the one hand, self-identifying as a heterosexual is a way to position oneself within a discourse so as not to create the (mis)impression of gay authenticity. Moreover, revealing one's heterosexuality can help to convey the idea that "heterosexism should be as much an issue for straight people as racism should be for white people."[32] On the other hand, "coming out" as a heterosexual can be a heteronormative move to avoid gay and lesbian stigmatization. It can function not simply as a denial of same-sex desire but to preempt the attribution of certain stereotypes to one's sexual identity. The assertion of heterosexuality, stated differently, is (functionally, if not intentionally) both an affirmative and a negative assertion about sexual preferences ("I sleep with persons of the opposite, not the same, sex") and about the normalcy of one's sexual relationships ("therefore I am normal, not abnormal").

Keith Boykin, former director of the Black Gay and Lesbian Leadership Forum, maintains that "heterosexual sexual orientation has become so ingrained in our social custom, so destigmatized of our fears about sex, that we often fail to make any connection between heterosexuality and sex."[33] Boykin is only half right. The socially constructed normalcy of heterosexuality is not due solely to the desexualization of heterosexuality in mainstream political and popular culture. It is due also to the sexualization of heterosexuality as normative and to the gender-norm presumptions about heterosexuality—that it is the normal way sexually to express one's gender.[34]

Moreover, it is not simply that homosexuality is sexed that motivates or stimulates homophobic fears about gay and lesbian relationships. These fears also relate to the fact that homosexuality is stigmatized and is perceived to be an abnormal way sexually to express one's gender.[35] The disparate social meanings that attach to gay and lesbian identities on the one hand and straight identities on the other make individual acts of heterosexual signification a cause for concern.

Recently, I participated in a workshop where one of the presenters "came out" as a heterosexual in the context of giving his talk. This sexual identity disclosure engendered a certain amount of whispering in the back row. Up until that moment, I think many people had assumed the presenter was gay.

After all, he was sitting on a panel discussing sexual orientation and had participated in the Gay and Lesbian section of the American Association of Law Schools. There were three other heterosexuals on the panel, but everyone knew they were not gay because everyone *knew* them; they had all been in teaching for a while, two were very senior, and everyone knew of their spouses or partners. Everyone also knew that there was a lesbian on the panel. She, too, had been in teaching for some time and had been out for many years. Apparently, few of the workshop participants knew very much about the presenter who "came out." Because "there is a widespread assumption in both gay and straight communities that any man who says something supportive about issues of concern to lesbian or gay communities must be gay himself,"[36] there was, at the very least, a question about his sexuality. Whatever his intentions were for "coming out," whatever his motivations, his assertion of heterosexuality removed the question.

And it is the politics behind the removal of the question—the politics of sexual identity signification—that we should be concerned about. Is it an act of resistance or does it reflect an acquiescence to existing sexual identity social meanings? Consider, for example, the television situation comedy *Spin City*, in which Michael Boatman played the role of Carter Heywood, an openly gay black male character. Boatman is clearly very comfortable with the role and is "believably gay"—perhaps, for some, "too believably gay." Thus, in an article in *Essence* about Boatman we learn rather quickly that Boatman is not in fact a gay man—he just plays one on television. We learn, too, that it was not Heywood's sexuality that attracted Boatman to the role (he had not set out to play a gay man), but rather Heywood's career. The relevant text reads: "It was Heywood's job description (a civil rights attorney who joins the mayor's office) rather than his sexuality that attracted the 32-year-old actor to the groundbreaking sitcom. 'We've been exposed to the stereotype of swishy gay men,' explains the *happily married* acting veteran."[37] The text thus removes the question about Boatman's (homo)sexuality.

I became sensitized to the politics of heterosexuals "coming out" in the context of reading about James Baldwin. Try to find a piece written about Baldwin and count the number of lines before the author comes out as heterosexual. Usually, it is not more than a couple of paragraphs, so the game ends fast. The following introduction from a 1994 essay about Baldwin is one example of what I am talking about: "The last time I saw James Baldwin was late autumn of 1985, when my wife and I attended a sumptuous book party."[38]

....

In this case, the game ends immediately. Independent of any question of intentionality on the author's part, the mention of the wife functions as an identity signifier to subtextually "out" his heterosexuality. We *read* "wife," we *think* heterosexual. My point here is not to suggest that the essay's overall tone is heterosexually defensive; I simply find it suspicious when heterosexuals speak of their spouses so quickly (in this case the very first sentence of the essay) when a subject (a topic or a personality—here, James Baldwin) implicates homosexuality.

There is no point wondering what the author was "doing" with Baldwin in Paris. The game is over. The possibility of a gay subtextual reading of the text vis-á-vis the author's relationship with Baldwin and/or the author's sexual identity is rendered untenable by the rhetorical deployment of the "wife." Her presence in the text operates not only to signify and authenticate the author's heterosexual subject position but also to signify and functionally (if not intentionally) stigmatize Baldwin's gay subject position. The author engages in what I call "the politics of the 3Ds"—disassociation, disidentification, and differentiation. The author is "different" from Baldwin (the author sleeps with women), and this difference, based as it is on sexual identity, compels the author to disassociate himself from and disidentify with that which makes Baldwin "different" (Baldwin sleeps with men).

Heterosexual significations need not always reflect the politics of the 3Ds. In other words, the possibility exists for heterosexuals to point out their heterosexuality without reauthenticating heterosexuality. Consider, for example, the heterosexual privilege list that I give below. While each item on the list explicitly names—outs—heterosexuality, in none of the items does heterosexuality remain unproblematically normative.

As a prelude to the list, I should be clear that the list is incomplete. Nor do the privileges reflected in it represent the experiences of all heterosexuals. As Bruce Ryder observes: "Male heterosexual privilege has different effects on men of, for example, different races and classes. . . . In our society, the dominant or 'hegemonic' form of masculinity to which other masculinities are subordinated is white, middleclass, and heterosexual. This means that the heterosexual privilege of, say, straight black men takes a very different shape in their lives than it does for straight white men."[39] My goal in presenting this list, then, is not to represent every heterosexual man. Instead, the purpose is to intervene in the normalization of heterosexual privileges. With this intervention, I hope to challenge the pervasive tendency of heterosexuals to see homophobia as something that puts others at a disadvantage and not something that actually advantages them.

Heterosexual Privileges: A List

1. Whether on television or in the movies, (white) heterosexuality is always affirmed as healthy and/or normal (black heterosexuality and family arrangements are still, to some degree, perceived to be deviant).

2. Without making a special effort, heterosexuals are surrounded by other heterosexuals every day.

3. A husband and wife can comfortably express affection in any social setting, even a predominantly gay one.

4. The children of a heterosexual couple will not have to explain why their parents have different genders—that is, why they have a mummy and a daddy.

5. (White) Heterosexuals are not blamed for creating and spreading the AIDS virus (though Africans—as a collective group—are blamed).

6. Heterosexuals do not have to worry about people trying to "cure" their sexual orientation (though black people have to worry about people trying to "cure" black "racial pathologies").

7. Black heterosexual males did not have to worry about whether they would be accepted at the Million Man March.

8. Rarely, if ever, will a doctor, on learning that her patient is heterosexual, inquire as to whether the patient has ever taken an AIDS test and if so, how recently.

9. Medical service will never be denied to heterosexuals because they are heterosexuals (though medical services may not be recommended to black people because they are black).

10. Friends of heterosexuals generally do not refer to heterosexuals as their "straight friends" (though nonblack people often to refer to black people as their "black friends").

11. A heterosexual couple can enter a restaurant on their anniversary and be fairly confident that staff and fellow diners will warmly congratulate them if an announcement is made (though the extent of the congratulation and the nature of the welcome might depend on the racial identities of the couple).

12. White heterosexuals do not have to worry about whether a fictional

film villain who is heterosexual will reflect negatively on their heterosexuality (though blacks may always have to worry about their racial representation in films).

13. Heterosexuals are entitled to legal recognition of their marriages throughout the United States and the world.

14. Within the black community, black male heterosexuality does not engender comments like "what a waste," "there goes another good black man," or "if they're not in jail, they're faggots."

15. Heterosexuals can take jobs with most companies without worrying about whether their spouses will be included in the benefits package.

16. Child molestation by heterosexuals does not confirm the deviance of heterosexuality (though if the alleged molester is black, the alleged molestation becomes evidence of the deviance of black [hetero]sexuality).

17. Black rap artists do not make songs suggesting that heterosexuals should be shot or beaten up because they are heterosexuals.

18. Black male heterosexuality does not undermine a black heterosexual male's ability to be a role model for black boys.

19. Heterosexuals can join the military without concealing their sexual identity.

20. Children will be taught in school, explicitly or implicitly, about the naturalness of heterosexuality (they will also be taught to internalize the notion of white normativity).

21. Conversations on black liberation will always include concerns about heterosexual men.

22. Heterosexuals can adopt children without being perceived as selfish and without anyone questioning their motives.

23. Heterosexuals are not denied custody or visitation rights of their children because they are heterosexuals.

24. Heterosexual men are welcomed as leaders of Boy Scout troops.

25. Heterosexuals can visit their parents and family as who they are, and take their spouses, partners, or dates with them to family functions.

26. Heterosexuals can talk matter-of-factly about their relationships with their partners without people commenting that they are "flaunting" their sexuality.

27. A black heterosexual couple would be welcomed as members of any black church.

28. Heterosexual couples do not have to worry about whether kissing each other in public or holding hands in public will render them vulnerable to violence.

29. Heterosexuals do not have to struggle with "coming out" or worry about being "outed."

30. The parents of heterosexuals do not love them "in spite of" their sexual orientation, and parents do not blame themselves for their children's heterosexuality.

31. Heterosexuality is affirmed in most religious traditions.

32. Heterosexuals can introduce their spouses to colleagues and not worry about whether the decision will have a detrimental impact on their careers.

33. A black heterosexual male does not have to choose between being black and being heterosexual.

34. Heterosexuals can prominently display their spouses' photographs at work without causing office gossip or hostility.

35. (White) heterosexuals do not have to worry about "positively" representing heterosexuality.

36. Few will take pity on a heterosexual on hearing that she is straight, or feel the need to say, "That's okay" (though it is not uncommon for a black person to hear, "It's okay that you're black" or "We don't care that you're black" or "When we look at you, we don't see a black person").

37. (Male) heterosexuality is not considered to be symptomatic of the "pathology" of the black family.

38. Heterosexuality is never mistaken as the only aspect of one's lifestyle, but is perceived instead as merely one more component of one's personal identity.

39. (White) heterosexuals do not have to worry over the impact their sexuality will have personally on their children's lives, particularly as it relates to their social lives (though black families of all identity configurations do have to worry about how race and racism will affect their children's well-being).

40. Heterosexuals do not have to worry about being "bashed" after leaving a social event with other heterosexuals (though black people of all sexual orientations do have to worry about being "racially bashed" on any given day).

41. Every day is (white) "Heterosexual Pride Day."

I have argued that one of the ways to contest gender and sexual orientation hierarchy is for heterosexual men to detail their social experiences on the privileged side of gender and sexual orientation. In advancing this argument, I do not mean to suggest that the role of these men is to legitimize "untrustworthy" and "self-interested" victim-centered accounts of discrimination. There is a tendency on the part of dominant groups (e.g., males and heterosexuals) to discount the experiences of subordinate groups (e.g., straight women, lesbians, and gays) unless those experiences are authenticated or legitimized by a member of the dominant group. For example, it is one thing for me, a black man, to say I experienced discrimination in a particular social setting; it is quite another for my white male colleague to say he witnessed that discrimination. My telling of the story is suspect because I am black (racially interested). My white colleague's telling of the story is not suspect because he is white (racially disinterested). The racial transparency of whiteness—its "perspectivelessness"[40]—renders my colleague's account "objective."[41]

The problem of racial status (in)credibility is quite real. Consider how Cornel West alludes to it in the following anecdote about his inability to get a cab in New York City:

> After the ninth taxi refused me, my blood began to boil. The tenth taxi refused me and stopped for a kind, well-dressed, smiling female fellow citizen of European descent. As she stepped in the cab, she said, "This is really ridiculous, is it not?"
>
> Ugly racial memories of the past flashed through my mind. Years ago, while driving from New York to teach at Williams College, I was stopped on fake charges of trafficking cocaine. When I told the police officer I was a professor of religion, he replied, "Yeh, and I'm the Flying Nun. Let's go, nigger!" I was stopped three times in my first ten days in Princeton for driving too slowly on a residential street with a speed limit of twenty-five miles per hour. . . . Needless to say, these incidents are dwarfed by those like Rodney King's beating. . . . Yet the memories cut like a merciless knife at my soul as I waited on that godforsaken corner. Finally I decided to take the subway. I walked three long avenues, arrived late, and had to catch my moral breath as I approached [my appointment with] the white male photographer and white female

cover designer. I chose not to dwell on this everyday experience of black New Yorkers. And we had a good time talking, posing, and taking pictures.[42]

Here West is connecting two problematic episodes. His racial representations of these episodes reflect concerns about his racial credibility. His narrative suggests that he is worried about how his readers will read him (is he a trustworthy witness?) and thus *read* the events he describes (do they reflect racism?). West understands that he is (or, rather, will be constructed as) an unreliable witness to his own racial victimization. That is, he is fully aware that as a black man his racial story (like his racial identity) is suspect. Thus, he rhetorically deploys a "disinterested" witness to legitimize and authenticate his racial narrative—the woman "of European descent." She can be trusted. She is white and respectable—"well-dressed" and "smiling." To the extent that she confirms West's racial interpretation of the cab story—"This is really ridiculous, is it not?"—the notion is forwarded that West is not racially imagining things; in fact, his race is interfering with his ability to get a cab. The employment of whiteness to racially authenticate West's first story renders West's second story (in which West is called a "nigger") more believable.[43]

Men invested in exposing their privileges should be careful not to replicate the kind of authentication strategy reflected in West's anecdote. They should not perform the legitimation function that the white woman's challenge to racism performs in West's text. To the extent that male heterosexuals participate in discourses on gender and sexuality, they should not create the (mis)impression that, because they do not experience the subordinating effects of patriarchy and heterosexism, their critiques of patriarchy and/or heterosexism are more valid and less suspect than the critiques propounded by lesbians, straight women, and gay men.

Assuming that the identification/listing of privileges methodology I have described avoids the problem of authentication, one still might wonder whether the project is sufficiently radical to dismantle gender and sexual orientation hierarchies. Certainly the lists I have presented do not go far enough. They represent the very early stages in a more complicated process to end gender and sexual orientation discrimination.

The lists, nevertheless, are politically valuable.[44] For one thing, the items on the lists reveal that men enforce and maintain their gender privileges through the personal actions they take and do not take every day. For another, to the extent that the lists focus our attention on privileges, they invite men to think about the extent to which they are unjustly enriched because of certain aspects of their identities.

To be sure, men will not be eager to learn or quick to accept the notion that they are unjustly enriched. The realization and acknowledgment of unjust enrichment carries with it the possibility of disgorgement. However, to the extent that men actually come to see their privileges as forms of unjust enrichment (and the lists help men do precisely that), they are more likely to take notice of the ways in which unjust enrichment operates systemically.

None of this is to say that awareness and acknowledgement of privilege is enough. Resistance is needed as well. But how does one resist? And what counts as resistance? With respect to marriage, for example, does resistance to heterosexual privilege require heterosexuals to refrain from getting married and/or attending weddings? It might mean both of those things. At the very least, resistance to identity privilege would seem to require "critical acquiescence": criticizing, if not rejecting, aspects of our life that are directly linked to our privilege. A heterosexual who gets married and/or attends weddings but who also openly challenges the idea that marriage is a heterosexual entitlement is engaging in critical acquiescence.

In the end, critical acquiescence might not go far enough. It might even be a cop out. Still, it is a useful and politically manageable place to begin.

NOTES

1. See *Washington v. Davis,* 426 U.S. 229, 246–48 (1976) (requiring a showing of discriminatory intent to establish an equal protection claim). For two classic critiques of the standard, see Alan D. Freeman, "Legitimizing Racial Discrimination through Antidiscrimination Law: A Critical Review of Supreme Court Doctrine," *Minnesota Law Review* 62 (1978): 1049; and Charles R. Lawrence III, "The Id, the Ego, and Equal Protection: Reckoning with Unconscious Racism," *Stanford Law Review* 39 (1987): 317.

2. See Stephanie Wildman, *Privilege Revealed: How Invisible Preference Undermines America* (New York: New York University Press, 1996).

3. See Karen D. Pyke, "Class-Based Masculinities: The Interdependence of Gender, Class, and Interpersonal Power," *Gender and Society* 10 (1996): 527 ("Conventional theoretical perspectives on power . . . view micro level power practices as simply derivative of macrostructural inequalities and overlook how power in day-to-day interactions shapes broader structures of inequality").

4. See Wildman, *Privilege Revealed.*

5. See Peggy McIntosh, "White Privilege and Male Privilege: A Personal Account

of Coming to See Correspondences through Work in Women's Studies," in *Power, Privilege and Law: A Civil Rights Reader,* ed. Leslie Bender and Daar Braveman (St. Paul, Minn.: West Publishing, 1995), 22.

6. See Judith Butler, *Gender Trouble: Feminism and the Subversion of Identity* (New York: Routledge, 1990): 136–39 (describing the performative aspect of gender); see also Devon W. Carbado and Mitu Gulati, "Working Identity," *Cornell Law Review* 85 (2000): 1259 (discussing identity performance as a function of a strategic response to specific institutional norms).

7. See Judith Butler, "Performative Acts and Gender Constitution: An Essay in Phenomenology and Feminist Theory," *Theater Journal* 40 (1988): 519, 523 ("The body becomes its gender through a series of acts which are renewed, revised and consolidated through time"). But see Bruce Wilshire, *Role Playing and Identity: The Limits of Theatre as Metaphor* (Bloomington: Indiana University Press, 1982) (arguing that gender is not a performance).

8. For a discussion of the concept of false necessity in legal theory, see Roberto M. Unger, *False Necessity: Anti-Necessitarian Social Theory in the Service of Radical Democracy* (New York: Cambridge University Press, 1987).

9. See Carbado and Gulati, "Working Identity" (arguing that people work their identities to avoid discrimination).

10. See Brent Staples, "Parallel Time," in *Brotherman: The Odyssey of Black Men in America,* ed. Herb Boyd and Robert L. Allen (New York: One World, 1995) (discussing the author's attempts to appear harmless while walking at night by whistling Vivaldi).

11. See Carbado and Gulati, "Working Identity" (discussing the costs and burdens of working one's identity).

12. Ibid. (arguing that working one's identity is work); see also Elizabeth V. Spelman, " 'Race' and the Labor of Identity," in *Racism and Philosophy,* ed. Susan E. Babbitt and Sue Campbell (Ithaca: Cornell University Press, 1999), 202–15.

13. See Barbara Flagg, "Was Blind, But Now I See: White Race Consciousness and the Requirement Of Discriminatory Intent," *Michigan Law Review* 91 (1994): 953, 963; McIntosh, "White Privilege and Male Privilege."

14. Flagg, "Was Blind, But Now I See," 963, 957.

15. Ibid., 970–71.

16. Ibid., 957.

17. McIntosh, "White Privilege and Male Privilege," 23.

18. See ibid., 25–26. See also bell hooks, *Feminist Theory: From Margin to Center* (Boston: South End Press, 1984), 54–55 (interrogating whiteness).

19. McIntosh, "White Privilege and Male Privilege," 6, 23.

20. Of course, not all men are empowered by patriarchy in the same way. Race, class, and sexual orientation shape the nature of men's relationships to patriarchal privilege. Perhaps it is more accurate to say, then, that patriarchy gives to (some) men (more than others) what it takes away from (some) women (more than others); the

disempowerment of (some) women (more than others) is achieved through the empowerment of (some) men (more than others). See Pyke, "Class-Based Masculinities," 527, 531 ("The effects *of* gender on interpersonal power relations are not one-dimensional. Hierarchies *of* social class, race, and sexuality provide additional layers of complication. They form the structural and cultural contexts in which gender is enacted in everyday life, thereby fragmenting gender into multiple masculinities and femininities").

21. See Simone Beauvoir, *The Second Sex* (New York: Knopf, 1957 [1949]).

22. Here, too, my comments about race, class, and sexual orientation pertain.

23. Andrea Dworkin and Catharine Mackinnon, *Pornography and Civil Rights: A New Day for Women's Equality* (Minneapolis: Organizing against Pornography, 1988), 22–23.

24. McIntosh, "White Privilege and Male Privilege," 23.

25. See, e.g., Robert Vorlicky, "(In)visible Alliances: Conflicting 'Chronicles' of Feminism," in *Engendering Men: The Question of Male Feminist Criticism,* ed. Joseph A. Boone and Michael Cadden (New York: Routledge, 1990), 275–76 (discussing universal manhood in the context of women's outrage toward men for the gang rape of a New York jogger).

26. Lee Edelman, "Redeeming the Phallus: Wallace Stevens, Frank Lentricchia, and the Politics of (Hetero)sexuality," in *Engendering Men: The Question of Male Feminist Criticism,* ed. Joseph A. Boone and Michael Cadden (New York: Routledge, 1990), 50.

27. Ibid.

28. Marlon T. Riggs, "Black Macho Revisited: Reflections of a SNAP! Queen," in *Black Men on Race, Gender, and Sexuality: A Critical Reader,* ed. Devon W. Carbado (New York: New York University Press, 1999), 307.

29. In some sense, heterosexuals are out all the time, kissing comfortably in public, sharing wedding pictures at work, announcing anniversaries, etc. These are not the practices I am referring to when I suggest that perhaps heterosexuals should develop a practice of "coming out." For none of the foregoing heterosexual significations challenge the socially constructed normalcy of heterosexuality. Further along in this essay, I provide an indication of how heterosexuals *might* be able to assert their heterosexuality without further entrenching heterosexual normalcy.

30. Houston A. Baker Jr., " 'You Cain't Trus' It': Experts Witnessing in the Case of Rap," in *Black Popular Culture,* ed. Gina Dent (Seattle: Bay Press, 1992), 132.

31. Ibid.

32. Bruce Ryder, "Straight Talk: Male Heterosexual Privilege," *Queen's Law Journal* 16 (1991): 303.

33. Keith Boykin, *One More River to Cross: Black and Gay in America* (New York: Doubleday, 1997).

34. See Francisco Valdes, "Queers, Sissies, Dykes, and Tomboys: Deconstructing

the Conflation of 'Sex,' 'Gender,' and 'Sexual Orientation' in Euro-American Law and Society," *California Law Review* 83 (1995): 1.

35. See ibid. See also Sylvia A. Law, "Homosexuality and the Social Meaning of Gender," *Wisconsin Law Review* (1998): 187 ("Disapprobation of homosexual behavior is a reaction to the violation of gender norms, rather than simply scorn for the violation of norms of sexual behaviors."); and Elvia R. Arriola, "Gendered Inequality: Lesbians, Gays, and Feminist Legal Theory," *Berkeley Women's Law Journal* 9 (1994): 103, 122 (observing that gay identities are often theoretically connected to gender).

36. Ryder, "Straight Talk: Male Heterosexual Privilege," 303.

37. Michael Boatman, "Acting 'Out,'" *Essence*, September 1997, 78 (emphasis added).

38. Leon Forrest, "Evidences of Jimmy Baldwin," in *Relocations of the Spirit*, ed. Leon Forrest (Emeryville, Calif.: Asphodel Press/Moyer Bell, 1994), 267.

39. Ryder, "Straight Talk: Male Heterosexual Privilege," 292.

40. See Kimberlé Williams Crenshaw, "Foreword: Toward a Race-Conscious Pedagogy in Legal Education," *Southern California Review of Law and Women's Studies* 4 (fall 1994): 33, 35 (employing the term "perspectivelessness" to describe the ostensibly race-neutral way in which law is taught).

41. Peter Halewood comments on this problem from a white heterosexual male perspective: "Because I am white and male, the Article is more likely to be accepted (or ignored) by colleagues as a scholarly application of scholarly ideas than it would be if written by a black female professor. A black female author of this piece would probably encounter more skepticism about the method, claims, and motives of the article and would probably be viewed, at least by some, as being oversensitive and making trouble for her mostly white and male colleagues" (Halewood, "White Men Can't Jump: Critical Epistemologies, Embodiment, and the Praxis of Legal Scholarship," *Yale Journal of Law and Feminism* 7 [1995]: 1, 6 n.14). To avoid *contributing* to this authentication of whiteness and delegitimation of blackness, Halewood argues that "rather than approaching the subject of law and subordination as neutral, theoretical experts or as political vanguardists, white male legal academics must recognize the legitimacy—even the superiority—of certain 'outsider' perspectives on these issues, and assume the role of secondary contributors to the development of scholarship in these areas" (7).

42. Cornel West, *Race Matters* (Boston: Beacon, 1994), xv–xvi.

43. For a very thoughtful discussion of the role of race in Cornel West's scholarship and especially in his popular book, *Race Matters,* see Dwight A. McBride, "Transdisciplinary Intellectual Practice: Cornel West and the Rhetoric of Race Transcending," *Harvard BlackLetter Journal* 11 (1994): 157–82.

44. See McIntosh, "White Privilege and Male Privilege."

KARA KEELING

"JOINING THE LESBIANS":
CINEMATIC REGIMES OF BLACK
LESBIAN VISIBILITY

The set of film texts and discourses that comprise, enable, sustain, and react to the emergent "black lesbian and gay film" movement can provide an occasion for a critical engagement with the very regime of visibility within which "black lesbian and gay film" achieves its coherence as a category. This critical engagement might provide a more nuanced and viable vocabulary through which to construct and discuss "black lesbian film" (the set of films and the scholarly and fan texts produced about them that are recognizable as "black lesbian") than that currently accessible in the commonly deployed binary oppositions between "visibility" and "invisibility," "giving voice" and "silence." In other words, the existence of a set of films identifiable as "black lesbian films," however loosely or strictly defined, provides an opportunity to engage critically with the nexus of forces that produce the need for "black lesbian film" as yet another term in the late-capitalist logic of product differentiation and target markets. This genre of films also reproduces "black lesbian" as a category that secures the logic of the post–Cold War multicultural state even as it indexes some of that which challenges such logic.

In a well-known essay "New Ethnicities," Stuart Hall identifies and characterizes a shift within the general strategies of black cultural politics. This shift, according to Hall, "is best thought of in terms of a change from a struggle over the relations of representation to a politics of representation itself."[1] What Hall refers to as the "relations of representation" involved a struggle on the part of black British cultural workers to "come into representation," to make themselves visible and vocal as black (British) subjects in ways that contest and counter "the marginality, the stereotypical quality and the fetishized nature of images of blacks" by providing what those cultural workers considered to be "positive" alternatives to that imagery. The idea of the relations of representation as Hall describes it thus involved a critique of existing images and notions of blackness. In the shift to a "politics of representation," the "relations of representation" was not replaced so much as it was redeployed and intensified. The "politics of representation" to which Hall refers can be understood, therefore, as a cultural strategy predicated on the criticism of existing "representations of blackness," including, importantly, even those "positive" images produced as counters to stereotypical and "negative" images of blackness.

Hall points out that the politics of representation, particularly in the black British culture about which he was writing, but also as it emerged in the United States, can be understood as the "effect of a theoretical encounter between black cultural politics and the discourses of a Eurocentric, largely white, critical cultural theory which in recent years has focused so much analysis on the politics of representation."[2] One of the most salient and far-reaching effects of this encounter is what Hall identified as "the end of the innocent notion of the essential black subject." Without an essential black subject with which to ground a politics or lodge a critique of existing representations (or of perceptible absences from the mechanisms of representation), one is, as Hall points out, "plunged headlong into the maelstrom of a continuously contingent, unguaranteed, political argument and debate: a critical politics, a politics of criticism."[3]

Significantly, in order to illustrate the shift he was characterizing, Hall points to films, stating, "to me, films like *Territories, Passion of Remembrance, My Beautiful Laundrette* and *Sammy and Rosie Get Laid*, for example, make it perfectly clear that . . . the question of the black subject cannot be represented without reference to the dimensions of class, gender, sexuality and ethnicity."[4] Within the context of U.S. cultural politics, both the creation and the scholarly analysis of "black lesbian and gay" film and video have emerged out of an encounter between black cultural politics and the discourses and practices of a visibly white "lesbian and gay" (and, later, "queer") social and political movement that now includes as one of its tentacles the theoretical innovations known as "queer theory."[5]

Hall's claim that the theoretical encounter between "black cultural politics" and "the discourses of a Eurocentric, largely white, critical cultural theory" is "always an extremely difficult, if not dangerous, encounter"[6] provides an initial context for a discussion of "black lesbian and gay film" produced within a U.S. context. A part of the difficulty of that encounter,

. . . .

while casting suspicion on the very terms within which the encounter is perceived as "dangerous," "black lesbian and gay film" was not "innocently" conceived as an essentialized category and subsequently corrupted by its contact with white queer practices, including queer theory, into an ambivalent, destabilizing and unstable force of identification and desire that results in a critical politics; rather, it was born that way.[7]

It is precisely at the nexus between the two representational strategies that Hall describes—the spatio-temporal point at which the "relations of representation" shifts toward the "politics of representation"—that "black queer film" is born within U.S. culture. The emergence of "black lesbian and gay film" in the United States can be understood as itself a critique both of the notion of an essential black ethico-political subject and of the construction of an undifferentiated "lesbian and gay" collectivity. "Black lesbian and gay film" critiques existing constructions of black subjectivity and of lesbian and gay subjectivity simultaneously.

"NOW WE THINK AS WE FUCK":[8] AN ANTIDOTE TO INNOCENT NOTIONS

In an essay published in 1993, Michelle Parkerson announced "the birth of a notion," the emergence of "a new generation of gay and lesbian filmmakers of color" that "has begun to produce imagery countering" the "invisibility and social stigma" characteristic of existing "images of black lesbians and gay men."[9] Parkerson described her newborn subject, perceptible in the latest wave of black lesbian and gay filmmaking, according to the critical terms available to her, those describing the "silence," "invisibility," and "stereotyping" of "black lesbians and gay men." Within this context, it has been said that the "new generation of gay and lesbian filmmakers of color" (a cultural movement for which Parkerson's own cinematic work helped to forge a path) counters the existing stereotypes and breaks the silences that have characterized "black lesbian and gay" representation and existence prior to that generation's hard-earned access to film and video making.

Rigorously interrogating "established modes of looking," Marlon Riggs's foundational and influential film *Tongues Untied* (1989)—a film that touches on most of the central preoccupations evident in the recent wave of black lesbian and gay filmmaking in the United States—dealt a blow to the black subject(s) it inherited, subject(s) constructed in and through the assimilationist politics of the Civil Rights movement and the nationalism of the Black Power movement, by challenging its viewers to see "black male bodies" differently (and, as David Van Leer points out, by focusing on "the tension between seeing and knowing.")[10] Riggs's work presents expressions of blackness that are inconsistent with those "official" representations of black subjectivity that insist that "black" is essentially macho, masculine, heterosexual, and ultimately, amenable to functioning smoothly as part of the moral fabric of a nation held together in large part by the ties that bind the nuclear family. In this way, Riggs's work throws into question the regime of truth that authorizes "official" conceptions of blackness.

If Riggs's *Tongues Untied* ruminates on a range of issues and concerns with which "black lesbian and gay film" continues to engage, then it is clear that, like *Tongues Untied*, "black lesbian and gay film" itself emerges as a force pushing black American cultural politics toward a "politics of representation" and away from a reliance on the relations of representation wherein black is necessarily beautiful (as long as it conforms to the strictures imposed by the currently accepted notion of the essential black subject). In other words, "black lesbian and gay film" emerges as already caught within a critical politics in which any "innocent notion" of an essential black subject (or, as I indicate below, an essential "lesbian" or "gay" subject) is foreclosed.

As Riggs's critique in *Tongues Untied* of the absence of black gay men from the gay male social milieu in San Francisco's Castro District makes clear, "black lesbian and gay film" emerges also as a way of resisting the marginalization and the exclusion of black homosexuality and of black lesbians and black gay men within existing (white) U.S. lesbian and gay culture and politics. "Black lesbian and gay film" was born as itself "a politics of criticism," a cultural expression of a multiplicity or a multifarious "we" that renders identity itself problematic. Serving on the one hand as a critical force in attendance at the end of the "innocent notion of the essential black subject" and on the other hand as a term that stubbornly prevents (white) "lesbian and gay" cultural politics from comfortably proclaiming the innocent construction of their subject(s), many "black lesbian and gay" visual cultural practices eschew innocent notions and highlight instead their own intimacy with danger.

Riggs's films *Tongues Untied* and *Black Is, Black Ain't* and those films' commentators demonstrate that the category "black lesbian and gay" is wholly inside the construction of both "blackness" and "lesbian and gay." But, it also is part of what needs to be expunged vigilantly and repeatedly from "black" and from "gay" and "lesbian" in order to render each category artificially coherent and discrete. Yet, any separation of "black lesbian and gay" into two categories ("black" and "lesbian and/or gay") presumed to be autonomous can be effected only violently. This is a point that Essex Hemphill makes emphatically in *Tongues Untied* in response to the question, "come the final throw down, what is he first, 'black' or 'gay?' "—a homophobic query leveled against black gay men in the name of racial solidarity. Hemphill's admonition to other black gay men charging them to respond to that question emphasizes the violence with which the separation of "black" from "gay" is enacted: "You know the answer, the absurdity of that question. How can you sit in silence? How do you choose one eye over the other? This half of the brain over that? Or, in words this brother might understand; which does he value most? His left nut or his right? Tell him." "Black lesbian and gay film" collects the excesses unleashed each time "blackness" is wrenched violently from "lesbian" and/or "gay" and vice versa and makes what it collects visible as an expression of life that currently is recognizable as "black lesbian and gay," a collectively created expression fashioned to ensure its own survival and, hence, productive of its own excesses.[11]

While it clearly is the case that the emergence of a black lesbian and gay film movement, however underfinanced and small, puts into circulation images of black lesbian and gay existence that duel with stereotypes and untie tongues regarding the range of historical experiences to which the category "black lesbian and gay" lays claim, continuing to rely on a celebratory notion of visibility that is counterposed positively to a binary opposite ("invisibility") reduces the complicated critique inherent in "the birth of a notion" to an "innocent" insistence on "positive images." If, as Pratibha Parmar explains in an essay published in the same collection that includes Parkerson's observations discussed above, black lesbian and gay filmmakers and other queer filmmakers of color "do not speak from a position of marginalization but more crucially from the resistance to that marginalization,"[12] then the regimes of articulation and of visibility through which black lesbian and gay filmmakers speak and make visible various expressions of black lesbian and gay existence need to be rigorously interrogated so that the "resistance" that (in)forms the coming into representation of black lesbian and gay film and video makers does not settle into a comfortable complicity with the very forms of domination, oppression, and exploitation that the birth of "black lesbian and gay film" itself critiques.

One of the ways that the regimes of visibility in which images of black lesbian and gay expression might be interrogated is through attention to what those regimes dictate must be hidden in order for black lesbian and gay images to appear as such. If the regime of visibility that authorizes black lesbian and gay images to cohere and be recognizable as such is itself a product of those movements that have become victorious by conceding to aspects of the existing hegemonic constructions of race, gender, and sexuality, then that which remains hidden in or obscured by those images still might retain the capacity to further challenge the dominant hegemonies set in motion by a politics of representation now predicated on black lesbian and gay visibility.

Put another way, I am arguing here that the appearance of black lesbian and gay images is made possible through a regime of visibility that has conceded to currently hegemonic notions of "lesbian and gay sexuality" and to the primacy of binary and exclusive gender categories in the articulation of sexuality. The critical reception of those images has colluded with that regime by privileging the terrain of the visible. A black queer critical project that might intervene in the solidification of those dominant conceptions of black lesbian and gay sexuality—conceptions of sexuality whose main force is toward integration into existing paradigms of gender, race, and sexuality— involves interrogating that which has been hidden within or obscured by the processes of the production and consumption of those images. Such a critical project (which could be understood, following Roderick A. Ferguson's compelling conceptualization, as a "queer of color critique")[13] might be advanced in an effort to valorize what has been forgotten, sacrificed, or compromised in the struggle for hegemony waged on the terrain of the visible. If, as Walter Benjamin has argued so eloquently and influentially, history belongs to the victors, and if regimes of visibility are sites of historical struggles over dominant meanings and over what socio-political formations will garner legitimacy via representation, then a queer critical project interested in mining the terrain of the invisible might offer a way to direct the legacy of queer historical and theoretical projects toward assisting in the valorization of organizations of sexuality capable of sustaining forms of sociality that provide ways of transfiguring currently oppressive and exploitative relations.[14] I offer the following examination of Cheryl Dunye's film The Watermelon Woman as an example of a queer interpretative project that begins by interrogating the regime of visibility in which "black lesbian" appears and moves into a consideration of what that regime renders invisible in its efforts to produce the ethico-political subject "black lesbian."

Black lesbian film gained entry into the U.S. film industry's dominant marketing logics when Cheryl Dunye's 1996 feature film was picked up for distribution by First Run Features. While *The Watermelon Woman*'s success (as determined by its ability to find a distributor) indicates that transformations are taking place within the logic whereby audiences are consolidated and recognized as capable of valorizing cultural productions, it also highlights the extent to which previously innovative social formations are not immune to being used as vehicles through which socio-economic relations are able to remain more or less the same.

"WE CALLED THEM 'WOMEN-LOVERS' "; OR, SOME OF THE THINGS THAT ARE FORGOTTEN WHILE "THE WATERMELON WOMAN" IS "LIVING WITH PRIDE"[15]

Reframed within the context of a visual terrain that is the product of dominant historical processes and, hence, supportive of hegemonic relations in oftentimes contradictory ways, discussions of "black lesbian visibility" must take into consideration questions concerning what needs and interests are being furthered by the images that currently are recognizable as "black lesbian." To the extent that it retains from the images it designates as "black lesbian" only that which reproduces "black lesbian" as a recognizable category, "black lesbian film" produces its own excesses, tossing aside or failing to perceive in the image it designates as "black lesbian" that which does not reproduce the sense of "black lesbian" that "black lesbian film" currently needs for its survival as a generic designation and, in some cases, as a viable commodity. Yet, what "black lesbian film" often throws out of the image it designates as "black lesbian" includes precisely that which might challenge the logical connections that currently rationalize existing social relations, including some of those that support homophobia, classism, heterosexism, sexism, and racism.

Like the other texts that comprise "black lesbian film" and "black lesbian film culture," this essay constructs its object of analysis (in this case, "black lesbian film" itself) in order to enter into the "continuously contingent, unguaranteed, political argument and debate" that it claims is staged by that object. Itself a critical politics, "black lesbian film" participates in a political debate in which even the constitution of its set of referents (and, hence, of those whom "black lesbian film" claims to be representative) is not guaranteed by the terms of the debate. Each selection of what will be included in the category "black lesbian," of what will be retained from the appearance of an image that is recognizable as "black lesbian," is simultaneously an exclusion of those elements that threaten the appearance of "black lesbian."

While the preceding statement might seem simply tautological, it opens the possibility that "black lesbian" itself might be troubled by the appearance of images that reveal an alternative past for "black lesbian" and by the articulation of other interested claims to "black lesbian." As an expression of a multifarious "we" glued together by common sensations and perceptions, "black lesbian" critiques those emergent socio-political forces that organized themselves as "black," as "lesbian," and as "women" during the late 1960s and throughout the 1970s. "Black lesbian" does so by presenting itself as that which has been rendered invisible within each of those categories as they consolidate particular constituencies in whose interests the current formulations of those categories function. To the extent that elements of the socio-political forces represented in "black," "lesbian," and "women" have been distilled to varying degrees and in contradictory ways into the conceptions of the world that sustain the post–Cold War multicultural state while at the same time providing a common vocabulary with which to, on the one hand, elucidate and argue against the racism, sexism, and homophobia that continues to inform U.S. political economy and, on the other hand, argue for the U.S. state's ongoing reformation, "black lesbian" retains a sense of "resistance" to the hegemony of those distillations within prevalent conceptions of the world.[16]

In other words, "black lesbian" still can provide a salient critique of the sexism and heterosexism of dominant articulations of "blackness," of the racism and heterosexism of dominant articulations of "women," and of the racism of dominant articulations of "lesbian." Because it registers as "resistant" within prevalent conceptions of the world, however, "black lesbian" has garnered a type of political transparency that should trouble it. Currently, the designation "black lesbian" is perceived as itself a guarantor of a radical or at least a progressive politics.[17]

The increased (though certainly not overwhelmingly so) visibility of "black lesbians" within U.S. popular culture must be understood within the context of a visual terrain in which "black lesbian" is perceived to be that which indexes (though never neatly) a set of lived experiences that are thought to be productive of knowledges that necessarily guarantee a radical politics. Because "black lesbianism" points to sexual networks and racially inflected experiences that currently provide hegemonic formations with their racialized, sexualized outside, "black lesbian" can be invoked as an illustration of the threats facing the moral fabric of the nation and, as Sharon Patricia Holland points out, as "the perfect answer to the problem of feminism."[18] The increased visibility of "black lesbians," whether received in celebratory or accusatory terms, thereby dissimulates the extent to which "black lesbian" already is the product of a series of exclusions and negotiations that have enabled the category to become perceptible within the terms of those conceptions of the world whose interests the visual terrain secures. For these reasons, the version of "black lesbian" most commonly perceptible in popular culture is one that has been parsed into the terms whereby it might be recognized as "black lesbian" according to dominant conceptions of the world. The "black lesbian" currently capable of becoming visible might force dominant conceptions of the world to retool the mechanisms whereby they rationalize existing relations so that the visible "black lesbian" might exist within a reformed version of those relations. Yet, it is precisely because "black lesbian" can carry out this reformist operation that any embrace of "black lesbian" as a guarantor of a radical or transformative politics should be tempered with a critical consideration of the set of needs and interests her appearance furthers.

Cheryl Dunye's *The Watermelon Woman* provides additional insight into the nexus of "needs" and "interests" that a visible "black lesbian" currently serves. The film provides a fictional past for "black lesbian" that Cheryl (the film's main character) ultimately fashions into a past in which she finds "hope," "inspiration," "possibility," and "history." By so doing, *The Watermelon Woman* provides insight into what must be rendered "invisible" in the image "black lesbian" in order for "black lesbian" to become "visible."

The Watermelon Woman has been received as a film in which the "typically invisible bodies" of "black lesbians" are "rendered visible in a number of ways."[19] The narrative of the film follows Cheryl (a character who identifies herself as "a black lesbian filmmaker" and who is played by Cheryl Dunye), in her efforts to excavate a story about a black actress who appeared in several "mammy" roles in Hollywood films and who is credited in those films as "the Watermelon Woman." While conducting research, Cheryl uncovers evidence of an erotic relationship between "the Watermelon Woman" (aka "Fae Richards" and "Faith Richardson") and a white female director, Martha Page. Based on the evidence she uncovers regarding Richardson's relationship with Page, Cheryl concludes, "I guess we have a thing or two in common, Miss

Richards: the movies and women." The interracial relationship between Fae and Martha thus provides the initial context within which "the Watermelon Woman" becomes visible as "black lesbian."

During the course of her research, Cheryl talks to "Shirley Hamilton," a character who remembers Fae Richards as "quite a looker" who "used to sing for all us stone butches." Perhaps most significantly, however, Cheryl's research ultimately leads her to "June Walker," a character played by Cheryl Clarke, a writer whose theoretical and creative work during the late 1970s and early 1980s were part of a movement that provided a vocabulary through which a political articulation of "black lesbian" as a critique of "black," "lesbian," "woman," "patriarchy," and "capitalism" emerged. Clarke's character in the film, June, Fae's lover until her death, writes a letter to Cheryl in which June explains that she thinks that the mammy roles Fae played "troubled [Fae's] soul." In the letter, June implicates Martha Page in that vexed history. June's letter implores Cheryl to leave Page out of the movie on Fae's life. Speaking about Fae as part of a collective "we," June asserts, "She did so much, Cheryl. That's what you have to speak about. She paved the way for kids like you to run around making movies about the past and about how we lived then. Please, Cheryl, make our history before we are all dead and gone. But, if you are really in 'the family,' you better understand that our family will always only have each other."

June's comments draw attention to the way that "black lesbian" might be policed to keep some "in the family" and others out of "our family." Yet, the documentary that Cheryl makes about Fae Richard's life similarly reveals Cheryl's own choices about the value of the information she uncovers and, importantly, about the utility of that information to an enabling construction of "black lesbian." Cheryl tailors the documentary about "the Watermelon Woman" presented at the end of the film in order to provide, as Cheryl explains, "hope," "inspiration," "possibility," and a "history" that would rationalize and support the existence of Cheryl herself, as a "black lesbian filmmaker." Cheryl explains the choices she makes in crafting a historical narrative about Faith Richardson's life in the monologue, which introduces the film within a film. Cheryl explains that the historical narrative June provides of her life with Fae validates a different "world" than that which Cheryl inhabits as a "black lesbian filmmaker." In response to June's interrogation into Cheryl's interest in the relationship between Fae and Martha, Cheryl explains, "I know she meant the world to you, but she also meant the world to me, and those worlds are different."

Each world, Cheryl's and June's, is authorized via access to a different sheet of the past,[20] and Cheryl makes it clear that the narrative she will tell is one that will validate and legitimate her existence, not June's: "What [Fae] means to me, a twenty-five-year-old black woman, means something else. It means hope. It means inspiration. It means possibility. It means history. And, most importantly, what I understand is that I'm gonna be the one who says, I am a black lesbian filmmaker who's just beginning. But I'm gonna say a lot more and have a lot more work to do."

The fictional "biography of the Watermelon Woman" that Cheryl presents at the end of *The Watermelon Woman* legitimates the "black lesbian film-maker" as "the one" who will become visible as "black lesbian" by invoking a sheet of the past that supports Cheryl's needs and interests as they have been presented throughout *The Watermelon Woman,* a past wherein interracial lesbian desire is part and parcel of "black women's" participation in Hollywood and so continues to inform their entry into it. The world that Cheryl claims is hers, as "a twenty-five-year-old black woman," is one in which her professional aspirations demand that she articulate herself into the emergent market category of "black lesbian filmmaker" in a way that will register within the terms of that market.

With the character Cheryl, Dunye ruminates on the conditions for the success of her own film, *The Watermelon Woman.* The first feature-length "black lesbian film," *The Watermelon Woman* is a conjunction between the previously existing categories of "black film" and "lesbian film." The film's articulation into a category recognizable as "black lesbian film" proceeds according to the logic that currently governs post-70s Hollywood; on the film's promotional poster and video cover, the film is proclaimed to be "*Go Fish* Meets *She's Gotta Have It!*" Cheryl Dunye and Guinevere Turner (from the "lesbian film" *Go Fish*) are singled out in the promotional materials as the film's "stars" and they are named and featured prominently on the poster, both smiling.[21] The choice to feature both Dunye and Turner in the promotional materials indicates that it is via the logic of an interracial "lesbian" relationship that the first "black lesbian feature film" to be picked up for distribution appears.

The marketing decision to feature Turner instead of Valarie Walker, the black actress who plays "Tamara," the other primary character in the film, is mirrored in the final account of "the Watermelon Woman's" life that Cheryl provides. That film-within-a-film begins with a shot of "Martha Page" and "Faith Richardson." While Fae's relationship with Martha Page, although not described explicitly as "lesbian," is granted an eroticism that provides the governing logic behind the film's embrace of Fae as a "black lesbian" foremother, June Walker's relationship with Fae is relegated via the voice-over narrative to the status of "special friend," a rhetorical move that un-self-consciously reproduces the homophobic discourse through which same-sex erotic attachments are obscured and rendered illegitimate within dominant conceptions of the world. Fae's relationship with June, the way she sang for the "stone butches" in the bar, etc., do not appear to be part of the past that enables Cheryl to find "hope," "inspiration," or her "history." Those who exist on a sheet of the past that might support a narrative that would challenge the construction of "black lesbian" that Cheryl provides are relegated by Cheryl's narrative to a "different" world, one that is incommensurate with that in which "black lesbian" can appear and circulate proudly in films.

Yet, because it re-creates the processes whereby Cheryl chooses what from the available past will support her own needs and interests as a "black lesbian filmmaker" and, hence, what will appear in the image that the film-within-a-film designates and puts into circulation as "black lesbian," *The Watermelon Woman* allows for a different possibility to be perceived in the image that Cheryl calls "black lesbian," one that remains hostile to the world Cheryl claims as hers because it is inassimilable into that world's logic. That possibility might collect the "stone butches," the "special friends," "the studs," "the femmes," "the woman-lovers," and "the queers" that were part of the working-class social milieu to which Fae Richards herself belonged and make those ambivalent, destabilizing, and unstable forces of desire and community cohere as a collective expression of a multifarious "we" that complicates any innocent notion of "the one" who says, "I am a black lesbian filmmaker." The multifarious "we" that challenges formulations of "the one . . . black lesbian" also drags "into the maelstrom of a continuously contingent, unguaranteed, political argument and debate," even the conception of the world in which an "I" will be perceived to be writing as a "black queer film scholar" who authoritatively (even if passionately) cautions against "joining the lesbians" in favor of the (re)constitution of a multifarious "we."

NOTES

1. Stuart Hall, "New Ethnicities," in *Stuart Hall: Critical Dialogues in Cultural Studies*, ed. David Morley and Chen Kuan-Hsing (New York: Routledge, 1996), 442.
2. Ibid., 443.

3. Ibid., 444.

4. Ibid.

5. When taken up within academic discourse, black lesbian and gay film critiques simultaneously the disciplinary formation of "black studies" and of "queer studies"; as such, it is an integral part of the project called "black queer studies." In the introduction to *Plum Nelly: New Essays in Black Queer Studies,* a special issue of *Callaloo,* Jennifer DeVere Brody and Dwight A. McBride argue that "black queer studies" can offer "a kind of trans-disciplinary critique" to both queer studies and black studies simultaneously. See Jennifer DeVere Brody and Dwight A. McBride, "Introduction," *Callaloo* 23.1 (2000): 286. Throughout the present discussion, I reserve the designation "black queer" as a currently accessible marker of the excesses produced by the "black lesbian and gay" project.

6. Hall, "New Ethnicities," 443.

7. By claiming that black lesbian and gay film emerges as a critical politics in which black cultural politics and (white) lesbian and gay socio-political philosophy and practice are inseparable, I am not arguing for the category's "hybridity" (if "hybridity" assumes the prior existence of at least two relatively autonomous parts that are combined into a new "hybrid" entity). As should be clear from what follows, what I am saying does not lend credence to the homophobic assertion that homosexuality is a European import into blackness, nor does it support the racist insistence on expunging "blackness" from "queerness." On the contrary, I am insisting that "black" and "queer" must be thought together.

For a similar argument that holds that "black" and "queer" infect each other at their origins, see Sharon Patricia Holland, *Raising the Dead: Readings of Death and (Black) Subjectivity* (Durham: Duke University Press, 2000) 145, 174–81; and Sharon Patricia Holland, "Bill T. Jones, Tupac Shakur and the (Queer) Art of Death," *Callaloo* 23.1 (2000): 384–421. For arguments concerning the co-constitution of sexual categories with other racial and ethnic formations in the United States, see, for instance, David L. Eng, *Racial Castration: Managing Masculinity in Asian America* (Durham: Duke University Press, 2001); and Roderick A. Ferguson, *Aberrations in Black: Toward a Queer of Color Critique* (Minneapolis: University of Minnesota Press, 2004).

8. This quotation is from a poem that Essex Hemphill recited in Marlon Riggs's film *Tongues Untied.*

9. Michelle Parkerson, "Birth of a Notion: Towards Black Gay and Lesbian Imagery in Film and Video," in *Queer Looks: Perspectives on Lesbian and Gay Film and Video,* ed. Martha Gever, John Greyson, and Pratibha Parmar (New York: Routledge, 1993), 234.

10. David Van Leer, "Visible Silence: Spectatorship in Black Gay and Lesbian Film," in *Representing Blackness: Issues in Film and Video,* ed. Valerie Smith (New Brunswick: Rutgers University Press, 1997), 161.

11. That "black lesbian and gay" is productive of its own excesses is clear when one considers, (1) the multiplication of categories (e.g., lgbt) that exploded out of "lesbian and gay's" inability to adequately represent the constituents for which it provided an entry into representation; (2) the embrace within much academic and some activist discourse of the category "black queer" that grows out of a critique of "lesbian and gay's" exclusivity; and (3) the designation "same-gender loving," a concept defined against "black lesbian and gay" and "black queer" as part of a strategy to distance the articulation of black homosexualities from expressions of white homosexualities.

12. Pratibha Parmar, "That Moment of Emergence," *Queer Looks: Perspectives on Lesbian and Gay Film and Video,* ed. Martha Gever, John Greyson, and Pratibha Parmar (New York: Routledge, 1993), 5.

13. Ferguson, *Aberrations in Black.*

14. In *The Witch's Flight: The Cinematic, the Black Femme, and the Image of Common Sense,* a work in progress, I develop the argument that what is perceptible in a cinematic image is "common sense" where "common sense" is understood according to Antonio Gramsci's formulation of that category.

15. The first quote here is from *Living with Pride: Ruth Ellis @ 100,* where Ruth Ellis (who at the time was a one-hundred-year-old black woman who claimed she "never was in what you call a closet" and who had lived for thirty-four years in a relationship with a woman nicknamed "Babe") explains, "I didn't know anything about lesbians. We called them women lovers. But I read that book, *The Well of Loneliness.* That put me wise to some things." The quotes in the subtitle refer to the titles of Cheryl Dunye's 1996 film *The Watermelon Woman* and Yvonne Welbon's 1999 documentary about Ruth Ellis's life, *Living with Pride: Ruth Ellis @ 100.*

16. For an early construction of black lesbianism as a form of "resistance," see Cheryl Clarke, "Lesbianism: Act of Resistance," in *This Bridge Called My Back,* ed. Cherríe Moraga and Gloria Anzaldúa (New York: Kitchen Table; Women of Color Press, 1981), 128–37.

17. Sharon Patricia Holland puts forth the possibility that in the contemporary United States, "being a black lesbian is always already a political state of existence" (*Raising the Dead,* 129).

18. See Holland, *Raising the Dead,* 124–48, for a consideration of the political pitfalls and possibilities within the latter use of "the black lesbian."

19. Laura L. Sullivan, "Chasing Fae: *The Watermelon Woman* and Black Lesbian Possibility," *Callaloo* 23.1 (2000): 450. In another analysis of the film, Mark Winokur points out that Cheryl/Dunye (character/filmmaker) "creates a black lesbian body in order to recover her own" in an essay that focuses primarily on the way that Dunye's film "creates a representation of the negative oedipal stage of both identification and desire for the body of the black lesbian mother" (Winokur, "Body and Soul: Identifying (with) the Black Lesbian Body in Cheryl Dunye's *Watermelon Woman,*" in *Recovering the Black Female Body: Self-Representations by African American Women,* ed.

Michael Bennett and Vanessa D. Dickerson [New Brunswick: Rutgers University Press, 2001], 244, 245).

20. For an explanation of "sheets of the past" as they might be accessed through cinema, see Gilles Deleuze, *Cinema 2: The Time-Image,* trans. Hugh Tomlinson and Robert Galeta (Minneapolis: University of Minnesota Press, 1989), 98–125.

21. Valarie Walker, the black actress who plays Tamara, Cheryl's best friend in the film, and a character that, arguably, is just as significant as Turner's Diana, is not mentioned and does not appear on the poster. Clearly, the promotional materials cannot feature every actress in the film. Yet, the choice not to feature Walker but rather Turner, recognizable from Rose Troche's film *Go Fish* as the "trendy, pretty, young Lesbian who is having trouble finding love," is indicative of, among other things, the extent to which *The Watermelon Woman*'s financial success was thought to reside in its ability to be recognizable as a "black lesbian film" according to the contours of existing categories.

CHARLES I. NERO

WHY ARE THE GAY GHETTOES WHITE?

Marlon Ross points out that at least since World War II the guiding ideal for homosexuals as a distinct minority has been multiculturalism—"the idea that gays and lesbians constitute a fluid minority, whose particular virtue grows out of the fact that they exist inside of every other culture."[1] Nevertheless, gay communities formed in the 1970s as part of what Jeffrey Escoffier calls the gay territorial economy "marked by the spread of gentrification and neighborhood development" fall far short of any multicultural ideals.[2] The so-called gay ghettoes in large U.S. urban areas have been mostly comprised of white males. Clearly, the multicultural guiding ideals about homosexuality as a subculture and the homogeneity of the so-called gay ghetto create a paradox of contemporary gay life.

Although writers in both popular and scholarly genres have noted this paradox of contemporary gay life, they have seldom accounted for it adequately. A typical failed explanation appears in Steve Hogan and Lee Hudson's *Completely Queer: The Gay and Lesbian Encyclopedia,* where under the entry "ghetto" they remark: "A distinctive factor of black lesbian and gay life has been that a higher percentage of African American lesbians and gay men live outside gay and lesbian ghettoes than their white counterparts."[3] Hogan and Hudson offer no further explanation about why the gay ghettoes are white or why African American lesbians and gay men do not live in them in larger numbers. The reticence of scholars to explore the whiteness of the gay ghettoes might suggest that the answer is simply a matter that black people regardless of sexuality prefer to stick to their own kind. However, I believe that the answer is more complex and that it raises important questions for thinking about contemporary gay life: Why is gay housing and community formation primarily a white and male phenomenon? Does gay community formation deliberately exclude women and people of color? Does gay housing and community formation mirror post–World War II suburbanization, which, by and large, excluded people of color? These questions must be answered if gay community formation is ever to live up to its multicultural ideals.

In this essay I seek to answer some of these questions by critically engaging Lawrence Knopp's pioneering research about the formation of gay neighborhoods. In the process of engaging Knopp, I wish to point to two areas addressed (albeit insufficiently) in his research that can help us to understand the homogeneity of the gay ghetto. One of those areas is the degree to which gay strategies have focused on integrating into the middle classes; the other is the purpose of white hostility toward African Americans. These two areas are actually interdependent and, historically, have reinforced each other. Knopp's work contains, I believe, the seeds for a cogent analysis of the ways that racialization operates in the gay world as a "fundamental organizing principle," to use the words of political scientists Michael Omi and Howard Winant.[4] It is thus important for us to reexamine Knopp's work to glean from it the ways that race was deployed as a principle for organizing a white and gay housing enclave in the midst of a majority African American city.

Omi and Winant's theory of racial formation is particularly useful for this exploration into Knopp's work because it pays attention to the way that racial dynamics function at both individual (micro) and collective (macro) levels. At the same time, their theory stresses continuity and reciprocity between individual and collective social relations. As an example, Omi and Winant give racial discrimination, which they state is at a collective level a set of "economic, political and ideological/cultural practices" that have "obvious consequences for the experience and identities of individuals. It affects racial meaning, intervenes in 'personal life,' [and] is interpreted politically." Rather than analytically distinct categories, the individual and the collective are continuous and reciprocal. At the collective or macro level Omi and Winant contend that race is a matter of the formation of social structures, which they understand as a series of "sites" or "regions of social life with a coherent set of constitutive social relations." Typical sites for the formation of racial structures in advanced capitalist societies include the capitalist economy, the patriarchal family, and the liberal democratic state as well as culture. They state: "In the cultural realm, dress, music, art, language and indeed the very concept of 'taste' has been shaped by the racial consciousness and racial dynamics, for instance in the absorption of black musical forms into the white 'mainstream.' "[5]

Omi and Winant's attention to culture is especially useful for the study of the gay world. Culture and culture-building, as the folklorist John Roberts states, "is a recursive, rather than linear, process of endlessly devising solutions to both old and new problems of how to live under ever-changing social, political, and economic conditions. While culture is dynamic and creative as it adapts to social needs and goals, it is also enduring in that it changes by building upon previous manifestations of itself."[6] Gay men have created a culture, or a subculture as some insist, that has allowed them to survive, to recognize fellow gays, and even to prosper in a relentlessly, and sometimes brutal, heterosexualizing world. In large part, this culture expresses itself as gay sensibility. Although gay sensibility notoriously defies precision, Michael Bronski observes that gay sensibility is, on the one hand, a strategic negotiation with the dominant world insofar as it "aims to gain some entry into, some acceptance by the mainstream culture" and, on the other hand, refers to the "consciously created" meanings that have arisen from gay people's "own analyses, experiences, and perceptions."[7]

One aspect of gay sensibility that requires more attention is racism, or, more specifically, the ways in which the gay and straight worlds cooperate in the production of racial and gender hostility toward black men. In the next section I explore this production through an examination of recurring controlling images of black gay men in film and television. These images shape "the racial consciousness and racial dynamics," to use Omi and Winant's language, of gay community formation.

RACE AND GAY NEIGHBORHOOD FORMATION IN NEW ORLEANS

San Francisco's Castro District is perhaps the most well-known gay community in the world. The creation of the Castro is an oft-repeated narrative that sometimes assumes mythic dimensions. Gay men fleeing oppression in small towns across North America arrived in San Francisco. Finding anonymity in the city and the ability to derive an income apart from a familial structure, these men created "a gay Israel" in San Francisco.[8] Once established, gay men initiated community renewal projects, which "helped to make the city beautiful and alive."[9]

Lawrence Knopp's study of gentrification in the Faubourg Marigny in New Orleans, a small but densely populated area adjacent to the famous French Quarter, presents rigorous and innovative research that sheds much-needed light on gay neighborhood formation. Knopp's research includes a doctoral dissertation in geography and several articles in refereed journals and anthologies. Not only is Knopp's research rigorous, it is also innovative because of its interdisciplinary approach. He uses the methods of geography and demography, as well as methods more often associated with sociology, journalism, and history. The result is that his studies are exacting in their precision and also highly engaging.

Knopp's study is particularly interesting for me because I grew up, attended school and college, and worked in New Orleans. Having come out as a gay man in New Orleans, I was familiar with the neighborhood and surrounding environs that Knopp describes. Perhaps my familiarity with the city led me to notice that Knopp was not particularly adept at explaining the racial homogeneity of the Faubourg Marigny. When I lived in New Orleans, particularly during the years between 1974 and 1983, the Faubourg Marigny appeared to be almost exclusively comprised of white gay men. In his research Knopp confirms my memories about the racial and gender homogeneity of the Faubourg Marigny.

Given that Knopp is such a sophisticated scholar, it is somewhat surprising that he is unable to satisfactorily explain the racial and gender makeup of the Faubourg. Rather than offering an explanation, Knopp merely restates the paradox that gayness is multicultural yet gay neighborhoods are overwhelmingly white and male. As Knopp explains: "Gay identity in the United States is skewed in terms of class, race, and gender, i.e., that while homosexual desire and behaviors are multiclass and multiracial phenomena involving both women and men, the self-identification of individuals as gay is more of a white, male, and middle-class phenomenon. This is because it is easier, economically and otherwise, for middle-class white males to identify and live as openly gay people than it is for women, non-whites, and non-middle-class people."[10] Needless to say, my initial reaction to this explanation was one of astonishment at its lack in exploring in complex ways the relationship between wealth, gender, and race. Although Knopp hints at this complicated relationship in his own research, especially when he shows how the accumulation of wealth through the acquisition of real estate is socially constructed and manipulated, it appears that he is not willing to think in complicated ways about the intersection of race and homosexuality.

On further reflection about Knopp's explanation, it dawned on me that it is possible that he conceives of race in traditional terms that focus solely on difference. For instance, one case where race becomes important in his studies is when he points out that the gays in the Faubourg often interacted violently with African Americans in adjacent communities. In order to address this issue and to offer a critique of Knopp's work that takes race into account in discussing gay neighborhood formation in the Faubourg Marigny, I have used my own knowledge about New Orleans, supplemented by further research. What follows is thus a racially conscious engagement with Knopp's research that points out some of the ways in which race matters as a factor in creating a white and male gay ghetto.

Knopp attributes the gentrification of the Faubourg Marigny to three events: "The movement of a small number of predominantly gay middle-class professionals to Marigny during the 1960s"; "a movement for historic preservation in the neighborhood, organized primarily by gay men"; and "the arrival of speculators and developers, who again were mostly gay, in the mid-to-late 1970s" (46). Although Knopp does not state as much, whiteness (and concomitantly the exclusion of black men and to a significant extent lesbians) mattered in all three events.

First, the gay middle-class professionals who moved to the Faubourg Marigny in the 1960s were men hired to work at the newly created University of New Orleans (UNO). Knopp does not identify them racially, but at that time whiteness was an implicit criterion for employment at UNO, which was founded, during the last days of legalized segregation in 1958, as Louisiana State University at New Orleans. Until the late 1980s, most black professionals in higher education worked at one of the three historically black universities in the city—Dillard University, Xavier University, and Southern University of New Orleans—rather than at UNO. This fact of employment segregation is important for Knopp to consider because informal networks were to play a crucial role in the gentrification of the Marigny. Racially segregated workplaces made it highly unlikely that middle-class black and white gay males would create racially integrated informal networks.

Second, by emphasizing historical preservation, white gays practiced racial and class "tribalism" whereby they identified their interests with those of other middle- and upper-class whites. Historical preservation has a long history in New Orleans that is very much associated with local white elites. The Vieux Carre Commission, which regulated development in the French Quarter, was established by local white elites in 1936. The initiator of the gay housing movement in the Faubourg Marigny was a white gay architect who lived part of the year in San Francisco's gay Castro. According to Knopp, this architect purchased property in the Faubourg in 1971 and used his connections with other white middle- and upper-class gay men to encourage gay gentrification there. These men created the Faubourg Marigny Improvement Association (FMIA) and they emphasized historic preservation. The FMIA cultivated their connections with city officials, successfully lobbied the mayor and city council for land use regulations, and held candidate forums at election time. The success of the FMIA had notable consequences beneficial to middle- and upper-class whites. Local politicians and new zoning regulations made historical preservation a priority in the Faubourg, which had the very practical effect that bank financing and insurance became easier for single men to get.

These middle-class white gay men extended their successes to working-class white gay men when the speculators and developers who brought about the gay gentrification of the Faubourg focused on creating a market for all kinds of housing in the neighborhood among gays. Knopp observes that one real estate broker in particular encouraged "as much in-migration, home-ownership, and renovation in Marigny as was humanly possible, regardless of the in-migrant's class status" (53). His targets included gay men employed in the low-wage service sector who otherwise would not have had access to the housing market. One of Knopp's interviewees recalled that this group included "all the waiters and all the gay people and all the people that were his friends in the Quarter that always wanted houses. . . . Just nobody was ever going to look for that type of person. It was a natural! . . . He was the first person to go after that market" (53). Neither the interviewee nor Knopp, however, address the racial composition of the gay men in the low-wage service sector. My own experience and engagement with gay businesses during this time period informs me that most of these men were, in fact, white.

Exploiting personal and friendship networks that had been established because of shared sexual—and racial and gender—identities was crucial at this stage of gentrification in the Marigny because real estate firms and other speculators resorted to using illegal maneuvers. These schemes allowed members of the local gay community to secure financing for virtually the entire purchase price of the home and enabled first-time home buyers and others of relatively modest means to avoid down payments and invest instead in renovations. Most of these first-time buyers were young gay men who had been recruited into the housing market by other gay men involved in the real estate business. Knopp points out that one real estate firm employed at its peak fifty-two agents, "nearly all of whom were gay" (84). Once again, Knopp is silent about the racial composition of this group.

The consequence of these schemes was that gay men, regardless of social class, received access to housing and the wealth that accrues from home ownership. One interviewee told Knopp: "I was a schoolteacher and I was making $400 a month . . . I saved $1200. The biggest savings of my life! . . . I bought [my first] house for $7500" (83). Knopp estimates that these schemes enabled "hundreds of gay first-time home buyers to enter the housing market" in what was essentially "a conscious and deliberate project of developing social and economic resources with New Orleans' and Marigny's gay community" (87). Black gay men and women were excluded from participating in home ownership in the Faubourg Marigny because they were neither a part of the informal networks of middle-class gay men nor were they employed in the low-wage service sector of gay-owned businesses.

One reason for the exclusion of black gay men that I would like to explore further is the historical meaning of the hostility of whites toward African Americans. Since emancipation, white racial hostility toward blacks has had a material dimension. At the end of the nineteenth century the black journalist and activist Ida B. Wells-Barnett pointed out how lynching benefited whites when she carefully demolished the image of the black male rapist of white women. According to Wells, lynching was nothing more than an "excuse to get rid of Negroes who were acquiring wealth and property and thus keep the race terrorized and 'keep the nigger down.' "[11] More recent pioneering scholarship in "white studies" confirms Wells's view. For instance, Thomas A. Guglielmo has shown that in the 1940s and 1950s Chicago's Italians became increasingly anti-black as they learned to emphasize their identities as "whites" and that "whiteness was not some meaningless social category, but something that carried considerable power and provided them with innumerable resources."[12] In their particular case, the resources included low-interest loans, backed by the Federal Housing Authority, to purchase homes in neighborhoods whose alleged value rested on excluding blacks.

Admittedly, white hostility takes a particular form when directed at black gay men. In the next section I address a hostile representation that I observe in the American media. The sheer repetition of this image points to the racialization of gay identity and requires us to ask questions about the role that this form of media hostility plays in the distribution of material resources among gays.

CONTROLLING IMAGES OF BLACK GAY MEN

In *Lianna* (1983), John Sayles's landmark film about the coming out of a suburban, white middle-class housewife, a college football coach makes the following comment: "I had a player once, a halfback, a hell of a runner.

Anyhow, I found out in the middle of the season that he, uh you know, he liked guys. I'd recruited this kid out of high school, watched him develop four years and I had no idea. I mean, he was a Black kid. I didn't even know they had them that way!"[13] The coach's humorous remark underscores twin aspects of the racism and homophobia that keep black gay men invisible or marginal on American film screens. On the one hand his comment refers to the racist idea that African American males are hyper-virile and cannot be gay. On the other hand, the coach's remarks underscore America's homophobic preoccupation with white masculinity, particularly the conditions that purportedly produce homosexuality. From these two interrelated perspectives black gay men simply cannot exist, or, if they do, their existence is an anomaly that must be explained.

Here I borrow Patricia Hill Collins's term "controlling images" to illuminate the continuing explanations for the existence of black gay men in white discourses. Collins points out that in white discourses about black women, controlling images help "to make racism, sexism, and poverty appear to be natural, normal, and an inevitable part of everyday life."[14] The impostor—which also includes the sexually voracious black stud who is not really a gay man since he exists only to satiate white male desire—is the predominate controlling image of black gay men. The impostor is similar to the caricatures of black gay men that E. Patrick Johnson discusses in his dazzling work *Appropriating Blackness*. Using examples such as the "Men On . . ." skit in the 1980s television show *In Living Color*; the Black Power writings by Eldridge Cleaver and Amiri Baraka; and the performances by the comic Eddie Murphy, Johnson shows how such caricatures "work to signify black masculinity and heterosexuality as authentic and black homosexuality as trivial, ineffectual, and, indeed, inauthentic."[15] In addition, Johnson illuminates how black-created caricatures of black gay men "exemplify the complex process through which black male heterosexuality conceals its reliance on the black effeminate homosexual for its status."[16] While homosexuality becomes an inauthentic expression of gender in black discourses, my focus on controlling images pays attention to sites where an always economic racial formation occurs. Like the controlling images of black women as mammy, jezebel, and welfare queen, the ubiquitous image of the black gay male as an impostor or a fraud naturalizes and normalizes the exclusion of black gay men from sites of territorial economies where wealth is created.

As a controlling image, the impostor in white discourses ironically stands as a representation for gay presence while simultaneously deflecting attention away from practices that exclude and marginalize black men. Philip Brian Harper has called attention to this irony in film, noting that since the Black Power era of the late 1960s, representations of black gay characters have functioned "to buttress (often specifically by *challenging*) normative conceptions of race, sexuality, and gender identity."[17]

Film and drama since the 1960s that have included black gay men frequently include a narrative in which characters in the film or we in the audience discover that the character of the black gay man is an impostor or a fraud. In effect, the black gay male's appearance is a masquerade. This narrative necessitates a pivotal scene (or scenes) of exposure in which the black gay male character is revealed to be a fraud. In Shirley Clarke's classic documentary *Portrait of Jason* (1967) the title character presents himself in several guises. In one, Jason describes his work on getting a cabaret act together; in another, he discusses his work cleaning houses. Jason even describes his childhood and his tortured relationship with his father. Eventually Clarke and her assistant, either by providing Jason with alcohol and marijuana or by incessant taunting, expose Jason as just another two-bit hustler and hanger-on.[18]

Mart Crowley's *The Boys in the Band* (1970), the first Hollywood film whose sole focus was queer male culture, uses the black character Bernard (Reuben Greene), as well as a variety of other white gay ethnic and social types, to represent the multiculturalism characteristic of the gay world. The play and filmed version of it is set at a birthday party given by Michael for a friend. Philip Brian Harper astutely points out that although Crowley attempts "to convey the sense of idyllic egalitarianism that putatively characterizes gay relations, in supposed contradistinction to 'mainstream' society," we are never allowed for a moment "to forget exactly from where [Bernard] came from to arrive" as a guest at Michael's party.[19] Bernard is pegged by one of the characters as a "pickaninny" from the Detroit ghettoes who helps to organize the musical relief.[20] Bernard's scene of exposure occurs during the climactic telephone game when each player must call the one person he loves and confess that love. Bernard comes off as the absolute embodiment of Eldridge Cleaver's twisted logic that black homosexual men have a "racial death wish" that expresses itself in outrage and frustration due to their inability "to have a baby by a white man."[21] Bernard reveals that the only man he has ever loved and for whom he still pines is the white man for whom his mother works as a domestic servant.

In the mid-1970s Antonio Fargas played two delightfully queeny characters. As Bernstein in Paul Mazursky's, *Next Stop, Greenwich Village* (1976), he claims to be half-Jewish and becomes a friend to a group of bohemians with artistic aspirations in 1950s New York.[22] As Lindy in Michael Schultz *Car Wash* (1976), Fargas got to deliver the famous quip "I'm more man than you'll ever be, and more woman than you'll ever get."[23] However, both characters were frauds. Bernstein was revealed to be just a guy from the projects and his Jewish ancestry a pathetic fabrication. Despite his famous quip, Lindy is ultimately the disposable "sissy" and, as revealed in the final encounter between the film's two authentic black men—the black nationalist and the exconvict—not a real man whose life matters. As Vito Russo in *The Celluloid Closet* aptly stated, "Lindy is only a cartoon" whose "effect in the end was just that of the safe sissy who ruled the day in the topsy-turvy situations of Thirties comedies."[24]

The controlling image of the black gay man as an impostor continues to animate representations of black gay men in film. The impostor shows up in some of the most critically lauded films and dramatic works. Neil Jordan's *The Crying Game* derives its dramatic impact from exposing the black female character's penis.[25] Arguably, Jennie Livingston's *Paris Is Burning!* operates in a manner similar to *The Crying Game* by exposing black and Latino women as men. In the filmed production of John Guare's *Six Degrees of Separation* Paul (Will Smith) is a sociopathic black gay man who gains entry into the house of upper-middle-class whites by pretending to be the son of Sidney Poitier. Eventually, he is found out and exposed as just another black gay hustler. His fraudulence is even malevolent, however, since he is held responsible both for the homosexual seduction and the suicide of a naive, young white male from the American heartland.[26] Even representations of black gay men that appear to be progressive rely to a considerable extent on fraudulence. With this in mind, I wish to discuss here in greater detail three incarnations in an independent film, Kevin Smith's *Chasing Amy*, and in the television shows *Spin City* and *Six Feet Under*.

Although Kevin Smith's *Chasing Amy* pioneered the portrayal of bisexuality, the black gay male character Hooper X (Dwight Ewell) is a throwback to Bernstein in *Next Stop, Greenwich Village*, and Bernard in *The Boys in the Band*, as is evident from the scenes of exposure. One scene takes place at a comic book conference in a special session devoted to minorities. Hooper discusses his comic book creation "White Hating Coon," whose heroic main character is named Maliqua. Hooper gives a speech peppered with inflammatory Afrocentric discourse with allusions to black militant icons such as Malcolm X, H. Rap Brown, and Louis Farrakhan. After an audience member challenges Hooper contending that all blacks really want to be white, Hooper takes out a gun and fires it into the audience shouting, "black rage."[27] Later in the scene we learn that the entire interaction, including the gunfire, is a hoax and that Hooper is gay. What is noteworthy about this scene is that Hooper's gayness posits him, much as *The Boys in the Band*'s Bernard, as the antithesis of militant black masculinity. Hooper's queerness offers the viewer the potential to derive a laugh from the speculation that the angry, frightening militant black man is, in actuality, a queer.

Hooper's fraudulence is, like Paul's in *Six Degrees of Separation*, also malevolent. When Hooper realizes that a young African American boy recognizes him as the author of the nationalist "White Hating Coon," Hooper stops his queeny behavior and turns on a black macho pose. This scene shows that Hooper's nationalism has no ethical basis; it is merely a front and a means for a profit. Hooper truly lives up to what his name implies, as he is all sound and fury, ultimately, signifying nothing. As a black gay impostor, Hooper is the apotheosis of his own comic creation, "White Hating Coon," ultimately showing the hilarity of black gay presence.

Spin City, which ran on ABC from 1996 to 2002, is a "workplace" situation comedy involving the staff of the mayor of New York City. Carter Sebastian Heywood (Michael Boatman) is a black gay activist in charge of minority affairs. Although the depiction of Carter as an openly gay black man is a progressive move, much of the humor about Carter recalls the impostor by revealing him to be a fraud. In numerous episodes Carter's fraudulence is exposed through playing on his position as a gay activist. In one of these episodes Carter leads a hunger strike against a corporation that plans to tear down buildings occupied by working-class people. However, a news crew captures Carter on camera eating doughnuts because he claims to have hypoglycemia. The show most often displays Carter's fraudulence in the long-running gag that implies that he and the sexist, racist, and homophobic Stuart Bondek (Alan Ruck) are ideal companions for each other. The running gag about their rightness for each other includes elements such as showing them finishing each other's sentences, spending holidays together, and arguing with each other like an old married couple. By the end of the series, the two have even moved in together, although they have not had sex. Carter and Stuart are unaware of how perfect they are for each other even though they are fiercely jealous of each other's sexual partners.

The idea that Carter and Stuart are a perfect couple is based on what television critic Daniel Mendelsohn calls "the ancient comedic formula . . . in which an attractive boy-girl pair are clearly 'right' for one another but kept from hooking up."[28] In *Spin City* the resulting tension produces some of the most hilarious moments in the show, but at Carter's expense. Since Carter is putatively the principled black gay activist and his coworkers acknowledge Stuart as sleezy, one wonders what the writers of the show believe Carter and Stuart share that make them "right" for each other. The most obvious possibility is that both are defined by socially agreed-on disreputable sexual identities. But, in this case, the writers reveal their homophobia by equating sleeze with homosexuality. The casting of a black man as the queer political activist was clever, but the show nevertheless relied on a controlling image of black gay men as fraudulent.

HBO's *Six Feet Under* is the latest entry to perpetuate the image of black gay men as impostors. The postmodern ironic sensibility of *Six Feet Under* seems to challenge prevailing conventions, but the show's African American gay male character has been transformed from the soul of the show into its lost soul. In the show's first season the African American Keith Charles (Matthew St. Patrick) appeared to be the show's moral center—the equivalent of a gay role model. Keith was completely comfortable with being "out." Further, Keith's ethical standards led him to break off a relationship with his closeted love interest, the show's costar David Fisher (Michael C. Hall) who was, for all intents and purposes, the white equivalent of a black buck: a brutal, irresponsible, sexual adventurer.

As the show developed over four seasons, Keith seemed to become "blacker." This transformation is significant for Keith's character for two reasons. First, Keith's blackness seems to mean an incompatibility with gayness to the show's writers and creators. This point was made quite clear in the third-season episode "Timing and Space," in which Keith became the source of humor at a gay party because he was completely ignorant about camp sensibility. Since Keith was the only black gay man present, the show seemed to support the belief that blacks are alien to gay sensibilities, such as camp. Moreover, Keith's complete ignorance about gay forms of culture seemed incongruous with the persona that had been established in the first season when the show implied that Keith belonged to a sizable network of gay men because he was active in queer social, religious, and political organizations.[29]

Second, the show presents blackness as savage and unredeemable. In a series that is about family dysfunction, the writers reveal a distressing double standard. White families have eccentricities, but black families are violent and criminal. In fact, in the opening episode of the third season, "Perfect

Circles," Keith explains that his violent, threatening behavior is just his way of showing that he is comfortable with his lover! As Keith is more associated with blackness, he retreats further and further from the first season's out and proud character. In season four, Keith, who has been fired from his job as a policeman and who works for a private security firm, now pretends to be straight to his coworkers. Keith's character may morph (as is the nature of an ongoing television series), but at the time of this writing his character continues the controlling image of black gay men as fraudulent.[30]

This controlling image of black gay men, which is produced by straights and gays, provides ideological support for the exclusion of black gay men from full participation in queer cultures. Anecdotal evidence suggests that this exclusion is widespread. Bars have been especially notorious for excluding black men through the practice of "carding," in which doormen and bouncers request an unreasonable amount of identification as a requirement for admission. Marlon Riggs includes in his brilliant 1989 documentary *Tongues Untied* a sequence in which an African American gay man becomes outraged after a white doorman requests five forms of picture identification to enter a bar. Interestingly, this belief that the admission of too many black men will cause a bar to lose its desirability for white patrons mirrors the social reality of housing. Sheryll Cashin, in *The Failures of Integration,* repeatedly observes that in housing "whites place a premium on homogeneity,"[31] and, further, that "where blacks or Latinos exist in large numbers, whites flee."[32] This practice of white separatism led Marlon Riggs to conclude that while living in San Francisco's overwhelmingly white and gay male Castro District, he became "an invisible man," possessing "no shadow, no substance. No history, no place. No reflection."[33] Riggs surmised that for all intents and purposes, in the gay Castro he had become "an alien, unseen, and seen, unwanted."

Brian Freeman, a member of the performance art group Pomo Afro Homo, echoes Riggs's remarks in the 1997 documentary *The Castro.* Freeman recalls being surprised and shocked repeatedly by the overwhelming presence of white men when he moved into the district. Not only were all of the men white, but their prominent attire, which became known as "the clone look," aped the white working-class male. Since working-class white males historically had been the foot soldiers in struggles against African Americans joining labor unions, black gay men may have been reluctant to embrace the clone look and participate in romanticizing it. Is it any wonder, then, that the two black members of the Village People, a popular 1970s disco group whose members dressed in clone attire, donned military costumes? Apart from the clothing style and its racialized class allusions, Freeman remembers being shocked by the racial insensitivity he found in the district's bars. One club, he remembers, held a celebration of southern plantation life replete with confederate memorabilia and images of black servants![34]

The persistence of controlling images of black gay male fraudulence in white discourse reveals white hostility toward black gay men. Racial hostility is important to consider in light of the pivotal role it has played in housing. As I show in the next section, white racial hostility has material benefits.

RACE, RACISM, CLASS, AND HOUSING

Historically, housing has been a major site for racial formation in the United States. Melvin Oliver and Thomas Shapiro, in their impressive volume *Black Wealth/White Wealth*, identify with precision the race-based policies of the state that "collectively enabled over thirty-five million families between 1933 and 1978 to participate in homeowner equity accumulation" but also "had the adverse effect of constraining black Americans' residential opportunities to central-city ghettos of major U.S. metropolitan communities."[35] The story begins during the Great Depression with the creation of the Home Owners Loan Corporation (HOLC), which refinanced tens of thousands of mortgages in danger of default or foreclosure. Of more importance, the HOLC introduced standardized appraisals of the fitness of properties for financing, and government agents used racial criterion that negatively impacted black people. Oliver and Shapiro state that

> government agents methodically included in their procedures the evaluation of the racial composition or potential racial composition of the community. Communities that were changing racially or were already black were deemed undesirable and placed in the lowest category. The categories, assigned various colors on a map ranging from green for the most desirable, which included new, all-white housing that was always in demand, to red, which included already racially mixed or all-black, old, and undesirable areas, subsequently were used by Federal Housing Authority (FHA) loan officers who made loans on the basis of these designations. (17)

The FHA was inaugurated in 1934 to bolster the economy and increase employment by aiding the construction industry. The FHA ushered in the modern mortgage system, which enabled people to buy homes on small down payments and at reasonable interest rates with lengthy repayment periods. The FHA's success was immediate and remarkable as housing starts doubled in the seven years after it was inaugurated. However, the FHA's policies worked against black people. Some policies indirectly impacted black people by favoring the financing of houses in suburbs over those in central cities. Other policies, however, were more direct. Notably, in its *Underwriting Manual*, the FHA upheld racial segregation and the use of restrictive covenants because it feared that property values would decline if "a rigid black and white segregation was not maintained" (18).

Contemporary institutional racism in the forms of mortgage lending practices and of redlining solidified segregated housing patterns. Oliver and Shapiro call attention to a 1991 Federal Reserve study of 6.4 million home mortgage applications by race and income that disclosed that "commercial banks rejected black applicants twice as often as whites nationwide," and that "the poorest white applicant . . . was more likely to get a mortgage loan approved than a black in the highest income bracket" (19–20). Discriminatory policies based on exclusion have provided "cumulative advantages" in wealth for white Americans and "cumulative disadvantages" for blacks (51). Based on their study of the 1987–1989 Survey of Income Participation administered by the United States Census Bureau, this means quantifiably that, on average, black households have almost no net financial assets (an accurate measure of wealth since it is the value of all assets less debts, including equity in home and vehicles). Among whites, Oliver and Shapiro note, the situation differs considerably: "Modest net financial assets are held in households from upper-white collar, lower-white collar, and upper-blue-collar origins amounting to $9,000, $9,500, and $8,744 respectively" (62). Although whites from lower-blue-collar backgrounds trail far behind fellow whites, their median net financial assets of $3,890 are almost four thousand times greater than blacks in upper-white-collar positions! Oliver and Shapiro estimate that in housing alone "institutional biases deprive the current generation of blacks of about $82 billion worth of assets" (169).

The cumulative effect of racial exclusion has been to confine blacks to the bottom of our social hierarchy. The legal scholar Derrick Bell, in *Faces at the Bottom of the Well: The Permanence of Racism*, affirms this view when he states, "Americans achieve a measure of social stability through their unspoken pact to keep blacks on the bottom—an aspect of social functioning that more than any other has retained its viability and its value to general stability from the very beginning of the American experience down to the present day."[36] When white gay men practice this exclusion in housing, they are participating in that "unspoken pact to keep blacks on the bottom."

CONCLUSION

Oliver and Shapiro consider suburbanization possibly "the greatest mass-based opportunity for home ownership and wealth accumulation in American history" (147). Gay neighborhood formation, Escoffier's "Territorial Economy" of the 1970s, is the "queered" spawn of 1950s suburbanization. Certainly, the example of gay gentrification of the Faubourg Marigny resulted in the equivalent of a queer male Levittown, the Long Island suburb that was built on a mass scale and was eminently affordable thanks to accessible financing, yet as late as 1960 had not a single black resident among its total population of 82,000 (147). Admittedly, differences exist between a suburb like Levittown and an urban neighborhood like the Faubourg Marigny, yet both are outposts of whiteness—one in the city, the other in the suburb—and both came into existence through policies that made the inclusion of whites and the exclusion of people of color appear normal and even natural. It is my view that the widely circulated image of the black gay impostor plays a role in allowing gay and non-gay whites to bond and to exclude black gay men.

In her famous essay "Notes on Camp," Susan Sontag prophesized that "homosexuals have pinned their integration into society on promoting the aesthetic sense."[37] Successful television shows in the new millennium like *Queer Eye for the Straight Guy, Will and Grace,* and *Queer as Folk,* with their overbearing images of gayness as whiteness and as correct taste, certainly proves Sontag correct.[38] But her prophecy was already evident in the 1970s with the formation of gay neighborhoods such as the Faubourg Marigny. Historical preservation was a strategy based on aesthetic taste that allowed mostly white gay men to accumulate wealth, one of the means for integrating into mainstream culture. The degree to which racialization through processes of inclusion and exclusion is significant for the formation of gay neighborhoods is seldom discussed. However, the fairly widespread controlling image of black gay men as impostors suggests that our exclusion from gay neighborhoods may be crucial for the formation of white inner-city outposts. In a sense, the malevolent black gay impostor legitimates the sense of fear that leads whites to prefer to live in racially homogenous neighborhoods. Ultimately, this fear undermines the social justice rhetoric of the queer movement.

NOTES

1. Marlon B. Ross, "Some Glances at the Black Fag: Race, Same-Sex Desire, and Cultural Belonging," *Canadian Review of Comparative Literature/Revue Canadienne de Littérature Comparée* (1994): 193–219.

2. Jeffrey Escoffier, "The Political Economy of the Closet: Notes Toward an Economic History of Gay and Lesbian Life before Stonewall," in *Homo Economics: Capitalism, Community, and Lesbian and Gay Life,* ed. Amy Gluckman and Betsy Reed (New York: Routledge, 1997), 124.

3. Steve Hogan and Lee Hudson, *Completely Queer: The Gay and Lesbian Encyclopedia* (New York: Holt, 1997), 18.

4. Michael Omi and Howard Winant, *Racial Formation in the United States: From the 1960s to the 1980s* (New York: Routledge, 1986), 66.

5. Ibid, 67.

6. John W. Roberts, *From Trickster to Badman: The Black Folk Hero in Slavery and Freedom* (Philadelphia: University of Pennsylvania Press, 1989), 11.

7. Michael Bronski, *Culture Clash: The Making of a Gay Sensibility* (Boston: South End Press, 1984), 12–13.

8. Frances Fitzgerald, *Cities on a Hill: A Journey through Contemporary American Cultures* (New York: Simon and Schuster, 1986), 48.

9. Manuel Castells, *The Rise of the Network Society* (London: Blackwell, 2000), 62.

10. Lawrence M. Knopp Jr., "Gentrification and Gay Neighborhood Formation in New Orleans: A Case Study" in *Homo Economics: Capitalism, Community, and Lesbian and Gay Life,* ed. Amy Gluckman and Betsy Reed (New York: Routledge, 1997), 47. (Subsequent cites appear as page numbers in the text.)

11. Ida B. Wells-Barnett, *Crusade for Justice: The Autobiography of Ida B. Wells,* ed. Alfreda M. Duster (Chicago: University of Chicago Press, 1970), 64.

12. Thomas A. Guglielmo, *White on Arrival: Italians, Race, Color, and Power in Chicago, 1890–1945* (Oxford: Oxford University Press, 2003), 169.

13. *Lianna,* dir. and screenplay by John Sayles, Metro-Goldwyn-Mayer, 1983.

14. Patricia Hill Collins, *Black Feminist Thought: Knowledge, Consciousness, and the Politics of Empowerment* (Boston: Unwin Hyman, 1990), 68.

15. E. Patrick Johnson, *Appropriating Blackness: Performance and the Politics of Authenticity* (Durham: Duke University Press, 2003), 69.

16. Ibid., 74.

17. Philip Brian Harper, "Walk-On Parts and Speaking Subjects: Screen Representations of Black Gay Men," in *Black Male: Representations of Masculinity in Contempo-*

rary *American Art,* ed. Thelma Golden (New York: Whitney Museum of American Art, 1994), 142.

18. *Portrait of Jason,* dir. Shirley Clarke, Mystic Fire Video, 1967.

19. Ibid., 145.

20. *The Boys in the Band,* dir. William Friedkin, screenplay by Mart Crowley, Twentieth Century-Fox, 1970.

21. Eldridge Cleaver, *Soul on Ice* (New York: Dell, 1968), 100.

22. *Next Stop, Greenwich Village,* dir. Paul Masursky, Twentieth Century-Fox, 1976.

23. *Car Wash,* dir. Michael Schultz, Universal Pictures, 1976.

24. Vito Russo, *The Celluloid Closet: Homosexuality in the Movies* (New York: Harper and Row, 1981), 229.

25. *The Crying Game,* dir. Neil Jordan, Miramax Films, 1992.

26. *Six Degrees of Separation,* dir. Fred Schepisi, screenplay by John Guare, MGM/UA, 1993.

27. *Chasing Amy,* dir. and screenplay by Kevin Smith, Miramax Films, 1997.

28. Daniel Mendelsohn, "I Want My Gay TV," *New York Magazine,* March 5, 2001, 35–36.

29. "Timing and Space," *Six Feet Under,* teleplay by Craig Wright, original airdate April 13, 2003.

30. "Perfect Circles," *Six Feet Under,* teleplay by Alan Ball, original airdate March 2, 2003.

31. Sheryll Cashin, *The Failures of Integration: How Race and Class Are Undermining the American Dream* (New York: Public Affairs, 2004), 10.

32. Ibid., 91.

33. *Tongues Untied,* dir. Marlon Riggs, Frameline, 1989.

34. *Neighborhoods: The Hidden Cities of San Francisco—The Castro* (aka *The Castro*), dir. Peter L. Stein, Wolfe Video, 1997.

35. Melvin L. Oliver and Thomas M. Shapiro, *Black Wealth/White Wealth* (New York: Routledge, 1997), 16. (Subsequent cites appear as page numbers in the text.)

36. Derrick Bell, *Faces at the Bottom of the Well: The Permanence of Racism* (New York: Basic Books, 1992).

37. Susan Sontag, "Notes on Camp," in *Against Interpretation* (New York: Farrar Strauss Giroux, 1986), 290.

38. Pay attention to the construction of "aesthetes" in these shows. Men are always the purveyors of elegance and taste, which is ironic, if not downright hateful, in the case of *Will and Grace.* Grace, the female protagonist, is an interior designer but lives in the apartment of Will, the white gay male protagonist. Presumably, Will provided the tasteful decorations for this apartment since Grace was unable to decorate her own apartment when she moved away from Will during one season of the show.

PART III

HOW TO TEACH THE UNSPEAKABLE:
RACE, QUEER STUDIES,
AND PEDAGOGY

BRYANT KEITH ALEXANDER

EMBRACING THE TEACHABLE MOMENT:
THE BLACK GAY BODY IN THE CLASSROOM
AS EMBODIED TEXT

As professors we rarely speak of the place of eros or the erotic in our classroom. Trained in the philosophical context of Western metaphysical dualism, many of us have accepted the notion that there is a split between the body and the mind. Believing this, individuals enter the classroom to teach as though only the mind is present and not the body. To call attention to the body is to betray the legacy of repression and denial that has been handed down to us by our professional elders.
—bell hooks, "Eros, Eroticism, and the Pedagogical Process"

"I think the new teacher's a queer," I turned around and saw they were talking about me, one false move and it would be all over, I could not drop my wrists or raise my voice. So I stood there up against the board arms folded pressed against my chest and looked without seeing or hearing until the children became a noiseless pattern—and all those years from when I sat among them stopped dead and I feared that they'd beat me up in the boys' room.—Perry Brass, "I Think the New Teacher's a Queer,"

The catchphrase "a teachable moment" identifies an intersection in time and space in which the ignorance of one person can be informed by another; and the conditions under which we live can be used to impart knowledge as well as to engage a critical dialogue. But while what is instructed in the moment is often verbal, by filling in gaps of knowledge or even figuratively "putting someone in their place," the demeanor and tenor of our articulated presence is also a potent component of the lesson taught.

For the black gay teacher, embracing the teachable moment, when it comes to talking about or through issues of sexuality and race, is not an issue that can be easily avoided. Our bodies are always already racially historicized, sexualized, physicalized, and demonized. In the classroom our presence is always already a disruption to the norms of our social construction. Talking about and presenting ourselves in the classroom as gay merely further illuminates the complexity of our character and the possibility of our beings. In "Face to Face with Alterity," Roger Simon states that the classroom is a place where one is constantly confronted with the incommensurability of that which cannot be reduced to a version of oneself. It is also the occasion on which such alterity can be returned. Engaged in this way, the assertion of particularities such as gay identity becomes a fundamental challenge to the nature of our participation in pedagogy.[1]

In the epigraph from of "Eros, Eroticism, and the Pedagogical Process," bell hooks identifies the tendency of many teachers to disengage when entering the classroom not only their bodies but also their sexualized human nature.[2] It is within this vein that I wish to explore the question of "teaching the unspeakable" as it relates to the overall focus of this book. In the process I wish to trouble the notion of "teaching the unspeakable" as well as reconstruct the tensive[3] negotiation of issues of sexuality in the classroom as "teachable moments."

While hooks in her essay refers to issues of desire between teachers and students, I am more interested in the notion of speaking about issues of sexuality, outing oneself, and positioning one's acknowledged gay body in the classroom. I am interested in constructing the *material fact* of the black gay body as subtext to the *material content* of the classroom.[4] In this case the course issues of gay/lesbian/transsexual/bisexual/queer/gender identity are not equated with the gay teacher per se, as if to declaim, "Of course a gay teacher would be teaching a course in queer theory!" I am interested in a situation in which the course content serves as the primary text and the gay identity of the teacher is the subtext through which the material, teaching, and classroom experiences are filtered.

I do not teach classes that have a "queer" designation—as in queer studies, or black gay fiction, or hetero/homo dichotomies. But as a black gay man, inevitably my own queer agenda[5] imbues the nature of my teaching in classes with titles like Oral Interpretation of Literature, Performing Culture, Oral

Communication, Instructional Theories in Communication, and Performance and Social Change. It is a part of my queer agenda that when speaking about social issues in the classroom I must address the political potency, the psychic disturbance, and the potential physical impact of those issues on my black gay body. The classroom is a space in which the personal is magnified, not diminished. What is unspeakable in the classroom is limited by the courage of those in the classroom. The situations I describe in the text following might aid me in my arguments because they poke and prod at the question: How can I not *not* speak the unspeakable?

When the in-class comments of students are suggestive of hatred and bigotry toward gays or other bodies that are "queer" to them, my body and voice representatively stand in place to address those issues. How can I not *not* address those issues that can cause harm to the physicalized or symbolically representative gay body, or the body of color, or the body marked by difference and the indifference of others—that is, my body? How must that remain unspeakable?

How can I not respond both as a teacher and as a black gay man when some of my "straight" black female students write papers in my class about the scarcity of "good black men," or about the "breakdown of the black family," or when they proceed to demonize black gay men for not "acting right," for not "being black," for not taking their "responsibility" as black men—thereby equating sexuality, character, and racial identity? How can I not *not* respond to those papers in articulated detail? In many ways these women are addressing their commentary *to* me, if not *at* me; the me who is unmarried, the me who speaks about his partner in class, the me who is *out* on campus, the me who defends the rights of many voices in class—including theirs, including my own. How must that remain unspeakable? In this teachable moment I want both to inform them of the complexity of my identity and to engage the promises and pitfalls of representation by speaking for other black gay men. I also want to signify on their own complex reifying identity that occasions the exchange. I want to say to them:

Dear Student,

I am first and always black—it is my history and my heritage marked and written in this dark flesh. It is the first thing noticed and remembered. My blackness has been predetermined by my divinely pure black parents with echoes from the dark continent of Africa. My blackness was germinated from a black seed, planted and nurtured in a black womb and harvested in black love. But that does not dictate my gender identity.

I am a man second, by genetics—a moment in time, a twist of fate, the balance of heat. As a black/man I bare a truth and a legacy, a stigma and a notable presence. I am remembered, reviled, and revered. I am what I am. My body signals a history, a societal dilemma, a passage, and a border crossing of the past, present, and the future. I see that your articulated desire can not be compromised and, yet, while our connected bodies may signal a race, the destiny of my desire can not be (re)directed, shackled, and dictated—not again!

I am homosexual, or dare I say it "gay," third, but not least—for this positionality signals a way of being that modifies and enhances, encodes and decodes, constructs and deconstructs the potential and possibilities of both being black and being a man. It is a positionality of divine betweenness. It also signals a history, a societal dilemma and a border crossing, both in time and space—but one fully engaged as the choice to follow an internal impulse, not clearly dictated like my black body or my male body, but the divine and dividing impulse to charter my own destiny.

My identity is mediated by the diaspora of my people, the design of my body and the object of my desire. I embrace myself as a black/man/ gay and celebrate the problematic and glorious intersection of that positionality—and dear student—while I have teased these individual strains from my complex identity, and enumerated them, please note that it has been for your benefit—for they are intricately interwoven into the tapestry of my being.[6] I also embrace your equally complex construction of self with the hope that somewhere we meet to celebrate our individuality and discuss the issues facing our community, without demonizing identity, lifestyles, or choices.

Respectfully submitted,

Your black gay teacher

That is what I want to say. That is what I say—knowing that the classroom is always mediated and that the confluence of geography, culture, language, and sexuality work in a tensive creation of identity leading to a performance that stands at the borders of social design.[7]

In their discussion of border pedagogy Stanley Aronowitz & Henry Giroux might describe these intersections as tensive sites where students and teachers "engage the multiple references that constitute different cultural codes, experiences, and languages. This means educating students to read these codes critically, to learn the limits of such codes, including the ones they use to construct their own narratives and histories."[8] Teaching occurs at those intersections where sanctioned content collides with lived experience—those moments when the "unspeakable" is spoken and the reverberation of social exchange ricochets and resonates in the classroom. Those moments when the personal becomes political and the pedagogical imperative is to articulate understanding without silencing voice—that of both the student and of the teacher.

I introduce in my classroom such public issues as California's Proposition 22 against same-sex marriage, and I state when the news of a hate crime against gays and lesbians appears on the last page of the *Los Angeles Times* and does not even make the nightly news. I introduce these issues as teachable moments to comment and critique on the logics that undergird the politics of positionality and the potency of absence.

When gay students out themselves in class, I take it as a personal accomplishment. This is not because I have created a safe space; for the classroom is never a safe space but is always filled with risk and challenge to the epistemological claims and ontological notions of who we are. Rather, I feel a personal sense of accomplishment because these students know that I will support them. They know that, if necessary, my black gay body will stand next to theirs in a barricade against ill will, and it will stand as a force for positive representation and identification of our gay identity by voicing our articulated experience in the classroom.

Yet, in spite of this, it is not my way to announce to the class that I am gay, to place this information on the pedagogical agenda as if to say: *Hi, My name is Professor Alexander, this is SPCH 468: Performance and Social Change, we will meet on Thursday evening from 4:20–8:00, and by the way I am gay.* No. That is not a part of my agenda—for I don't feel it necessary to out myself in ways that seem gratuitous and self-serving. "The articulation of identities in a pedagogical encounter cannot be reduced to a personal desire for cultural acknowledgement. What's at stake must be written [spoken] in different terms."[9] In terms marked by the occasion of the telling, and in moments in which my gay identity does not seemingly play a role in the specificity of the moment, I claim the privilege ritually afforded to heterosexuals, who present themselves without the need to self-identify.

Yet, I have outed myself on campus. In public performances scheduled during Black History Month, during Women's History Month, and during AIDS Awareness Week and Gay Pride Week I engage in formalized, publicized events in which queer folk of every color, shape, and size claim space and exercise voice to self-identify. During these publicly sanctioned windows of opportunity we politicize the personal (as if the personal is not always already politicized). On those days we stand up and speak out for those who cannot or will not speak for themselves and to those who would erase our lives.

I participate in these activities on my campus knowing that students will be attending; inviting my students to attend; and knowing that some will want to talk about these performances in class and others will not. It becomes a part of my pedagogy to have myself fully present in the presence of my students. For "we always teach, at some level, the personal but usually unspoken story of ourselves in the world. We teach with ourselves as our own most effective visual aids." The difficulty is deciding which part of the public/ personal dichotomy is addressable versus the personal that is private.[10]

I argue here that the classroom is a "liminal space" with contesting cultural performances. The classroom and the broader institution of schooling/ education is a rite of passage.[11] I argue that the classroom is "a symbolic arena where students and teachers struggle over the interpretations of metaphors, icons, and structures of meanings, and where symbols have both centripetal and centrifugal pulls"—forcing us together and pulling us apart.[12] In addition to the performance of education, which is fraught with policies and procedures that are cemented in ritual practice, issues of sex, gender, and race come to mediate the educational endeavor.

I further argue that black gay teachers are positioned betwixt and between the traditions of the academy and the social and cultural structures that impact our lives. The act of silencing the multiple realities of our lives results not only in sanitizing our lived experience but also threatens to reduce the potential of our teaching effectiveness.[13] For surely, the fullness of our beings and the fullness of our identity serves as the equipment with which we teach. The question becomes how do we negotiate the tensiveness that exists between our personal ways of being in the world with the traditions and tensions of the classroom? Are our personal lives unspeakable in the classroom? And, in marking our lives as unspeakable, are we not silencing ourselves and reifying the very oppressions that we resist?

As a black gay man, I realize that my body is a contested site. I realize that students may sense my difference and immediately cast me as other, since in the words of bell hooks, "so much of the quest for phallocentric manhood . . .

rests on a demand for compulsory heterosexuality."[14] In this case my black gay identity becomes counterintuitive to the historicized nature of black masculinity, an ideal that has been socially constructed and maintained. I become subject to a critique based in a "dick-thing masculinity."[15] Along with this, there is the risk that my authority as a teacher may also be questioned. This, of course, is in alignment with a society in which homophobic fear is still evidenced in tragic acts of violence, and fear and ignorance about the spread of AIDS casts all gay bodies as diseased and finds particular dis-ease in the black gay body. With this in mind the thought of outing oneself in the classroom is always already equated with risk: risk to the physical body, of course, but also risk to pedagogical authority. But not to engage the fullness of our character—when necessary, when doing so would make a meaningful impact—is to risk missing the teachable moment.

A STUDENT PERFORMING DRAG IN THE CLASSROOM

At one point in my beginning Oral Interpretation of Literature class I received from a student an analysis paper for a prose performance. I was amused by the student's selection, an excerpt from Meryl Cohn's *Do What I Say: Ms. Behavior's Guide to Gay and Lesbian Etiquette,*[16] which is a trade book in the camp etiquette genre. The student constructed his performance around his vision of Ms. Behavior as an overly exaggerated hyperbolic drag queen dishing out advice to would-be-drag queens and the ill-advised "natural" woman.

I was further amused when the student pranced into the performance space on six-inch stiletto heels like a high-stepping carnival performer, his stylized version of femininity. Other than his shoes and his affected manner his drag was suggestive, as all drag is suggestive. He wore black corduroys and a red shirt—of the polo variety. He resisted shaving his facial hair—a vandike (his male drag). If the dualism of his appearance forestalled the believability of his drag, he circulated pictures of himself done up—his face beat[17] with make-up and full dark lips, wearing a larger-than-life black wig and a form-fitting black dress that emphasized his ample bosom—Maria Callas, I believe, on steroids. The size of his faux breasts and the thinness of the dress revealed a white brassiere—a documented fashion faux pas that competed against his pedagogical credibility on drag etiquette.

In thinking about this performance I am disturbed and amused at how the student actor reconstructs the audience from students in the classroom to audience members at a drag show, blurring the lines while knowing that the classroom is always a site of performance and drag is always relative. And I also begin to think about the shifting roles of teacher-student, performer-audience, spectacle and spectators in the classroom. I begin to think, like Jane Gallop, that "pedagogical positions are like drag performances."[18]

I am intrigued by the student's pedagogical performance as he instructs the class on the proper decorum for being a drag queen. His method calls attention to the spectacle of instruction while it speaks to the spectacle of gender performance. But I am not as interested in his campy delivery—this bigger than life queen who has found her/his way to the runway of my classroom—with unsuspecting and captive viewers. I am interested and amused by the other students in the class. They are a motley crew. During previous discussions related to issues of sex/sexuality/gender, they have silently asserted their heterosexuality by performing "het-texts"—stories of male-female desire, masculine zeal, and fatal femininity as if to extend the expected heteronormative standard of gender performance into my classroom as an insurgent act of performative resistance against what they know is my queer identity.

I muse on their response to Ms. Behavior. They giggle and guffaw as she walks in her stiletto heels allowing the point and balance of that performative act to dictate her body gesture. They issue embarrassed smiles when she/he talks about the dilemmas and challenges of finding size 15 pumps. They direct resentful stares when she/he speaks of the negotiation of dressing rooms—praying for a sign that says, "unisex" so that she/he does not have to make the choice. But he, the man in performance, has made some clear choices.

I notice one of the boys sitting in the back of the room. In class he previously did a performance of Hercules—his idealized masculine idol—in a text called "The Choices of Hercules."[19] In his performance (of gender) he preened and flexed his sculpted physique and beamed over an idealized feminine construct in the text. He is eye candy for the girls in the class (and for some of the boys). But now Hercules is cowering in the corner, his body angled to the wall as he takes sneak peeks at the spectacle of femininity that is Ms. Behavior. Ironically, in his own performance text his character makes a choice between two women: the first is called Labor, the second is called Pleasure. Whereas Pleasure was "beautiful as a summer day," Labor "was not as beautiful as the other, [but] had a countenance pure and gentle." The student chooses Labor over Pleasure.

Ms. Behavior speaks about the labor that is gender performance. Yet

Hercules is performing resistance, for while in both his performance and the one he is viewing, woman is what Parama Roy calls a "concept-metaphor." His performance uses the construction of woman to substantiate his own masculinity and heterosexuality, and therefore he could not endorse the femininity performed by his classmate—thereby questioning the very construct of gender performance and his own identity.[20] Hercules looks back and forth between the picture in his head, the drag queen—every bit the femme fatale, and the male in performance; they are the same and not the same. He smiles then passes the pictures on quickly, as if embarrassed—this time refusing to make the choice of Labor over Pleasure.

During the performance I also muse at the women in the class who perform as a tensive audience of their drag queen big sister. She/he both challenges their comfort in femininity and confirms the constructedness of femininity as well as their enculturation into a cult of beauty. When Ms. Behavior instructs them on the danger of blue eye shadow, the negotiation of their first pair of heels, and the process of finding the right formal dress, they nod and giggle like sorority girls acknowledging secret fashion tips.

At the end of the performance all of the students rush to ask questions. The men want to know about the negotiation of wearing heels (and how long it took him to learn). The women confirm the performance of gender—not this student in drag or his character, but how his instruction parallels their own performance of gender. They begin to tell stories, sharing their own personal successes and failures. Yet, to find their comfort in the complex issues of gender performance and sexuality (as presented by Ms. Behavior), they must reject the pedagogical trigger of their body memory—as same and not the same.

The students invalidate the meaningfulness of the message by relegating the performance as spectacle when they say, "That was funny. You're so funny." For them, spectacle is something that amuses, shocks, and dumbfounds, but does not inform. Spectacle is only something that draws attention to and marks the difference between the normal and the not normal, performance and performativity, the thing and the thing done—establishing distance between the drama of the actor and the aesthetic distance of the spectator. As Judith Hamera suggests about the dancing female body in another context, Ms. Behavior "troubles the performative boundaries that separate laboring novice and transcendent virtuosic [female], reconceiving the typical plot of spectacular, autonomous agency to which such bodies [fe/male] are generally consigned."[21]

And it is in that moment that I decide I must intervene. I intervene knowing that I am going to make a spectacle of myself, but I am hoping that they don't see me exclusively as a gay-identified man coming to the rescue of a drag queen in distress, but rather that they see me as their teacher (who is gay) engaged in a moment of instruction, which can also be a moment of rescue and recovery. As I walk to the front of the room, I keep in check my own pastiche image as teacher.

I feel the need to address the student's performance as it meets the assignment, as it acts as a construction and deconstruction of femininity, and how this relates to the nature of the students' comments. I feel the need, as I often feel the need, to deconstruct my position as teacher in moments in which the socio-political aspect of the curriculum or course content are in tension with the personal aspects of how I carry myself in the world and the things that I value. I need to remind them that for our purposes performance has to be *dulce et utile,* sweet and useful—the aesthetic crafted with intention. Like my teaching, it must be carefully crafted to inform about content, while signaling larger issues of decorum and the social politics that dictate our lives. I need to ask them to look at the intention of the performance, which seems to be far more than simply fulfilling the assignment.

How does the performance of Ms. Behavior inform us? We knew that the presenter is gay because he has mentioned it often. I have created a space where that is commonplace; for if I am going to be comfortable in my own queer identity I must find ways to fuse that aspect of myself with everything else that I am, including my role as teacher—and thus give space for others to walk in relative ease in the classroom. It is not my desire to flaunt the implicit and/or explicitness of my difference, but to present myself as authentically as I can, to be fully present in the classroom and to use the fullness of my identity as the tools with which I teach.

The student's performance of gender helps to denaturalize the everydayness of gender performance. He magnifies the constructedness of gender by placing his body on those illusory borders that separate and signify what it performatively means to be a "woman" and what it performatively means to be a "man." As teachers we also place our bodies in the instructional gaps negotiating the tensions that often exist between our teaching persona and the fullness of our being. Our sexualized and racialized bodies always signal a history, an enfleshed knowledge that may or may not, to our students, obviously inform our pedagogy and our orientation to the subject matter.[22] Yet, in this pedagogical performance we come to see not only how Ms. Behavior narrates gender performance but also how we are implicated in that process as actors and spectators, engaging our own performance and reviewing the performances of others.

The student's performance opens up a space where we can come to question the very notion of "misbehaviors" as they relate to the expected performances of sex, sexuality, and gender, reduced to issues of heteronormativity—knowing, of course, that within a technocratic construction of education,[23] the body of the teacher is constructed as straight, if not neutered, conferring intellectual knowledge without "libidinal complications."[24] The pedagogical performance of Ms. Behavior forces us to realize that as teachers/performers in the classroom we are trapped in the spectatorial gaze of our students. We are positioned somewhere in the binary between parody and reality, between the real and the not real, and the choices between our personal Pleasure and the Labor of pedagogy.

As I stand in front of the class engaged in the pedagogical performance of commentary and critique, I think about the imaginary picture of myself in drag that is circulating around the room, the me and the not me.[25] Somewhere between my praise of the performance and the admonishment of the audience, the students see my biases and my allegiances. They see the imaginary slip of my drag-teacher performance showing, if not literally dragging,[26] beneath the presumed objectivity of the teacher. And I wonder if for them somehow my queer identity competes against my pedagogical credibility.

Somewhere between my comments on the performance and my clarification of the issues, lies the me and the not me. The black gay man in me has challenged the impression of the "straight" teacher and the sanitized nature of classroom discourse around issues of race, sex, sexuality, and gender that had so often signaled my classroom experience as a student. Cheryl Johnson refers to this as engaging "disinfecting dialogues" in order "to sanitize [and] deodorize the 'funkiness' of racism and sexism" in the classroom.[27] Such knowledge is considered dangerous: "Many kinds of knowledge are dangerous: dangerous because they destabilize established common-sense worldviews; dangerous because they pull the veil away from oppression, discrimination and suffering, making for uncomfortable confrontation with these issues."[28]

And now in the classroom I am trapped in the tensive negotiation of viewing and responding to performances of sexuality and sexualized performances, and how my own desire and disdain becomes a politicized variable. Yet I know that this is not a trap, as much as it is the quest of good pedagogy—

to question not only what to teach and how to teach it—but why? The condition of tensiveness does not signal strife and resistance as much as it reveals the contrasts and conflicts in which teachers infuse their teaching—an academic intellectual knowing tempered with a personal sense of being in the world.

So I must respond to Hercules's questions and accusations about my objectivity and the notion of promoting a homosexual agenda in the classroom.

Dear Student—

In this class I speak from the position of the teacher and a person in the world.

In this class I speak with the express intent in clarifying issues, challenging thoughts, encouraging critical introspection, and helping students to see "themselves as members of a broader social community, responsive and responsible to it."

In this class I speak as a teacher who has some degree of academic accomplishment, but not at the expense of the person that I am or would like to be.

In this class I speak as a teacher, but as a teacher who is Black, and a teacher who is gay. My academic knowledge is filtered through the person that I am. Sometimes that knowledge influences other aspects of my life. But most often the history of my being, the history of being black in this country, the history being gay in this country and my history of being a black gay academic—all temper and direct my understanding of academic issues and direct my teaching. It happens to help recoup the past and redirect the future.

So my comments related to Ms. Behavior are not designed to promote a "homosexual agenda" but rather a critical examination of the performance as it met the assignment and the accompanying social critique it offered on the construction of gender.

While I appreciate your questions, I would also ask that you reflect on why you asked those questions. Does the performance of "misbehavior" challenge you in some ways that question your notions of the normal? Would you prefer to silence such dissent? To question whether Ms. Behavior or I are trying to promote a homosexual agenda is also to have us question whether you are promoting an agenda of heteronormativity; therefore, you become some legislator of what is moral and normal. Are you setting yourself up as the arbiter of good taste? And since I am black and Ms. Behavior is Latino and we are gay, and you are a self-identified straight white man asking the questions, should these be factored into our discussion as well?

How does this performance work in tension with your own? Here, I am speaking directly to your performance of prose, not the constructedness of your gender performance—though that would be an interesting project. Do you see the relationship between this text and your own choices, meaning "The Choices of Hercules"? Can you engage in that critical endeavor?

Respectfully submitted,
Your black gay teacher

TO TEACH OR NOT TO TEACH?

"To teach the unteachable" is not only a question about whether or not the black gay or lesbian teacher should out himself/herself in the classrooms or even about the intersections of race and sexuality. Rather the question is about addressing the borders that mark the territories of blackness, masculinity, femininity, sexuality, and pedagogy. The question is, do we want to use our bodies as a necessary bridge to forge (in my case) a new black masculine mystique that in its very existence and persistence is a critique of sexism, misogyny, patriarchy, phallocentrism, and homophobia? The answer is linked to our desire to engage a project for all black folk—gay or straight—to address the legislation of desire and the constraint of individual agency.

The notion of the "unspeakable" forestalls the possibility of enlightenment and resists the embracing of "the teachable moment." This is the challenge; for as Cornel West says, "our truncated public discussion on race [or sexuality] suppresses the best of who and what we are as a people, because we fail to confront the complexity of the issues in a candid and critical manner."[29] I also echo Adrienne Rich in "If Not with Others, How?" when she says: "My hope is that the movement we are building can further the conscious work of turning Otherness into a keen lens of empathy, that we can bring into being a politics based on concrete, heartfelt understanding of what it means to be Other."[30]

Ultimately, the classroom is a site of possibility. It is a "contested terrain in which competing ideologies collide, and transformation is already an incipient possibility."[31] We must all seize the teachable moment because, according to Manthia Diawara, "such [action] is both political and theoretical: it refers to and draws on existing traditions; represents the actor [teacher] as occupying a different position in society; and interpellates the audience's responses to emerging images of black [gay and lesbian] people."[32]

The question of pedagogy is not what to teach, but how to teach it.[33] How do we show our students the substance of our character and what constitutes a brave and bold pedagogy? As bell hooks quotes Thomas Merton in his essay on pedagogy, "Learning to Live": "If the purpose of education is to show students how to define themselves 'authentically and spontaneously in relation to the world,' then we can best teach if we are self-actualized."[34] So, how can we not *not* teach about race and sexuality? We do it not necessarily through the *material content* of the course, but through our conviction and the *material fact* of our black gay bodies in the classroom, which always already signals a teachable moment.

NOTES

1. Roger I. Simon, "Face to Face with Alterity: Postmodern Jewish Identity and the Eros of Pedagogy," in *Pedagogy: The Question of Impersonation,* ed. Jane Gallop (Bloomington: Indiana University Press, 1995), 90.

2. bell hooks, "Eros, Eroticism, and the Pedagogical Process," in *Between Borders: Pedagogy and the Politics of Cultural Studies,* ed. Henry A. Giroux and Peter McLaren (New York: Routledge, 1994), 113.

3. In performance terminology the word "tensive" is used not in relation to tension, as in strife or friction, but to the dramatic elements that exist in any dynamic, rhetorical situation or text that contributes to stasis and promotes the actualization of intent or possibility.

4. Here I am playing with Frantz Fanon's notion of "the fact of Blackness" to refer to both the material facticity of the body and the social construction of what it means to be black. See Franz Fanon, *Black Skin, White Masks* (New York: Grove Press, 1967), 116.

5. I use the term "queer agenda" to focus on the personalized issues that impact my life as a gay man. I do not use the term in the same vein as those ultraconservatives or religious fanatics who would suggest a "radical homosexual agenda" that would include concentrated recruitment efforts. But while I see my queer agenda to be pedagogical in nature—to teach, inform, and enlighten—I also see an incommensurable separation between "my" queer agenda and my pedagogical agenda as a classroom teacher. It is not my aim at any point to teach perceivably gay and lesbian students "how to be gay" (see the short piece in the *Chronicle of Higher Education,* April 7, 2000, p. A12).

6. At the Black Queer Studies in the Millennium conference, in making these delineations, Dwight McBride asked about the problematics of creating this kind of "hierarchy of identity." In a playful exchange, in which I addressed him as "Dear Dwight," I acknowledged the complex issues involved but added that as teachers we must meet our students where they are with the hope of moving them above and beyond, or further inward or outward, extrapolating the known to the unknown. The delineating hierarchy expressed in my letter "Dear student" is a reflection more of the student's process than mine. This process also begins to question the claiming and prioritizing of certain identities above others. It begins to question how we construct ourselves and how we are not only constructed by others, but also how others make claims and demands on and investments in our identity. Members of our "racial" community demand that we "act black." Members of our "sex category" demand that we "act like a real man (or woman)." Members of our "gender community" demand that we engage in the politics of representing—as in being "out." The delineations and hierarchy set forth in this passage is my preliminary attempt to tease through issues of representation, accountability, and identity constructions that are no more problematic in the realm of gay identity constructions than they are in "straight" notions of normalcy.

7. Issues of racial identity at geographical borders that mark difference are explored by Sangeeta Tyagi in "Writing in Search of a Home: Geography, Culture, and Language in the Creation of Racial Identity," in *Names We Call Home: Autobiography on Racial Identity*, ed. Becky Thompson and Sangeeta Tyagi (New York: Routledge, 1998), 43.

8. Stanley Aronowitz and Henry A. Giroux, eds., *Postmodern Education: Politics, Culture, and Social Criticism* (Minneapolis: University of Minnesota Press, 1991), 118–19.

9. Simon, "Face to Face with Alterity," 90.

10. Indira Karamcheti, "Caliban in the Classroom," in *Pedagogy: The Question of Impersonation,* ed. Jane Gallop (Bloomington: Indiana University Press, 1995), 138–46. I further play with Karamcheti's idea in my own article, "Performing Culture in the Classroom: An Instructional (Auto)Ethnography," *Text and Performance Quarterly* 19.4 (1999): 271–306.

11. Victor Turner, "Images and Reflections: Ritual, Drama, Carnival, Film, and Spectacle in Cultural Performance," in *The Anthropology of Performance*, ed. Victor Turner (New York: Performing Arts Journal Publications, 1986), 25.

12. Peter McLaren, *Schooling as a Ritual Performance: Towards a Political Economy of Educational Symbols and Gestures* (New York: Routledge, 1993), 6.

13. Herb Green offers a similar notion when he says, "The act of silencing the multiple-realities that I experience as a gay man, and an African-American, in order to stay in line with the prescribed rules of academic training/reasoning/disciplining,

has had a profound effect on the way in which I write, giving me the sense that I am not writing in dialogue but in response to what is deemed rational, meaningful, and worth critical examination" (Green, "Turning the Myths of Black Masculinity Inside/ Out," in *Names We Call Home: Autobiography on Racial Identity*, ed. Becky Thompson and Sangeeta Tyagi (New York: Routledge, 1998), 255.

14. bell hooks, "Reconstructing Black Masculinity," in *Black Looks: Race and Representation* (Boston: South End Press, 1992), 112.

15. bell hooks, *Outlaw Culture: Resisting Representation* (New York: Routledge, 1994), 94.

16. The excerpt is taken from "Donning a Dress, Do Real Men Do Drag?" in Meryl Cohn's *Do What I Say: Ms. Behavior's Guide to Gay and Lesbian Etiquette* (New York: Houghton Mifflin, 1995), 54–58. Sergio's (the student in this performance) drag name is Sabrina.

17. "Beat" is a term used by "female impersonators/allusionists" to describe a heavy contoured application of makeup.

18. Jane Gallop, "Knot a Love Story," *Yale Journal of Criticism* 5.3 (1992): 217.

19. James Baldwin, "The Choices of Hercules," in *The Book of Virtues*, ed. William J. Bennett (New York: Simon and Schuster, 1993), 390–92.

20. Parama Roy, "As the Master Saw Her," in *Crusing the Performative*, ed. Sue-Ellen Case, Phillip Brett, and Susan Forster (Bloomington: Indiana University Press, 1995), 119.

21. Judith Hamera, "The Romance of Monsters: Theorizing the Virtuoso Body," *Theatre Topics*, 10.2 (2000): 150. In this quote Hamera is actually referring to Naoyuki Oguri.

22. Toni Morrison uses the construction of "genderized, sexualized and racialized" to describe the world context in which she writes "unencumbered by dreams of subversion or rallying gestures at fortress walls" (Morrison, *Playing in the Dark: Whiteness and the Literary Imagination* [Cambridge, Mass.: Harvard University Press, 1990], 4–5).

23. Technocratic models conceptualize teaching as a discrete and scientific understanding, embracing depersonalized solutions for education that often translate into the regulation and standardization of teacher practices and curricula, and rote memorization of selected "facts" that can easily be measured through standardized testing. As such the role of the teacher is reduced to that of an uncritical, "objective," and "efficient" distributor of information. See Pepi Leistyna and Arlie Woodrum, "Context and Culture: What is Critical Pedagogy?" in *Breaking Free: The Transformative Power of Critical Pedagogy*, ed. Pepi Leistyna, Arlie Woodrum and Stephen Sherblom, (Cambridge, Mass.: Reprint Series No. 27. Harvard Educational Review, 1996), 1.

24. Roy, "As the Master Saw Her," 119.

25. Here I am capitalizing on Judith Hamera's argument when she writes about "the conflation of the body and identity and, in turn, fore-grounding the 'impossibil-

ity of obliterating the 'difference' that comprises representation—specifically here, the difference between the 'me' (my body/identity), the 'not/me' (*not* my identity), and the 'not-not *me*' (*maybe* my body/identity and maybe not)" (Hamera, "Emotional/ Theoretical Response to HIV Education through the Performance of Personal Narrative," in *HIV Education: Performing Personal Narrative,* ed. Frederick Corey [Tempe: Arizona State University Press, 1993], 54).

26. Eric Partridge suggests that "[drag] describes the petticoat or skirt used by actors when playing female parts" and that the word derives from "the drag of the dress (on the grounds), as distinct from the non-dragginess of trousers" (quoted in Roger Baker, *Drag: A History of Female Impersonation in the Performing Arts* [New York: New York University Press, 1994], 17).

27. Cheryl Johnson, "Disinfecting Dialogues," in *Pedagogy: The Question of Impersonation,* ed. Jane Gallop (Bloomington: Indiana University Press, 1995), 129.

28. Debbie Epstein and James T. Sears, *A Dangerous Knowing: Sexuality, Pedagogy and Popular Culture* (London: Cassell, 1999), 1.

29. Cornel West, *Race Matters* (New York: Vintage Books, 1994), 4.

30. See Adrienne Rich, "If Not with Others, How?" In *New Worlds of Literature,* ed. Jerome Beaty and John P. Hunter (New York: Norton, 1996), 786–91.

31. Elyse Pineau, "Critical Performative Pedagogy: Fleshing Out the Language of Liberatory Education," paper presented at the Conference for the Pedagogy of the Oppressed, University of Nebraska, Omaha, February 1995, 6.

32. Manthia Diawara, "Black Studies, Cultural Studies: Performative Acts," in *Race, Identity and Representation in Education,* ed. Cameron McCarthy and Warren Crichlow (New York: Routledge, 1993), 265.

33. Roger Simon defines pedagogy as "a term which signals the practical synthesis of the question, 'What should be taught and why?' with considerations as to how that teaching should take place" (Simon, *Teaching against the Grain: Texts for a Pedagogy of Possibility* [New York; Monthly Review Press, 1992], 55).

34. Quoted in hooks, "Eros, Eroticism, and the Pedagogical Process," 118.

KEITH CLARK

ARE WE FAMILY?
PEDAGOGY AND THE RACE
FOR QUEERNESS

> What interests me most in the work I do . . . is the thirst
> among students and faculty, but especially among students—
> black students, white students—for a way to talk about these
> things, a vocabulary that allows them to talk about race in a
> manner that is not diminishing, demeaning, reductive or ad
> hominem. Race is a very difficult thing to talk about, because
> the conversation frequently ends up being patronizing, guilt
> ridden, hostile or resentful. But for those interested in the
> study of literature and the writing of literature, it is some-
> thing you have to confront and think about.
> —Toni Morrison, quoted in Katharine Driscoll Coon, " 'A
> Rip in the Tent': Teaching (African) American Literature"

One of the unanticipated benefits of participating in the Black Queer Studies
in the Millennium conference was that it prompted a much-needed self-
assessment, a kind of professional reality check regarding the choices I make
as a teacher of African American literature. The event occasioned an extended metapedagogical moment, as I pondered my position in the classroom as more than just titular authority as "professor." I began to consider all
that informs my choices—the texts I include as well as exclude, the language
of the syllabus, my pedagogical mission. In effect I had to consider what
Bryant Keith Alexander has aptly called "performing in the classroom"—the
professorial persona that I present; a veritable corporeal sign system that is
textualized and miscontextualized, read professionally, intellectually, racially,
sexually, and even physically.[1] For instance, a student will invariably "read"

my hair, and will do so usually in ways such as, for example, on one occasion when a white male "complimented" me on my ability to fuse two ostensibly antithetical personae: the "cool" English professor (since dreadlocked hair is consistently read as "countercultural") and the denizen of the rarefied ivory tower, a space considered patently uncool.

I think Toni Morrison's impassioned comments about the difficulties inherent in "talking race" speak to my anxieties about what the editors of this volume, E. Patrick Johnson and Mae G. Henderson, have called "teaching the unspeakable." I had to unpack my own anxiety about the extent to which I will address issues of sexual orientation not so much in textual terms but in personal ones. This self-evaluation, to be candid, was discomfiting. In theorizing what she deems "engaged pedagogy," bell hooks opens an interrogative space for exploring how the "teacherly" and "private" selves intersect and potentially collide: "Engaged pedagogy does not seek simply to empower students. Any classroom that employs a holistic model of learning will also be a place where teachers grow, and are empowered in the process. That empowerment cannot happen if we refuse to be vulnerable while encouraging students to take risks. Professors who expect students to share confessional narratives but who are themselves unwilling to share are exercising power in a manner that could be coercive."[2] Though the basic accuracy of hooks's claims is unimpeachable, the notion of a mutually open, reciprocal exchange between professor and student nevertheless might trouble the pedagogical waters for some. Though I routinely and unswervingly foreground issues related to same-sex desire in the works I teach, hooks's comments forced me to confront my ambivalence about teaching a course devoted solely to black gay and lesbian literature. Is it because I imagine that my vaunted status as "brother-professor" might be compromised in the eyes of some students— that I might exacerbate what Bryant Keith Alexander correctly calls the problematic culturally based equation that cool plus authenticity equals authority?[3] Ultimately, I have had to reevaluate how I, in hooks's terms, can "empower" students in ways that are not "coercive," in ways that don't replicate hegemonic pedagogical models where the professor's privileged position as centered subject becomes the locus of power and domination; becomes disempowering and de-voicing when attempting to do otherwise.

In rethinking the personal-professional-sexual nexus, I found George Haggerty's essay " 'Promoting Homosexuality' in the Classroom" especially provocative though problematic. He unequivocally designates the classroom a politicized and sexualized zone: "As gay and lesbian faculty members, we have a duty to give our gay and lesbian students—all our students, really—the tools they need to *achieve a sexual identity* in a society that is determined to make that identity an impossibility. That duty includes being open about our own sexuality, of course; it also means being open to the sexualities of the texts and the sexualities of the students."[4] He then adduces that "*Gay and lesbian professors have to teach their students to be gay and lesbian, that is, because few people in authority inside or outside the academy can or will.*"[5] This conceptualization of the classroom as a site that inexorably melds the personal, textual, and sexual is one that I certainly comprehend in our fervently conservative, anti-gay climate, but it evinces a number of knotty problems. First and foremost, Haggerty seems to mandate that we proselytize if not cheerlead, that we indoctrinate students with *the* "correct" way to be gay. This pedagogical subject construction presupposes that there exists a priori some form of "queerness" that needs only to be mapped out and navigated. In this rather prescriptive framework, our students are reduced to willing supplicants awaiting our "sexual identity healing," to invoke a song title from a late R&B icon (whose surname is ironically apropos in this discussion).

Absent from Haggerty's presumptive guidelines for instructors is an acknowledgment of an intersubjective professorial subject—one who is more composite than monolith. David Román thoughtfully explodes the notion of an unencumbered, unified "queer" identity in "Teaching Differences: Theory and Practice in a Lesbian and Gay Studies Seminar": "What happens, for instance, when one considers differences related to the construction of a self-identity that are drawn from, say, ethnicity, race, gender, or spiritual expression? By weighing the implications of such self-fashioning, which is based on a diverse field of difference, we were able to recognize the fluidity of self-constructions, thus questioning the entire phenomenon of historically determined forms of self-presence that are based only on marks of sexuality."[6] Indeed, what *does* become of issues regarding class and racial/ethnic affiliation vis-à-vis the "teaching of students how to be gay or lesbian"? Is the underlying assumption that all of the professors are white, and that all of the "queers" are male? Are questions of race and class subsumed by the privileged—at least in this context—identity of sexual orientation? What about professors who themselves have not reconciled their sexual and professional selves? And what about a nongay-identified professor whose raised consciousness can be marshaled in the struggle to combat homophobia? Certainly, there could be other instances in which a professor's "modeling" could contribute to a student's self-actualization and self-awareness. But a compulsory "homo-sexualizing" of the classroom constitutes a sort of "QC" or queer correctness, by which some professors may be deemed insufficiently "queer" if they are not "out" in ways deemed acceptable. I am reminded here of a bracingly honest assertion by Ian Barnard: "Any US politics, no matter how coalitional its compass, that identifies itself in terms of sexual orientation only (e.g., queer nation or lesbian and gay studies for example) will be a white-centered and dominated politics, since only white people in this society can afford to see their race as unmarked, as an irrelevant category of analysis."[7] We must be cognizant of our students' multisubjectivities, the array of identities that encompasses race, ethnicity, gender, sexuality, religion/spirituality, and class. Stratifying identities potentially fragments our students' multifaceted selves in ways that undermine our desire to enlighten and empower.

Even when this scenario of a gay-identified professor modeling to a presumed gay student "to be gay" is "homo-racial," an experience of a then-undergraduate friend of mine attests to the potential pitfalls of personalizing and sexualizing the classroom. The friend relates how his African American literature professor (both student and instructor being black) commented on a gay issue and called on my friend for corroboration in a "you-got-my-back" moment. My friend, a senior at the time, was in the inchoate stages of "confronting" his gay identity, and he thus suffered a great deal of consternation at being outed in this way. I certainly acknowledge that we must be vigilant in countering heterocentric pedagogical praxes and uncloseting same-sex silences in the texts we study. But just as important, in the race for queerness we must guard against imposing our own idiosyncratic "codes of queer conduct" when we are unsure as to when and where our students enter our classrooms in terms of their personal and sexual identity formation.

Of course, I'm not naive enough to view the classroom as a depoliticized zone, because of the very fact that I, my students, and the texts we read are all raced, gendered, and sexualized by virtue of the cubbyholes into which our culture demands we be slotted. However, I had not fully considered the implications of what David Román calls the "subject positions that we bring into our classrooms both through our syllabi and through our own position(s)."[8] To be sure, the selection of texts and composing of syllabi are indeed assertions of pedagogical agency. But the political dimension of pedagogy was illuminated for me when a same-gender-loving[9] friend, a newly minted high school instructor (the undergraduate in my previous anecdote), declared that not only was he planning to teach *Go Tell It on the Mountain,* but that he planned on *going there*—of specifying for his eleventh graders the novel's homoerotic under- or overpinnings. His valiant act of instructional intervention demonstrates how the way we present texts is as important as the selection of those texts. Unbeknownst to this friend, he modeled how I must be vigilant and proactive in unveiling same-gender-loving issues, more vehement in disrupting *hetero-textist* pedagogical paradigms. At professional meetings, I now routinely engage friends and instructors of African American literature who profess a sensitivity and commitment to dismantling hegemonic teaching practices. For instance, I ask them whether, when teaching venerated works like *Invisible Man,* if they do a thorough reading of episodes such as that between the Invisible Man and "Young Emerson." Recall that in this scene a white male assumes that racial and financial privilege entitles him to fetishize and lure the neophyte invisible man's black body. While engaging my colleagues, I also inquire as to whether their intertextual reading of Ellison includes a gloss on Whitman's *Calamus* poems, which the text invokes by name. Such conversations often leave me beleaguered and perplexed about the layers of invisibility under which many of us labor no matter how noble our intentions.

Writing this essay also enabled me to think of my syllabi as more than a listing of great works and literary luminaries. They are, in fact, our students' first engagement of our pedagogical positions and objectives. I have noticed that, in addition to the de rigueur language extolling "diversity" and condemning all forms of racial, political, and gender oppression, some professors have begun including language on their syllabi proscribing utterances that may be construed as "racist, sexist, or homophobic." Certainly, I applaud the commitment to fostering a respectful, hostility-free atmosphere. However, this gesture, much like "promoting homosexuality," seems wellintentionally wrongheaded, amounting to a policing of forms of speech that we've deemed unacceptable. If our declarations of "openness and diversity" are to be more than glorified shibboleths, we must be mindful of the invaluable teaching moments we might squander by attempting to circumscribe student language. At such moments, we can exploit our professorial subject positions by offering students a compelling countervoice, one that challenges their often shortsighted assumptions about race, gender, or sexuality.

One such moment occurred in my twentieth century African American literature survey during a discussion of Ann Petry's short story "Miss Muriel." "Dottle Smith," a black male character described as having a "very fat bottom which sort of sways from side to side as he walks" and as "seeming kind of ladylike" (36), evoked a devaluative response from a black woman student. Echoing the characters who uttered these remarks, she expressed her distaste for what she labeled the character's "effeminacy" and "queerness" (she then launched into a screed about "theater people," several of whom she insisted behave in similarly repulsive "ladylike" fashion). This moment reminded me of a comparable incident related by Elizabeth Swanson Goldberg, who wrote about her experience of screening the film *Six Degrees of Separation* for an audience she described as "first year students at a largely white, upper-middle-class, Midwest university." Upon seeing rapper-cum-actor Will Smith in bed with a white male hustler, "the auditorium full of students erupts into a chorus of disgusted moans, groans, and simulated retching sounds."[10] Similarly, after some of my black students expressed an equally palpable disdain for Petry's "Dottle Smith," I articulated how their response reenacted the very prejudices that Petry's story exposes as potentially malignant: how different communities, irrespective of the race, gender, class, or sexual orientation of its denizens, can promote dangerously exclusive practices that endanger the community's overall welfare. I'm not sure whether the imposing of an authoritative classroom discourse would permit students the freedom to engage texts in their own language, no matter how biased and odious we may find it. Thus, such reflexive moments, when classroom dynamics replicate textual ones, are potentially lost when we try to "legislate" student discourse by outlawing certain language in our syllabi. Doing so might have the unintended effect of censoring opposing voices and sanitizing the classroom, making it far less safe than we might have imagined. Ultimately, I was grateful for my student's passionate albeit parochial response, for it permitted me to begin dismantling the "hierarchy of hate"[11] where one group, in this instance a few African American students, perpetuates the very hegemonic attitudes that in other contexts would designate them alien and Other.

To conclude this essay, I offer three relatively practical strategies for "teaching the unspeakable," ones that inform the way I structure all of my literature courses. First, we must continue to foreground and voice same-gender-loving issues, thereby disrupting the ways that many teachers/scholars approach "canonical" black authors and texts. Along with the dearth of critics writing about textual same-gender-love from a racial perspective—and I applaud fellow scholars such as Charles Nero and Dwight McBride for their trenchant work that has interrupted the critical hegemony that renders some topics as "white" or taboo—there is a tendency to approach "great works" and writers from a heterotextual perspective. So when I teach Langston Hughes's sanctioned, canonical "blues" poems, I also distribute largely unanthologized ones such as "Café: 3 am" and "Port Town" so that students can grasp the full trajectory of Hughes's artistic imagination and the sexual ambiguousness that permeated his work and life. Attending to and voicing the sexual silences in much of black writing will help to counter the putative notion that the towering and pathbreaking voices of Baldwin and Audre Lorde are the *only* black authors exploring same-gender-love issues. Instead of fetishizing these two literary icons, we must resituate them as part of a continuum of writers who textualize sexual difference in ways both overt and covert.

Second, along these same lines we must contest the fiction that black writers and their protagonists—I'm speaking primarily of black male authors here—categorically subscribe to heterocentric constructions of black subjectivity. We need to challenge the apotheosizing of characters such as Bigger Thomas from *Native Son* and the eponymous Invisible Man from Ellison's novel, characters whom critics have installed as the official portraitures of black literary subjectivity, an installation that sanctions a phallocentric, monodimensional form of sexual subjectivity. These works, and many of the professors teaching them, valorize a deformed narrative of heteronormative sexuality while simultaneously exposing and repudiating racist, classist cultural norms that disembody and paralyze the protagonists.[12] Our pedagogical mission should be to establish alternative models of subjectivity that challenge heterosexist ones embedded in black men's canonical texts. This can be achieved in several ways—first, by reassessing the "canonical" texts we privilege. Instead of consistently teaching either the fulsomely praised *Go Tell It on the Mountain* or the hyperanthologized "Sonny's Blues" as the "official" Baldwin works, we can introduce students to more ambitious and enriching novels like *Another Country* or *Just above My Head* or even nonfiction such as "The Male Prison" or "Here Be Dragons." We can also revisit undervalued but critically acclaimed writers such as Chester Himes (*Yesterday Will Make You Cry*) and John A. Williams (*Clifford's Blues*), authors who are summarily excluded from syllabi but who imagine black male sexuality as fluid and multivalent. Moreover, we must unloosen our attachment to the canon by including authors such as Ann Allen Shockley, Pearl Cleage, Randall Kenan, and Sapphire, as well as anthologies such as Charles Rowell and Bruce Morrow's *Shade,* where the stories of younger gay male authors amplify sexual difference. By de-emphasizing sacrosanct authors and a static narrative of black sexuality, we begin to explore the interstices of black literary subjectivity, entering the pedagogical other country where same-sex desire is often elided as a salient dimension of subject formation.

Finally, we must fashion a lexicon for *black male intimacy,* sexual or non-sexual. The late critic Michael Cooke once remarked that a prominent black male protagonist was "not cut out for the rigors of intimacy."[13] I think this phrase captures the constricting narrative of black maleness, where cultural fictions of black men as hypermasculine and phallocentric vitiate alternative models that include not only same-sex desire but also what Eve Sedgwick has called *homosocial desire,* which for me involves black men's desire for intimacy regardless of orientation. My own scholarship has attempted to witness against this master narrative of black literary masculinity by exploring black male desire through the trope of community. Thus a work such as *Go Tell It on the Mountain* becomes as much a narrative about the different ways in which black men attempt to love each other, or at least negotiate the terms of intimacy, as it is a psycho-religious drama about "dysfunctional" Harlemites, perfidious preachers, or even an angst-ridden gay adolescent. More contemporary works such as Ernest Gaines's *A Lesson before Dying* also lend themselves to interrogating how authors counter the notion that male intra-racial intimacy is unspeakable by demonstrating that it takes sexual *and* nonsexual forms. Hence, we should attempt to expand notions of intimacy and not single-mindedly focus on same-gender sex and sexuality. As scholars cognizant of how hegemonic practices are legitimized and perpetuated, we must guard against the refetishizing or re-"Mandingoizing" of black bodies by replacing phallocentric hermeneutical practices with homocentric ones—for instance, removing straight Bigger Thomas from the summit of black male protagonists and elevating gay Rufus Scott. This seemingly homocentric gesture merely mimics the very heterosexist pedagogical practices we all vigorously oppose.

The Black Queer Studies conference has inaugurated a critical dialogue about the intersection of race and sexuality and its position in our pedagogical space. My modest proposal for teaching the unspeakable requires that we continue to combat unflaggingly the litany of well-rehearsed "isms" and phobias while being simultaneously transgressive and self-evaluative. Still, in the race for queerness we must not hastily and haphazardly erect a new hegemonic model that sanctions a parochial construction of "queerness," one that essentializes gayness and erases other forms of Otherness.

NOTES

I am indebted to the legacy of the late scholar-activist Barbara Christian. My title riffs on her trenchant essay "The Race for Theory," which first appeared in *Cultural Critique* 6 (1987): 51–63 and has been widely reprinted. I would also like to thank E. Patrick Johnson for directing me toward material germane to my topic.

1. Bryant Keith Alexander, "Performing Culture in the Classroom: Excerpts from an Instructional Diary," in *The Future of Performance Studies*, ed. Sheron Dailey (Annandale, Va.: National Communications Association, 1999), 170–80.

2. bell hooks, *Teaching to Transgress: Education as the Practice of Freedom* (New York: Routledge, 1994), 21.

3. Alexander, "Performing Culture in the Classroom," 172.

4. George E. Haggerty, " 'Promoting Homosexuality' in the Classroom," in *Professions of Desire: Gay and Lesbian Studies in Literature*, ed. George E. Haggerty and Bonnie Zimmerman (New York: Modern Language Association of America, 1995), 12; emphasis added.

5. Ibid., 13; emphasis added.

6. David Román, "Teaching Differences: Theory and Practice in a Lesbian and Gay Studies Seminar," in *Professions of Desire: Lesbian and Gay Studies in Literature*, ed. George E. Haggerty and Bonnie Zimmerman (New York: Modern Language Association of America, 1995), 115–16.

7. Ian Barnard, "Fuck Community; or, Why I Support Gay-Bashing," in *States of Rage: Emotional Eruption, Violence, and Social Change*, ed. Renee Curry and Terry L. Allison (New York: New York University Press, 1996), 77.

8. Román, "Teaching Differences," 113–14.

9. The term "same-gender-loving" has been adopted by many gays of color in lieu of "queer," a pejorative for many that connotes a privileged white gay and masculinist status. This act of "signifying" is reminiscent of many black women writers, scholars, and activists' use of the term "womanist" (e.g., Alice Walker, Barbara Christian) as a counterreferent to "feminist," which is widely considered the purview of economically and academically privileged white women and one that excludes the experiences of women of color.

10. Elizabeth Swanson Goldberg, "The Way We Do the Things We Do: Enunciation and Effect in the Multicultural Classroom," in *Teaching African American Literature: Theory and Practice*, ed. Maryemma Graham, Sharon Pineault-Burke, and Marianna White Davis (New York: Routledge, 1998), 151–52.

11. Ibid., 155. Goldberg attributes this phrase to Sharon Pineault-Burke, one of the co-editors of the volume in which Goldberg's essay appears.

12. Black feminist scholar and cultural critic Karla FC Holloway speaks eloquently to the heterosexual—and in my thinking, hetero-textual—bias that pervades public sexual discourse, which black women's writing has resisted through its forthright

treatment of sexual relationships between women in works such as *The Color Purple*. Her comments about homophobia as an antidote for racial victimization are apropos vis-à-vis black men's virulent homophobia (e.g., the feverish anti-gay rhetoric that dominated the 1960s Black Arts movement) and its twin, extreme phallocentrism, which pervades much of black men's writing prior to the 1970s. Though Holloway addresses lesbianism specifically, her assertions resonate in terms of perceptions of black gay male sexuality: "The public's discomfort with sexuality between and among women within African American literatures reflects the discomfort of our public cultures with sexuality and passion that resist patriarchy and its power as it is instead enabled, sustained, and shared . . . between women. After all, the bias of heterosexuality promises one of the few spheres of privilege in our culture that is equally available to whites and blacks. It is as if the 'normative' promise of heterosexuality's masculinist authority promises to extend this norm and its authority to our communities whose ethnicity has historically devalued and challenged any expressive power. So, the abusive and conservative sexual ethics of homophobia are generated in some significant measure from the veneer of power that heterosexuality has successfully asserted in black and white communities. Public denigration of queerness perversely uplifts a publicly denigrated ethnicity" (Holloway, *Codes of Conduct: Race, Ethics, and the Color of Our Character* [New Brunswick: Rutgers University Press, 1995], 55). Concomitantly, Holloway's observations find their analogue in public and popular misperceptions and misrepresentations of black gay men (for instance, the execrable, homophobic "comedy" routines of stars such as Eddie Murphy [his 1982 film *Raw*] and Damon Wayans [as the gratuitously effeminate "film critic" on the sketch comedy series *In Living Color* in the early 1990s]); see E. Patrick Johnson, *Appropriating Blackness: Performance and the Politics of Authenticity* (Durham: Duke University Press, 2003, 48–75). Black men's writing has traditionally done little to trouble this notion. Canonical texts such as *Native Son* and *Invisible Man,* along with second-tier but widely known works such as Chester Himes's *If He Hollers Let Him Go,* may be more muted in their disdain for same-sex intimacy, but these works nevertheless uphold a patriarchal ideal. The protagonists who populate these works consistently enact masculinist sexual praxes, which permit them to extricate themselves from truncated positions as black and thereby devalued subjects.

13. Michael G. Cooke, *Afro-American Literature in the Twentieth Century: The Achievement of Intimacy* (New Haven: Yale University Press, 1984), 59.

MAURICE O. WALLACE

ON BEING A WITNESS:
PASSION, PEDAGOGY, AND THE
LEGACY OF JAMES BALDWIN

Since spring 1996 I have had, on three occasions, the indescribably gratifying experience of teaching an advanced seminar exclusively devoted to what I have come to call "The Voice and Vision of James Baldwin." Out of this seminar came some of the most brilliant undergraduate papers I think I shall ever see. Among them, Nicholas Boggs's essay "Of Mimicry and Little Man, Little Man," a title riffing, of course, on Homi Bhabha's infinitely important piece "Of Mimicry and Man," ranks the most stunning of all. It is, as far as I know, the only scholarly treatment in print of Baldwin's little-known children's book, *Little Man, Little Man*. To his credit, Dwight McBride had the editorial acumen to recognize Boggs's visioned originality by publishing this undergraduate talent in the collection *James Baldwin Now*.

The Voice and Vision of James Baldwin seminar produced a great deal more, however, than the eloquent materiality of recuperative papers and publications about Baldwin, arguably black America's most prolific witness in the twentieth century. More to the point—for many of my students, but especially for the black gay, lesbian, or still yet questioning student—quite apart from my often inexpert pedagogical designs, Baldwin's own sometimes public, sometimes private, but always personal pains to negotiate an identic equilibrium of racial and sexual subjectivity illumined with a power all their own a model interiority intent on turning out "an honest man and a good writer." Accordingly, Baldwin's example allowed every student her or his own identitarian angst and created out of the intimately delineated architecture of the seminar room a doubly intellectual and social space, however much institutionally vexed, in which one might be, in relative terms, safely *in* or safely *out* while simultaneously interrogating, by course design, the politics of the homosexual closet as a still more intimate, spatially conceived speech act mimetically recast in the muted closed-door discussions of the classroom. For what students of Baldwin inevitably discover about him is his own vexed relationship to gay and queer identity politics. "The phenomenon we call 'gay' has always rubbed me the wrong way," he said on more than a one occasion.[1] In spoken discourse, at least, Baldwin insisted that sexuality was a private affair, as, for example, when he told filmmaker/photographer Sedat Pakay: "I don't think it's anybody's business whatever goes on in anybody's bedroom, you know. But in my own case I can see that it is . . . a very big issue for a lot of people . . . I have a certain kind of puritan thing about two things. A certain kind of privacy, which I think is everybody's right. Certainly mine. And a certain kind of pride. The life that I actually live . . . is very different from the life people imagine and my involvement with men, with women and what I say about them . . . [and it is] not to be talked about to the world."[2]

Baldwin's claim to privacy here is not simply a complaint of his celebrity ("In my own case . . . it is . . . a very big issue for a lot of people"). Rather, to live unmolested by the symbolic intrusion of others on what one does in the coverture of his bathroom or bedroom "is everybody's right." And it is precisely this safety that gay identity, so thoroughly overdetermined in the Western imagination, jeopardizes for Baldwin. He will not forbear the whole Western world "rubb[ing him] . . . the wrong way" while it projects its guilty queerness onto his scapegoated body. Despite his significant resistance to the homosexual referent "gay," though, anyone who reads nearly any Baldwin work continuously from *Go Tell It On the Mountain* in 1953 to *The Evidence of Things Not Seen* in 1985 sees in them very clearly that his disposition toward sex is at least congruent with the identity sign "queer" as it has come recently to signify so many expressions of sexual dissidence. The conundrum of sex and secrecy, of identity undecideability, faced by Baldwin here, however, exceeds his experiential particularity. Far more widely, it concretizes a conflict that gay, lesbian and bisexual students and teachers know intimately: that difficult choice between the subversive, despectacularizing power of subaltern silence, on the one hand—self-preserving as such a silence may yet be—and, on the other, the political urgency to speak one's queer mind decisively, precisely because the secrets concealed by one's *un*speaking— particularly in sexualized contexts like Baldwin's exchange with Pakay— permits an illusion of neutrality to let pass unchallenged what Joseph Chadwick describes as the "normal, institutionally and socially sanctioned current of homophobias."[3]

In other words, inasmuch as Baldwin's insistent hedgings of the identity questions put to him realize the very speech act of silence that Eve Sedgwick theorized in *Epistemology of the Closet,* he exemplifies "the phenomenon we call 'gay'" with its unavoidable "requisitions of secrecy and disclosures."[4] Specifically, Baldwin's skirting of the issue succeeds not according to "a particular silence" that refuses speech outright, "but a silence that accrues particularity by fits and starts, in the relation to the discourse that surrounds and differentially constitutes it."[5] Since we live in a world where the explicit exposure of the subject, as D. A. Miller has written, "would manifest how thoroughly he has been inscribed within a socially given totality,"[6] Baldwin's secrecy, his silence about *the* thing his interlocutor most wants to know, might seem, in Miller's words, a sort of "spiritual exercise by which the subject is allowed to conceive of himself as a resistance" to the relentlessness of overdetermination, thusly rendering him "radically inaccessible to the culture that would [or, in black situations, always has] otherwise entirely determine[d] him."[7] Under social conditions in which speech, in spite of its oppositional locutions, cannot but subtend the normativity of institutions that sanction and uphold the racist, homophobic disenfranchisement of even a potentially gay, lesbian, bisexual, or transgendered speaker who may also be, importantly and by native accident, black, Baldwin's secrecy withholds a secret that, according to a certain strain of thought advanced by Gayatri Spivak, "may not be a secret" to some—being closeted may be mostly situational—"but cannot be unlocked" by any homophobic agent.[8]

If, however, Baldwin's circumvention of the conclusive answer to Pakay's unrecorded query lends any amount of power to the forward motion of homophobia's heteronormativizing project, a project that has all along demanded his silence even when it has pretended to want to know, then his or any gay speaker's silence is complicit with the very machinations of homophobia that his secrecy was to have foiled, machinations that may still yet carry out their violence should his secret get out. If it is the protection of one's life or limbs that a gay subject's silence aims to ensure, then under this counterlogic, not coming out, *not speaking,* may not, frankly, be an option either. It is no more safe in closet contexts to keep a secret that cannot be kept safe from becoming known *as* a secret (though the content of it, *the* thing, may never come to light) than it is to openly divulge one's queer compulsions since the homophobic requires nothing in the way of proof but rather only a picturable possibility.

The quandary of concealment and confession, of private living and the public politics of sex—emblematized here and throughout Baldwin's career as a self-avowed witness to things racial and sexual, seldom seen with honest intelligibility—is, I have discovered, an entirely teachable absurdity that black students especially, straight and gay, may come to appreciate quickly. Not least because the speech act according to which Sedgwick defines the homosexual closet is shown to have had an earlier and sometimes contemporaneous life in those racial passing narratives that enliven so much fascination (and, perhaps, latent fear) in African American literature courses. That is, as I have argued elsewhere,[9] the selfsame speech act that now names the homosexual closet has also functioned in some African American writing to conceal a similarly overdetermined and anathematized racial truth, one animated by fantasies of another class of illicit sex and made familiar to a present generation of students by the ever more complicated politics of racial identity and affiliation in our multiracial and mixed-race (if still, practically speaking, black and white) American reality.

What is, then, for so many of my students the exhaling occasion to interrogate these two critical closet positions connectively with the historical "problem" of biology and blackness from the institutional loophole of retreat and safety that is the queer classroom, these discussions have led, more than a few times, to an unforeseeable eventuality for which I suppose I should have been more pedagogically prepared. While there is no intent in the classroom conversations I speak of to coax the closeted student out (or to cajole the *out* back *in* because, as Baldwin once said, "there is nothing more boring . . . than sexual activity as an end in itself and a great many people who came out . . . should reconsider"), the effect of these conversations was to afford some students, at least, the critical courage to publicly assert and maintain a gay or lesbian or bisexual identity. What was for me in the first two or three of these coming out occurrences the considerably awkward circumstance of my students sufficient faith *in* me to come out *to* me, became in latter instances only a trifle less awkward. Not merely because I was, in the first of these instances, anxious about how personal things might get but because, I was not sure, as I am not today entirely sure, what precisely my students' faith *in* me was asking *of* me. To keep a secret? Or to aid in negotiating the daunting task of getting the secret out "safely"? These experiences have compelled me to think and rethink the unpredictable nuances that frequently obtain between pedagogical practices that understand black gay and lesbian studies to be a body of knowledge—a subfield, in other words—for intellectual inquiry and, finally, consumption, and those that take for their first aim the black gay, lesbian, bisexual, or transgendered student and the protection of his or her socio-intellectual freedom and well-being. While I cannot pretend to have resolved the question of what queer pedagogy is or means exactly in black contexts or whether a distinction needs to be made at all between the subfield and pedagogical technique, I do aver, with Paulo Freire, that insofar as "a careful analysis of the student-teacher relationship, at any level, inside or outside of school, will reveal its fundamentally narrative character" and "this relationship involves a narrating subject (the teacher) and a patient listening object (the student),"[10] then new pedagogical models are exigent in and out of the gay and lesbian studies or queer classroom, models that do not rely on the obsessive, disciplining fixity of active/passive positionalities that only serve to sediment heteronormative illusions of properly "straight" pedagogical relations. What I am advancing here instead is a pedagogical praxis that may very well be queer to the degree that the term's most recent—albeit contested—hope to signify a plurality of sexualities and sex acts is embraced (or not) by black gays and lesbians. What I am proposing is a pedagogical praxis that is dialogically creative, necessarily undisciplined, and misbehavedly liberatory. I have in mind a pedagogy, as my earlier attention to the interrogations of the closet were meant to convey, that is at once "problem posing" (Freire) and positively transferential (Freud).

Problem-posing pedagogy—"consider[ing] neither abstract man nor the world without people, but people in their relations with the world"[11]—conceives of the gay, lesbian, bisexual, and transgendered student as conscious actors in the educational experiment, rejects a pedagogy of information deposit-making and explores the problems per se of being-in-the-world and being-for-others as sexual dissidents, with an attendant commitment, in the consequential productions of knowledge that these exercises yield, to liberate minds and bodies. In a phrase, what is urgent in the academy today is a more productively intrepid philosophy and practice of teaching that are inflected by the sexual realism of our time. I call this exigency a *pedagogy of passion.*

By pedagogy of passion, I mean to refer to a wholly public performance of professorial self-abandonment to embodied knowledge, an epistemology of identity for which the materiality of the flesh, its shades and its desires, is ground zero. Inasmuch as embodied knowledge, remarked or unremarked, is requisite to the constitution of a social self—my subjecthood obtains at the moment I am recognized in my body, at precisely the moment I am called forth—passionate pedagogy *witnesses* in the familiarly Baldwinian sense that it testifies "to whence I came, where I am. Witness[es] to what I've seen and the possibilities that I think I see."[12] I take Baldwin's resignation to the duty of witnessing, "an obligation . . . impossible to fulfill,"[13] to be fully commensurate with the French philosophers' belief in the inherent paradox of all passionate pursuits: in the words of Steven Shaviro, "Passion does not inhere in a subject or substance, it does not qualify anything; its specificity is that of an adjective without a noun. . . . Passion is precisely a movement without an aim. In its grasp, I am carried away from myself, carried away from the state in which mastery and possession are possible. It is not that my desire is frustrated by a cruelly indifferent fate; that, in itself, would be easy enough to bear. But much harder to endure is the discovery that the force which defeats me is the very one which sustains me."[14] In distilling Maurice Blanchot and Georges Bataille in a single work, Shaviro highlights what is familiarly and simultaneously black (oppositional), queer (unfixed), and progressive (dynamically just) about the sort of pedagogy of passion Baldwin's *witness* inspires. As the subject (teacher) divests herself or himself of the narcissistically inseminatory habits of the totalitarian teaching relations criticized by Freire as "the 'banking' concept of education," oppressively 'straight' protocols of classroom culture, "arguments based on [titular] 'authority' are no longer valid."[15] Rather, "authority," nothing more or less than the accumulated credibility of critical truth claims, proceeds from the demonstrated surrender of the subject (the impassioned teacher) to a more dialogical relationship with the erstwhile objects of knowledge deposit (the teacher's students), a relationship that may be understood in the abstract as "queer" insofar as the reformed relationship between student and teacher, in Freire's model, hinges on mutual desires of virtual sameness. In forsaking the learned will to mastery beneath historically insipid pedagogical practices, "the teacher-of-the-students and the students-of-the-teacher cease to exist and a new term emerges: teacher-student with students-teachers."[16]

The liberative potential of passionate pedagogy is not entirely a consequence of its curiously "queer" ambitions, however. It lies not in the muscular production of passionate professing so much as in a performance of professorship that is also, odd as it may sound, a performance, creative and requisitely dialogical, of the transference relationship—idealized in Freud, Jung, and Lacan—between the troubled analysand and the ministering analyst who is the "subject-supposed-to-know" (Lacan). Importantly, the vaguely psycho-dramatic analogy I am insisting on here is not one arbitrarily drawn. In Friere's theorization of the narrative function in teaching, the patient-student sitting listening at the feet of her or his teacher resembles no one so much as the student-patient in transferential relation to her doctor (from the Latin *doçere*, to teach).

According to Freud, transference occurs in psychoanalysis (and is, in fact, essential to psychoanalysis) when the patient, in regarding the doctor as the "subject-supposed-to-know" invests the doctor with the qualities of past authority figures (the father or mother, usually) once held by the patient to be the chief keepers of the mysteries of knowledge. Consequently, this transference becomes fraught with many of the same psychic ambivalences that attach to the original authority figures and often results, problematically, in the analysand falling in love with (or hating) the analyst. In either case, the analysand's simultaneous demand and desire is for requited affection.[17] Later, Jung revised Freud to argue that the deeper desires of the analysand were not exactly sexual but spiritual, the longing for a god. According to Thomas King, "Freud had maintained that our libido was fundamentally sexual; but Jung came to understand the libido in a broader sense, and at its center he saw [in effect] a religious passion."[18] By encouraging this "passion" Jung sought, with near-idol charm, to inspire his patients toward more active *self*-analysis since the analyst is fully aware of the impossibility of herself or himself ever possessing the truth about the patient that the patient demands for her or his cure, which may be accomplished only through the power of the patient. Little by little, an inner "function" develops at the analyst's provocations and "gather[s] to itself the excessive esteem that had been projected onto him."[19] As a result, does the analysand achieve shared personhood with the analyst as a self-conscious actor in both the analysand and the analyst's higher learning?[20]

Not a few times have I been in the place of the analyst, the imagined father-lover of my students—some black, some also queer, some queer though not black, but all vexed by the dire politics of race and sex everywhere around them—at home, in the dorm, on athletic teams, in locker rooms and seminar rooms alike. (I say this in no way to flatter myself but to point to the incredibly totemic power of the transference dynamic.) When I've "doctored" well, the silenced and stigmatized have occasionally found their voices. Not long ago, I received a note from a black student enrolled in a seminar on identity and diversity that I co-taught with black feminist critic Karla FC Holloway as part of the advanced freshman curriculum at Duke called FOCUS (First-Year Opportunity for Comprehensive Unified Study):

Professor Wallace,

I didn't get to tell you . . . but I wanted to say to you again how much of
an impact this FOCUS program has made in my life. PLEASE be convinced of its necessity and in the work that you and [Professor] Holloway . . . put into it. However trite this may sound, you [two] have given
my experiences a voice; you have valid[ated] so much of what for so
long has been [invalidated] in my life. I have never felt so emotionally
connected to a subject like this, and it makes me almost shameful when
I tell you that I am in tears in writing this. . . . [T]his D[iversity] and
I[dentity course] has helped . . . it has made me realize a lot about the
emotional nature of the things we discuss. . . . Thank you. I can never
show you how much gratitude I have.

Sincerely,
Gregory[21]

It is worth pointing out that "Gregory" was already a brilliant student, as
precocious as any first-year student I have ever met, when he came to our
seminar. But what I believe he discovered, possibly for the first time in his
young identity-vexed life, was a validation of his social and spiritual strivings
from an Other (his teachers) that, in the end, was turned inward by an elusive
inner function toward that self-validation leading us all to "a voice."

Although there is little I experience in the course of a semester more
gratifying than receiving a note like Gregory's, to usher Gregory to voice is
not, alone, enough. With the passionate eloquence of black gay and lesbian
writers like Baldwin, Hughes, Melvin Dixon, Audre Lorde, Pat Parker, and
Bill T. Jones now at his command, he has a language, if not a black and queer
lexicon, of body and pen and tongue.

Gregory's message to me was flattering, I confess. In its flattery, though,
was also a vague epiphany that has persuaded me all the more of James
Baldwin's significance to the consideration of pedagogy and black queer
studies addressed in this volume, and to my decision to bring his life and
work to bear on my pedagogical philosophy. While nothing Gregory said in
his note explicitly recalls Baldwin, it is the tone of the missive that compels
me to return to Baldwin here at this essay's end. Gregory speaks the same
tongue as Baldwin's John Grimes; Gregory's "cure" ("I have never felt so
emotionally connected") and John Grimes's conversion at the conclusion of
Baldwin's *Go Tell It on the Mountain* represent the positive results of the

passionate transferential pedagogy I have here theorized, the queerness of which is nowhere more plainly dramatized than in Baldwin's first novel. Who does not remember Baldwin's ending and John's haunting conversion? On the threshing-floor "the evening of the seventh day, when, raging, he had walked out of his father's house," John was "saved."[22] There, raging and weeping, wrestling with demons in the dust, John lay. "He began to shout for help, seeing before him the lash, the fire, and the depthless water, seeing his head bowed down forever, he, John, the lowest among these lowly. And he looked for his mother, but her eyes were fixed on this dark army—she was claimed by this army. And his father would not help him, his father did not see him" (202). It is Brother Elisha—John's new Sunday-school teacher—who "prayed [John] through" (217). Like the analysand to the analyst under the conditions of transference, John "was distracted by his new teacher . . . admiring the timbre of Elisha's voice, much deeper and manlier than his own, admiring the leanness, and grace, and strength, and darkness of Elisha in his Sunday suit" (13). To the extent that the student predicament in black and queer classroom contexts is analogous to that of the Jungian analysand in search of a spiritual cure, a predicament recapitulated in novel form in *Go Tell It on the Mountain,* then praying the silenced, the stigmatized, and the struggling through is, in a phrase, what I have aimed to do all along as teacher and mentor to not a few individuals like Gregory. The *feeling* of our exchange, though not its content, Baldwin anticipated, with characteristic elegance, in the exchange between Elisha and John in the novel's final pages.

> "I been praying for you little brother," Elisha said, "and I sure ain't going to stop praying now."
> "For me," persisted John, his tears falling, "for *me.*"
> "You know right well," said Elisha, looking at him, "I ain't going to stop praying for the brother what the Lord done give me." . . .
> John, staring at Elisha, struggled to tell him something more—struggled to say—all that could never be said. Yet: "I was down in the valley," he dared, "I was by myself down there. I won't never forget. May God forget me if I forget." (219–20)

While the life and work of James Baldwin have been of immeasurable instrumentality to me in pedagogical contemplations of the project of black queer studies, it may be that, in the final analysis, Brother Elisha is the patron "saint" of our labor as teachers.

I extend thanks of the most profound sort to Suzanne Schneider, a Duke graduate student in English, for her generous and meticulous criticism of this paper's first and second drafts. What praise this piece may merit is owed to her nearly as much as to me; what failings may be judged in it, however, are mine entirely.

1. Richard Goldstein, "Go the Way Your Blood Beats: An Interview with James Baldwin," in *James Baldwin: The Legacy*, ed. Quincy Troupe (New York: Simon and Schuster, 1989), 182.

2. *James Baldwin, from Another Place*, dir. Sedat Pakay, Hudson Filmworks Inc., 1973.

3. Joseph Chadwick, "Toward an Antihomophobic Pedagogy," in *Professions of Desire: Lesbian and Gay Studies in Literature*, ed. George Haggerty and Bonnie Zimmerman (New York: Modern Language Association of America, 1995), 32.

4. Eve Kosofsky Sedgwick, *Epistemology of the Closet* (Berkeley: University of California Press, 1993), 68. Note, too, that "even an out gay person deals daily with interlocutors about whom she doesn't know whether they know or not; it is equally difficult to guess for any given interlocutor whether, if they did know, the knowledge would seem very important" (68).

5. Ibid., 3.

6. D. A. Miller, "Secret Subjects, Open Secrets," in *The Novel and the Police* (Berkeley: University of California Press, 1988), 207.

7. Ibid., 195.

8. Gayatri Chakravorty Spivak, *A Critique of Postcolonial Reason: Toward a History of the Vanishing Present* (Cambridge, Mass.: Harvard University Press, 1999), 190.

9. Maurice Wallace, *Constructing the Black Masculine: Identity and Ideality in African American Men's Literature and Culture, 1775–1995* (Durham: Duke University Press, 2002).

10. Paulo Freire, *Pedagogy of the Oppressed* (rev. ed.), trans. Myra Bergman Ramos (New York: Continuum, 1998), 52.

11. Ibid., 62.

12. James Baldwin, quoted in *Conversations with James Baldwin* (Jackson: University of Mississippi Press), 225.

13. Ibid.

14. Steven Shaviro, *Passion and Excess: Blanchot, Bataille, and Literary Theory* (Tallahasse: Florida State University Press, 1990), 32, 136.

15. Freire, *Pedagogy of the Oppressed*, 61.

16. Ibid.

17. For a concise statement of Freud's theory of transference, see Freud, "Observa-

tions on Transference—Love," in *The Freud Reader,* ed. Peter Gay (New York: Norton, 1989), 378–87.

18. Thomas M. King, "Jung and Catholic Spirituality," *America* 180.11 (1999): 13.

19. Ibid.

20. Of course, the analyst in this scenario must also guard against counter-transference (falling in love with or, conceivably, hating the patient) based on the analyst's own repressed, unreconciled issues. A misstep could be personally and professionally ruinous. The analyst must never lapse into the treacherous belief that she or he is or can be, in the real, the idol of the patient's projecting imagination.

21. The message was sent to me by email November 29, 2001, and, except for the clarifying interpolations I have bracketed, is quoted word for word. Only the student's name has been changed.

22. James Baldwin, *Go Tell It on the Mountain* (New York: Laurel 1985), 202. Subsequent citations appear as parenthetical page numbers in the text.

PART IV

BLACK QUEER FICTION:

WHO IS "READING" US?

JEWELLE GOMEZ

BUT SOME OF US ARE BRAVE LESBIANS:

THE ABSENCE OF BLACK LESBIAN FICTION

In preparing this essay I felt it was necessary to first examine the "us" expressed in my title before moving on to consider who is reading us and thinking about how we'd be found by our readers. It was in my quick survey of the literature available for discussion that I confirmed my suspicions that the "us"—that is, published black lesbian fiction writers and poets—is an ever-shrinking population.

I then returned to some of the seminal texts in black lesbian culture and politics to find out why the optimism of the 1980s had not produced the flock of black lesbian writers that I had expected would grow out of those early independent publishing efforts. Why hadn't *Loving Her, ZAMI,* and *The Color Purple* inspired the dozens of black lesbian novels I had been waiting for? Or if they had been inspirational, what had happened to the black lesbian writers who would have taken to the path following their muse?

I discovered the focus of my thoughts and my title as I revisited the groundbreaking black feminist anthology *All the Women Are White, All the Blacks are Men, But Some of Us Are Brave* (1982), which embodies much of the feminist energy that helped fuel the proliferation of black lesbian literature in the 1980s. The essays, although not explicitly lesbian, held a promise for a new dawning of black women's politics and creativity that seemed to naturally include lesbians. However, the years following that publication have not delivered on that promise.[1]

My need to look back also grows out of my sense that queer studies is at an important crossroads, and that the quality of our path ahead, as always, depends significantly on our acknowledgment and examination of the disparate political/historical contexts that have led to where we are now.

While our histories have often overlapped, black lesbians and black gay men have experienced repression and invisibility in vastly different ways. After all, sexism is alive and well in all facets of our culture. It will take a concerted effort on the part of those invested in black queer academic studies to avert the serious crisis that is currently in the making as a result of the insidious misogyny that plagues our culture. The invisibility of black lesbians is already an "epidemic" in many academic arenas—black/African studies, women's studies, literature, and sociology. The affliction of invisibility is in danger of spreading to queer studies as well.

In my effort to examine this crisis I began with the idea of exploring the work of black lesbian fiction writers in the current publishing atmosphere, where AIDS activism and the higher visibility of queer people in the popular media seem to have inspired a burst of publication activity. How black lesbians are published—commercially or independently—has a major effect on visibility, so I also noted who the publishers were as well as who was being published. I was especially concerned with the fate of fiction that features black lesbians. More specifically, I was concerned with black lesbian characters who are presented within a social, cultural, and political context that reflects other lesbians and lesbians of color (I frequently use this latter term as a reminder that the invisibility discussed here cloaks all lesbians of color not just black lesbians).

It is the *representation* of black lesbian lives, not simply its analysis and deconstruction that has the most immediate, broad-based and long-lasting cultural and historical impact. Only by telling our stories in the most specific, imagistic, and imaginative narratives do the lives of black lesbians take on long-term literary and political significance. This representation, especially as created by black lesbians, continues to occupy an inordinately small space in the world of literature. This is especially alarming in view of the active presence of black lesbian writers during the blossoming of contemporary lesbian culture in the 1970s and 1980s. What quickly became obvious as I looked for texts to consider was that there is less contemporary black lesbian fiction to discuss today than there was before the so-called gay literary boom of the early 1990s.

In 1983 I wrote an essay for *Home Girls: A Black Feminist Anthology,* edited by Barbara Smith. In that essay I wrote: "The shadow of repression has concealed the black lesbians in literature in direct proportion to her invisibility in American society. Women of color, as a whole, have long been perceived as the least valuable component in our social and economic system—the group with the least economic power and the smallest political influence. Not surprisingly, we are the least visible group not only in the fine arts, but also in the popular media, where the message conveyed about lesbians of color is that she does not even *exist*, let alone use soap, drive cars, drink Coke, go on vacations or do much of anything else."[2] I reexamined the table of contents of that collection of essays, poems, and stories to ground myself in where my own work and that of others had come from. I estimated that about four-fifths of the thirty-seven women included in the collection were lesbians (or bisexual), and in most cases they placed their writing within a lesbian context. The majority of women in the collection who are today still writing material directly related to lesbian life, culture, or politics are doing so not through fiction or poetry but rather through nonfiction, a category that has grown dramatically. Authors like Barbara Smith, Gloria Akasha Hull, and Alexis DeVeaux are writing essays and biographies, which are the genres being boosted by publishers because the academic market is so lucrative.

But what of the women writing fiction or poetry, the genres in which the nonacademic reading public would have the most interest? Only a few of the writers from the *Home Girls* anthology were still publishing fiction or poetry with lesbian-centered narratives or references. Ann Allen Shockley, who authored the first black lesbian novel, *Loving Her* (1974), as well as the first collection of black lesbian short stories, *The Black and White of It* (1980), hasn't written a new book in over a decade. The same is true for short story writer Becky Birtha. Poets Michelle Clinton and Kate Rushin have each had only one collection of poems published (by independent presses) in the years since *Home Girls* first appeared.

Of the writers in that collection, only poet Cheryl Clarke, fiction writer Donna Allegra, and myself have in the intervening years published fiction or poetry regularly in independent and mainstream journals. In Clarke's case as well as my own, our volumes of fiction and poetry have been published by Firebrand Books, an independent feminist publisher. Donna Allegra finally had her *first* collection of fiction produced by Alyson Publications, a gay independent press, in 2000.

If considered individually rather than as a single unit, the Combahee River Collective, whose seminal statement on black feminism is included in the anthology, would represent an even larger number of lesbian writers in *Home Girls*. The group included activist/thinkers such as Evelynn Hammonds, now a professor at Harvard, and Margo Okazawa-Rey, a professor at Mills College, both of whom write non-fiction. Still, this accounting would bring the percentage of surviving black lesbian writers down even further.

More than twenty years after what now, in retrospect, seems like a time of abundance, the support circles for black lesbian writers are gone: no new Combahee River Collective has emerged to lend political support to black lesbian creative life. There is also no contemporary equivalent of the Jemima Collective, which on the East Coast nurtured the early fiction and poetry of lesbians of color like Donna Allegra and Linda Jean Brown. Allegra, as mentioned earlier, just had her first book published and Brown self-published her own book of fiction. Both writers were, in the mid 1970s, part of the collective, which founded *Azalea,* a literary magazine by and for lesbians of color (which published my first fiction and also that of Sapphire). *Azalea*'s West Coast sister, *Ache,* was founded in the 1990s, but in recent years it has produced few issues. So not only are those who started writing in my generation disappearing, but it remains a mystery where the next generation of fiction writers and poets is honing its skills and distributing its work.

To further examine the field I looked at anthologies produced after *Home Girls* (which has remained in print). Fifteen years later the first collection of black lesbian coming out stories was published by Lisa C. Moore's independent publishing venture Red Bone Press. The anthology, *Does Your Mama Know,* features about forty-five contributors, of whom only about six are already regularly published authors. Of that number only two—Shay Young-blood and Alexis DeVeaux—have books published by mainstream/corporate presses, and neither is most widely known for work set in a predominantly lesbian context. The other published lesbian writers in the collection are all represented by independent and/or feminist, not mainstream, presses.

In continuing my survey I looked at the reference work *Contemporary Lesbians Writers of the United States* (1993), edited by Sandra Pollack and Denise D. Knight, which is the first of its kind. Of the one hundred women included, sixteen are black; furthermore, three of those have passed on (Audre Lorde, Pat Parker, and Terri Jewell). Again, most of the black lesbians included have not been published by mainstream presses; and those who have been, such as Jacqueline Woodson, have not traditionally been known for fiction primarily grounded in the lesbian context or community. Again, each of the writers mentioned above is openly lesbian, but their narratives have, with some exceptions, taken place in a nonlesbian context, which means that their reputations are more likely to be as black writers than as lesbian writers.

Another resource is Eric Brandt's *Dangerous Liaisons* (1999), an important exploration of the construction of black queer social and political life. It features a number of black lesbians, but the book is a collection of essays, so most of the contributors are nonfiction writers. Again, only my work and that of Cheryl Clarke includes fiction and poetry about the black lesbian experience in the context of other lesbians, and, primarily, noncorporate, independent presses publish our work.

Writing about the black lesbian experience in the context of other lesbians is the pivotal concern in my discussion. In reviewing the numbers presented by these valuable texts, it seems that the key is that what gets published by the larger presses is inversely related to how centrally the black lesbian characters are situated within a lesbian/queer community and experience. If corporate publishers seem comfortable in selling black lesbians at all, it is only as the subject of someone else's academic examination or where the context of the lives of the black lesbian characters is not necessarily queer or black.

In this element, black lesbians have a parallel with black gay men. Marketing executives at commercial publishers are interested in black queer characters who are singular, whose sexuality is marginal or ambivalent, and who are in transition, or tragic, or even better—comic. The equivalent of this would be if publishers produced books only about black people who lived in white neighborhoods, or books only about Native Americans in history who lived within the walls of U.S. forts. This approach not only makes black lesbians one-dimensional but also ensures that the stereotypes about lesbian life and culture are reinforced. The world of social organizations, literary magazines, cultural events, political actions, and music festivals that black lesbians have helped to create remain invisible.

Not since Celie and Shug found each other in *The Color Purple* (1982) has the mainstream publishing world even considered that black lesbians might find happiness with each other, much less find their way into print. This is not to dismiss the value of writers who do not make the lesbian experience central to their narrative. There are countless perspectives that one might take as an artist, and any writer (whether lesbian or not) who dares to postulate the existence of lesbians, bisexuals, and transgendered people in our society is doing a service by lifting the veil of invisibility. Alice Walker, April Sinclair, Sapphire, and Gloria Naylor have each contributed to shedding light on the lives of queer black women.

But the whole lives of black lesbians, not simply the most assimilated aspects, must be explored in order for us to be really seen. This is not to suggest a black lesbian ghetto, isolated from other aspects of life, must dominate the narrative. But a fully dimensional black lesbian character exists in many worlds, not just the heterosexual one. A sense of community (meaning here a perceived commonality, connective relationships, and a shared sense of history and familiarity with common ideas) has historically been at the core of much of the successful writing by black fiction authors. Ranging from Frances I. W. Harper, Dorothy West, Zora Neale Hurston, Chester Himes, John A. Williams, Toni Cade Bambara, Walter Moseley, and Toni Morrison to Oprah Book Club choice Breena Clarke or hip hop novelist Paul Beatty—all of this work presumes a larger, living community that is the ground from which the story and characters spring. The early efforts of groups such as Jemima and publications like *Azalea* were just such purveyors of that sense of community for black lesbians.

Writers who pursue this wholeness by contextualizing black lesbians within a queer community and/or a black lesbian community are ignored by mainstream presses. The resultant problems arise because it is the corporate publishers (as indicated by recent headlines about antimonopoly lawsuits against them) who have the strongest distribution networks and are afforded the most attention by critics and the best shelf space in chain bookstores. More and more corporate publishers and chain bookstores are working hand in hand to maximize profits by narrowing the market. Who, they ask, needs that great little novel that only sells thirty thousand copies when you can sell the latest blockbuster? My answer would be: black lesbians; as well as those readers who realize the benefit of reading literature by someone who doesn't, on the most obvious levels, look and act just like they do.

It's important to remember that even poet and activist Audre Lorde could not interest a mainstream publisher in her important biomythography *ZAMI: A New Spelling of My Name*. The volume finally was published in 1983 by Persephone, a small feminist press, and it has continued to be reprinted by other publishers in the United States and around the world since that time. If Lorde were looking for a publisher for *ZAMI* now, however, there would be no Persephone Press to pick it up. A good number of the other independent, feminist presses in the United States that would have stepped in to support black lesbian work are also no longer in existence. After publishing more than one hundred titles, Firebrand Books, the premier lesbian literary press, has been sold; Cleis is now a "queer" press publishing Gore Vidal; Spinsters Ink is on the verge of closure; Naiad Books is still functioning in a reduced way and under new management; and Kitchen Table: Women of Color Press has been gone for quite some time.

More than twenty years after my first short story was published in *Azalea* along with the work of twenty-two others, it looks like there are fewer black lesbian fiction writers circulating their work than there were in those hopeful, early days. All is not completely lost, however. Redbone Press just published *The Bull Jean Stories* (1998), a collection by emerging writer Sharon Bridgeforth. And Donna Allegra was able to find a home for her work with Alyson Publications.

A second aspect of my concern is, then, not only who will read us but how they will find us. How books are chosen for publication and where they can be sold has a direct affect on where those black lesbian writers can be found. Unless the authors or publishers personally carry the book from store to store across the nation there is little guarantee book buyers will ever hear of it. Unlike the physical world where things have at least three dimensions, there is a monodimensionality to the thinking of most corporate publishers, who identify one aspect of a book that can be marketed and focus all attention there. It is a tried-and-true method of selling anything, from used cars to corporate logos. In publishing, the range of aspects considered interesting is being narrowed down more and more, as marketing experts dominate the acquisition of manuscripts. In the general media, gay has come to mean "white, male, and middle class," unless you're Ellen, who stands in for what it means to be a "gay woman" since the word lesbian isn't even allowed.[3] Similarly, publishing executives reinforce simplified formulas that they hope will guarantee mammoth sales. A major ingredient in that formula is that lesbians be situated within a heterosexual context.

With the narrowing of the market it has become more difficult for independent publishers to maintain themselves. This in turn means that those of us publishing on those margins are squeezed out even further. What specifically does this mean for writers and for academic programs? The specialized programs—black/women/queer studies—were the fruit of the Civil Rights and Black Power movements of the 1960s, of the women's liberation movement of the 1970s, and of the activism around the AIDS epidemic of the 1980s and 1990s. The growth of these programs has, to some degree, kept interest alive in those movements, and in doing so it has helped to heighten the marketability of nonfiction texts. Anthologies devoted to various specialties have become a cottage industry, occasionally including fiction. This leaves fiction writers and poets, for the most part, facing a brick wall. The handwriting on that wall says: "Write an essay about yourself and your 'condition,' never mind developing a narrative or poetic voice and its gestalt, which might say something about not just your condition but about the condition of the world."

For some programs, such as women's studies and gender studies, the decreased availability of subjective narrative texts encourages a retreat from the progressive politics that helped to create them. It means that black lesbians will not be represented as active, progressive members of society but will merely be examined under a discursive microscope. The quicksand of racism, sexism, heterosexism, and consumerism sucks down the authentic voices of lesbians of color interested in telling their own stories. The field is then left open only to theoreticians whose interests are abstract and impersonal, and to academic careerists whose concerns are primarily professional.

Queer studies instructors might well find themselves in the position of creating classes in which they further reinforce the marginalization of lesbians of color because there is so little of their fiction or poetry available to use. Women's studies chairs attempting to justify budgets and faculty may decrease lesbian courses in favor of "broader" areas of study; at one university, the women's studies chair defended such a reduction by stating that lesbians are not an international issue. Clearly missing from that decision-making process were the stories of Makeda Silvera in Canada, Barbara Burford in Great Britain, or other vital cultural touchstones such as the lesbian film *Fire* from India, or the German film *Everything Will Be Fine*, both of which feature lesbians of color.

African American or black studies programs have already indicated that queerness is not a black issue and so may be dismissed. It is almost without exception that my visits to college campuses can engage the financial support of the college's black group or department but not their active participation. I can count on one hand the number of black student groups or departments that, while I was on campus at the invitation of another program, have responded to my direct offer to meet with them or to visit a class. Black studies professors are not interested in black lesbians.

Black queer academics are in the unique position to bridge this gap and to return to the tradition of resistance, which characterized the movements that engendered the programs in which they teach. By remembering progressive politics and feminism, the root factors of all specialized programs and departments, those who teach black queer classes do not just examine but also aid social change. By searching not just Amazon.com but also the independent presses themselves, a few new black lesbian voices (and new work by the old standbys) can be discovered. When instructors repeatedly query publishers and their sales representatives about more black lesbian fiction and poetry for use in their courses, they are making space for black lesbians' voices. They are also signaling to distributors and publishers that those voices are as crucial to the field as the voices of those who make their living off of analyzing black lesbian culture.

At this crossroads queer academics can speak for the full queer community and not be satisfied with the mainstream ideal of queerness as it appears in popular fiction, television sitcoms, or blonde HBO melodramas. In the final paragraph of my essay in *Home Girls* I wrote: "Nature abhors a vacuum and there is a distinct gap in the picture where the Black lesbian should be. The Black lesbian writer must recreate our home, unadulterated, unsanitized, specific and not isolated from the generations that have nurtured us."[4] It should be an urgent concern for all of us that, despite the rhetoric, the tenure-track jobs, online publishing, Ellen, and marches on Washington, in the beginning of the new millennium black lesbians are less visible than we were twenty years earlier.

Our colleagues in academia are now challenged to not drift away from the activism that helped open the doors to their positions. Educators do help shape the coming generations. By making conscious, active choices, teachers can keep the lives of black lesbians from continuing to be obscured by the shadows.

A syllabus is a terrible thing to waste.

NOTES

1. See Gloria T. Hull, Patricia Bell Scott, and Barbara Smith, eds., *All the Women Are White, All the Blacks Are Men, But Some of Us Are Brave: Black Women Studies* (Old Westbury, N.Y.: Feminist Press, 1982).

2. Jewelle Gomez, "A Cultural Legacy Denied and Discovered: Black Lesbians in Fiction by Women," in *Home Girls: A Black Feminist Anthology,* ed. Barbara Smith (New York: Kitchen Table; Women of Color Press, 1983), 110.

3. The title of the cable show *The L Word,* while clever, unconsciously reinforces the perceived illicit nature of the word lesbian.

4. Gomez, "A Cultural Legacy Denied and Discovered," 122.

MAE G. HENDERSON

JAMES BALDWIN'S *GIOVANNI'S ROOM:* EXPATRIATION, "RACIAL DRAG," AND HOMOSEXUAL PANIC

In James Baldwin's *Giovanni's Room* (1956), geographical expatriation combines with the literary act of racial expatriation—or what I call "racial drag"—
to create a space for the exploration of the homosexual dilemma within and
beyond the social and geographic contours of post–World War II America.
In some respects, literary masquerade, which Roger Berger describes in another context as "the literary equivalent of passing," becomes the counterpart
of Baldwin's geographical expatriation.[1] And though some argue that blackness functions as an absent presence in Baldwin's text, it is important to
recognize that the author's project not only necessitates a male protagonist,
but one defined in terms of racialized whiteness. Further, Baldwin's flight to
Paris, along with his "flight to whiteness," or "racial drag," may be regarded as
a way to open up a space of possibility for subjects at that time not available
to black writers in the United States. By literarily crossing the racial divide,
and literally crossing the national divide, the author repositions himself at a
site that interrogates the borders and boundaries of nation, gender, and
sexuality.

Written during Baldwin's early years in Europe, *Giovanni's Room* thus
becomes the textual analogue to the author's personal expatriation. Moreover, the absence of black characters in the novel obviously defied the prevailing tacit assumption of the American critical establishment—in some ways
confirmed by Baldwin's precursor and self-proclaimed "spiritual father,"
Richard Wright—that black authors must write about what was euphemistically, and characteristically, referred to as "the Negro problem." *Giovanni's Room* therefore signified for its author a liberation from what had
been construed, if not always assumed, as the traditional burden of the Negro

writer. If allowing his characters to perform in "racial drag," or "whiteface," freed the author to interrogate the complexities of gendered, national, and sexual identity—uncomplicated by the issue of racialized blackness—then actual geographical expatriation must have freed Baldwin to explore, outside the sexually and politically repressive climate of postwar America, the complexities of his own identity as writer, as American, and as homosexual. The erasure of blackness in his second novel thus enabled Baldwin to examine the complex personal, social, sexual, and cultural dimensions of identity uncomplicated by the extraliterary preoccupation with "the Negro problem." Focusing on the paradoxical and self-contradictory issues of subjectivity in a space that provided for the author both a sense of literary as well as social freedom, the text poses the following questions: What is it to be a (white) American and an expatriate? What is it to be a homosexual and a man?

Baldwin locates his narrative in Paris, modeling his characters on the American expatriates and Parisians associated with *le milieu,* or *demimonde,* habitués of the city's gay bars and cafés in the 1950s. And although Baldwin's characters perform in racial drag, it is clear that the narrative preserves the emotional tone of the author's own experiences in Paris. And while some critics suggest that the French setting links homosexuality with the alien, exotic, or outlandish, Paris also functions as a site configuring both cultural possibility and transgression. Indeed, as Baldwin recalls in "A Question of Identity," published two years before the appearance of *Giovanni's Room,* "Paris [was], according to legend, the city where everyone loses his head, and his morals, lives through at least one *histoire d'amour,* ceases, quite, to arrive anywhere on time, and thumbs his nose at the Puritans—the city, in brief, where all become drunken on the fine old air of freedom."[2]

Baldwin's novel, which was rejected by his American publisher, appeared during the era of U.S. McCarthyism and the cold war, a historical moment described by Stephen Whitfield as an era "which prescribed that men were men and women were housewives," and where "the overriding fear of [the] American parent . . . was that a son would become a 'sissie.' "[3] In this atmosphere, sexual deviance or "perversion" was linked to "subversion," and the job of the government was, in the words of the Reverend Billy Graham, to expose "the pinks, the lavenders, and the reds who have sought refuge beneath the wings of the American eagle."[4] In other words, to be a "good American" meant to be "a real man."[5] It seems fairly evident, then, that during this postwar period of conservative sexual and political mores in America, Baldwin's appropriation of whiteness constituted a strategic decision to assume—for artistic, if not, strictly speaking, personal reasons—a certain self-distancing in relation to a second, thinly veiled, autobiographical novel. At the same time, the author chooses in this novel to address front and center an issue that had appeared only peripherally in his first novel—the conundrum, as he might have put it, of homosexuality.

More importantly, however, Baldwin's literary performance of racial passing provides for the author a position from which to cast his critical gaze on the Other, while creating a subject position that allowed him both to explore his own sexual variance or "difference" and to critique the dominant national construction of masculinity. Thus Baldwin produces a highly mediated reverse passing narrative in which he appropriates whiteness as a way of exploring the contours of his own sexuality (thus, in effect, redeploying the strategy that Toni Morrison attributes to Anglo-American writers who serviceably deployed blackness to alleviate the insecurities of white identity).[6] In other words, Baldwin's literary masquerade, and racial imposture, enables the author to examine internal aspects of the complex self by occupying a position of radical otherness. Even thirty years later, in his essay "Here Be Dragons," Baldwin emphasizes the dialectics and dialogics of identity underlying his fictional mask: "Each of us, helplessly and forever, contains the other—male in female, female in male, white in black and black in white. We are part of each other."[7] Further, Baldwin's intensely ambivalent identification with his character is attested not only by the deployment of the autobiographical "I" in his fictive autobiography, but also by the epigraph from Walt Whitman— that most irreverent and profane of American poets—noted for his celebration of America as well as his open avowal of homoeroticism. In his self-referential, Whitmanesque epigraph, "I am the man, I suffered, I was there," Baldwin affirms the role of witnessing and suffering as profoundly constitutive of identity.

Giovanni's Room, explores the homosexual dilemma as one of expatriation or exile—from nation, from culture, from body. Creating a character who projects the image of the quintessential American or, as the French call him, *Monsieur l'American*—Baldwin's white American protagonist, David, demonstrates the author's preoccupation with the relation between identity and culture and, more specifically, the cultural constructions of nationality and masculinity.

In 1949, Baldwin's controversial article attacking Richard Wright, "Everybody's Protest Novel," appeared in *Zero* magazine; in that same year, the magazine published "Preservation of Innocence," a rarely cited essay that has, until recently, remained unanthologized, is as crucially important to his project as his first essay. In some respects, these essays are companion pieces, the former addressing the issues of gender and race and the latter gender and sexuality. In "Everybody's Protest Novel" Baldwin critiques the dehumanizing images of black masculinity circulating in the American (and African American) literary imaginary, images constructing the black man as Christlike "Uncle Tom" (Harriet Beecher Stowe) or alternatively, monsterlike "Bigger Thomas" (Richard Wright). If, in the earlier essay, Baldwin denounces Wright's protest fiction, and its corollary, Stowe's sentimental fiction, in "Preservation of Innocence" he critiques the contemporary, popular noir detective fiction of Raymond Chandler and James Cain. Addressing America's remarkable preoccupation with the aggressively violent and virile male, Baldwin observes: "In the truly awesome attempt of the American to at once preserve his innocence and arrive at a man's estate, that mindless monster, the tough guy, has been created and perfected; whose masculinity is found in the most infantile and elementary externals and whose attitude towards women is the wedding of the most abysmal romanticism and the most implacable distrust."[8]

Anticipating Eve Sedgwick's "homosexual panic" thesis by several decades, Baldwin describes the violence and brutality of the popular detective fiction as "compelled by a *panic* which is close to madness." "These novels," argues Baldwin, "are not concerned with homosexuality but with *the ever-present danger of sexual activity between men.*"[9] Baldwin not only implies here that the enactment of male violence constitutes the foundation of homosocial bonding, but, further, that the production of American masculinity, and more specifically the aggressive (white) male heterosexual subject, is predicated on "an abysmal romanticism and the most implacable distrust" of woman as well as on a maniacal fear and anxiety of male homosexual activity.

In this essay, Baldwin articulates the problem of representing masculinity in much the same terms that he used to critique the representation of race in "Everybody's Protest Novel." Like the production of black masculinities— the emasculated (effeminate) "Uncle Tom" or his later reincarnation as the monstrous predator, Bigger Thomas—the production of the nonvirile, non(re)productive (white) male functions not only to alleviate the anxieties menacing the white American male subject, but indeed to produce a nationally inflected notion of racialized masculinity. Addressing the allegation that homosexuality constitutes a transgression of both culture and nature,

Baldwin observes: "We arrive at the oldest, the most insistent and the most vehement charge faced by the homosexual: he is unnatural because he has turned from his life-giving function to a union which is sterile."[10] Homosexuality is thus constructed as a transgression of both Nature and Society—in what Freud would describe as an urge toward *thanatos* rather than *eros*. Once more Baldwin suggests that the creation of the authentically (hypo)masculine national subject necessitates the production of the inauthentic, sterile, effeminate, non(re)productive homosexual subject. Baldwin takes up this issue more explicitly five years later (two years before the publication of *Giovanni's Room*) in "The Male Prison," a critique of Andre Gide's *Madeleine:* "The argument . . . as to whether or not homosexuality is natural seems to me completely pointless—pointless because I really do not see what difference the answer makes. It seems clear, in any case, at least in the world as we know it, that no matter what encyclopedias of physiological and scientific knowledge are brought to bear the answer can never be Yes. And one of the reasons for this is that it would rob the normal—who are simply the many— of their very necessary sense of security and order, of their sense, perhaps, that the race is and should be devoted to outwitting oblivion—and will surely manage to do so."[11]

Yet, as Baldwin seeks to demonstrate, this seeming dual transgression of nature and culture—this "phenomenon as old as mankind"—also undeniably exists in both nature and culture. We cannot, argues Baldwin, "continue to shout 'unnatural' whenever we are confronted by a phenomenon as old as mankind; a phenomenon, moreover, that nature has maliciously repeated in all of her domain. If we are going to be natural then this is part of nature; if we refuse to accept this, then we have rejected nature and must find another criterion."[12]

Baldwin concludes by stating that "experience [construed as nature] . . . to say nothing of history [construed as culture] seems clearly to indicate that it is not possible to banish or falsify any human need without ourselves undergoing falsification or loss."[13] The author's moral formulation here can be rearticulated in terms of the risks attendant to the psychological processes of denial ("banish or falsify") and self-negation ("falsification or loss"). It is precisely such denial and self-negation, along with their consequences, that Baldwin's protagonist will confront in *Giovanni's Room*.

In classically circular form, the narration's end is in the beginning. The narrative opens with David, a white American living in France, contemplating the literal reflection of his own visage, filtered through the prism of the morning's rays refracted through the window of the "great house" he has rented in the south of France. In this Lacanian moment of narcissistic self-speculation, the narrator ironically and palimpsestally recognizes in his own likeness an ancestral image evoking a national past as dark as David's own: "My reflection is tall, perhaps rather like an arrow, my blond hair gleams. My face is like a face you have seen many times. My ancestors conquered a continent, pushing across death-laden plains, until they came to an ocean which faced away from Europe into a darker past."[14] The literal reflection of the narrator's own image, along with the figurative reflection on the historical past that has brought him to his present personal dilemma, combine to fade into a spectral reflection returning him to a mythically phantasmagoric national past: the darkness of David's vision and the complexity of his dilemma are fused with the dark deeds of his ancestors that still haunt the national imaginary. Bound by his own image—a reflection of what Baldwin elsewhere calls "the male prison" or "the prison of . . . masculinity"—the narrator attests to a disturbing, but revealing, connection to the ancestors who are associated with death and darkness. For who could these ancestors be but the western Europeans, who had to "cross death-laden plains" to reach their end, who conquered the continent with African and Native American blood on their hands? Just as his ancestors were forced to turn inward and face "a darker past" after their journey across America to the Pacific, David has been made to face himself after crossing not a continent, but the Atlantic. For David, too, is guilty—and guilt-ridden. The evocation of his ancestors identifies David's loss of innocence with that of America, even at the moment of its incipiency. Like his ancestors, whose violence and violation have laid claim to a continent and destroyed an indigenous people, David's emotional violence and moral violations have wrought destruction, not only to others, but to himself as well. Ironically, however, this moment of narcissistic self-contemplation yields the narrator a complex moment of intersubjectivity, one connecting David with an ambiguously complex historical and cultural past, a past that necessarily shapes the present. It is a moment of self-contemplation that constructs subjectivity as a site of mediation between the present and the past, the personal and the historical, the self and the other.

Notably, this rather striking passage opening Baldwin's novel echoes the closing of another American expatriate narrative, F. Scott Fitzgerald's *The Great Gatsby*. In the wake of the murder of Jay Gatsby, another prototypical American innocent, the narrator, Nick Carraway, makes the following statement: "Gradually I became aware of the old island here that flowered once for

Dutch sailors' eyes—a fresh, green breast of the new world. Its vanished trees . . . had once pandered in whispers to the last and greatest of all human dreams; for a transitory enchanted moment man must have held his breath in the presence of this continent, compelled into an aesthetic contemplation he neither understood nor desired, face to face for the last time in history with something commensurate with his capacity to wonder."[15]

If, in this passage, Fitzgerald inscribes the innocence and freshness of the New World encounter, the "transitory enchanted moment" compelling "aesthetic contemplation" in the face of "something commensurate to [man's] capacity to wonder," Baldwin's passage evokes a vision of the ravages and destruction consequent on its discovery, the blood-guilt of its violent colonial origins. And unlike Fitzgerald's Gatsby, who "did not know that [the dream] was already behind him," David is all too aware of the "death-laden plains," facing "away from Europe into a darker past." If Baldwin's fellow expatriate and literary precursor concludes his narrative with an elegy to the end of American innocence, Baldwin's opening reconstructs the national narrative as one predicated on originary guilt, or perhaps, more complexly, on an "innocence" entangled with and inseparable from a concomitant "guilt."

Structurally this meditation on the distant historical past is followed by a recollection of David's more recent past—and the events that have brought him to this narrative moment. By conjoining an expatriate (or leave-taking) narrative with an emergence (or "coming-out") narrative—both relatively "new" genres in American and African American fiction—the author also provides the template for a uniquely hybrid narrative. And, although images of voyage and travel are clearly structuring tropes in the novel of expatriation, critic Jacob Stockinger expands this notion by demonstrating that these same tropes are also classic topoi in what he names "homotextuality," or the homosexual text. As in the expatriate text, spatiality in the homotext becomes a privileged topos, and the negotiation of space—the crossing of borders and boundaries—a strategic deployment in the narrative of (homo)sexual emergence. David's real story, then, begins with a journey, a prototypical flight in which, as Stockinger would describe it, the "external itinerary corresponds to an internal journey of self-discovery."[16]

The topoi of journey and exile are central to Baldwin's narrative in which expatriation figures both as a geographical and a psychological construct. David thus embarks not only on a physical journey but also an inward one, and his exile is not only from America, but also from self-knowledge. As such, David's quest leads him in pursuit of a reassuring essentialized identity that is coherent, fixed, and unitary—an identity, in other words, that is outside of history and culture. By the end of his journey, David achieves a complex vision of self that is mediated by history, a history recapitulated by his individual experiences. And he will recognize the impossibility and, indeed, undesirability, of preserving his state of innocence.

In assuming the aspect of the generic confessional narrative, David's burden is to seek expiation, or atonement, for becoming the agent of tragedy for Giovanni, his lover; for becoming the agent of unhappiness for Hella, his fiancée; and, ultimately, for becoming the agent of despair to himself. Because the mode of the confessional invites a psychoanalytical reading, it is in this context that David's early development becomes most meaningful. David is the son of an amiable, but weak-willed, father, and of a mother of strong character. And although David's mother died when he was very young and an aunt steps in to take her place, the primal nexus of the novel turns on the relation between mother and son: David's maternal memories dominate his childhood. Thus Baldwin offers a variation on the classic psychoanalytic explanation for homosexuality: the aunt, an overbearing phallic mother surrogate, refigures the conventional dominating mother. In reconstructing the Freudian family romance, Baldwin therefore follows the then popularized contemporary notions linking male homosexuality to maternal fear and fixation. Infantile nightmares and fantasies of his dead mother haunt David, representing a threatening Medusa-like fusion of sex and death, fascination and revulsion: "I scarcely remember her at all, yet she figured in my nightmares, blind with worms, her hair as dry as metal and brittle as a twig, straining to press me against her body; that body so putrescent, so sickening soft, that it opened, as I clawed and cried, into a breach so enormous as to swallow me alive" (17).

The threat of becoming absorbed into m/other, of losing identity, seems to animate the protagonist's fear of the menacing maternal. This inability to separate from the m/other thus leads to a rejection of the anaclitic choice. As Freud explains in "On Narcissism: An Introduction," the adult choice of love objects for the homosexual is based not on the anaclitic choice of the mother, but the self: "We have found, especially in persons whose libidinal development has suffered some disturbance, as in perverts and homosexuals, that in the choice of their love object they have taken as their model not their mother but their own selves."[17] It seems clear that Baldwin was aware of, and to some extent drew on, the notion of homosexuality that links it with unresolved oedipal desire, as theorized by Freud in the 1910 edition of *Three Essays on the Theory of Sexuality*. These writings, along with Freud's study of Leonardo da Vinci, provide the classic formulation that homosexual men "proceed from a narcissistic basis, and look for a young man who resembles themselves and whom they may love as their mother loved them."[18] Following the currently fashionable Freudian formulation of homosexuality, the narrator's ambivalence toward the mother, coupled with his father's distance, creates confusion for young David that is only compounded by his brief but frightening adolescent homosexual encounter with a childhood schoolmate, Joey. Refiguring his fears of the maternal, David's encounter with Joey, one that initially evokes feelings of love and joy, is transformed into a fear of "the black opening of a cavern in which [he] would be tortured until madness came, in which [he] would lose [his] manhood." Thus, while the homosexual encounter protects against maternal absorption, it also threatens the protagonist with ablation. As a consequence, David makes the decision "to allow no room in the universe for something which shamed and frightened [him]" (30). His flight from the past, from homosexual intimacy, and from himself ultimately launches him, ironically, on a journey toward what he perceives to be self-discovery. The early portrait of David emerges as an identifiable American social type—a middle-class white male whose life has been caught up in the "constant motion and ennui of joyless seas of alcohol . . . blunt, bluff, hearty, and totally meaningless relationships . . . and forests of desperate women." The purpose of his eventual flight to Europe, he says in the American argot, is "to find himself," but perhaps it may be more aptly described as an attempt to "lose"—or escape—himself. Clearly, Baldwin's idea of identity, based as it is on a model of depth psychology and the accompanying notion of interiority, would seem to reflect either a modernist fiction of integral identity or, alternatively, a structuralist model of "deep" and "surface" identity. Whichever the paradigm, the narrative ultimately decenters this modernist and/or binary conception of identity, ostensibly figured by a protagonist in exile from his more "authentic" or "deeper" homosexual identity. Rather, as we shall see, the protagonist will model homosexual identity on something closer to a postmodernist paradigm based on the notions of self-difference, or the "otherness" of the self.

In France, David meets Hella Lincoln, an American woman (whose name evokes classic femininity linked to the notion of female emancipation) who has come to Paris to study painting. When David, in an attempt to reclaim that which he experiences as lack—an American notion of masculinity predicated on the conventions of heterosexual coupling and children—proposes marriage, Hella travels to Spain to think about his proposal. Remaining behind in Paris, David joins a friend, Jacques, with whom he frequents a local gay bar popular among *le milieu*. In the bar, David encounters the "knife-blade lean, tight-trousered boys" and "*les folles* screaming like parrots the details of their latest love affairs." In this carnivalesque atmosphere, David confronts phantasmally perverse and grotesque images of masculinity and femininity. What he confronts there, of course, are distorting mirrors of the self that he fears and represses. It is in this raucously transgressive liminal space that David first meets the expatriate Italian bartender, Giovanni. It is surely not lost on the reader that Baldwin models his two characters, some-what ironically as it turns out, after the biblical David (whose name means "loving") and Jonathan (whose name is translated as "God has given"), figures whose fabled love, it is said, surpassed "the love of women."[19] The remainder of the story recounts the disastrous consequences of David's affair, his subsequent denial and desertion of Giovanni and, finally, his futile attempt at reunion with Hella.

Giovanni's Room is structured by a series of parallel relationships and encounters centered around David: the brief encounter with Joey and the more extended affair with Giovanni both parallel and contrast with the seduction of Sue, a rather pathetic white American expatriate in Paris whom David seduces in an attempt to test his virility, and the longer relationship with his fiancée Hella. Baldwin, however, makes the struggle between David and Giovanni the central focus of the novel, with this relationship configuring the dangers and seduction of homosexuality for David.

Throughout the novel, David's world is ordered according to his perception of relationships, which fall into three general categories: relations between parents and children, inscribing familial identity; relations between men and women, inscribing gender/sexual identity; and relations between Europeans and Americans, inscribing national identity. Narratively, there exists between parents and children a lack of connection, an absence of communication, contact, and nurturance. Giovanni has fled to France after the stillborn birth of his son. David has grown up without a mother, and is unable to relate filially to his father. The union between David and Giovanni thus figures that of a motherless son and a childless father, a reconfiguration, or symbolic displacement, of the Freudian family romance.

Curiously, however, the relationship between men and women, particularly husbands and wives, bears some resemblance to the relationship between parents and children. Husbands and men in general take on the attributes of children—youth, innocence, weakness, and irresponsibility, while wives and women assume the attributes of maturity—experience, strength, and responsibility. David describes his father as "at his best, boyish and expansive," while he sees his mother in her photograph as "straight-browed with . . . eyes set in the head" in such a fashion as to suggest a "strength as various as it was unyielding" (20). The peasant women in the south of France are regarded as virtual widows, although most of them have husbands still living. As the narrator observes, "They might have been the sons of these women in black, come after a lifetime of storming and conquering the world, home to rest and be scolded and wait for death, home to those breasts, now dry, which have nourished them in their beginnings" (89). At the end of the novel, watching Hella pack to leave after she discovers him with a sailor in a homosexual bar, David stands in the doorway, "the way a small boy who has wet his pants stands before his teacher" (216). Before his Italian landlady, he feels like "a half-grown boy, naked before his mother" (95).

Throughout the novel, the men are defined in their relationships with women as children, sometimes naughty and sometimes charming, but perpetually and regardless of age, childlike. Males seem to inhabit a condition of prelapsarian innocence, and it is the effort to preserve this putative innocence, the author suggests, that makes it impossible for them to become men; they remain arrested in a state of eternal childhood. And, significantly, these essentialized constructions circulate transnationally in Baldwin's narrative.

In a world where men are children, the classic Jamesian expatriate confrontation between American innocence and European experience can be only superficial at best; yet David is represented as the American who seeks—no matter the price and against all odds—to preserve that innocence. In Europe, David seeks to preserve, or perhaps more accurately, to recover the innocence that covers over the "secret" of his homosexual desire. Julia Kristeva's notion of the *abject* is useful here in understanding David's complex reaction to Giovanni and to the homosexual subculture that forms the backdrop to their relationship.[20] Abjection refers to the feelings of revulsion and seduction experienced by the subject in encountering an "other", a reaction triggered by certain images, literal or fanciful. What is unique about the abject, as Kristeva explains, is that it fails to distinguish or differentiate between the self and the other, the ego and the object. Rather, abjection represents a momentary separation or "border" between the as-yet-unformed ego and the production, or rather expulsion, of that part of the self, which is, in effect, discharged from the self and thereby rendered abject or "other." As theorist Judith Butler explains it, "the boundary of the body as well as the distinction between internal and external is established through the ejection and transvaluation of something originally part of identity into a defiling otherness." Butler further explains that the "alien is effectively established through this expulsion" and the "construction of the 'not-me' as the abject establishes the boundaries . . . which are also the contours of the subject." Thus, not only does the abject mark the relation between self and other ("between ego and [its] objects"), it also marks the border between "inner" and "outer," thus forming the binary distinction that stabilizes and consolidates the coherent subject.[21]

In *Giovanni's Room*, David, in effect, abjects Giovanni and the sign of homosexual subculture under which he functions. As a figure of repulsion and seduction, love and danger, and fear and desire, Giovanni holds for David a deadly attraction—fearful in the rejection, unbearable in the acceptance. In a series of images associated with the room in which Giovanni lives—images invoking aversion and loathing—David seeks to expel—or abject—both his love and his terror. It is this room, formerly the maid's quarters, a place metonymically connected with Giovanni, that David finds disgusting and repulsive. Associated with images of dirtiness, disorder, and decomposition, Giovanni's room, functioning as the abject repository of his emotions and fears in relation to his own body and sex, embodies all that from which David so desperately desires to flee. For him, the yellow light in the center of the room "hung like a diseased and undefinable sex." In projecting his desire to expel the aversive self, to abject Giovanni, David perceives Giovanni's room as the repository of the "garbage" of "Giovanni's regurgitated life": "The table was loaded with yellowing newspapers and empty bottles and it held a single brown and wrinkled potato in which even the sprouting eyes were rotten. Red wine had been spilled on the floor; it had been allowed to dry and it made the air in the room sweet and heavy" (115). Not only does Giovanni's room—for which the closest analogue is clearly the "closet"—represent David's association of homosexuality with dirtiness and filth, it also becomes a spatial metaphor for his claustrophobic sense of self-entrapment. Thus, unlike Stockinger, who identifies the homosexual space as typically "a closed and withdrawn place that is transformed into a redeeming space," Baldwin constructs the homosexual space as more typically the closet, that contorting secret place of shame in which dwells, as Oscar Wilde's "lover-in-disgrace," Lord Alfred Douglass, so famously put it, "the love that has no name" (a formulation that invokes, of course, Baldwin's collection *No Name in the Street*).[22]

If David feels himself enclosed, locked, buried within the walls of the room, Giovanni tries "with his own strength, to push back the encroaching walls." Yet, for David it was Giovanni who was "dragging him to the bottom of the sea," who made him feel that he could not move, that his "feet were being held back by water" (152, 140). Returning to the Freudian oedipalization of homosexuality, Giovanni's room becomes the watery tomb in which David fears drowning, the equivalent of the phantasmal embrace of his mother's decaying body (and later Hella's embrace), which functions as the womb in which he fears being swallowed alive.

It would seem that, for Baldwin, the sign of homosexuality both defines and empties agency: David feels caught and helpless in a quagmire from which there is no exit. At the same time, his reactions suggest that, for him, "the boundaries of the body" delimit the boundaries of the social, thereby invoking Mary Douglas's notion that "the body is a model that can stand for any bounded system." As such, "its boundaries can represent any boundaries which are threatened and precarious."[23] What the analogy here between body and society suggests is that David's dilemma is a consequence not only of repressed desire but also that such desire is defined as transgressive by a society that positions him here not only as victimizer but as victim as well. That is, his own repression and ambivalence, manifested as internalized homophobia, is a consequence of social sanctions that pathologize or criminalize homosexual identity and activity.

The extreme and solipsistic self-seclusion generated by such fears is represented in recurring self-reflexive images suggesting David's emotional self-absorption. The framing of the tale, which begins and ends with images of David's reflection in mirrors and windows, reinforces the dominant motif of self-confinement, or the "male prison." Thus, the rooms and enclosed spaces in *Giovanni's Room* become sites of liminality—sites that carry the potential of redemption but that inevitably fail to become transformative. Significantly, Giovanni's room is something of a work in progress, and his attempts to remodel it signify not only a futile attempt to transform his own life but also a failure to create a space in his universe for homosexuality. Symbolically, on one wall, "a lady in a hoop skirt and a man in knee breeches perpetually walked together, *hemmed in by roses*" (113; emphasis added). Albeit doomed from the start, Giovanni's efforts to destroy the walls of his room signify his efforts to destroy the confining walls of heterosexuality. Nevertheless, the wall ("destined never to be uncovered") remains a monument to the durability and rigidity of the codes that bolster the edifice of heterosexuality.

The great house in the country, on the other hand, represents another *limen* in which the protagonist fails, this time to achieve with Hella the potential of heterosexuality. Clearly, David feels comfortable neither in Giovanni's room nor in the great house; rather, he remains 'betwixt and between' homosexual desire and the heterosexual imperative. In endeavoring to preserve his innocence by retreating into a safety zone of conventional domesticity, David seeks conformity to prevailing gendered conventions and norms. Thus, his need to preserve an image of purity demands that he deny Giovanni and deceive himself. It was Giovanni, he tells himself, who had "awakened the awful beast in him." Given Baldwin's self-acknowledged relationship with his nineteenth-century precursor Henry James—that is, his acknowledgment of James's literary influence ("James became, in a sense, my master. It was something about point of view, something about discipline")[24]—the evocation of James's short story "The Beast in the Jungle" seems not unwarranted.[25] Eve Sedgwick's rereading of the Jamesian story as one of "intense male homosocial desire" is, after all, fully anticipated and confirmed by Baldwin's critique of American detective fiction in the late 1940s in his essay "Preservation of Innocence." In fact, Baldwin's text draws its power, in part, from its ability to make manifest the repressed or latent meaning of what Sedgwick describes as James's "long act of dissimulation."[26] As suggested at the outset of this essay, Sedgwick's compelling notion of "homosocial panic" is, finally, one that recuperates Baldwin's own term. It would seem that Baldwin's Giovanni and James's John Marcher both become victims of "homosexual panic." In *Giovanni's Room*, David repeatedly refers to his "panic"—as, for example, when he speaks of the "panic caused in me" when one of his army consorts is court-martialed for homosexual conduct. Nonetheless, Baldwin's agenda is very different from that of the "Master." If Marcher's final posture is, as Sedgwick describes it, one of "irredeemable self-ignorance that enforces the heterosexual compulsion," Baldwin's character, as we shall see, is at least poised on the precipice of a self-knowledge that has the potential to absolve him from "homosexual panic."[27]

As a victim of internalized homophobia, David's sexual anxiety expresses itself in an identification with the dominant heterosexual subjectivity and heternormative script. "People have dirty words for—for the situation," stammers David to Giovanni, "besides, it *is* a crime—in my country and, after all, I didn't grow up here, I grew up *there*." Although acknowledging

implicitly the social construction of the "natural," David continues to criminalize and pathologize homosexuality.

It is David's bondage to what Baldwin calls elsewhere "the American ideal
of masculinity" that prevents him from acknowledging his feelings for Giovanni. Trapped within his own body and self-image, David in effect ful-
fills the prophecy of Jacques, an aging Belgian-born American homosexual
businessman, who warns him that should he continue to "play it safe long
enough" he would "end up forever trapped in [his] own dirty body, forever
and forever and forever" (77). It is Giovanni, however, who delivers the most
serious indictment of David's narcissistic sense of "purity": "You are just like
a little virgin, you walk around with your hands in front of you as though you
had some precious metal . . . You will never give it to anybody, you will never
let anybody *touch* it. You want to be *clean* . . . You want to leave Giovanni
because he makes you stink. You want to despise Giovanni because he is not
afraid of the stink of love. You want to *kill* him in the name of all your lying
little moralities" (187). As a prototypical American ("Monsieur l'American")
David represents a construction of whiteness that rests on a conception of
human nature that derives fundamentally from an American puritanical
notion associated with the repression of the body and its sinfulness. It also
depends on a perception of the world as morally unambiguous, stable, and
fixed, one based on what Giovanni astutely identifies as a philosophy of life
comparable to the "English melodrama." His comparison is apt. David conceives of life, as in the melodrama, in terms of absolutes: absolute good and
evil, absolute right and wrong. It is a perspective that makes self-deception
imperative: David ultimately realizes that such absolute values force Americans to devise a system of evasion and illusion designed to make themselves
and the world conform to a monolithic mold. This is, of course, the view of
the world that initially motivated David's flight to Europe, a perspective that
could not accommodate the shame and fear associated with his first youthful
homosexual encounter.

But when, in Europe, David comes face to face with homoerotic desire, his
flight and denial lead swiftly and inevitably to disaster and, finally, tragic self-
awareness. David must ultimately assume responsibility for Giovanni's execution for the murder of his former boss, a flamboyantly homosexual old
aristocrat. David must also, at last and unavoidably, come to terms with
homoerotic desire. His relationship with Giovanni exposes the falseness and
the guilt underlying David's seeming innocence. In the end, it is not the
European Giovanni who has corrupted David, but David, the American, who

has misled and deceived not only Giovanni, but himself and others as well. The traditional Jamesian theme thus undergoes an ironic reversal in the Baldwinian revision: the American corrupts the European, not so much through experience as through an inability to accept the consequences of experience. It is Giovanni who leaves an Edenic Italian village to discover in Paris a new kind of life in his relationship with David. He responds to their encounter, moreover, with love, recognition, and acceptance—not evasion, denial, and deception.

Giovanni's answer to the English melodrama, as he characterizes David's worldview, is *la vie practique* in which arrangements are made not on the basis of moral absolutes but on the imperatives of love and commitment. What perverts the homosexual relationship, the author suggests here, is not the nature of its love but the absence of love. The absence of love is also what perverts the heterosexual relationship, as in the case of David, who uses women like Sue and Hella as objects on which to test his "manhood." David betrays himself and makes his female consorts unknowing co-conspirators in his desperate desire to find refuge within the boundaries of conventional heterosexuality: "I wanted to be inside again, with the light and safety, with my manhood unquestioned, watching my woman put my children to bed. I wanted the same bed at night and the same arms and I wanted to rise in the morning, knowing where I was. I wanted a woman to be for me a steady ground, like the earth itself, where I could always be renewed" (137–38). Clearly, the heterosexual body here represents for David the site of manhood and "legitimate surrender": "[Hella] smelled of the wind and the sea and of space and I felt in her marvelously living body the possibility of *legitimate surrender*" (159; emphasis added). But his efforts ultimately fail, in part because both he and Hella do not understand that the construction of the feminine is "itself a category of the patriarchy." For this reason, the female "cannot ever become a refuge for the homosexual"—whether as sister, mother, lover, or wife; neither can the feminine ever become "a model of identification."[28]

For Baldwin, the expatriate becomes a trope for the homosexual who cannot reconcile his body and desire. The expatriate, who is more conventionally constructed as a stranger in a strange land, becomes, in Baldwin's vision, a stranger at home—a stranger unto himself, one whose body is exiled from desire. On a broader level, however, Baldwin seems to suggest that in the New World (American) experience, nature and culture are in an antithetical relationship, dissociated by puritanical imperatives. It is the Law of the

Father (patriarchal and religious) that has marked "the duality of good and evil," as Baldwin describes it in "Preservation of Innocence." The sexual union of Giovanni and David potentially breaks down the opposition between nature and culture, making homoeroticism a symbolic enactment of the reconciliation of these two principles, and thus restoring harmony between experience and history as well as nature and culture—both exemplified by what Baldwin regards as the inexpressibly complex conundrum of being human. David, however, views his love for Giovanni as a transgression against the laws of culture, essentially the Law of the Father, inscribed in the tenets of Puritanism. His "transgression," however, only reinforces the prohibition that the original homoerotic act attempted to destroy. In David's cultural consciousness, the original unity has never existed because he is unable to defy or deny the cultural imperatives of his uniquely American experience. Unable to accept the contradictions of his identity, David finds that the cost of social acceptance is the inability to achieve personal fulfillment.

The framing and flashback devices that structure the novel create a juxtaposition of images that embodies its central dialectic—the conflict between the pull of the self from within and of society from without, or more particularly, the conflict between homosexual desire and the heterosexual imperative. For example, part 1 concludes with David's cleaning out the house that he and Hella have rented in the south of France. The house—clean and large, with airy, spacious rooms—is associated with heterosexuality, marriage, and family. When Hella leaves after discovering that David has concealed his homosexuality from her, the Italian caretaker of the house informs him, "It is not good . . . it is not right for a young man like you to be setting alone in a great big house with no woman." Her advice is that David "must go and find . . . another woman . . . and get married, and have babies" (92). Opposed to these images of domesticity is David's memory of Giovanni's room, which concludes part 2. Giovanni's room, a small, airless, closetlike space that is filled with dirt, clutter, and disorder, is associated with death, decay, and homosexuality—images expressing David's inner chaos.

The recurrent pattern of imagery in *Giovanni's Room* is both specular and spatial, and together they establish the symbolic framework of the novel. The opening scene, in which David scrutinizes his inverted self-image in front of a windowpane, establishes a symbolic code of what Luce Irigaray describes as the specular "logic of the same."[29] In her rereading of Freud, Irigaray argues that the male subject defers and/or masters the death drive (*thanatos*) through a process of "specular [self] deplication." Thus, in the speculation of his own specularity (what Irigaray calls "specula(riza)tion"), David sees his desired image reflected and repeated as the "same through the mirror" of the Other [Woman]. What David fails to see, however, is that the mirror images is an inverted image—one that leads, at least potentially, to a recognition of self-difference—or the "otherness" of the self.

There seem, however, to be two specular modes operating in the text: one in which reflections reveal a hidden—or repressed—self, and another in which the reflections reveal a false and/or illusionary self. Other specular images reinforce this pattern: The photographs of David's dead mother, the projection of the image of a broken-down movie queen to describe the seduced Sue; the narrator's "unguarded eyes," which reflect to a passing sailor the gaze of envy and desire. All combine to reinforce the specular logic of the novel and to symbolize the ordering of David's world, which is based on "elaborate systems of evasions, of illusion, designed to make . . . the special-ists in self-deception . . . and the world appear to be what they and the world are not" (30).

The recurrent images of mirror and water also evoke the myth of Nar-cissus, who seeks to possess his likeness as it is reflected in the mirror created by the surface of the water. The myth integrates the water and mirror imagery of the novel, and the implicit onanism of the tale of Narcissus provides an ironic key to David's dilemma. David, like Narcissus, is trapped in his own self-image, the specular logic of the same. He cannot escape what Baldwin describes in "The Male Prison" as "the tyranny of his own personality." Narcissus's attempted self-embrace leads to his drowning in the self, so to speak, just as David's self-absorption (rather than absorption by the other) will result potentially in his destruction, a fate symbolically prefigured in his fears of being swallowed alive.

The specular symbolic framework, reflecting David's "specular ego," is complemented by the spatiality of the architectural imagery. Indeed, the title of the novel alerts the reader to the dominant spatiality structuring the narrative. A series of images of enclosed, interior spaces (including bars, cars, rooms, walls) suggests spatial limitation and entrapment epitomized in the image of Giovanni's room.

Thus the spatial and specular imagery form an axis of meaning around which is constructed the symbolic framework of the novel, and these two modalities intersect in the dominant spatial imagery of the room and the specular imagery of the water/mirror. In the final scene, the narrator again postures before his mirror, which becomes the site of intersection of the specular and the spatial: "The body in the mirror forces me to turn and face it. And I look at my body, which is under sentence of death. It is lean, hard, and cold, the incarnation of a mystery. And I do not know what moves in this body, what this body is searching. It is trapped in my mirror as it is trapped in time and it hurries toward revelation" (222–23). The mirror thus both enframes and sentences the body. David's existence would seem to remain entrapped in time and space—in history and society. His only hope is revelation.

It is, however, in the fusion of these two symbolic modes—the spatial and the specular—that the novel is resolved on a symbolic plane. Of course, while the structural and symbolic frameworks contain the potential for resolution, it is not at all certain that David will break through the surface of the mirror/ water and find release from a self-absorptive self. David has yet to discover that freedom comes from attachment and that he must commit himself to a meaningful relationship—surrender himself to another—before he can claim himself.

In the conclusion to the novel, the narrator achieves a revelatory vision, disclosing to him the illusoriness of his own self-image. The days of his innocence (childhood) have departed and now he must accept the responsibilities of experience (manhood): "*When I was a child, I spake as a child, I understood as a child, I thought as a child: but when I became a man, I put away childish things*" (223). In "Preservation of Innocence," Baldwin remarks that it is the "recognition of . . . complexity" that is the "signal of maturity"; it is this recognition which "marks the death of the child; and the birth of the man."[30] David thus realizes that in order to achieve salvation, his false, mirror image must be destroyed. "I long to make this prophecy come true," he writes, "I long to crack that mirror and be free" (223). The protagonist thus will be able to achieve maturation and manhood only when he is able to release himself from the false images created by puritanical preconceptions of the debasement of the body—as well as constructions of American masculinity based on what Baldwin elsewhere describes as "an ideal so paralytically infantile that it is virtually forbidden—as an unpatriotic act—that the American boy evolve into the complexity of manhood."[31] Only when David is free to recognize the complexity of self-difference will he be able to achieve manhood.

Fiction writers frequently employ a character to speak self-referentially on the author's own creation. In most of Baldwin's fiction, his protagonists are

. . . .

self-reflexively figured as musicians, writers, actors, or artists. Remarkably, in *Giovanni's Room* the protagonist-as-artist is never developed, despite the fact that Hella poses as a disillusioned art student and Giovanni is figured as an amateur violinist. In neither instance, however, does the association with the artistic advance character development or meaning.

One would not normally consider David in the role of artist; but as narrator of the tale he does assume the role of storyteller, and as such it is his narration that structures the text. To understand the structure of the narrative, we must recall, on the one hand, Giovanni's comparison of the American perspective to the melodrama: "Life is certainly not the English melodrama you make it. Why that way, life would be unbearable" (108–9); and, on the other hand, to the murder mystery: "*Chez toi* [declares Giovanni] everything sounds extremely feverish and complicated, like one of those English murder mysteries. To find out, to find out, you keep saying, as though we were accomplices in a crime" (107).

If Giovanni's analogy is accurate, then one would expect to discover elements of both of these generic modes in the construction of narrative. Steven Carter suggests the affinities between these two genres: "The point is that the mystery novel is well adapted to a world view which makes a sharp distinction between opposing ways of life and which pictures one as overtly healthy and the other as surreptitiously destructive."[32] Carter's definition bears a striking similarity to that of the melodrama, a literary form that generally expresses a conflict of good and evil in absolute terms. Like the narrator in the murder mystery, David opens his story with an indirect allusion to the perpetrator of a crime: "Giovanni [is] about to perish, sometime between this night and this morning, on the guillotine" (10). Continuing the parallel to the murder mystery, the remainder of the tale reveals the circumstances and motivations leading up to the crime. Just as the investigator uses deductive logic and his knowledge of human nature to solve the murder mystery, so David uses an imaginative reconstruction of his knowledge of the principles involved to re-create the murder of Guillaume and the execution of Giovanni. More importantly, however, David uses his own past—along with his evolving self-knowledge that is a consequence of recognizing that the past is bound up with the present—to reconstruct the events that have lead both him and Giovanni to their present tragic but potentially redemptive state.

Using the conventions of the melodrama, then, David tells a tale based ostensibly on his conception of the conflict of moral right and wrong and good and evil. However, he offers a narrative that reveals, in spite of himself, his own "fortunate fall" from innocence into knowledge. Moreover, David presents a story line based appropriately on the use of flashbacks, which link a series of past actions (the mystery) to the present (the revelation). Thus David, in his narrative strategy and perspective, creates a fusion of the elements of melodrama and the murder mystery.

Though arguably David is as much a victim as are Giovanni and Hella, it is not quite so evident that David functions as both detective and criminal (although it is Guillaume who immediately provokes the offense that will lead Giovanni to his death). Like the criminal in a detective story (and the villain in the melodrama) David must create a web of deception and illusion in order to survive, and, at the same time, preserve the (hetero)normative social order. David thus functions simultaneously as a detective who sets about unraveling the mystery of his own identity as well as the consequences of his actions. Like the fictional detective, David must discover a way of perceiving reality in the midst of illusion and deceptions. At the conclusion of the novel, and not without a sense of tragic irony, David reveals himself to be a victim as well—a victim potentially doomed to remain forever entrapped in his specular logic of the same.

Still, and despite the generic parallels cited, neither David's narrative nor Baldwin's text can be passed off as a melodrama in which good triumphs over evil, or as a murder mystery in which the perpetrator of the crime is punished for wrongdoing. No matter how accurately David reconstructs his tale, it cannot be successfully translated into either of these forms. It is the author, who ultimately assumes narrative control by revealing both forms as inadequate. Baldwin's major characters, thus, can be judged neither according to the principles of the murder mystery nor the conventions of the English melodrama. Neither can they be judged according to moral absolutes: good and evil can be inseparable; guilt and innocence can be enmeshed and entangled; and that which is evil can sometimes have good consequences. The murder of Guillaume by Giovanni only appears to be the crime. The real crime, which leads to Giovanni's actions and to the destruction of three lives, is David's deception and dishonesty. David, like Giovanni, is culpable; and, like Giovanni, he suffers for his offenses. Giovanni's crime, however, is one of passion and therefore more venial than David's.

On another level, however, it is the social construction of American masculinity that Baldwin perceives to be the real culprit; it is "the heroes of Mickey Spillane" and the "swaggering of Hollywood he-men,"[33] as well as the binarisms on which American masculinity gets constructed—"the cowboys and Indians, good guys and bad guys, punks and studs, tough guys and softies, butch and faggot, black and white"[34]—that account for the panic underlying the American notion of masculinity, an idea, or *ideal* (as Baldwin would have it), in which is rooted American conceptions of sexuality. Appropriately, then, the novel ends in paradox, moral ambiguity, and ambivalence, as the image of David's affirming his own guilt is juxtaposed with the image of the "innocent" Giovanni on his way to the guillotine. Baldwin has incorporated elements of popular detective fiction and murder mystery into his story, only to subvert them in the end. He has parodied these genres just as he has parodied a way of life, and he has written a story that is antimythological in its challenge to the illusions, deceptions, stereotypes, and hypocrisies that many Americans accept without question. David is not the blond-haired hero of American innocence, and Giovanni is not the dark-haired villain of European evil. Baldwin's novel aims to debunk the traditional American myths of innocence and purity—as well as popular stereotypes and conventions of masculinity. Like Baldwin himself, David, his expatriate protagonist in racial drag, must divest himself of conventional notions of masculinity before he can achieve self-realization or, to use an overused term but one that deserves some recuperation, "authenticity." But authenticity is not so easily come by. In Baldwin's vision, authenticity entails a complex engagement not with our deepest, truest self (a psychoanalytic fiction), but with the complexities of a self that is neither (or perhaps both) "male [and/] or female, straight [and/] or not, black [and/] or white."[35] Here Baldwin would seem, at least implicitly, to conjoin notions of authenticity and complex subjectivity in order to open a space for the affirmation of self-difference—or the recognition of the otherness of the self.

In the final image closing David's narrative (and Baldwin's novel), the torn pieces of Jacques's envelope, in which was enclosed the letter (a metaphor for the text) informing David of Giovanni's execution, momentarily "dance in the wind" that "[carries] them away." Yet, the "wind blows some of [the torn pieces] back" to the David. Such an image would seem to remind the protagonist, as well as the reader, that the key to Baldwin's narrative rests in how we negotiate the claims of the past, in this instance a specifically American past—some of which we can productively use and some of which must be released; some of which we must claim, at least in terms of responsibility, and some of which we must disclaim.

While David fails in narrative time to come to terms with himself or his dilemma, the act of writing *Giovanni's Room* represents, for the author, a significant step, a "slaying of dragons," so to speak that is necessary in coming to terms with his own homosexuality and vision of America, but perhaps most importantly, in becoming an honest writer. As Baldwin commented in an interview with Richard Goldstein, "If I hadn't written that book I would probably have had to stop writing altogether."[36] Indeed, although Baldwin chose to perform in racial drag in his first explicit treatment of homosexuality, his later works explore black homosexuality as a theme and trope central to his vision of a reconstructed America and a reconstructed masculinity. The perspective offered by "another country" (geographical and imaginary) is central to his moral vision. In *Another Country,* (1962) and in his final novel, *Just Above My Head,* (1979) homosexuality and the self-authenticity achieved in Europe are used to represent the potential of the individual to transcend and transform the limitations imposed by national culture and gender proscription. *Giovanni's Room,* then, was vital to Baldwin's artistic and social vision, and expatriation has remained a trope, in his subsequent works, for crossing borders and breaking the boundaries of convention when they stifle the capacity of the individual to grow, love, and create.

NOTES

1. Roger A. Berger, "The Black Dick: Race, Sexuality, and Discourse in the L.A. Novels of Walter Mosley—African American Detective Novels," *African American Review* 31.2 (1997): 281–95.

2. James Baldwin, "A Question of Identity," in *The Price of the Ticket* (New York: St. Martin's Press, 1985), 93.

3. Stephen Whitfield, *The Culture of the Cold War* (Baltimore: Johns Hopkins University Press, 1990), 43.

4. Quoted in ibid.

5. Ibid., 44–45.

6. See Toni Morrison, *Playing in the Dark: Whiteness and the Literary Imagination* (New York: Vintage, 1993).

7. Baldwin, "Here Be Dragons," in *The Price of the Ticket,* 690.

8. James Baldwin, "Preservation of Innocence," in *James Baldwin: Collected Essays* (New York: Library of America, 1998), 597.

9. Ibid., 599; emphasis added.

10. Ibid., 595.

11. Ibid., "The Male Prison," in *James Baldwin: Collected Essays,* 232.

12. Baldwin, "Preservation of Innocence," 595.

13. Ibid., 596.

14. James Baldwin, *Giovanni's Room* (New York: Laurel, 1988 [1956]), 7. Subsequent citations appear as parenthetical page numbers in the text.

15. F. Scott Fitzgerald, *The Great Gatsby* (New York: Charles Scribner's Sons, 1953), 182.

16. See Jacob Stockinger, "Homotextuality: A Proposal," in *The Gay Academic*, ed. Louie Crew (Palm Springs, Calif.: ETC Publication, 1978), 27–28.

17. Sigmund Freud, "On Narcissism: An Introduction" in *General Psychological Theory* (New York: Touchstone, 1997), 69.

18. See Sigmund Freud, *Leonardo da Vinci: A Study in Psychosexuality* (New York: Vintage Books, 1947 [1916]).

19. David says to Jonathan: "Thy love to me was wonderful, passing the love of women" (2 Samuel 1:26; King James Version).

20. See Julia Kristeva, *The Powers of Horror: An Essay in Abjection* (New York: Columbia University Press, 1982).

21. See Judith Butler, *Gender Trouble: Feminism and the Subversion of Identity* (New York: Routledge, 1990), 133.

22. Though often associated with Oscar Wilde, the original phase, "the love that has no name," is from a sonnet titled "The Two Loves" that was written by Wilde's lover, Lord Alfred Douglass. I am indebted to my friend and colleague Chip Delany for this clarification.

23. See Mary Douglass, *Purity and Danger: An Analysis of the Concepts of Pollution and Taboo* (New York: Routledge, 1966).

24. David Leeming, *James Baldwin: A Biography* (New York: Henry Holt, 1994), 254.

25. See Henry James, *The Beast in the Jungle* (New York: Wildside Press, 2003 [1903]).

26. See Eve Sedgwick, "The Beast in the Closet: James and the Writing of Homosexual Panic," in *Sex, Politics, and Science in the Nineteenth-Century Novel*, ed. Ruth B. Yeazell (Baltimore: Johns Hopkins University Press, 1991).

27. For a suggestive, but somewhat different, treatment of Baldwin's *Giovanni's Room* as an intertext for James's "Beast in the Closet," see Bryan R. Washington, *The Politics of Exile* (Boston: Northeastern University Press, 1995).

28. See Thomas E. Yingling's *Hart Crane and the Homosexual Text* (Chicago: University of Chicago Press, 1990), 53.

29. See Luce Irigaray, *This Sex Which Is Not One* (Ithaca: Cornell University Press, 1985).

30. Baldwin, "Preservation of Innocence," in *James Baldwin: Collected Essays*, 597.

31. Baldwin, "Freaks and the American Ideal of Manhood," in *James Baldwin: Collected Essays*, 815.

32. Steven Carter, "Ishmael Reed's Neo-Hoodoo Detection," in *Dimensions of Detective Fiction,* ed. Larry Landrum, Pat Brown, and Ray Brown (Madison: University of Wisconsin Press, 1976), 270.

33. Baldwin, "The Male Prison" in *James Baldwin: Collected Essays,* 235.

34. Baldwin, "Freaks and the American Ideal of Manhood," in *James Baldwin: Collected Essays,* 815.

35. Ibid.

36. James Baldwin, "Go the Way Your Blood Beats: An Interview with James Baldwin," in *James Baldwin: The Legacy,* ed. Quincy Troupe, (New York: Simon and Schuster, 1989), 176.

FAEDRA CHATARD CARPENTER

ROBERT O'HARA'S *INSURRECTION:*

"QUE(E)RYING" HISTORY

I hold a play in my hands. The play is Robert O'Hara's *Insurrection: Holding History*. Neatly bound in a slim, paperback volume, the cover features an intriguing graphic: a black-and-white photograph of dark, wrinkled hands. With fingers gently interwoven, the aged and weathered appearance of these hands seems to suggest a long and arduous life, encouraging me to wonder how this photograph serves as a clue to the pages within. Noting the deep lines and swollen knuckles, I imagine the leathery calluses that are invisible to my eyes, hidden by the graphic's limited dimensions. I also recognize that the appearance of these hands—these corporeal texts—represents a powerful mode of historic documentation. This striking visual prompts me to ponder: Can history be *held?*

Evoking the play's critical line of inquiry, the cover photo does indeed foreshadow the rich, multifaceted discourse found within the pages of O'Hara's play. In questioning the sanctity of written historical narratives, the very premise of *Insurrection: Holding History* compels its audience to reconsider habitual assumptions regarding historical documentation. In encouraging its audience to constantly reassess the authority granted to the written word—especially in terms of how traditional archives treat issues concerning race, sex, and gender—O'Hara's play prompts us to ask: Can history be truly (truthfully) held? Can it be fully contained within the grasp of a hand, the fold of an arm, or the cover of a book?

In O'Hara's play, Ron—a gay African American graduate student at Columbia University—wrestles with the canonical, politicized subjectivity of the academy. In so doing, his character simultaneously embodies and disrupts notions of a traditional, historical narrative. Although Ron's double-minority status challenges the normative simply through his presence in the play, his scholarly pursuits (he is writing his thesis on American slave insurrectionists) also offer the play's author an opportunity to question the power granted to conventional modes of historic documentation and the institutions they serve. Furthermore, by staging intersections and conflations of time, place, space, and perspective (Ron and his 189 year-old great-great-grandfather T. J. are transported back into time) *Insurrection: Holding History* uses the fantastical to emancipate African American history and identity from the bondage of compulsive white heteronormativity. It is this liberation—this revolt—that fully discloses the meaning of the play's title: *Insurrection: Holding History.* In dramatizing an insurrection against the limiting perspectives of conventional archives, O'Hara's play presents history—and identity—as fluid experiences that cannot be fully confined or categorized within the metaphorically "dusty" pages of an authoritative text.

Although this movement toward, in the words of Helene Keyssar, the "deprivileging of absolute, authoritarian discourses" conjures concepts inherent in Bakhtinian theory as well as other aspects of postmodernism, O'Hara extends these concepts of nonlinearity and multiplicity by revealing the performativity of history itself.[1] History (like performance) may be documented or reenacted, but in so doing it will inevitably elude the notions of absolute truth and/or objective mediatization due to the fact that "repetition marks it as 'different.' "[2] Acknowledging this difference, O'Hara's play rebels against the suggestion of control and containment that "holding" implies. In light of this revelation of the fluidity inherent in the recollection of past experiences, I propose here that O'Hara "queers" the authoritative notion of history by emphasizing the performative role that history plays in shaping our social identities and consciousness.

In applying the term "queer" to O'Hara's work, I play upon the term's usage as it is articulated by David Eng who proposes that queer "has been resignified in a rather open and capacious context—one that can be used simultaneously to discuss the politics of the personal, to question a spectrum of personal identities, to act against normalizing ideologies, and to resist the historical terror of social phobia and violence."[3] Eve Kosofsky Sedgwick also notes that queer can refer to "the open mesh of possibilities, gaps, overlaps, dissonances and resonances, lapses and excesses of meaning when the constituent elements of anyone's gender, of anyone's sexuality aren't made (or *can't be* made) to signify monolithically."[4] And within the discourse of queer theory, as Annamarie Jagose aptly observes, queer is unique in that "its definitional indeterminacy, its elasticity, is one of its constituent characteristics."[5] My understanding of queer is shaped not only by these assertions but also by the suggestion of a distinctive cultural aesthetic—what Jack Babuscio would term as a "gay sensibility"—one that revels in the performance of incongruity, individualism, and identity.[6]

By subscribing to these uses of the term queer, I contend that O'Hara's *Insurrection: Holding History* queers history by emphasizing history's own performativity and, in doing so, dismantles the monolithic authority of normalizing ideologies associated with historic discourse. This queering of history occurs within O'Hara's play in three distinct ways: (1) through the script's form and language, *Insurrection* critiques the rigid and linear organizational categories that have been used to construct our traditional narratives; (2) through its spectacular plot, the play dramatizes the innate multiplicity of historical perspective, thereby denying the existence of a singular authoritative truth; and (3) through the physical presence of a gay character and a queer aesthetic, *Insurrection* opens a space for alternative concepts of sexual orientation, race, and gender identity to exist within our historicized imaginations and imagined histories.

I write of historicized imaginations and imagined histories not to wholly disregard the authenticity of past experiences, but to illustrate further the validity of substantiating history as inclusive of—and beyond—the assemblage of individual interpretations and ideologies. History is fashioned and its documentation is inevitably filtered through the lens of its archivist, who—unwittingly or consciously—impresses himself or herself upon the record. In *Insurrection: Holding History,* O'Hara calls attention to this complication through characters who personify the silenced and erased histories of the minoritized subject. In creating a sphere for alternative images to exist within a predominately white, masculine, and heterosexist interpretation of history, *Insurrection: Holding History* explosively defies any monopolization of territory, creating instead a boundless space of inclusion and diversity. It is this yielding of space that permits myriad personal and collective histories to coexist—an openness initially introduced through the play's use of dramatic form.

Rebelling against a linear chronology or concrete locale, O'Hara notes that the time and place of *Insurrection: Holding History* is "Now and Then" and "Here and Now"[7] thus making both positional categories ambiguous and fluid. To further emphasize his rejection of the established spatiotemporal order, the dramatist also notes that "this play should be done as if it were a Bullet Through Time" (6), suggesting imagistically that the play itself charges between temporalities, thereby creating holes and gaps as it ricochets back and forth between past and present. These are the holes—spaces in-between the layers of time and place—that contain the promise of multiplicity and possibility. Thus, from its very structure, *Insurrection* dramatizes Homi Bhabha's assertion that the liminal spaces between primary organizational categories provide rich and fertile ground for the production and proliferation of diverse identities and ideologies.[8]

O'Hara not only incorporates notions of slippage and liminality through the manipulation of time and place, but he also promotes a sense of indeterminacy through the naming of the play's characters. For example, according to O'Hara's stage directions, the character of Nat Turner is referred to as "NAT TURNER who is the INSURRECTIONIST, who is the SLAVE, who is the PROPHET, who is the HATCHET MURDERER" (8)—titles that encompass both passive/positive and aggressive/negative identities. Metonymically, these titles illuminate the slippage of identity itself, not only revealing how the character's identity is shaped by each and all of these descriptives, but also suggesting how various scenarios, relationships, and communities can create contrasting notions of identity for a single historical subject. Furthermore, O'Hara specifies that the actor who portrays Nat Turner also portrays Ova Seea Jones, the overseer of the slave plantation against whom O'Hara's Nat Turner rebels. Bound within one performing body are the characteristics of two opposing and discordant representations, thus further emphasizing the notion that variance—even disparity—can exist within a shared space.

Just as *Insurrection* assumes a non-Aristotelian structure to evade linear rigidity and evoke a sense of diversity, its use of punctuation, capitalization, and African American vernacular works toward dehierarchizing language by desubstantiating the authority of what is "correct" and "proper." This desubstantiation is most clearly apparent and visible when one reads the written text as demonstrated in the following excerpt:

> NAT: that cain't reach me.
> i'm too high.
> don't mean nuthin ta me them words in there cain't
> move me cos ya see i gots me a ROCK that i stand upon
> the BOOK of Gawd is my foundation the WORDS of
> CHRIST is my ROOT
> and i'm heah ta tell YOU
> I'M. DONE. HEAH. (84)

As a written document, the manipulation of its language—including the full capitalization of selected words and phrases; the use of the lower-case personal pronoun "I"; the resistance to capitalizing the first word of sentences; and the insistence of constructing staccatolike punctuated phrases such as "I'M. DONE. HEAH."—empowers the text to perform its own insurrection by rebelling against the norms of writing, spelling, and grammar. In queering the sacred propriety of written English, O'Hara challenges the traditional protocols of this organizational category ("proper" English) and creates a space for deviation and difference.

Personifying this space, the play's highly educated, black, gay, male protagonist Ron exhibits various markers of acculturation, thereby granting him full access to travel through the different spaces (and spaces of difference) suggested within the play. The fluidity of Ron's particular journey, however, is most clearly identified through the play's oral and auditory performance rather than through its written text. Through the voiced word, Ron's vacillation between the speech and rhythm of African American idiom and the speech of his university-educated, "white" counterparts is representative of the diverse cultural experiences he embodies, thereby dramatizing both the collision and deconstruction of the assumed societal norms explored within the play. Through the navigational tools of language, Ron travels with ease between the spheres of his existence, creating—through linguistic models of communication—distinctive expressions that help shape the complexity of his self-identity, as well as how he is perceived and identified by others.

In illustrating the slippage experienced within identificatory practices, O'Hara queers the concept of history by placing all of the variants described above within the historically momentous—and well-documented—experience of American slavery, specifically the tempestuous and explosive event of Nat Turner's failed slave rebellion. In examining the peculiarities of American slavery, O'Hara demonstrates how historic events are interpreted from various perspectives and cannot be fully classified within a singular authoritative narrative. Thus, it is no coincidence that O'Hara chooses Nat Turner's rebellion—a historical topic rich with contestation—to examine how history is repeatedly reworked and reinterpreted.

It was on August 22, 1831, in Southampton County, Virginia, that Nat Turner, motivated by a succession of divine "visions," led sixty to eighty fellow slaves in one of America's most bloody slave revolts. The thirty-one-year-old Turner and his army of rebels charged through the farms of South-ampton, crudely killing between fifty-five and sixty-five white men, women, and children. Although most of the rebels were caught shortly after the insurrection, Turner himself managed to escape captivity for more than three months until finally, on October 30, he was apprehended. While in jail awaiting his trial, Turner was interviewed by the young white lawyer, Thomas R. Gray, to whom he furnished his "confessions." Shortly after, on November 5, the court passed its judgment and announced Nat Turner's death sentence. Turner was executed—by hanging—six days later.

In the opening prologue of *Insurrection: Holding History,* the stage directions state that "RON READS *a version of* THE CONFESSIONS OF NAT TURNER" (7). Noting that Ron is reading "a" version versus "the" version immediately places into question the authenticity of any version of Nat Turner's confessions. Even the casual student of African American history will recall that there is the fictionalized account of Nat Turner's rebellion, entitled *The Confessions of Nat Turner* (1967), by William Styron, as well as Thomas Gray's allegedly authentic record of Nat Turner's confession—a document that is also entitled *The Confessions of Nat Turner* (1831).[9] What O'Hara makes clear with his own ambiguity is the relative inauthenticity of either version: just as Nat Turner's original confession represents one version of what happened, the literary musings of Gray and Styron are renderings of writers' historicized imaginations. This is especially poignant considering that Thomas Gray's work claims to be a truthful and certified rendition of Nat Turner's account. What is clear on reading Thomas Gray's *Confession,* however, is that it is Gray's voice—Gray's language and perspective—that inserts itself within the text and impresses itself on the reader. In this case, the usurpation of space goes so far as to deny the supposed speaker/subject of these confessions the autonomy and authority of his own voice. As for *The Confessions of Nat Turner* by William Styron, the controversy lies not in the Pulitzer Prize–winning novel's factual accuracy (it is, after all, written as a piece of fiction), but in its portrayal of Nat Turner—a portrayal that caused a storm of heated debate soon after the novel was published. Some of the most potent condemnations of Styron and his novel are found in the critical collection from 1968 titled *William Styron's Nat Turner: Ten Black Writers Respond,* edited by John Henrik Clarke.[10] In this seething compilation of essays, it is argued that Styron's depiction of Turner suffers grossly from negative stereotypes, resulting in a characterization that "was little more than a reflection of Styron's own racial and sexual fantasies about black people."[11]

In dramatizing the contestation surrounding the Nat Turner rebellion, O'Hara does not attempt to ridicule the fictionalizations that have preceded his own, but rather conjures them to reinforce the idea that history is often transformed as it passes through individuals and generations.[12] Not only does O'Hara's play dramatize this phenomenon, but the experiences of Ron, the play's protagonist, suggest that after becoming a witness to the events preceding the insurrection, he will approach his own scholarly endeavors in a new way. Initially studying Nat Turner's rebellion with the analytical distance of scholarly retrospection, Ron wrestled with the value of his dissertation topic, exploding with frustration: "for some reason i got it in my crazy head that Nat Turner was IT. i mean who the hell needs another paper on slavery . . . i have nothing new to say about him or slavery there's nothing new about the fact that he lost his mind and started slashin' folks" (18). After experiencing the rebellion, however, Ron is privy to an alternative perspective—one that promises to inform his thesis in a unique and original manner. No longer seeing the rebellion through the linear, authoritative lens of a distanced historicist, Ron's journey into an alternate space and time opens up new modes of thought and intellectual possibility, suggesting that his future treatment and documentation of history will not be limited by conventional academic practice.

By entertaining the possibility of new epistemological methods, O'Hara challenges the authority of the written archive and validates the significance of oral history and corporeal experience, thereby queering the sanctity of the page. This is forcefully illustrated when Ron, an ivy-league member of America's college-educated middle class, learns his most challenging and revelatory lessons from T. J., an "uneducated" former slave. It is T. J. who teaches Ron, a doctoral student, a life-altering lesson: that one's knowledge of history—filtered through theory and opinion rather than first-hand experience—will inevitably suffer from a lack of "real" understanding and insight:

> T. J.: HUSH UP!
> you now nuthin
> you know letters on paper
> you know big words
> connected ta little ideas
> you know nuthin . . .
> i LIVED it!!
> you. the one Watchin'! (85–86)

Encouraging us to own our personal and collective histories, O'Hara uses T. J.'s character to reveal that experience is more valuable than hearsay; and that the written word bears no greater rigor or weight than that which is spoken and heard. This, of course, is historically poignant when one recognizes that the majority of enslaved Africans in America were denied the ability to concretize their own histories through the written word, thus relying on traditions of oral history and storytelling. What *Insurrection: Holding History* demands is that both its protagonist and audience recognize the wealth and value of oral history as a methodology of preservation. While it is true that an animate archive undergoes transformation with time, it is also clear—as evidenced by the documents surrounding Nat Turner's rebellion— that the written word is equally susceptible to interpretation and mutation; thus, neither form of historic documentation need take priority over the other. O'Hara's play seems to suggest that, in the spirit of queered inclusivity, all factors and methods of historic documentation should share space—and status—within our cultural records.

It is this quality of openness that inspires O'Hara to treat the corporeal body as an alternative archival text, suggesting (like the photograph featured on the play's softback cover) that the material body—and the cultural memories it contains—can represent a uniquely powerful form of historic documentation. Again, O'Hara illustrates this esoteric truth through the character of Ron's 189-year-old great-great grandfather T. J., who, as noted by the stage directions, can only move "his left eye and the middle toe of his right foot" (7). As the play unfolds, it is revealed that the idiosyncrasies of T. J.'s aged body serve as living chronicles of his familial history: T. J.'s father lost his left eye as punishment for looking at a white woman; his mother lost all her toes—except the middle toe on the right foot—when, as a young woman, she ran way with T. J. to escape her life of enslavement.

Further concretizing the notion of the "body as text," O'Hara creates a scene in which Nat and his fellow insurrectionist Hammet trace the letters of the alphabet on their backs, literally *holding* the memory and meaning of these letters in their skin:

> NAT: you been studin' 'em letters?
> HAMMET: i been studin' 'em.
> NAT: let me see one of 'em A's then.
> (*HAMMET moves to NAT's Back.*
> *With his Finger he begins Drawing the letter "A."*)
> HAMMET (*Slowly*): . . . arrow.
> . . . stick.

NAT: nah do me on 'em B's.

HAMMET: *(Concentrates):* . . . stick.

. . . rock. rock.

NAT: do that one again and don't speak it this time.

(HAMMET thinks. then begins drawing As
he does he still speak BUT
he makes sure NAT can't hear him.
As HAMMET finishes his 2nd "B"
NAT turns around to him,
HAMMET smiles confidently.)

okay nah befo' we split i'm gon' teach you a new one.

(NAT begins drawing the letter "C" on HAMMET's Back.)

moon.

this letter "C."

(he points to sky)

think "see" "moon."

"C." (38–39)

For the enslaved Africans in O'Hara's play, pen and paper—overt evidence of their quotidian insurrections—would invite the danger of discovery, and thus they are compelled to teach and learn in creative and clandestine ways. Out of necessity, Nat and Hammet use fingers as writing utensils while the flesh of their naked backs becomes the ideal canvas on which to write. The power of these innovative acts and the significance of their bodily instruments, however, extend far beyond the concern for secrecy. By literally embodying the abstract, O'Hara's characters grant the letters of the alphabet with material significance, conferring them with the conceptual "realness" of an arrow, sticks, rocks, and the moon. In so doing, they hold the annals of remembrance in their skin, transforming their physical bodies, as well as their intellectual selves, into carriers of practical experience as well as knowledge. Furthermore, when Nat advises Hammet to write his "B" again, but "don't speak it this time," he queers the protocols of communication by prioritizing this alternative form of tangibility over the visual and audible signs normally associated with written language. Illustrating how "the bent back of Nat Turner is metaphor for revolution, where the lash is repulsed and replaced by the letter,"[13] O'Hara depicts a scene of multivalent mutinies, disclosing revolutionary ways in which the enslaved and oppressed lay claim to the world around them. In staging this scenario, O'Hara substantiates his characters' ownership of the English language, granting them the authority to transcribe—and dictate—how their black bodies will be represented by (and through) the written word.[14]

It is this recurrent queering of traditional protocols in *Insurrection: Holding History* that not only kicks open a space expansive enough to accommodate a gay presence in the play, but also allows Ron (and his love interest Hammet) to give voice to queer identities—present and past. In an interview by *American Theatre* magazine, O'Hara speaks of his incentive as a gay, black male to create a space in which an individual of his multiple identificatory markers could exist: "I began to wrestle with the idea of trying to figure out what I would have been like and where I would have fit in the past. All of me. Not just my blackness, not just my irreverence, and not just my sexuality—but all of me."[15] Writing from this perspective, O'Hara attempts to dissect the monolithic shadow of slavery by viewing it through issues of sexuality—a perspective that emphasizes the sexual politics, exploitation, and oppression inherent in the "peculiar" institution known as the American slave trade.

Insurrection's queered examination of slavery reverberates with powerful images that emphasize both sexuality and sexualized behavior. When Ron and T. J. travel through time and find themselves amid the slaves on the Mo'tel plantation, they are catapulted into the past via T. J.'s bed. The landing of the bed on Massa Mo'tel not only represents the obvious (the bed as a "sexual site"), but the symbol of the bed itself—and its deathly weight—disrupts the normalcy of the scene while simultaneously representing a powerful image of sexual imprisonment and oppression. Moreover, the landing of the bed is also "Signifyin(g)" on the quintessential Judy Garland film *The Wizard of Oz*.[16] A rifling referent that hosts its own layered subtext, O'Hara's conjuring of both Judy Garland and *The Wizard of Oz* introduces a "queer aesthetic" to his play, emphasizing notions of performativity through the theatricality and ironic humor of "camp."

When Susan Sontag wrote her seminal essay *Notes on Camp*, she set the groundwork for critics and scholars such as Jack Babuscio to further elucidate how camp speaks to—and through—a decidedly gay sensibility.[17] According to Babuscio, the basic features of camp are irony, aestheticism, theatricality, and humor. While "any highly incongruous contrast between an individual or thing and its context or association" marks the irony found in camp, camp's aestheticism is defined by its fantastic, stylized, exaggerated, individualized, and "unnatural" affect.[18] In terms of theatricality, camp celebrates the exposure of life as performance, relishing in the practice of role playing and the conflation of reality versus theater, and actualization versus impersonation. While the humor of camp often erupts as a bitter wit (a wit that discloses the recognition of ironic incongruities as well as the hostility and fear experienced by socially oppressed subjects), Babuscio notes that "because camp combines fun and earnestness, it runs the risk of being considered not serious at all . . . Camp, through its introduction of style, aestheticism, humour and theatricality, allows us to witness 'serious' issues with temporary detachment, so that only later, after the event, are we struck by the emotional and moral implications of what we have almost passively absorbed. The 'serious' is, in fact, crucial to camp. Though camp mocks the solemnities of our culture, it never totally discards the seriousness of a thing or individual."[19] As prefaced by Babuscio, O'Hara temporarily distances his audience from the horrors of slavery in order to increase the velocity of the moral and emotional blow that will inevitably strike their consciousness as the play progresses.

Although it is O'Hara's intent to recognize the terror of American slavery (in particular, he references the sexual objectification endured by enslaved Africans), the playwright does not want the depravity of this aspect of slavery to subsume the spectator's experience, but rather he insists on creating a theatrical experience that is as queer as the form, content, and protagonist of his play. For this reason, the very beginning of the plantation scene in the play opens with a "*FULL-THROTTLE, NO-HOLDS-BARRED, 11:00, BROADWAY, SHOWSTOPPING BRING DOWN THE HOUSE, PRODUCTION NUMBER, Chains and all*" song-and-dance number called "He's Dead" (32–33). Referring to Massa Model's "death-by-bed-landing," this high-flying scene infiltrates the script with the iconic camp reference to *The Wizard of Oz*, making slavery camp by subversively holding up the emotional weight of slavery for questioning through its musical theatricalization. True to the play's spirit and form, O'Hara applies the gay aesthetic of camp to create incongruous scenes marked by their self-conscious theatricality and humor. Thus, in one play, the monolithic topic of American slavery is viewed as both a subject of comedy as well as a subject of tragedy. Once again, O'Hara emphasizes the inclusive notion of multiplicity—one in which even emotional disparities can coexist within a queer space.

While the landing of the bed riffs on the divaesque qualities of Judy Garland and the camp fantasy of *The Wizard of Oz*, its sexual connotations help to underscore sexuality as the centralizing motif in a queer theoretical paradigm. Another example of the subtextual sexual references within

O'Hara's portrayal of slavery occurs when the Clerk Son informs Ron that a double room will cost him "35 bucks" (28). Considering the vacillation this scene portrays as it repeatedly shifts between the past and present, the term "bucks" is pointedly charged with dual meaning. As a form of contemporary slang, "bucks" is a term for American currency; however, it also has a far less innocuous etymological history. Used in a demeaning and derogatory manner during American slavery, "bucks" was used in reference to black men, framing them in terms of their perceived breeding potential, sexual prowess, brute strength—and, befittingly, economic value. Although the usage of the term "bucks" is a subtle double entendre, it also serves as a powerful reminder of how the oppression, control, and regulation of sexual behavior were essential factors within the capital machine of American slavery.

Not all of O'Hara's sexually charged references, of course, are as subtle as the reference to "35 bucks." Such is the case of Ova Seea Jones's order for the stripping and whipping of Izzie Mae and Ron. As punishment for not collecting enough cotton, Ova Seea Jones orders Izzie Mae to take off her clothes. As the scenario unfolds, the stage directions emphasize the slow, methodical way in which she undresses, noting that *"She begins stripping off one layer—then another"* until she is stripped naked (43). Once Izzie Mae is naked, Ova Seea Jones orders Buck Naked to tie her to the Whippin' Post, at which time he proceeds to whip Izzie Mae, thus enacting a punishment which carries the obvious subtext of sadistic fantasy. When Ron dares to protest against this abuse and humiliation he, too, is ordered to strip totally naked. Before forcing T. J. to whip his own great-great-grandson, Ova Seea Jones ravishes Ron's bodily orifices and *"examines RON's Face, Teeth, Chest, Groin and Ass with Whip"* (47), symbolically raping Ron with the same brutal fervor with which he molested Izzie Mae. Animating the observations of Darieck Scott, the violation of both Ron and Izzie Mae discloses how the "rape of black women" and the "emasculation/castration of black men"—two common tropes in African American literature and history—are generally portrayed as parallel and analogous. Even more significantly, however, the whipping scene encourages the audience to ponder the possibility of the sexual subordination, domination, and abuse experienced by enslaved men at the hands of their white masters, thereby offering the opportunity to revise assumptions regarding black male subjectivity. As Scott succinctly notes: "a liberated black male identity must not only involve the recovery of the memory of the black male body's violation, but also the recovery of the painfully acquired knowledge of other modes of being male than the model of phallocentric mastery."[20] Thus, by subjecting the gay male and the enslaved female to the same type of assault, O'Hara not only dramatizes the shared experience of violence and violation (which, in accordance with a queer theoretical paradigm, aligns these two varying subjects in their struggle against the same oppressive forces), but he also forces his audience to contemplate the multivalent experiences of black male subjectivity and sexuality.

Of course, the audience of *Insurrection* is directly confronted with their own potential prejudices and preconceptions when Ron's great-great-grandfather T. J. casually asks his grandson: "You a faggot ain't ya?" (23). The effect is jarring—not so much due to the crassness of the term, but rather due to the nonchalance with which T. J. tosses off such an explosive epithet. After a moment of measured patience, Ron responds to the usage of the term, explaining to his great-great-grandfather: "Only faggots are allowed to call each other faggots. No. body. else." (24). Within this relatively short exchange, O'Hara explores the emotional impact of the term "faggot" which, like the term "nigger" and "queer," has been subsumed by disidentificatory practices in order to nullify its power as an oppressive and derogatory term.[21] In utilizing "faggot," O'Hara exposes the slippage inherent in language, demonstrating how the meanings of words can fluctuate between definitions and interpretations among those who employ them. Just as this essay assumes and interpolates "queer" as a term of empowerment and inclusivity, Ron's explanation of "faggot" illustrates the existence of a community with its own cultural codes, consisting of—as well as beyond—African Americans. Moreover, when Ron publicly assumes the identity/name of Faggot while "in the past," he not only blatantly rebels against Ova Seea Jones, but also demonstrates an aggressive masculinity unparalleled by his heterosexual counterparts. Ron, as (a) Faggot, is far from "ineffectual"; instead, he is the quintessential insurrectionist—a fierce rebel fighting against the institutions of racism and heterosexism.

Just as disidentification is a source of strength for Ron, it is also a strategy of empowerment employed by one of the most unlikely of characters—that of Buck Naked. Although the character of Buck Naked is listed as the "1 Cracker" within the play, his character—the *"PO' WHITE TRASH indentured servant"* (32)—is referenced by Mistress Mo'tel as "THE LAZIEST NIGGA I GAT" (36). Buck Naked confirms his allegiance to the enslaved blacks by asserting, "just cos i'm different don't make me no different" and insisting that "i bends just as low picks just as much hauls just as many works just as hard as any otha nigga in heah n' i be damned if'n you gon walk all through me just cos I'm day n' you nite!" (76). As the inside "outsider," Buck Naked is strengthened by his alliance with the enslaved blacks, bringing into question the practice of self-identification and demonstrating how one can be empowered by laying claim to labels or epithets that may be interpreted as derogatory. Even more significantly, Buck Naked's identification with the enslaved blacks suggests a blurring of the racial and cultural categories of identity, thus inevitably queering the conceptual binaries of racial difference.

O'Hara's most direct and powerful representation of queer(ed) identity, however, is created through his depiction of the relationship between Ron and the slave insurrectionist, Hammet. Through these characters, *Insurrection* expands the definition of masculinity and opens the possibilities of sexual orientation for black men within our historical archives and present-day portrayals. In referencing the era of American slavery, O'Hara sheds light on the fact that there has been little scholarly attention addressing the sexuality and private sexual practices among enslaved blacks, thereby exposing yet another element of African American identity that has suffered under a practice of silence, dismissal, and denial. Furthermore, as Charles Nero astutely observes, despite the indisputable absence of substantial documentation regarding homosexuality among enslaved men and women, the existence of laws (and the execution of sentences) forbidding sexual acts among enslaved men is evidence in itself that such relationships did, indeed, exist.[22] Thus, the relationship between Ron and Hammet is one that gives presence to a tradition of absence, demonstrating that homosexuality, like heterosexuality, is a natural proclivity among other possibilities. Verifying that homosexuality is a viable and unaffected possibility, T. J. quips that he knew Ron was a "faggot" the day he was born: "I knew when you was just 22 hours old you popped outta Lillie and the next thang I knew she had you stuffed in my face cryin' 'bout how cute you was I knew then 22 hours was all it took not even a full day old" (23). In suggesting that Ron was "born gay," O'Hara portrays Ron's attraction to other men as a natural phenomenon and dramatizes how Ron is physically and metaphysically drawn to Hammet:

> (*HAMMET motions.*
> RON *begins to move towards him, involuntarily.*)
> . . . uh could you explain how it is I'm moving uh in your
> direction without wanting to uh move . . . in . . . your . . .

(HE has reached HAMMET.)

...hi...

I'm—

(HAMMET motions at RON's mouth which opens fully, again
involuntarily.
RON is helpless.
Slowly, Silently, Gently HAMMET blows Sweet Air into RON's
open mouth.
He motions to RON's mouth again and it closes.
HAMMET smiles.
He disappears.
RON tries to Speak
but no words form.) (29–30)

Later in the play, Ron reciprocates this tender, sensual exchange by "blowing
sweet air" into Hammet's mouth (97). While the orality of these acts and the
usage of the word "blow" intentionally plays on the image of fellatio, the act
of "blowing sweet air" symbolizes more than just a sexual connection, invoking instead a spiritual connection between the two men. The sweet air that is
exchanged between Ron and Hammet is spiritual oxygen, a life-giving force
that impregnates each man with the soul of the other, thus filling up their
emotional gaps and voids. It is through his relationship with Hammet that
Ron finally feels complete and fully connected to his past.

Borrowing the words of Joseph Beam, Ron's love of Hammet opens up the
possibilities in which black men can love other black men, demonstrating
that love "is not rooted in any particular sexual, political, or class affiliation,
but in our mutual survival. The ways in which we manifest that love are as
myriad as the issues we must address."[23] In creating a space for the expression
and validity of both homosexual love (as illustrated between Ron and Hammet), as well as familial love (as illustrated between T. J. and Ron), O'Hara
expands notions of love and liberates the meaning of family. By including a
gay presence within the narrative of *Insurrection,* O'Hara illustrates how
the inclusion and acceptance of the multiple possibilities of our past—and
present—empowers us by filling in the spaces that provide our community a
sense of unity and wholeness.

Exposing the existence of "holes" and "gaps" within our traditional historical narratives, *Insurrection: Holding History* reveals that an attempt to
document, isolate, and categorize the singular truths of history and identity

is a slippery, and inevitably problematic, slope. Portraying how historical interpretation generally excludes perspectives outside of the compulsive, heteronormative sphere, O'Hara uses the language, dramatic form, and narrative of *Insurrection: Holding History*—as well as the bodies of its characters—to interrogate these institutionalized fissures. By challenging white, heteronormative notions of African American history and identity and their assumptions regarding race, sex, and gender, O'Hara not only queers the notion of a single authoritative perspective, but also creates a space for a queer history to be present.

True to his own vision of openness and inclusion, O'Hara welcomes the audience of *Insurrection: Holding History* to indulge in diverse and varied interpretations of his play: "I actually like to have people see the same exact thing onstage and have completely different takes on it. That's exciting to me. I love watching people from different cultures and different backgrounds sitting together laughing at the same thing and also at the same time choking on certain things—they have to ask themselves, What am I really laughing at? What are gay people getting that I'm not getting? That kind of questioning makes you realize who you are and what you can learn from other people."[24] Thus, by encouraging the diversity of his play's interpretations and meanings, O'Hara uses the Nat Turner insurrection to stage a revolt against the limitations of historic documentation in hopes of perpetuating the very multiplicity that his dramatization articulates, thereby promoting questions versus answers; possibilities versus absolutes.

The question remains, however, as to whether O'Hara's audiences can fully appreciate the prolific and fertile space this play creates. Does *Insurrection: Holding History*—a dramatic merging of the fantastical and theoretical—offer audiences substantive meanings and messages that they can fully grasp and understand? Like Ron's temporal journey back into time, does this complex work simply enslave our imaginations momentarily or does it actually offer us the possibility of holding our history, of touching, shaping, and revising our understanding of the past through the qu(e)erying (that is, the querying *and* queering) of our present?

If a perusal of selected reviews for the inaugural production of *Insurrection: Holding History* are any indication, the initial response to O'Hara's work—which premiered at the New York Shakespeare Festival/Joseph Papp Public Theater in 1996—reflects the play's inherent challenges as well as its canonical importance. Some theater critics, unaccustomed to the animated querying of sensitive topics such as American slavery and sexuality, failed to appreciate the commentary implicit in O'Hara's calculated camp and nonlinear narrative. Howard Kissel of the *Daily News* was not alone when he characterized *Insurrection* as a comedy with "cartoon sensibility"; dismissed the play's campish portrayal of Nat Turner's failed slave rebellion as being "largely like a 'Saturday Night Live' sketch"; and revealed his own limited interpretation of the play's treatment of sexuality by writing: "Only if you subscribe to the fashionable view that sexual minorities are kin to enslaved peoples does O'Hara's play seem at all logical."[25] Reflecting society's deep-rooted practice of habitual heteronormativity, Kissel's superficial and assumptive critique powerfully verifies the importance of—and need for—O'Hara's work. By challenging his audience with the irreverence of *Insurrection*'s content and form, O'Hara implores us to interrogate the sanctity surrounding institutions of power and thought, and, in so doing, he demonstrates that homosexuality—like heterosexuality—is a valid and intrinsic part of the history of human interaction.

Unlike Kissel, critics such as Peter Marks of the *New York Times* clearly understood this aspect of O'Hara's dramatic vision, noting that the playwright "creates a love affair between Ronnie and a slave, not only to show that homosexuality existed in the antebellum South, but to give a fuller portrait of life there." Although Marks was astute in his analysis of O'Hara's play, his intellectual appreciation of the work was tempered by what he deemed as the production's more "disjointed" and "disorienting aspects": "In 'Insurrection: Holding History,' O'Hara's time-bending comic fantasia at the Joseph Papp Public Theater, ideas about slavery, homosexuality and the value of scholarship collide and converge in ways that are both clever and confusing . . . Some of the confusion is playfully intentional: Mr. O'Hara . . . is toying with accepted notions about history, race and sexual identity to make a point about the ways in which Americans perceive—or fail to perceive—the lessons of the past. At many other times, however, the playfulness loses focus, and 'Insurrection' becomes muddled."[26]

In a 1998 interview/dialogue conducted by *San Francisco Chronicle* staff critic Steven Winn, O'Hara acknowledged, and defended, the lack of clarity noted in some reviews of his play: "The New York critics (of 'Insurrection') wanted me to write something more linear, something they could understand. But I don't always understand it. My job isn't to make you understand. It's to tell this story."[27]

While the confusion that some critics ascribe to the play may be rooted in its insistent intersections of time and place, the playfulness of O'Hara's play—initiated by the script's generous indulgence in camp and its use of cultural iconography—is also engendered by the text's intentional openness. Guided by his own directorial instincts, O'Hara (a graduate of Columbia University's MFA directing program and the director of the play's Public Theater production), wrote *Insurrection* with a deliberate capaciousness, thereby allowing the play's content to mirror its form: "I write so the director in me can direct on the page. That's why I don't use stage directions. If a scene calls for a bed to fly, I don't dictate all the mechanics."[28] Liberated, by design, from the authoritative stance of a controlling author, the text of *Insurrection: Holding History* models the play's predilection toward the "lived experience" rather than the written word. Just as Ron's journey questions the primacy of the text, the actual script of *Insurrection: Holding History* forfeits a significant degree of power over to the play's ever-changing performance—an apt dynamic considering its emphasis on the performative nature of both identity and history.

Despite the play's lukewarm reception by New York critics, *Insurrection: Holding History* won *Newsday's* 1996 Oppenheimer award for best new American play and continues to sustain a full production life.[29] In addition, O'Hara, a protégé of George C. Wolfe (O'Hara, in fact, was the assistant to the director for Wolfe's *Bring in da' Noise/Bring in da' Funk* and *Blade to the Heat* and served as the 1995–96 artist-in-residence at the Public Theater) has received numerous artistic accolades, including a 1995 Van Lier Fellowship at New Dramatists, a Rockefeller scholarship, the Mark Taper Forum's Sherwood award, the John Golden award, the TANNE fellowship, and the 1996 NEA/TCG residency for playwrights at the American Conservatory Theater. Furthermore, *Insurrection,* a dramatic work that fervently wrestles with issues of race and sexuality, provides rich and timely material for discussion in an academic environment currently consumed with identity politics, and, befittingly, it has enjoyed a life beyond the stage by becoming a popular text for study within the university setting.[30] However, it is O'Hara's fascination with the resurrection, with "re-membering," and with the recording of African American history in particular that places him firmly alongside today's most notable African American playwrights. Exhibiting the ambitiousness of August Wilson and the irreverence of Suzan-Lori Parks, O'Hara shares their common preoccupation with history—a theme that has inspired some of American theater's most celebrated work.

August Wilson, widely acknowledged as one of America's greatest playwrights, is close to completing his impressive and daunting goal of writing a play for every decade in the twentieth century. History, then, is paramount in the world of August Wilson: his plays attempt to document the social, political, and artistic forces that have shaped and informed African American life from the early 1900s to the present. Using African American folklore, music, and ritual as inspiring elements, Wilson's treatment of history animates and empowers the familiar, yet oblique, stories of our past. In creating, in the words of the playwright, "a kind of review, or re-examination, of history," Sandra G. Shannon contends that Wilson "goes beyond recording history merely to inform. By transforming select moments in black history into dramatic reenactments, he attempts *to forge new attitudes* among black Americans about their past and the role they played in its making."[31] The same, of course, can be said about O'Hara's work. And, just as *Insurrection: Holding History* chronicles a journey back into time—propelling its protagonist on a search for his origin, identity, and community—the dramas of August Wilson also detail a journey through the continuum of time to illustrate both a personal and collective African American odyssey.[32] Treating both the monumental and minute details of black life with the same consideration, Wilson's work—like that of O'Hara's—" 'rights' American history, altering our perception of reality to give status to what American history has denied the status of 'real.' "[33] Giving credence and substance to stories previously untold, both O'Hara and Wilson elaborate on our notions of identity and the African American experience.

Perhaps even more akin to the work of O'Hara, however, is the approach used by Pulitzer Prize–winning Suzan-Lori Parks in her efforts to retrieve and reconnect the present to the past: "Since history is a recorded or remembered event, theatre, for me, is the perfect place to 'make' history—that is, because so much of African-American history has been unrecorded, dismembered, washed out, one of my tasks as playwright is to—through literature and the special strange relationship between theatre and real-life—locate the ancestral burial ground, dig for bones, find bones, hear the bones sing, write it down . . . I'm working theatre like an incubator to create 'new' historical events . . . I'm re-membering and staging historical events which, through their happening on stage, are ripe for inclusion in the canon of history."[34] Parks's playful, circuitous, and often opaque treatment of history is not only evident in the daring content of her plays, but, like the structure of

Insurrection: Holding History, it is also reflected in the cutting-edge form of her work. Like O'Hara, Parks frees her scripts from set descriptions and involved stage directions; she rejects standard rules of English grammar, spelling, and syntax; and she opts to set her plays with a "fluid sense of time and place" and a "multidirectional structure of events."[35] And, similar to O'Hara, Parks mocks the premise of scholarly documentation and challenges assumptions of academic authority as evident by her use of both "real" and fictionalized footnotes. At times, these footnotes are integrated into the dialogue of her plays (as in the case of *Imperceptible Mutabilities in the Third Kingdom*), in other instances (as particularly prevalent in *The America Play*) footnotes are placed outside of the dialogue and are thereby reserved solely for the edification and/or amusement of her reading audience. Thus, as noted by Harry J. Elam Jr. and Alice Rayner, Parks not only "satirizes the process of critical interpretation, and points out the impossibility of determining the Real," but she plays "with the status of the peripheral text as a sign for marginalized experience. Where are those footnotes in performance? Like the exclusions of history, they are on the side."[36]

Suzan-Lori Parks, August Wilson, and O'Hara all share in their fervent attempt to liberate the marginalized African American experience from the sidebars of history. Of course, what separates *Insurrection: Holding History* so strikingly from the work of Suzan-Lori Parks and August Wilson is O'Hara's exploration of African American (homo)sexuality—a topic that is still a relatively uncultivated terrain within the African American dramatic canon. Although there are dramatists of color placing gay and lesbian characters and issues on the page—Brian Freeman, Cherríe Moraga, and Oliver Mayer among them—their work has yet to receive the critical attention (and production opportunities) that their artistry—and their lives—deserve. This, of course, reflects the very issue at hand in *Insurrection: Holding History:* there are stories that have been denied, silenced, ignored, and forgotten that need to be told—and retold.

Like "a Bullet Through Time," *Insurrection: Holding History* tells such a story, triggering elements of form and content to blast open space and allow its audience to fill in the void with the multiplicity of their own personal truths and collective histories. By successfully illustrating how a queer theoretical paradigm can be used to illuminate issues regarding race and gender through the centralizing lens of sexuality, O'Hara not only uses the precarious lessons of history to assert a new set of answers but, more importantly, he proposes a new line of inquiry: Are the issues of race, gender, and sexuality inherently interdependent? And if so, how do they inform one another in revelatory ways on and beyond the stage?

NOTES

1. Helene Keyssar, *Feminist Theater and Theory* (New York: St. Martin's Press, 1996), 110.

2. Peggy Phelan, *Unmarked: The Politics of Performance* (New York: Routledge, 1993), 146.

3. David L. Eng, "Out Here and Over There: Queerness and Diaspora in Asian American Studies," *Queer Transexions of Race, Nation, and Gender*, Special issue of *Social Text* 15(3–4): 50.

4. Eve Kosofsky Sedgwick, *Tendencies* (Durham: Duke University Press, 1993), 8.

5. Annamarie Jagose, *Queer Theory: An Introduction* (New York: New York University Press, 1996), 1.

6. Jack Babuscio, "Camp and Gay Sensibility," in *Gays and Film*, ed. Richard Dyer (New York: Zoetrope, 1984). I would be remiss if I did not acknowledge the contention that exists in the black gay and lesbian community surrounding the term "queer," a term that for many is troubled by its associations with white middle-class privilege. In "Punks, Bulldaggers, and Welfare Queens: The Radical Potential of Queer Politics?" in this volume, [36], Cathy Cohen writes: "Despite its liberatory claim to stand in opposition to static categories of oppression, queer politics and much of queer theory seem in fact to be static in the understanding of race, class, and gender and their roles in how heteronormativity regulates sexual behavior and identities." To this end, E. Patrick Johnson directly addresses the oft-ignored imbrications of race, class, and queer theory through his coinage and application of the term "quare." See his " 'Quare' Studies, or (Almost) Everything I Know About Queer Studies I Learned from My Grandmother," in this volume, 125. Inspired by the African American vernacular tradition, Johnson suggests that the concern with race and class inherent in "quare studies" reflects the diversity that queer theory proposes to address yet habitually fails to fully encompass. My use of the term queer could justifiably be supplanted by Johnson's "quare"; however, while Johnson articulates that "quare studies is a theory of and for gays and lesbians of color" (127), my application of the term "queer" attempts to hold queer theory to its theoretical promise of inclusivity, capaciousness, and open possibility. Furthermore, in this essay I intentionally play on the term "querying." I am interested in the idea of how O'Hara's "queering" of history is simultaneously a "querying" of history: O'Hara's play questions, and thereby challenges, normative assumptions regarding history (as it is represented by the written, versus spoken, word) and African American identity.

7. Robert O'Hara, *Insurrection: Holding History* (New York: Theatre Communica-

tions Group, 1999), 5. Subsequent citations of this work appear as parenthetical page numbers in the text.

8. Homi K. Bhabha, *The Location of Culture* (New York: Routledge, 1994), 1–2.

9. William Styron, *The Confessions of Nat Turner* (New York: Modern Library, 1967); Thomas Gray, "The Confessions of Nat Turner," in *The Confessions of Nat Turner and Related Documents*, ed. Kenneth S. Greenberg (Boston: Bedford Books of St. Martin's, 1996), 38–58.

10. John Henrik Clarke, ed., *William Styron's Nat Turner: Ten Black Writers Respond* (Boston: Beacon Press, 1968).

11. Kenneth S. Greenberg, *"Introduction,"* in *Nat Turner: A Slave Rebellion in History and Memory* (Oxford: Oxford University Press, 2003), xvii. Although there are a number of scenarios and characterizations that Styron's critics found objectionable (among them, the portrayal of Turner lusting after a young white woman), of special note is some scholars' condemnation of Styron's depiction of a brief homoerotic experience between Nat Turner and another slave. Revealing their own homophobia (and sexism), these critics felt that such a portrayal was not only deviant but also feminizing (see Charles Joyner, "Styron's Choice: A Meditation on History, Literature, and Moral Imperatives," in *Nat Turner: A Slave Rebellion in History and* Memory, 179–213).

12. For further discussion regarding the mythology and fictions surrounding the historic treatment of the Nat Turner rebellion, see Clarke, *William Styron's Nat Turner*; Kenneth S. Greenberg, ed., *Nat Turner: A Slave Rebellion in History and Memory* (New York: Oxford University Press, 2003); Mary Kemp Davis, *Nat Turner before the Bar of Judgment: Fictional Treatments of the Southampton Slave Insurrection* (Baton Rouge: Louisiana State University Press, 1999); and Sterling Lecater Bland Jr., *Voices of the Fugitives: Runaway Slave Stories and Their Fictions of Self-Creation* (Westport, Conn.: Greenwood Press, 2000).

13. Cherríe Moraga, *Loving in the War Years: Lo Que Nunca Pasó Por Sus Labios* (Boston: South End Press, 2000), 171.

14. This emphasis on the lived experience of the black body reflects E. Patrick Johnson's assertion regarding the material emphasis of "quare" studies: "We must grant each other time and space not only to talk of the body but through it as well" ("'Quare' Studies," 132).

15. Jessica Werner, "Something to Die For: An Interview with the Playwright [Robert O'Hara]," *American Theatre* 15.2 (1998): 26.

16. For more on "Signifyin(g)" see Henry Louis Gates Jr., *The Signifying Monkey: A Theory of African-Amercian Literary Criticism* (Oxford: Oxford University Press, 1988).

17. Susan Sontag, "Notes on Camp," in *Against Interpretation* (New York: Farrar Strauss Giroux, 1986), 275–92.

18. Babuscio, "Camp and Gay Sensibility," 41.

19. Ibid., 48–49.

20. Darieck Scott, "More Man Than You'll Ever Be: Antonio Fargas, Eldridge Cleaver, and Toni Morrison's *Beloved*," in *Dangerous Liaisons: Blacks, Gays, and the Struggle for Equality*, ed. Eric Brandt (New Press, 1999), 237.

21. For more on "disidentification," see José Estaban Muñoz, *Disidentifications: Queers of Color and the Performance of Politics* (Minneapolis: University of Minnesota Press, 1999).

22. Joseph Beam, "Brother to Brother: Words from the Heart," in *In the Life: A Black Gay Anthology* (Boston: Alyson, 1986), 242.

23. In referencing the laws and sentences associated with homosexuality among enslaved blacks during the American slavery period, Charles Nero, in "Toward a Black Gay Aesthetic: Signifying in Contemporary Black Gay Literature" (in *Brother to Brother: New Writings by Black Gay Men*, ed. Essex Hemphill [Boston: Alyson, 1991]), cites A. Leon Higginbotham Jr.'s *In the Matter of Color: Race and the American Legal Process: The Colonial Period* (New York: Oxford University Press, 1978), as well as Jonathan Katz's *Gay/Lesbian Almanac* and *Gay History* (New York: Avon Books, 1976). In addition, Nero references the narrative of Esteban Montejo in *The Autobiography of a Runaway Slave*, trans. Jocasta Innes, ed. Miguel Bamet (New York: Random House, 1968), in which Montejo, discussing his experience of slavery in Cuba, reflects upon the rape of young Cuban slaves by their white masters as well as on the prevalence of "homoerotic sex and exclusively male families" among enslaved men.

24. Werner, "Something to Die For," 26.

25. Howard Kissel, "Getting a Rise Out of Nat Turner: 'Insurrection' Has Sketchy Way of Dealing with Tragedy, Injustice," Review of *Insurrection: Holding History*, by Robert O'Hara, *New York Daily News*, December 12, 1996, 53; similarly, Greg Evans of *Variety* refers to the production's "cartoonish characters" while Elyse Sommer, in her on-line magazine *CurtainUp.com*, observes that "O'Hara's humor bears the brush stroke of the cartoonist." Although Sommer notes that O'Hara's comedic stylization "is understandable since slavery was something so wildly unreal that it defies realistic, linear treatment," she argues that the "obvious *Saturday Night Live* roots" in the characterization of Mistress Mo'tel (played, in the Joseph Papp production, by former SNL regular, Ellen Cleghorne) "underscore our objections to the effect of [*sic*] play's comedic framework." In terms of the treatment of homosexuality, Sommer writes that the play "seems to spin out of control and lose its balance—as illustrated by the irreverence vis-à-vis slaves and their masters and the reverential and drawn-out love scene between Ron and the doomed-to-die rebel slave." Six years later, when reviewing the Berkshire Theatre Festival's 2002 production of the play, Sommer's critique of the love scene between Ron and Hammet becomes even more pointed: "The injection of the love relationship between Ron (Wayne Scott) and Hammet (Sekou Campbell), a young slave for whom words like gay and homosexual don't exist but who knows

that he likes boys, is quite touching but, now as then, seems a detour from the major 'holding history' theme." See Greg Evans, "Insurrection: Holding History," review of *Insurrection: Holding History*, by Robert O'Hara, *Variety*, December 16, 1996: 94 and Elyse Sommer, "Insurrection: Holding History," review of *Insurrection: Holding History*, by Robert O'Hara. *A Curtain Up Review*, December 14, 1996, http://www.curtainup.com/insurr.html.

26. Peter Marks, "Of Slavery and Sex in a Time Warp," review of *Insurrection: Holding History*, by Robert O'Hara, *New York Times*, December 13, 1996, C27.

27. Steven Winn, "Dialogue from Two Playwrights: Paula Vogel and Robert O'Hara Talk over the State of Theater," *San Francisco Chronicle*, January 4, 1998, 25.

28. Ibid. For critics such as Peter Marks ("Of Slavery and Sex in a Time Warp," C27), who concluded that O'Hara's role as playwright and director was "a decision that has mixed results," the inaugural production of the play may have suffered from the absence of a director with artistic objectivity and critical distance. Greg Evans of *Variety* noted that "The play itself is only partially successful—O'Hara would have been wiser to hand over his work to a director more critical than he himself proves to be—but it certainly shows a gutsy imagination that bodes well for the playwright and his audience." Furthermore, Elyse Sommers, highly critical of the 1996 production directed by O'Hara, is far more favorable in her 2002 review of *Insurrection*: "Under [Timothy] Douglas' smart direction and with a cast that seems to have coalesced into a loving, vitally connected family ensemble, *Insurrection* now adds up to an eminently watchable and more satisfying evening of theater."

29. *Insurrection: Holding History* has been produced by numerous theaters including San Francisco's American Conservatory Theater (1998), Phoenix's Planet Earth Theatre (1999), Stockbridge's Berkshire Theatre Festival (2002), and Los Angeles's Celebration Theater (2002).

30. The text *of Insurrection: Holding History* has been taught in college courses at Stanford University, University of California at Berkeley, and Occidental College, among others.

31. Sandra G. Shannon, *The Dramatic Vision of August Wilson* (Washington, D.C.: Howard University Press, 1995), 3; emphasis added.

32. As Kim Pereira notes in *August Wilson and the African-American Odyssey* (Urbana: University of Illinois Press, 1995), Wilson's journeys are structured around notions of "separation, migration, and reunion" (2). There are, of course, many well-known treatments of similar personal and communal odysseys that speak to the African and African American experience, including those that draw on the notion of "timetravel" as utilized in *Insurrection: Holding History*. In particular, Octavia Butler's novel *Kindred* (Boston: Beacon, 1988 [1979]) details the story of a young African American woman named Dana who is catapulted back into time to the slavery plantation owned by her ancestors. Although she experiences terrifying abuse as a slave, Dana—who is able to return to the present whenever her life is in grave danger—

continues her visitations in order to repeatedly save her hapless great-great-great grandfather, Rufus, and thereby ensure the promise of her own life. Also of note is the film *Sankofa* (1993). Written by Haile Gerima, *Sankofa* (a Ghanaian word meaning "one must return to the past in order to move forward") chronicles the story of an African American model, Mona, who is transported back into time—and into slavery—after posing for a photo shoot in an old slave fortress in Ghana. Transformed into a slave named Shola, with no recollection of her earlier life, *Sankofa's* protagonist takes her contemporary audience on a journey that reveals the unadulterated horrors of American slavery. I thank E. Patrick Johnson for pointing out the similarities among these particular texts.

33. Jay Plum, "Blues, History, and the Dramaturgy of August Wilson," *African American Review* 27 (winter 1993): 562.

34. Suzan-Lori Parks, *The America Play and Other Works* (New York: Theatre Communications Group, 1995), 4–5.

35. Jeanette R. Malkin, "Suzan-Lori Parks and the Empty (W)hole of Memory," in *Memory-Theater and Postmodern Drama* (Ann Arbor: University of Michigan Press, 1999), 156.

36. Harry J. Elam Jr. and Alice Rayner, "Echoes from the Black (W)hole: An Examination of 'The America Play' by Suzan-Lori Parks," in *Performing America: Cultural Nationalism in American Theater*, ed. Jeffrey D. Mason and J. Ellen Gainor (Ann Arbor: University of Michigan Press, 1999), 186.

BIBLIOGRAPHY

Abelove, Henry, Michelé Aina Barale, and David M. Halperin, eds. *The Lesbian and Gay Studies Reader.* New York: Routledge, 1993.

Agamben, Giorgio. *The Coming Community.* Minneapolis: University of Minnesota Press, 1993.

Alexander, Bryant Keith. "Performing Culture in the Classroom: Excerpts from an Instructional Diary." In *The Future of Performance Studies,* ed. Sheron Dailey. Annandale, Va.: National Communications Association, 1999. 170–80.

——. "Performing Culture in the Classroom: An Instructional (Auto)Ethnography." *Text and Performance Quarterly* 19.4 (1999): 271–306.

Alexander, M. Jacqui. "Redrafting Morality: The Postcolonial State and the Sexual Offenses Bill of Trinidad and Tobago." In *Third Woman and the Politics of Feminism,* ed. Chandra T. Mohanty, Ann Russo, and L. Torres. Bloomington: Indiana University Press, 1991. 133–52.

Alexander, M. Jacqui, and Chandra Talpade Mohanty, eds. *Feminist Genealogies, Colonial Legacies, Democratic Futures.* New York: Routledge, 1997.

Almaguer, Tomas. "Chicano Men: A Cartography of Homosexual Identity and Behavior." *differences* 3.2 (1991): 75–100.

Altman, Dennis. *The Homosexualization of America, the Americanization of the Homosexual.* New York: St. Martin's Press, 1982.

Anzaldúa, Gloria. "To(o) Queer the Writer: Loca, escrita y chicana." In *Inversions: Writing by Dykes and Lesbians,* ed. Betsy Warland. Vancouver: Press Gang, 1991. 249–59.

Appadurai, Arjun. "Disjuncture and Difference in the Global Cultural Economy." In *Colonial Discourse and Postcolonial Theory: A Reader,* ed. Patrick Williams and Laura Chrisman. New York: Columbia University Press, 1994. 324–39.

Aptheker, Herbert. "The Event." In *Nat Turner: A Slave Rebellion in History and Memory,* ed. Kenneth S. Greenberg. Oxford: Oxford University Press, 2003.

Aronowitz, Stanley and Henry Giroux. *Postmodern Education: Politics, Culture, and Social Criticism.* Minneapolis: University of Minnesota Press, 1991.

Arriola, Elvia R. "Gendered Inequality: Lesbians, Gays, and Feminist Legal Theory." *Berkeley Women's Law Journal* 9 (1994): 103–22.

Babuscio, Jack. "Camp and Gay Sensibility." In *Gays and Film,* ed. Richard Dyer. New York: Zoetrope, 1984. 40–57.

Baker, Houston A. Jr. *Blues, Ideology, and Afro-American Literature.* Chicago: University of Chicago Press, 1984.

———. " 'You Cain't Trus' It': Experts Witnessing in the Case of Rap." In *Black Popular Culture,* ed. Gina Dent. Seattle: Bay Press, 1992. 132–38.

Baker, Lee D. *From Savage to Negro: Anthropology and the Construction of Race, 1896–1954.* Berkeley: University of California Press, 1998.

Baker, Roger. *Drag: A History of Female Impersonation in the Performing Arts.* New York: New York University Press, 1994.

Baldwin, James. "The Choices of Hercules." In *The Book of Virtues,* ed. William J. Bennett. New York: Simon and Schuster, 1993. 390–92.

———. *Giovanni's Room.* New York: Laurel, 1988 [1956].

———. *Go Tell It on the Mountain.* New York: Laurel 1985.

———. *James Baldwin: Collected Essays.* New York: Library of America, 1998.

———. *Nobody Knows My Name: More Notes of a Native Son.* New York: Vintage, 1993.

———. *No Name in the Street.* New York: Dial, 1972.

———. *The Price of the Ticket.* New York: St. Martin's Press, 1985.

Bambara, Toni Cade. *The Black Woman: An Anthology.* New York: Mentor, 1970.

Barnard, Ian. "Fuck Community; or Why I Support Gay-Bashing." In *States of Rage: Emotional Eruption, Violence, and Social Change,* ed. Renee Curry and Terry L. Allison. New York: New York University Press, 1996. 74–88.

Bartlett, Neil. *Who Was that Man: A Present for Mr. Oscar Wilde.* London: Serpent's Tail, 1988.

Beam, Joseph. "Introduction: Leaving the Shadows Behind" and "Brother to Brother: Words from the Heart." In *In the Life: A Black Gay Anthology*, ed. Joseph Beam. Boston: Alyson, 1986. 13–18, 230–42.

———. "Making Ourselves from Scratch." In *Brother to Brother: New Writings by Black Gay Men,* ed. Essex Hemphill. Boston: Alyson, 1991. 261–62.

Beauvoir, Simone. *The Second Sex.* Knopf, 1957 [1949].

Beemyn, Brett, and Mickey Eliason, eds. *Queer Studies: A Lesbian, Gay, Bisexual, and Transgender Anthology.* New York: New York University Press, 1996.

Bell, Derrick. *Faces at the Bottom of the Well: The Permanence of Racism.* New York: Basic Books, 1992.

Bennett, Andrew, and Nicholas Royle. "Queer." *Introduction to Literature, Criticism and Theory.* London: Prentice Hall Europe, 1999. 178–87.

Berger, Roger A. "The Black Dick: Race, Sexuality, and Discourse in the L.A. Novels of Walter Mosley—African American Detective Novels." *African American Review* 31.2 (1997): 281–95.

Bergman, David. *Gaiety Transfigured: Gay Self-Representation in American Literature.* Madison: University of Wisconsin Press, 1991.

Berlant, Lauren, and Elizabeth Freeman. "Queer Nationality." In *Fear of a Queer Planet: Queer Politics and Social Theory,* ed. Michael Warner. Minneapolis: University of Minnesota Press, 1993. 193–229.

Berlant, Lauren, and Michael Warner. "What Does Queer Theory Teach Us about X?" *PMLA* 110 (May 1995): 343–49.

Bérubé, Allan, and Jeffrey Escoffier. "Queer/Nation." *Out/look: National Lesbian and Gay Quarterly* 11 (winter 1991): 12–14.

Bhabha, Homi. *Location of Culture.* New York: Routledge, 1994.

Black Is . . . Black Ain't. Dir. Marlon Riggs. Independent Film Series, 1995.

Bland, Sterling Lecater Jr. *Voices of the Fugitives: Runaway Slave Stories and Their Fictions of Self-Creation.* Westport, Conn.: Greenwood Press, 2000.

Blasius, Mark. *Gay and Lesbian Politics: Sexuality and the Emergence of a New Ethic.* Philadelphia: Temple University Press, 1994.

——, ed., *Sexual Identities, Queer Politics.* Princeton: Princeton University Press, 2001.

Boatman, Michael. "Acting 'Out.'" *Essence* (September 1997): 78.

Bourdieu, Pierre. *Distinction: A Social Critique of the Judgment of Taste.* Trans. Richard Nice. Cambridge, Mass.: Harvard University Press, 1984.

Bouthillette, Anne-Marie, and Yolanda Retter, eds. *Queers in Space.* Seattle: Bay Press, 1997.

Boykin, Keith. *One More River to Cross: Black and Gay in America.* New York: Doubleday, 1997.

The Boys in the Band. Dir. William Friedkin. Twentieth Century-Fox, 1970.

Brandt, Eric, ed. *Dangerous Liaisons: Blacks, Gays, and the Struggle for Equality.* New York: New Press, 1999.

Brass, Perry. "I Think the New Teacher's a Queer." In *New Worlds of Literature: Writings from America's Many Cultures,* ed. Jerome Beaty and J. Paul Hunter. New York: Norton and Company, 1983. 402–3.

Bravmann, Scott. *Queer Fictions of the Past: History, Culture, and Difference.* Cambridge: Cambridge University Press, 1997.

Bristow, Joseph, and Angelia R. Wilson, eds. *Activating Theory: Lesbian, Gay, Bisexual Politics.* London: Lawrence and Wishart, 1993. 33–52.

Britzman, Deborah. "Is There a Queer Pedagogy? or, Stop Being Straight." *Educational Theory* 45 (spring 1995): 151–66.

——. *Lost Subjects, Contested Objects.* Albany: State University Press of New York, 1998.

Brody, Jennifer DeVere, and Dwight A. McBride. Introduction to "Plum Nelly: New Essays in Black Queer Studies." *Callaloo* 23.1 (2000): 286–88.

Bronski, Michael. *Culture Clash: The Making of a Gay Sensibility.* Boston: South End Press, 1984.

Brown, Wendy. *States of Injury*. Princeton: Princeton University Press, 1995.

Butler, Judith. *Bodies That Matter: On the Discursive Limits of "Sex."* New York: Routledge, 1993.

——. *Gender Trouble: Feminism and the Subversion of Identity*. New York: Routledge, 1990.

——. "Performative Acts and Gender Constitution: An Essay in Phenomenology and Feminist Theory." *Theater Journal* 40 (1988): 519–31.

Butler, Octavia E. *Kindred*. Boston: Beacon Press, 1988.

Carbado, Devon W., and Mitu Gulati. "Working Identity." *Cornell Law Review* 85 (2000): 1259.

Carby, Hazel. *Race Men*. Cambridge, Mass.: Harvard University Press, 1998.

——. *Reconstructing Womanhood: The Emergence of the Afro-American Woman Novelist*. New York: Oxford University Press, 1987.

Carter, Steven. "Ishmael Reed's Neo-Hoodoo Detection." In *Dimensions of Detective Fiction*, ed. Larry Landrum, Pat Brown, and Ray Brown. Madison: University of Wisconsin Press, 1976.

Car Wash. Dir. Michael Schultz. Universal Pictures, 1976.

Case, Sue-Ellen. *The Domain Matrix: Performing Lesbian at the End of Print Culture*. Bloomington: Indiana University Press, 1996.

Cashin, Sheryll. *The Failures of Integration: How Race and Class Are Undermining the American Dream*. New York: Public Affairs, 2004.

Castells, Manuel. *The Rise of the Network Society*. London: Blackwell, 2000.

Castle, Terry. *The Apparitional Lesbian: Female Homosexuality and Modern Culture*. New York: Columbia University Press, 1993.

Chadwick, Joseph. "Toward an Antihomophobic Pedagogy." In *Professions of Desire: Lesbian and Gay Studies in Literature*, ed. George Haggerty and Bonnie Zimmerman. New York: Modern Language Association of America, 1995.

Champagne, John. *The Ethics of Marginality: A New Approach to Gay Studies*. Minneapolis: University of Minnesota Press, 1995.

Chandler, James. *England in 1819: The Politics of Literary Culture and the Case of Romantic Historicism*. Chicago: University of Chicago Press, 1998.

Chasing Amy. Dir. Kevin Smith. Miramax Films, 1997.

Chauncey, George. *Gay New York: Gender, Urban Culture, and the Making of the Gay Male World, 1890–1940*. New York: Basic Books, 1994.

Christian, Barbara. "The Race for Theory." *Cultural Critique* 6 (1987): 51–63.

Clarke, Cheryl. "The Failure to Transform: Homophobia in the Black Community." In *Home Girls: A Black Feminist Anthology*, ed. Barbara Smith. New York: Kitchen Table; Women of Color Press, 1983. 197–208.

——. "Lesbianism: Act of Resistance." In *This Bridge Called My Back*, ed. Cherríe Moraga and Gloria Anzaldúa. New York: Kitchen Table; Women of Color Press, 1981. 128–37.

Clarke, John Henrik., ed. *William Styron's Nat Turner: Ten Black Writers Respond.* Boston: Beacon Press, 1968.

Cleaver, Eldridge. *Soul on Ice.* New York: Dell, 1968.

Clum, John M. *Still Acting Gay: Male Homosexuality in Modern Drama.* New York: St. Martin's Press, 2000.

Cohen, Cathy. The *Boundaries of Blackness: AIDS and the Breakdown of Black Politics.* Chicago: University of Chicago Press, 1999.

——. "Contested Membership: Black Gay Identities and the Politics of AIDS." In *Queer Theory/Sociology,* ed. Steven Seidman. Oxford: Blackwell, 1996. 362–94.

Cohn, Meryl. *Do What I Say: Ms. Behavior's Guide to Gay and Lesbian Etiquette.* New York: Houghton Mifflin Company, 1995.

Collins, Patricia Hill. *Black Feminist Thought: Knowledge, Consciousness, and the Politics of Empowerment.* Boston: Unwin Hyman, 1990.

——. "The Social Construction of Black Feminist Thought." In *Words of Fire: An Anthology of African-American Feminist Thought,* ed. Beverly Guy-Sheftall. New York: New Press, 1995. 338–57.

Combahee River Collective. "The Combahee River Collective Statement." In *Home Girls: A Black Feminist Anthology,* ed. Barbara Smith. New York: Kitchen Table; Women of Color Press, 1983. 272–81.

The Commitments. Dir. Alan Parker. Lauren Films, 1991.

Cooke, Michael G. *Afro-American Literature in the Twentieth Century: The Achievement of Intimacy.* New Haven: Yale University Press, 1984.

Coon, Katharine Driscoll. "'A Rip in the Tent': Teaching (African) American Literature." In *Teaching African American Literature: Theory and Practice,* ed. Maryemma Graham, Sharon Pineault-Burke, and Marianna White Davis. New York: Routledge, 1998. 31–51.

Creekmur, Corey K., and Alexander Doty, eds. *Out in Culture.* Durham: Duke University Press, 1995.

Crenshaw, Kimberlé Williams. "Mapping the Margins: Intersectionality, Identity Politics, and Violence against Women of Color." *Stanford Law Review* 43 (1991): 1241–299.

——. "Foreword: Toward a Race-Conscious Pedagogy in Legal Education." *Southern California Review of Law and Women's Studies* 4 (fall 1994): 33–40.

Crimp, Douglas. "Right On, Girlfriend!" In *Fear of a Queer Planet: Queer Politics and Social Theory,* ed. Michael Warner. Minneapolis: University of Minnesota Press, 1993. 300–20.

Crosbie, Lynn, and Michael Holmes, eds. *Plush: Selected Poems of Sky Gilbert, Courtnay McFarlane, Jeffery Conway, R. M. Vaughan, and David Trinidad.* Toronto: Coach House Press, 1995.

The Crying Game. Dir. Neil Jordan. Miramax Films, 1992.

Davies, Carol Boyce et al. *Decolonizing the Academy: African Diaspora Studies.* New York: Africa World Press, 2003.

Davis, Angela Y. *Women, Race, and Class.* New York: Vintage, 1983.

Davis, Mary Kemp. *Nat Turner before the Bar of Judgment: Fictional Treatments of the Southampton Slave Insurrection.* Baton Rouge: Louisiana State University Press, 1999.

de Lauretis, Teresa. "The Essence of the Triangle, or Taking the Risk of Essentialism Seriously: Feminist Theory in Italy, the U.S. and Britain." *differences* 1.2 (1989): 3–37.

——. "Queer Theory: Lesbian and Gay Sexualities." *differences* 3.2 (1991): iii-xiii.

Delaney, Samuel. *The Motion of Light in Water: Sex and Science Fiction Writing in the East Village, 1957–1965.* New York: Plume, 1998.

Deleuze, Gilles. *Cinema 2: The Time-Image.* Trans. Hugh Tomlinson and Robert Galeta. Minneapolis: University of Minnesota Press, 1989.

D'Emilio, John. *Sexual Politics, Sexual Communities: The Making of a Homosexual Minority in the United States, 1940–1970.* Chicago: University of Chicago Press, 1983.

Dent, Gina, ed. *Black Popular Culture.* Seattle: Bay Press, 1992.

"Dialogue on the Lesbian and Gay Left." Duncan Conference Center, Del Ray Beach, Florida, April 1993.

Diamond, Elin, ed. "Introduction." *Performance and Cultural Politics.* New York: Routledge, 1996. 1–9.

Diawara, Manthia. "Black Studies, Cultural Studies: Performative Acts." In *Race, Identity and Representation in Education,* ed. Cameron McCarthy and Warren Crichlow. New York: Routledge, 1993. 262–67.

Doty, Alexander. *Making Things Perfectly Queer: Interpreting Mass Culture.* Minneapolis: University of Minnesota Press, 1993.

Douglas, Mary. *Purity and Danger: An Analysis of the Concepts of Pollution and Taboo.* New York: Routledge, 1966.

Drowne, Kathleen. "'An Irrevocable Condition': Constructions of Home and the Writing of Place in *Giovanni's Room.*" In *Re-Viewing James Baldwin: Things Not Seen,* ed. D. Quentin Miller. Philadelphia: Temple University Press, 2000.

Duberman, Martin, ed. *Queer Representations.* New York: New York University Press, 1997.

Duggan, "Making It Perfectly Queer." *Socialist Review* 22 (1992): 11–31.

Dunlap, David W. "Three Black Members Quit AIDS Organization Board." *New York Times,* January 11, 1996, B2.

Dworkin, Andrea, and Catharine Mackinnon. *Pornography and Civil Rights: A New Day for Women's Equality.* Minneapolis: Organizing Against Pornography, 1988.

Dyson, Micael Eric. *Between God and Gansta Rap.* New York: Oxford University Press, 1996.

——. "The Black Church and Sex." In *Race Rules: Navigating the Color Line.* Reading, Mass.: Addison-Wesley, 1996. 77–108.

Edelman, Lee. "Queer Theory: Unstating Desire." *GLQ* 2 (1995): 343–48.

——. "Redeeming the Phallus: Wallace Stevens, Frank Lentricchia, and the Politics of (Hetero)sexuality." In *Engendering Men: The Question of Male Feminist Criticism,* ed. Joseph A. Boone and Michael Cadden. New York: Routledge, 1990.

Elam, Harry J., and Alice Rayner. "Echoes from the Black (W)hole: An Examination of 'The America Play' by Suzan-Lori Parks." In *Performing America: Cultural Nationalism in American Theater,* ed. Jeffrey D. Mason and J. Ellen Gainor. Ann Arbor: University of Michigan Press, 1999.

Eng, David L. "Out Here and Over There: Queerness and Diaspora in Asian American Studies." *Social Text* 52–53, 15.3–4 (fall/winter 1997): 31–52.

——. *Racial Castration: Managing Masculinity in Asian America.* Durham: Duke University Press, 2001.

Epstein, Debbie, and James T. Sears, eds. *A Dangerous Knowing: Sexuality, Pedagogy and Popular Culture.* London: Cassell, 1999.

Epstein, Steven. "A Queer Encounter: Sociology and the Study of Sexuality." *Sociology Theory* 12.2 (1994): 188–202.

Escoffier, Jeffrey. "The Political Economy of the Closet: Notes toward an Economic History of Gay and Lesbian Life before Stonewall." In *Homo Economics: Capitalism, Community, and Lesbian and Gay Life,* ed. Amy Gluckman and Betsy Reed. New York: Routledge, 1997. 123–34.

Evans, Greg. "Insurrection: Holding History." Review of *Insurrection: Holding History,* by Robert O'Hara. *Variety,* December 16, 1996, 94.

Fanon, Franz. *Black Skin, White Masks.* New York: Grove Press, 1967.

Farajaje-Jones, Elias. "Ain't I a Queer?" Paper presented at the Creating Change Conference, National Gay and Lesbian Task Force, November 1995, Detroit.

Favor, Martin. *Authentic Blackness: The Folk in the New Negro Renaissance.* Durham: Duke University Press, 1999.

Ferguson, Roderick A. *Aberrations in Black: Toward a Queer of Color Critique.* Minneapolis: University of Minnesota Press, 2003.

Fiedler, Leslie. *Love and Death in the American Novel.* New York: Anchor, 1992.

Fisher, Gary. *Gary in Your Pocket.* Durham: Duke University Press, 1996.

Fitzgerald, F. Scott. *The Great Gatsby.* New York: Charles Scribner's Sons, 1953.

Fitzgerald, Frances. *Cities on a Hill: A Journey Through Contemporary American Cultures.* New York: Simon and Schuster, 1986.

Flagg, Barbara. "Was Blind, but Now I See: White Race Consciousness and the Requirement Of Discriminatory Intent." *Michigan Law Review* 91 (1994): 953–63.

Forrest, Leon. "Evidences of Jimmy Baldwin." In *Relocations of the Spirit,* ed. Leon Forrest. Emeryville, Calif.: Asphodel Press/Moyer Bell, 1994. 267–78.

Foster, Thomas, Carol Siegel, and Ellen E. Berry. *The Gay '90s: Disciplinary and*

Interdisciplinary Formations in Queer Studies. New York: New York University Press, 1997.

Foucault, Michel. *The History of Sexuality, Volume 1: An Introduction.* Trans. Robert Hurley. New York: Vintage, 1990.

Frankenberg, Ruth, ed. *Displacing Whiteness: Essays in Social and Cultural Criticism.* Durham: Duke University Press, 1997.

Fredrickson, George M. *The Black Image in the White Mind: The Debate on Afro-American Character and Destiny, 1817–1914.* Hanover, N.H.: Wesleyan University Press, 1987.

Freire, Paulo. *Pedagogy of the Oppressed.* Rev. ed. Trans. Myra Bergman Ramos. New York: Continuum, 1998.

Freeman, Alan D. "Legitimizing Racial Discrimination through Antidiscrimination Law: A Critical Review of Supreme Court Doctrine," *Minnesota Law Review* 62 (1978): 1049.

Freud, Sigmund. *Leonardo da Vinci: A Study in Psychosexuality.* New York: Vintage Books, 1947 [1916].

——. "Observations on Transference—Love." In *The Freud Reader,* ed. Peter Gay. New York: Norton, 1989.

——. "On Narcissism: An Introduction." In *General Psychological Theory.* New York: Touchstone, 1997.

Fuss, Diana. *Essentially Speaking: Feminism, Nature and Difference.* New York: Routledge, 1989.

——. *Inside/Out: Lesbian Theories, Gay Theories.* New York: Routledge, 1991.

Gallop, Jane. "Knot a Love Story." *Yale Journal of Criticism* 5.3 (fall 1992): 217–40.

Gamson, Joshua. "Must Identity Movements Self-Destruct? A Queer Dilemma." *Social Problems* 42 (1995): 390–407.

Gates, Henry Louis Jr. *The Signifying Monkey: A Theory of African-American Literary Criticism.* Oxford: Oxford University Press, 1988.

Gilroy, Paul. " 'Race,' Class, and Agency." In *There Ain't No Black in the Union Jack: The Cultural Politics of Race and Nation.* London: Hutchinson, 1987. 15–42.

——. " ' . . . To Be Real': The Dissident Forms of Black Expressive Culture." In *Let's Get It On: The Politics of Black Performance,* ed. Catherine Ugwu. Seattle: Bay Press, 1995. 12–33.

Gluckman, Amy, and Betsy Reed, eds. *Homo Economics: Capitalism, Community, and Lesbian and Gay Life.* New York: Routledge, 1997.

Goldberg, Elizabeth Swanson. "The Way We Do the Things We Do: Enunciation and Effect in the Multicultural Classroom." In *Teaching African American Literature: Theory and Practice,* ed. Maryemma Graham, Sharon Pineault-Burke, and Marianna White Davis. New York: Routledge, 1998. 151–77.

Golden, Thelma. *Black Male: Representations of Masculinity in Contemporary American Art.* New York: Whitney Museum of American Art, 1994.

Goldman, Ruth. "Who Is that *Queer* Queer?" In *Queer Studies: A Lesbian, Gay, Bisexual and Transgender Anthology,* ed. Brett Beemyn and Mickey Eliason. New York: New York University Press, 1996. 169–82.

Goldstein, Richard. "Go the Way Your Blood Beats: An Interview with James Baldwin." In *James Baldwin: The Legacy,* ed. Quincy Troupe. New York: Simon and Schuster, 1989. 180–95.

Gray, Thomas. "The Confessions of Nat Turner." In *The Confessions of Nat Turner and Related Documents,* ed. Kenneth S. Goldberg. Boston: Bedford Books of St. Martin's Press, 1996.

Green, Herb. "Turning the Myths of Black Masculinity Inside/Out." In *Names We Call Home: Autobiography on Racial Identity,* ed. Becky Thompson and Sangeeta Tyagi. New York: Routledge, 1996. 253–64.

Greenberg, Kenneth S., ed. *The Confessions of Nat Turner and Related Documents.* Boston: Bedford Books of St. Martin's Press, 1996.

——. *Nat Turner: A Slave Rebellion in History and Memory.* Oxford University Press, 2003.

Griffin, Farah. "Black Feminists and DuBois: Respectability, Protection, and Beyond." *Annals of the American Academy of Political and Social Science* 568 (March 2000): 28–40.

Gross, Kali N. "Examining the Politics of Respectability in African-American Studies." *University of Pennsylvania Almanac* 43, April 1, 1997.

Gross, Larry, and James D. Wood, eds. *The Columbia Reader on Lesbians and Gay Men in Media, Society, and Politics.* New York: Columbia University Press, 1999.

Guglielmo, Thomas A. *White on Arrival: Italians, Race, Color, and Power in Chicago, 1890–1945.* Oxford: Oxford University Press, 2003.

Gutman, Herbert G. *The Black Family in Slavery and Freedom, 1750–1925.* New York: Vintage, 1976.

Haggerty, George E. " 'Promoting Homosexuality' in the Classroom." In *Professions of Desire: Gay and Lesbian Studies in Literature,* ed. George Haggerty and Bonnie Zimmerman. New York: Modern Language Association of America, 1995. 11–18.

Halberstam, Judith. *Female Masculinity.* Durham: Duke University Press, 1998.

Halewood, Peter. "White Men Can't Jump: Critical Epistemologies, Embodiment, and the Praxis of Legal Scholarship." *Yale Journal of Law and Feminism* 7 (1995): 1–13.

Hall, Stuart. "Cultural Identity and Diaspora." In *Identity: Community, Culture, Difference,* ed. Jonathan Rutherford. London: Lawrence and Wishart, 1990. 222–37.

——. "New Ethnicities." In *Stuart Hall: Critical Dialogues in Cultural Studies,* ed. David Morley and Chen Kuan-Hsing. New York: Routledge, 1996. 441–48.

——. "Subjects in History: Making Diasporic Identities." In *The House That Race Built,* ed. Wahneema Lubiano. New York: Pantheon, 1997. 289–99.

Halperin, David. *Saint Foucault: Toward A Gay Hagiography.* New York: Oxford University Press, 1995.

Hamera, Judith. "Emotional/Theoretical Response to HIV Education through the Performance of Personal Narrative." In *HIV Education: Performing Personal Narrative*, ed. Frederick Corey. Tempe: Arizona State University Press, 1993.

———. "The Romance of Monsters: Theorizing the Virtuoso Body." *Theatre Topics* 10.2 (2000): 145–53.

Harper, Phillip Brian. *Are We Not Men? Masculine Anxiety and the Problem of African-American Identity.* New York: Oxford University Press, 1996.

———. "Eloquence and Epitaph: Black Nationalism and the Homophobic Impulse in Responses to the Death of Max Robinson." *Social Text,* no. 28 (1991): 68–86.

———. "Gay Male Identities, Personal Privacy, and Relations of Public Exchange: Notes on Directions for Queer Critique." *Social Text* 52–53, 15.3–4 (fall/winter 1997): 5–29.

———. *Private Affairs: Critical Ventures in the Culture of Social Relations.* New York: New York University Press, 1999.

———. "Walk-on Parts and Speaking Subjects: Screen Representations of Black Gay Men." In *Black Male: Representations of Masculinity in Contemporary American Art,* ed. Thelma Golden. New York: Whitney Museum of American Art, 1994.

Harris, Trudier. *Black Women in the Fiction of James Baldwin.* Knoxville: University of Tennessee Press, 1985.

Harrison, Daphne Duval. *Black Pearls: Blues Queens of the 1920s.* New Brunswick: Rutgers University Press, 1998.

Haver, William. *The Body of This Death: Historicity and Sociality in the Time of AIDS.* Stanford: Stanford University Press, 1996.

———. "Of Madmen Who Practice Invention to the Brink of Intelligibility." In *Queer Theory in Education,* ed. William Pinar. Mahwah, N.J.: Lawrence Erlbaum Associates, 1998. 349–64.

———. "Queer Research; or, How to Practice Invention to the Brink of Intelligibility." In *The Eight Technologies of Otherness,* ed. Sue Golding. London: Routledge, 1997. 277–92.

Hawkeswood, William G. *One of the Children: Gay Black Men in Harlem,* ed. Alex W. Costley. Berkeley: University of California Press, 1996.

Helen (charles). " 'Queer Nigger': Theorizing 'White' Activism." In *Activating Theory: Lesbian, Gay, Bisexual Politics,* ed. Joseph Bristrow and Angelia R. Wilson. London: Lawrence and Wishart, 1993. 97–117.

Hemphill, Essex, ed. *Brother to Brother: New Writings by Black Gay Men.* Boston: Alyson, 1991.

———. *Ceremonies.* San Francisco: Cleis Press, 2000 [1992].

Henderson, Mae. "Speaking in Tongues." In *Feminists Theorize the Political,* ed. Judith Butler and Joan W. Scott. New York: Routledge, 1992. 144–65.

Hennessy, Rosemary. "Queer Theory, Left Politics." *Rethinking Marxism* 17.3 (1994): 85–111.

Higginbotham, A. Leon Jr., *In the Matter of Color: Race and the American Legal Process: The Colonial Period*. New York: Oxford University Press, 1978.

Higginbotham, Evelyn Brooks. *Righteous Discontent: The Women's Movement in Black Baptist Church 1880–1920*. Cambridge, Mass.: Harvard University Press, 1994.

Hill, Mike, ed. *Whiteness: A Critical Reader*. New York: New York University Press, 1997.

Hogan, Steve, and Lee Hudson. *Completely Queer: The Gay and Lesbian Encyclopedia*. New York: Henry Holt, 1997.

Holland, Sharon Patricia. "Bill T. Jones, Tupac Shakur and the (Queer) Art of Death." *Callaloo* 23.1 (2000): 384–421.

——. *Raising the Dead: Readings of Death and (Black) Subjectivity*. Durham: Duke University Press, 2000.

Holloway, Karla FC. *Codes of Conduct: Race, Ethics, and the Color of Our Character*. New Brunswick: Rutgers University Press, 1995.

hooks, bell. *Black Looks: Race and Representation*. Boston: South End Press, 1992.

——."Eros, Eroticism, and the Pedagogical Process." In *Between Borders: Pedagogy and the Politics of Cultural Studies,* ed. Henry A. Giroux and Peter McLaren. New York: Routledge, 1994.

——. *Feminist Theory: From Margin to Center*. Boston: South End Press, 1984.

——. *Killing Rage: Ending Racism*. New York: Holt, 1995.

——. *Outlaw Culture: Resisting Representation*. New York: Routledge, 1994.

——. *Teaching to Transgress: Education as the Practice of Freedom*. New York: Routledge, 1994.

——. *Yearning*. Boston: South End, 1990.

Hull, Gloria T., Patricia Bell Scott, and Barbara Smith, eds. *All the Women Are White, All the Blacks Are Men, But Some of Us Are Brave: Black Women Studies*. Old Westbury, N.Y.: Feminist Press, 1982.

Hurston, Zora Neale. *Their Eyes Were Watching God*. New York: Harper and Row, 1990.

Hutchinson, Daryl. "Out Yet Unseen: A Racial Critique of Gay and Lesbian Legal Theory and Political Discourse." *Connecticut Law Review* (winter 1997): 1–68.

Ignatiev, Noel. *How the Irish Became White*. New York: Routledge, 1995.

Ingraham, Chrys. "The Heterosexual Imaginary: Feminist Sociology and the Theories of Gender." *Sociological Theory* 12 (1994): 203–19.

Irigaray, Luce. *This Sex Which Is Not One*. Ithaca: Cornell University Press, 1985.

Irwin, Robert McKee. *Mexican Masculinities*. Minneapolis: University of Minnesota Press, 2003.

Jackson, George. *Soledad Brother: The Prison Letters of George Jackson*. New York: Bantam Books, 1970.

Jagose, Annamarie. *Queer Theory: An Introduction*. New York: New York University Press, 1996.

James Baldwin, from Another Place. Dir. Sedat Pakay. Hudson Filmworks Inc., 1973.

James Baldwin: The Price of the Ticket. Dir. Karen Thorsen. Nobody Knows Productions, 1989.

James, Henry. *The Beast in the Jungle.* New York: Wildside Press, 2003 [1903].

Johnson, Barbara. "Nothing Fails Like Success." *A World of Difference.* Baltimore: Johns Hopkins University Press, 1987.

Johnson, Cheryl. "Disinfecting Dialogues." In *Pedagogy: The Question of Impersonation,* ed. Jane Gallop. Bloomington: Indiana Press, 1995. 129–37.

Johnson, E. Patrick. *Appropriating Blackness: Performance and the Politics of Authenticity.* Durham: Duke University Press, 2003.

——. "Feeling the Spirit in the Dark: Expanding Notions of the Sacred in the African American Gay Community." *Callaloo* 21 (1998): 399–418.

——. "SNAP! Culture: A Different Kind of 'Reading.'" *Text and Performance Quarterly* 3 (1995): 121–42.

Jones, Tamara. "Inside the Kaleidoscope: How the Construction of Black Gay and Lesbian Identities Inform Political Strategies." Unpublished essay. Yale University, 1995.

Jordan, Winthrop. *White over Black: American Attitudes Toward the Negro, 1550–1812.* New York: Norton, 1968.

Joyner, Charles. "Styron's Choice: A Meditation on History, Literature, and Moral Imperatives." In *Nat Turner: A Slave Rebellion in History and Memory,* ed. Kenneth S. Greenberg. Oxford: Oxford University Press, 2003.

Julien, Isaac, and Kobena Mercer. "True Confessions: A Discourse on Images of Black Male Sexuality." In *Brother to Brother: New Writings by Black Gay Men,* ed. Essex Hemphill. Boston: Alyson, 1991. 167–73.

Karamcheti, Indira. "Caliban in the Classroom." In *Pedagogy: The Question of Impersonation,* ed. Jane Gallop. Bloomington: Indiana University Press, 1995. 138–46.

Kelley, Robin D. G. "Looking to Get Paid: How Some Black Youth Put Culture to Work." In *Yo Mama's Disfunktional! Fighting the Culture Wars in Urban America.* Boston: Beacon, 1997. 43–77.

Kellner, Bruce. "Carl Van Vechten's Black Renaissance." In *The Harlem Renaissance: Revaluations,* ed. Amiritjit Singh, William S. Shiver, and Stanley Brodwin. New York: Garland, 1989.

Keyssar, Helene. *Feminist Theatre and Theory.* New York: St. Martin's Press, 1996.

King, Thomas M. "Jung and Catholic Spirituality." *America* 180.11 (1999): 1–23.

Kissel, Howard. "Getting a Rise Out of Nat Turner: 'Insurrection' Has Sketchy Way of Dealing with Tragedy, Injustice." Review of *Insurrection: Holding History,* by Robert O'Hara. *New York Daily News,* December 12, 1996, 53.

Knopp, Lawrence M. Jr. "Gentrification and Gay Community Development in a New Orleans Neighborhood." Ph.D. diss. University of Iowa, 1989.

——. "Gentrification and Gay Neighborhood Formation in New Orleans: A Case

Study. In *Homo Economics: Capitalism, Community, and Lesbian and Gay Life*, ed. Amy Gluckman and Betsy Reed. New York: Routledge, 1997. 45–64.

Kristeva, Julia. *The Powers of Horror: An Essay in Abjection*. New York: Columbia University Press, 1982.

Larsen, Nella. *Quicksand and Passing*, ed. Deborah E. McDowell. New Brunswick: Rutgers University Press, 1986.

Lauria, Mickey, and Lawrence Knopp. "Toward an Analysis of the Role of Gay Communities in the Urban Renaissance." *Urban Geography* 6.2 (1985): 152–69.

Law, Sylvia A. "Homosexuality and the Social Meaning of Gender." *Wisconsin Law Review* (1998): 187–98.

Lawrence, Charles R. III. "The Id, the Ego, and Equal Protection: Reckoning with Unconscious Racism." *Stanford Law Review* 39 (1987): 317.

Leeming, David. *James Baldwin: A Biography*. New York: Henry Holt, 1994.

Leer, David Van. "Visible Silence: Spectatorship in Black Gay and Lesbian Film." In *Representing Blackness: Issues in Film and Video*, ed. Valerie Smith. New Brunswick: Rutgers University Press, 1997. 157–82.

Leistyna, Pepi and Arlie Woodrum. "Context and Culture: What is Critical Pedagogy?" In *Breaking Free: The Transformative Power of Critical Pedagogy*, ed. Pepi Leistyna, Arlie Woodrum and Stephen Sherblom. Cambridge, Mass.: Harvard Educational Review, 1996. 1–11.

Leland, John. "Shades of Gray." *Newsweek*, March 20, 2000, 50.

Lianna. Dir. John Sayles. Metro-Goldwyn-Mayer, 1982.

Living with Pride: Ruth Ellis @ 100. Dir. Yvonne Welbon. Our Film Works, 1999.

Lorde, Audre. *Sister Outsider*. Freedom, Calif.: Crossing Press, 1984.

——. *Zami: A New Spelling of My Name*. Freedom, Calif.: Crossing Press, 1982.

Lowenthal. Michael. *Gay Men at the Millennium*. New York: Penguin, 1997.

Lubiano, Wahneema. "Mapping the Interstices between Afro-American Cultural Discourse and Cultural Studies: A Prologue." *Callaloo* 19.1 (1996): 68–77.

Madhubuti, Haki. *Black Men: Osolete, Single, Dangerous? The Afrikan American in Transition: Essays in Discovery, Solution, and Hope*. Chicago: Third World Press, 1990.

Malkin, Jeanette R. "Suzan-Lori Parks and the Empty (W)hole of Memory." In *Memory-Theater and Postmodern Drama*. Ann Arbor: University of Michigan Press, 1999.

Manalansan, Martin F. "In the Shadows of Stonewall: Examining Gay Transnational Politics and the Diasporic Dilemma." In *The Politics of Culture in the Shadow of Capital*, ed. Lisa Lowe and David Lloyd. Durham: Duke University Press, 1997.

Marks, Peter. "Of Slavery and Sex in a Time Warp." Review of *Insurrection: Holding History*, by Robert O'Hara. *New York Times*, December 13, 1996, C27.

Martin, Biddy. *Femininity Played Straight: The Significance of Being Lesbian*. New York: Routledge, 1996.

Martin, Robert K. *Hero, Captain, and Stranger: Male Friendship, Social Critique, and Literary Form in the Sea Novels of Herman Melville.* Chapel Hill: University of North Carolina Press, 1986.

Marx, Karl. "On the Jewish Question." In *The Marx/Engels Reader*, ed. Robert Tucker. New York: Norton, 1972.

McBride, Dwight A. "Can the Queen Speak? Racial Essentialism, Sexuality and the Problem of Authority." *Callaloo* 21.2 (spring 1998): 363–79.

——. "Transdisciplinary Intellectual Practice: Cornel West and the Rhetoric of Race Transcending." *Harvard BlackLetter Law Journal* 11 (1994): 157–82.

McDowell, Deborah. "The 'Nameless . . . Shameful Impulse': Sexuality in Larsen's *Quicksand* and *Passing.*" In *The Changing Same: Black Woman's Literature, Criticism, and Theory*, ed. Cheryl Wall. Bloomington: Indiana University Press, 1995. 78–97.

McIntosh, Mary. "Queer Theory and the War of the Sexes." In *Activating Theory: Lesbian, Gay, Bisexual Politics*, ed. Joseph Bristow and Angelia R. Wilson. London: Lawrence and Wishart, 1993. 33–52.

McIntosh, Peggy. "White Privilege and Male Privilege: A Personal Account of Coming to See Correspondences through Work in Women's Studies." In *Power, Privilege and Law: A Civil Rights Reader*, ed. Leslie Bender and Daar Braveman. St. Paul, Minn.: West Publishing, 1995.

McLaren, Peter. *Schooling as a Ritual Performance: Towards a Political Economy of Educational Symbols and Gestures.* New York: Routledge, 1993.

Mendelsohn, Daniel. "I Want My Gay TV." *New York Magazine*, March 5, 2001, 35–36.

Mercer, Kobena. "Decolonization and Disappointment: Reading Fanon's Sexual Politics." In *The Fact of Blackness: Frantz Fanon and Visual Representation*, ed. Alan Read. Seattle: Bay Press, 1999. 114–31.

Miller, D. A. *The Novel and the Police.* Berkeley: University of California Press, 1988.

Montejo, Esteban. *The Autobiography of a Runaway Slave*, ed. Miguel Barnet Trans. Jocasta Innes. New York: Random House, 1968.

Moraga, Cherríe L. *Loving in the War Years: Lo Que Nunca Pasó Por Sus Labios.* Boston: South End Press, 2000.

Moraga, Cherríe, and Gloria Anzaldúa, eds. *This Bridge Called My Back: Writings by Radical Women of Color.* New York: Kitchen Table; Women of Color Press, 1983.

Morrison, Toni. *Playing in the Dark: Whiteness and the Literary Imagination.* New York: Vintage, 1992.

Morton, Donald, ed. *The Material Queer.* Boulder: Westview, 1996.

——. "The Politics of Queer Theory in the (Post)Modern Movement." *Genders* 17 (fall 1993): 121–45.

Mossman, James. "Race, Hate, Sex, and Colour: A Conversation with James Baldwin." In *Conversations with James Baldwin*, ed. Fred L. Standley and H. Pratt Louis. Jackson: University of Mississippi Press, 1989. 46–58.

Moya, Paula M. L. "Postmodernism, 'Realism,' and the Politics of Identity: Cherríe Moraga and Chicano Feminism." In *Feminist Genealogies, Colonial Legacies, Democratic Futures*, ed. M. Jacqui Alexander and Chandra Talpade Mohanty. New York: Routledge, 1997. 125–50.

Moynihan, Daniel Patrick. *The Negro Family: The Case for National Action.* Washington, D.C.: Office of Planning and Research, U.S. Department of Labor, 1965.

Mudhurst, Andy, and Sally R. Munt, eds. *Lesbian and Gay Studies: A Critical Introduction.* London: Cassell, 1997.

Mumford, Kevin. *Interzones: Black/White Sex Districts in Chicago and New York in the Early Twentieth Century.* New York: Columbia University Press, 1997.

Muñoz, José Estaban. *Disidentifications: Queers of Color and the Performance of Politics.* Minneapolis: University of Minnesota Press, 1999.

Murphy, Timothy, and Suzanne Poirier, ed. *Writing AIDS: Gay Literature, Language, and Analysis.* New York: Columbia University Press, 1993.

Namaste, Ki. " 'Tragic Misreadings': Queer Theory's Erasure of Transgender Identity." In *Queer Studies: A Lesbian, Gay, Bisexual and Transgender Anthology*, ed. Brett Beemyn and Mickey Eliason. New York: New York University Press, 1996. 183–203.

Nancy, Jean Luc. *The Inoperative Community.* Minneapolis: University of Minnesota Press, 1991.

Neighborhoods: The Hidden Cities of San Francisco—The Castro (aka *The Castro*). Dir. Peter L. Stein. Wolfe Video, 1997.

Nero, Charles I. "Toward a Black Gay Aesthetic: Signifying in Contemporary Black Gay Literature." In *Brother to Brother: New Writings by Black Gay Men*, ed. Essex Hemphill. Boston: Alyson, 1991. 229–52.

Next Stop, Greenwich Village. Dir. Paul Mazursky. Twentieth Century-Fox, 1976.

Ng, Vivien. "Race Matters." In *Lesbian and Gay Studies: A Critical Introduction*, ed. Andy Medhurst and Sally R. Munt. London: Cassell. 215–31.

O'Hara, Robert. *Insurrection: Holding History.* New York: Theatre Communications Group, 1999.

Oliver, Melvin L., and Thomas M. Shapiro. *Black Wealth/White Wealth.* New York: Routledge, 1997.

Omi, Michael, and Howard Winant. *Racial Formation in the United States: From the 1960s to the 1980s.* New York: Routledge, 1986.

Painter, Nell. "Black Studies, Black Professors, and the Struggles of Perception." *Chronicle of Higher Education*, December 15, 2000, B7.

Park, Robert. *Race and Culture: Essays in the Sociology of Contemporary Man.* London: Free Press of Glencoe, 1950.

——. "Racial Assimilation in Secondary Groups." *American Journal of Sociology* 19 (1914): 606–23.

Parkerson, Michelle. "Birth of a Notion: Towards Black Gay and Lesbian Imagery in

Film and Video." In *Queer Looks: Perspectives on Lesbian and Gay Film and Video,* ed. Martha Gever, John Greyson, and Pratibha Parmar. New York: Routledge, 1993. 234–37.

Parks, Suzan-Lori. *The America Play and Other Works.* New York: Theatre Communications Group, 1995.

Parmar, Pratibha. "That Moment of Emergence." In *Queer Looks: Perspectives on Lesbian and Gay Film and Video,* ed. Martha Gever, John Greyson, and Pratibha Parmar. New York: Routledge, 1993. 3–11.

Patton, Cindy. "Performativity and Social Distinction: The End of AIDS Epidemiology." In *Performativity and Performance,* ed. Andrew Parker and Eve Kosofsky Sedgwick. New York: Routledge, 1995. 173–96.

Pereira, Kim. *August Wilson and the African-American Odyssey.* Urbana: University of Illinois Press, 1995.

Phelan, Peggy. *Unmarked: The Politics of Performance.* New York: Routledge, 1993.

Phelan, Shane. *Getting Specific.* Minneapolis: University of Minnesota Press, 1994.

——. *Identity Politics: Lesbian Feminism and the Limits of Community.* Philadelphia: Temple University Press, 1989.

——, ed. *Playing with Fire.* New York: Routledge, 1997.

Pineau, Elyse. "Critical Performative Pedagogy: Fleshing Out the Language of Liberatory Education." Paper presented at the Conference for the Pedagogy of the Oppressed, University of Nebraska, Omaha, February 1995.

Plum, Jay. "Blues, History, and the Dramaturgy of August Wilson." *African American Review* 27 (winter 1993): 561–67.

Podolsky, Robin. "Sacrificing Queers and Other 'Proletarian' Artifacts." *Radical America* 25.1 (January 1991): 53–60.

Portrait of Jason. Dir. Shirley Clarke. Mystic Fire Video, 1967.

Pyke, Karen D. "Class-Based Masculinities: The Interdependence of Gender, Class, and Interpersonal Power." *Gender and Society* 10 (1996): 527–31.

Queer Nation. "I Hate Straights" manifesto. New York, 1990.

Queers United Against Straight-Acting Homosexuals. "Assimilation Is Killing Us: Fight for a Queer United Front." *Why I Hated the March on Washington* (1993): 4.

Ransby, Barbara, and Tracye Mathews. "Black Popular Culture and the Transcendence of Patriarchal Illusions." *Race and Class* 35.1 (July-September 1993): 57–70.

Reagon, Bernice Johnson. "Coalition Politics: Turning the Century." In *Home Girls: A Feminist Anthology,* ed. Barbara Smith. New York: Kitchen Table; Women of Color Press, 1983. 356–68.

Reed, Aldolph L. Jr., "The 'Underclass' as Myth and Symbol: The Poverty of Discourse about Poverty." *Radical America* 24.1 (January 1990): 21–40.

Reid-Pharr, Robert. *Black Gay Man.* New York: New York University Press, 2001.

——. "The Shock of Gary Fisher." In *Dangerous Liaisons: Blacks, Gays, and the Struggle for Equality,* ed. Eric Brandt. New York: New Press, 1996. 243–56.

Remember Africville. Dir. Shelagh MacKenzie. National Film Board of Canada, 1992.

Rhodes, Jane. *Mary Ann Shad Cary: The Black Press and Protest in the Nineteenth Century.* Bloomington: Indiana University Press, 1998.

Rich, Adrienne. "Compulsory Heterosexuality and Lesbian Existence." In *Powers of Desires: The Politics of Sexuality,* ed. Ann Snitow, Christine Stansell, and Sharon Thompson. New York: Monthly Review, 1983. 177–206.

———. "If Not with Others, How?" In *New Worlds of Literature,* ed. Jerome Beaty and John P. Hunter. New York: Norton, 1996. 786–91.

Riggs, Marlon. "Black Macho Revisited: Reflections of a SNAP! Queen." In *Brother to Brother: New Writings by Black Gay Men,* ed. Essex Hemphill. Boston: Alyson, 1991. 253–57.

———. "Unleash the Queen." In *Black Popular Culture,* ed. Gina Dent. Seattle: Bay Press, 1992. 99–105.

Roberts, John W. *From Trickster to Badman: The Black Folk Hero in Slavery and Freedom.* Philadelphia: University of Pennsylvania Press, 1989.

Roediger, David. *Towards the Abolition of Whiteness.* London: Verso, 1994.

Roediger, David, and James Barrett. "Inbetween Peoples: Race, Nationality, and the 'New-Immigrant' Working Class." In *Colored White: Transcending the Racial Past,* ed. David Roediger. Berkeley: University of California Press, 2002. 138–68.

Román, David. "Teaching Differences: Theory and Practice in a Lesbian and Gay Studies Seminar." In *Professions of Desire: Lesbian and Gay Studies in Literature,* ed. George E. Haggerty and Bonnie Zimmerman. New York: Modern Language Association of America, 1995. 115–16.

Ross, Marlon B. "Some Glances at the Black Fag: Race, Same-Sex Desire, and Cultural Belonging." In *African American Literary Theory: A Reader,* ed. Winston Napier. New York: New York University Press, 2000. 498–522.

———. "White Fantasies of Desire: Baldwin and the Racial Identities of Sexuality." In *James Baldwin Now,* ed. Dwight A. McBride. New York: New York University Press, 1999. 13–55.

Rowell, Charles H. "Signing Yourself: An Afterword." In *Shade: An Anthology of Fiction by Black Gay Men of African Descent,* ed. Bruce Morrow and Charles H. Rowell. New York: Avon, 1996. 335–43.

Roy, Parama. "As the Master Saw Her." In *Crusing the Performative,* ed. Sue-Ellen Case, Phillip Brett, and Susan Forster. Bloomington: Indiana University Press, 1995. 112–29.

Russo, Vito. *The Celluloid Closet: Homosexuality in the Movies.* New York: Harper and Row, 1981.

Ryder, Bruce. "Straight Talk: Male Heterosexual Privilege." *Queen's Law Journal* 16 (1991): 303.

Scott, Darieck. "Jungle Fever? Black Gay Identity Politics, White Dick, and the Utopian Bedroom." *GLQ* 3 (1994): 299–332.

——. "More Man than You'll Ever Be: Antonio Fargas, Eldridge Cleaver, and Toni Morrison's *Beloved.*" In *Dangerous Liaisons: Blacks, Gays, and the Struggle for Equality,* ed. Eric Brandt. New York: New Press, 1999.

Scott, David. *Refashioning Futures: Criticism after Postcoloniality.* Princeton: Princeton University Press, 1999.

Scott, Joan V. "Experience." In *Feminist Theorize the Political,* ed. Judith Butler and Joan W. Scott. New York: Routledge, 1992. 22–40.

Sedgwick, Eve Kosofsky. "The Beast in the Closet: James and the Writing of Homosexual Panic." In *Sex, Politics, and Science in the Nineteenth-Century Novel,* ed. Ruth B. Yeazell. Baltimore: Johns Hopkins University Press, 1991.

——. *The Epistemology of the Closet.* Berkeley: University of California Press, 1990.

——. "Queer and Now." In *Tendencies.* Durham: Duke University Press, 1993. 1–20.

——. *Tendencies.* Durham: Duke University Press, 1993.

Seidman, Steven. *Difference Troubles: Queering Social Theory and Sexual Politics.* Cambridge: Cambridge University Press, 1997.

——. "Identity and Politics in a 'Postmodern' Gay Culture." In *Fear of a Queer Planet: Queer Politics and Social Theory,* ed. Michael Warner. Minneapolis: University of Minnesota Press, 1993. 105–42.

Shannon, Sandra G. *The Dramatic Vision of August Wilson.* Washington, D.C.: Howard University Press, 1995.

Shaviro, Steven. *Passion and Excess: Blanchot, Bataille, and Literary Theory.* Tallahassee: Florida State University Press, 1990.

Shende, Suzanne. "Fighting the Violence against Our Sisters: Prosecution of Pregnant Women and the Coercive Use of Norplant." In *Women Transforming Politics: An Alternative Reader,* ed. Cathy Cohen, Kathleen Jones, and Jones Tronto. New York: New York University Press, 1997. 123–35.

Shepherd, Reginald. *Some Are Drowning.* Pittsburg: University of Pittsburg Press, 1994.

Simmons, Ron. "Some Thoughts on the Issues Facing Black Gay Intellectuals." In *Brother to Brother: New Writings by Black Gay Men,* ed. Essex Hemphill. Boston: Alyson, 1991. 211–28.

Simon, Roger I. "Face to Face with Alterity: Postmodern Jewish Identity and the Eros of Pedagogy." In *Pedagogy: The Question of Impersonation,* ed. Jane Gallop. Bloomington: Indiana University Press, 1995. 90–105.

——. *Teaching against the Grain: Texts for a Pedagogy of Possibility.* New York: Monthly Review Press, 1992.

Sinfield, Alan. *Gay and After.* London: Serpent's Tail, 1998.

Six Degrees of Separation. Dir. Fred Schepisi. MGM/UA, 1993.

Smith, Barbara. "Home." In *Home Girls: A Black Feminist Anthology,* ed. Barbara Smith. New York: Kitchen Table Women of Color Press, 1983. 64–72.

——. "Queer Politics: Where's the Revolution?" *Nation* 257.1 (July 5, 1993): 12–16.

——. "Toward a Black Feminist Criticism." In *All the Women Are White, All the Blacks Are Men, But Some of Us Are Brave,* ed. Gloria T. Hull, Patricia Bell Scott, and Barbara Smith. Old Westbury, N.Y.: Feminist Press, 1982. 157–75.

Smith, Cherry. "What Is This Thing Called Queer?" In *Material Queer: A LesBiGay Cultural Studies Reader,* ed. Donald Morton. Boulder: Westview, 1996. 277–85.

Smith, M. G. "Social Structure in the British Caribbean about 1820." *Social and Economic Studies* 1.4 (August 1953): 55–79.

Smith, Neil. *Uneven Development: Nature Capital and the Production of Space.* Oxford: Basil Blackwell, 1990 [1984].

Smith, Valerie. *Not Just Race, Not Just Gender: Black Feminist Readings.* New York: Routledge, 1998.

Somerville, Siobhan. "Scientific Racism and the Emergence of the Homosexual Body." *Journal of the History of Sexuality* 5.2 (1994): 264–80.

Sommer, Elyse. "Insurrection: Holding History." Review of *Insurrection: Holding History,* by Robert O'Hara. *A Curtain Up Berkshire Review.* July 25, 2002.

——. "Insurrection: Holding History." Rev. of *Insurrection: Holding History,* by Robert O'Hara. Joseph Papp Public Theater, New York. *A Curtain Up Review.* December 14, 1996.

Sontag, Susan. "Notes on Camp." In *Against Interpretation.* New York: Farrar Strauss Giroux, 1986. 275–92.

Spade, Jane, and Craig Wilse. "Confronting the Limits of Gay Hate Crimes Activism: A Radical Critique." *Chicano-Latino Law Review* 21 (2000): 35.

Spelman, Elizabeth V. "'Race' and the Labor of Identity." In *Racism and Philosophy,* ed. Susan E. Babbitt and Sue Campbell. Ithaca: Cornell Univeristy Press, 1999. 202–15.

Spivak, Gayatri. *A Critique of Postcolonial Reason: Toward a History of the Vanishing Present.* Cambridge, Mass.: Harvard University Press, 1999.

——. *Outside In the Teaching Machine.* New York: Routledge, 1993.

Staples, Brent. "Parallel Time." In *Brotherman: The Odyssey of Black Men in America,* ed. Herb Boyd and Robert L. Allen. New York: One World, 1995. 358–65.

Stein, Arlene, and Kenneth Plummer. "'I Can't Even Think Straight': 'Queer' Theory and the Missing Sexual Revolution in Sociology." *Sociological Theory* 12 (1994): 178–87.

Stockinger, Jacob. "Homotextuality: A Proposal." In *The Gay Academic,* ed. Louie Crew. Palm Springs, Calif.: ETC Publications, 1978.

Stoler, Ann. *Race and the Education of Desire: Foucault's "History of Sexuality" and the Colonial Order of Things.* Durham: Duke University Press, 1995.

Strine, Mary. "Articulating Performance/Performativity: Disciplinary Tasks and the Contingencies of Practice." Paper presented at the National Speech Communication Association Conference, San Diego, November 1996.

Styron, William. *The Confessions of Nat Turner.* New York: Modern Library, 1967.

Sullivan, Andrew. "This Is a Religious War." *New York Times Magazine* (October 7, 2001): 52.

Sullivan, Laura L. "Chasing Fae: *The Watermelon Woman* and Black Lesbian Possibility." *Callaloo* 23.1 (2000): 448–78.

Thomas, Calvin. "Straight with a Twist: Queer Theory and the Subject of Heterosexuality." In *The Gay '90s: Disciplinary and Interdisciplinary Formations in Queer Studies,* ed. Thomas Foster, Carol Siegel, and Ellen E. Berry. New York: New York University Press, 1997. 83–115.

Tongues Untied. Dir. Marlon Riggs. Frameline, 1989.

Troupe, Quincy, ed. *James Baldwin: The Legacy.* New York: Simon and Schuster, 1989.

Turner, Victor. *The Anthropology of Performance.* New York: Performing Arts Journal Publications, 1986.

Tyagi, Sangeeta. "Writing in Search of a Home: Geography, Culture, and Language." In *Names We Call Home: Autobiography on Racial Identity,* ed. Becky Thompson and Sangeeta Tyagi. New York: Routledge, 1998. 43–52.

Unger, Roberto M. *False Necessity: Anti-Necessitarian Social Theory in the Service of Radical Democracy.* New York: Cambridge University Press, 1987.

Vaid, Urvashi. *Virtual Equality: The Mainstreaming of Gay and Lesbian Liberation.* New York: Anchor, 1995.

Valdes, Francisco. "Queers, Sissies, Dykes, and Tomboys: Deconstructing the Conflation of 'Sex,' 'Gender,' and 'Sexual Orientation' in Euro-American Law and Society." *California Law Review* 83 (1995): 1.

Valente, Joseph. "Joyce's (Sexual) Choices: A Historical Overview." In *Quare Joyce,* ed. Joseph Valente. Ann Arbor: University of Michigan Press, 1998. 1–18.

Vorlicky, Robert. "(In)visible Alliances: Conflicting 'Chronicles' of Feminism." In *Engendering Men: The Question of Male Feminist Criticism,* ed. Joseph A. Boone and Michael Cadden. New York: Routledge, 1990. 275–89.

Walcott, Rinaldo. "Beyond the 'Nation Thing': Black Studies, Cultural Studies, and Diaspora Discourse (or, the Post Black Studies Movement)." In *Decolonizing the Academy: African Diaspora Studies,* ed. Carol Boyce Davies et al. New York: Africa World Press, 2003.

———. ed. *Rude: Contemporary Black Canadian Cultural Criticism.* Toronto: Insomniac Press, 2000.

Walker, Alice. *In Search of Our Mothers' Gardens: Womanist Prose.* San Diego: Harcourt Brace Jovanovich, 1983.

Wallace, Maurice O. *Constructing the Black Masculine: Identity and Ideality in African American Men's Literature and Culture.* Durham: Duke University Press, 2002.

Warner, Michael, ed. *Fear of a Queer Planet: Queer Politics and Social Theory.* Minneapolis: University of Minnesota Press, 1993.

Washington, Bryan R. *The Politics of Exile.* Boston: Northeastern University Press, 1995.

The Watermelon Woman. Dir. Cheryl Dunye. First Run Features, 1997.

Weeks, Jeffrey. *Coming Out: Homosexual Politics in Britain, from the Nineteenth Century to the Present.* London: Quartet, 1983.

Welcome to Africville. Dir. Dana Inkster. 1991.

Wells-Barnett, Ida B. *Crusade for Justice: The Autobiography of Ida B. Wells,* ed. Alfreda M. Duster. Chicago: University of Chicago Press, 1970.

Werner, Jessica. "Something to Die For: An Interview with the Playwright [Robert O'Hara]." *American Theatre* 15.2 (1998): 26.

West, Cornel. "The Paradox of the Afro-American Rebellion." In *The Sixties without Apology,* ed. Sohnya Sayres, Anders Stephanson, Stanley Aronowitz, and Fredric Jameson. Minneapolis: University of Minnesota Press, 1984. 44–58.

——. *Race Matters.* Boston: Beacon Press, 1993.

White, E. Frances. *Dark Continent of Our Bodies: Black Feminism and the Politics of Respectability.* Philadelphia: Temple University Press, 2001.

Whitfield, Stephen, *The Culture of the Cold War.* Baltimore: Johns Hopkins University Press, 1990.

Wiegman, Robyn. *American Anatomies: Theorizing Race and Gender.* Durham: Duke University Press, 1995.

Wildman, Stephanie. *Privilege Revealed: How Invisible Preference Undermines America.* New York: New York University Press, 1996.

Wilshire, Bruce. *Role Playing and Identity: The Limits of Theatre as Metaphor.* Bloomington: Indiana University Press, 1982.

Wilson, Angelia R. "Somewhere over the Rainbow: Queer Translating." In *Playing With Fire: Queer Politics, Queer Theories,* ed. Shane Phelan. New York: Routledge, 1997. 99–111.

Wilson, William Julius. *The Truly Disadvantaged: The Inner City, the Underclass, and Public Policy.* Chicago: University of Chicago Press, 1987.

Winn, Steven. "Dialogue from Two Playwrights: Paula Vogel and Robert O'Hara Talk over the State of Theater." *San Francisco Chronicle,* January 4, 1998, 25.

Winokur, Mark. "Body and Soul: Identifying (with) the Black Lesbian Body in Cheryl Dunye's *Watermelon Woman.*" In *Recovering the Black Female Body: Self-Representations by African American Women,* ed. Michael Bennett and Vanessa D. Dickerson. New Brunswick: Rutgers University Press, 2001. 231–52.

Wolcott, Victoria. *Remaking Respectability: African American Women in Interwar Detroit.* Chapel Hill: University North Carolina Press, 2001.

Woolf, Virginia. *Mrs. Dalloway.* San Diego: Harcourt Brace Jovanovich, 1990.

Wynter, Sylvia. "1942: A New World View." In *Race, Discourse, and the Origin of the Americas: A New World View,* ed. Vera Hyatt and Rex Nettleford. Washington, D.C.: Smithsonian Institution Press, 1995.

——. "On Disenchanting Discourse: 'Minority' Literary Criticism and Beyond." In *The Nature and Context of Minority Discourse,* ed. Abdul Janmohamed and David Lloyd. New York: Oxford University Press, 1990.

Yarbro-Bejarano, Yvonne. "Sexuality and Chicana/o Studies: Toward a Theoretical Paradigm for the Twenty-First Century." *Cultural Studies* 13.2 (1999): 335–45.

Yingling, Thomas E. *Hart Crane and the Homosexual Text*. Chicago: University of Chicago Press, 1990.

Yu, Henry. *Thinking Orientals: Migration, Contact, and Exoticism in Modern America*. New York: Oxford University Press, 2001.

Žižek, Slavoj. *Looking Awry: An Introduction to Jacques Lacan Through Popular Culture*. Cambridge, Mass.: MIT Press, 1991.

CONTRIBUTORS

BRYANT KEITH ALEXANDER is a professor of performance and pedagogical studies in the Department of Communication Studies at California State University, Los Angeles. His research is centered on the trinity of performance, pedagogy, and culture but also extends into gender/queer studies. His work appears in *Callaloo, Text and Performance Quarterly, Theatre Topics,* and *The Communication Teacher* and in the books *The Future of Performance Studies: Race, and Family: Exploring Communication in Black, White, and Biracial Families.* He is coeditor (with Gary L. Anderson and Bernardo P. Gallegos) of *Performance Theories in Education: Power, Pedagogy, and the Politics of Identity* (2005).

DEVON W. CARBADO is a professor of law and American Studies and a member of the Advisory Board for African American studies at the University of California at Los Angeles where he teaches Constitutional Criminal Procedure, Criminal Adjudication, and Critical Race Theory. He has published articles in the *Harvard Women's Law Journal, Yale Law Review, Cornell Law Review, Harvard Civil Rights, Civil Liberties Law Review, Callaloo,* and *Berkeley Women's Law Journals.* He is also editor of and contributor to *Black Men on Race, Gender, and Sexuality: A Critical Reader* (1999), and coeditor (with Dwight A. McBride and Donald Weise) of *Black Like Us: A Century of Queer African American Fiction* (2002), as well as coeditor of (with Donald Weise) *Time on Two Crosses: The Collected Writing of Bayard Rustin* (2003).

FAEDRA CHATARD CARPENTER is a doctoral candidate in drama at Stanford University and a freelance dramaturge; she is a former resident dramaturge of Arena Stage in Washington, D.C. and Crossroads Theatre Company in New Brunswick, N.J. She is a visiting assistant professor of theatre at the University of Maryland, College Park.

KEITH CLARK is an associate professor of English and African American studies at George Mason University, where he teaches African American and American literature. His essays have appeared in *African American Review, Callaloo,* and the *Faulkner Journal.* He is the editor of *Contemporary Black Men's Fiction and Drama* (2001) and the author of *Black Manhood in James Baldwin, Ernest J. Gaines, and August Wilson* (2002).

CATHY J. COHEN is a professor of political science and director of the Center for the Study of Race at the University of Chicago. She is the author of *The Boundaries of Blackness: AIDS and the Breakdown of Black Politics* (1999) and coeditor (with Kathleen Jones and Joan Tronto) of *Women Transforming Politics: An Alternative Reader* (1997). She has published articles in numerous journals, including the *American Political Science Review, GLQ,* and *NOMOS,* and in selected edited volumes. In addition to her academic work, Cohen has been and continues to be politically active with organizations such as Black AIDS Mobilization (BAM!), the Audre Lorde Project, Kitchen Table: Women of Color Press, the Black Radical Congress, and African American Women in Defense of Ourselves, as well as in planning events such as Black Nations/Queer Nations? and African American Agenda 2000.

JEWELLE GOMEZ received her master's degree from the Columbia School of Journalism. She is from Boston, where she was on the original staff of *Say Brother,* one of the first black weekly television shows in the country. The author of three collections of poetry and a collection of short stories and of essays, she wrote the double Lambda Award–winning novel *The Gilda Stories.* Her stage adaptation of the novel was performed by Urban Bush Women in thirteen cities across the country. She is the former executive director of the Poetry Center and American Poetry Archives at San Francisco State University. She was on the founding board of GLAAD and is currently an advisory board member of the National Center for Lesbian Rights.

RODERICK A. FERGUSON is an associate professor of American studies at the University of Minnesota. He is the author of *Aberrations in Black: Toward a Queer of Color Critique* (2004).

PHILLIP BRIAN HARPER is a professor of English and of American studies at New York University. He is the author of *Framing the Margins: The Social Logic of Postmodern Culture* (1994), *Are We Not Men? Masculine Anxiety and the Problem of African-American Identity* (1996), and *Private Affairs: Critical Ventures in the Culture of Social Relations* (1999), and coeditor (with Anne McClintock, José Esteban Muñoz, and Trish Rosen) of *Queer Transexions of Race, Nation, and Gender,* a 1997 special issue of *Social Text.* He has published widely in journals such as *Callaloo, Art Journal, Diacritics,* and *Social Text.* Currently, he is at work on a manuscript on avant-garde aesthetic practice by black artists.

MAE G. HENDERSON is a professor of English at the University of North Carolina, Chapel Hill. She is the author of numerous articles on African American and feminist criticism and theory, pedagogy, and cultural studies and is editor of *Borders, Boundaries, and Frames* (1995), coeditor (with John Blassingame) of the five-volume *Antislavery Newspapers and Periodicals: An Annotated Index of Letters, 1817–1871* (1980), and author of the widely anthologized essay "Speaking In Tongues: Dialogics, Dialectics, and the Black Woman Writer's Literary Tradition." Her collected essays, *The Interpretation* *of Tongues: Reading Black Women Writing,* and her monograph on black expatriate writers are forthcoming.

SHARON P. HOLLAND is an associate professor in the Department of English and acting associate dean in LAS at the University of Illinois, Chicago. She is the author of *Raising the Dead: Readings of Death and (Black) Subjectivity* (2000), for which she won the Lora Romero prize. She is working on a book on misogyny, as well as on a novel.

E. PATRICK JOHNSON is an associate professor and director of graduate studies in the Department of Performance Studies and African American Studies at Northwestern University. As a performance artist/poet, he has written and directed a number of theatrical productions, and he has performed for national and international audiences such as in his recent one-man show "Strange Fruit." He has published essays in *Callaloo, Text and Performance Quarterly, Journal of Homosexuality,* and *The Drama Review.* He is the author of *Appropriating Blackness: Performance and the Politics of Authenticity* (2003). He is working on an oral history of black gay men of the South.

KARA KEELING is an assistant professor of media and cultural studies in the Department of Communication Studies at the University of North Carolina at Chapel Hill. She is coeditor (with Colin MacCabe and Cornel West) of *Racist Traces and Other Writing: European Pedigrees/African Contagions* (2003). Her writing has appeared in the *Black Scholar* and *Qui Park* as well as elsewhere.

DWIGHT A. MCBRIDE is Leon Forrest Professor and chair of African American studies at Northwestern University. He is the editor of *James Baldwin Now* (1999), coeditor (with Devon Carbado and Donald Weise) of *Black Like Us* (2002), and author of *Impossible Witness* (2002) and *Why I Hate Abercrombie and Fitch* (2005).

CHARLES I. NERO is an associate professor in the Department of Theater and Rhetoric at Bates College where he teaches courses in the African American Studies Program. His writings about black gay literature have been widely anthologized. Currently, his projects include a book about black gay literature, a study of the biblical Queen Esther's role in African American literature, and a study of black and white men's relationships in film.

MARLON B. ROSS is a professor of English and of African American and African studies in the Carter G. Woodson Institute at the University of Virginia. He is the author of *The Contours of Masculine Desire: Romanticism and the Rise of Women's Poetry* (1989) and *Manning the Race: Reforming Black Men in the Jim Crow Era* (2004).

RINALDO WALCOTT is an associate professor and Canada Research Chair of Social Justice and Cultural Studies at the Ontario Institute for Students in Education at the University of Toronto. He is the author of *Black Like Who? Writing Black Canada* (1997) and the editor of *Rude: Contemporary Black Canadian Cultural Criticism* (2000). He is founder and editor of the online journal *New Dawn: The Journal of Black Canadian Studies*.

MAURICE O. WALLACE is an associate professor of English at Duke University and the author of *Constructing the Black Masculine: Identity and Ideality in African American Men's Literature and Culture, 1775–1996* (2002). His research interests include critical theory, American cultural studies, African American literature and culture, and nineteenth-century American literature, with a more recent interest in African American poetics. He is currently at work on a book on James Baldwin.

INDEX

192; and pedagogy, 259, 266; and performativity, 137

Performativity, 136; and blackness, 142, 144; and performance, 137

Policy Institute of the National Gay and Lesbian Taskforce, 47

Portrait of Jason, 236

"Preservation of Innocence," 88 n.14, 301

Privilege: and gender, 191, 195–98; and heterosexuality, 198–206; and race, 191, 193–95

Quare: definition of, 125; uses of, 126–27

Quare studies, 127, 135, 136, 147–50; and the black church, 149; and performance, 140–41

Queer: as a term, ix, 6, 7, 8, 22–25, 29, 36, 128, 129, 152–53 n.10, 184 n. 3, 324

Queer activism, 22, 28, 29, 31

Queer nation, 5, 23, 31

Queer of color critique, xi, 218

Queer politics, 22–25, 28, 30–31, 34–35

Queer Shopping Network, 33

Queer studies, 9, 10, 109, 110; and black studies, 6, 86; and class, 128; history of, 4; and race, 128

Queer theory, 22–23, 161; and class, 130; and race, 129, 147

Queers United Against Straight-Acting Homosexuals, 29, 30

Race: and black studies, 111; and ideology, 162, 176; and queer studies, 5, 110–11; racial formation, 229–30; and sexuality

Riggs, Marlon, 94–95, 133, 141–42, 145–47

Robinson, Max, 115, 116

Rogers, Alva, 121–22 n.2

Roosevelt, Theodore: and European immigration, 55

Rowell, Charles, 95–96, 98

Sedgwick, Eve, 5, 22, 128, 324; and the closet, 169–76, 278; and homosexual panic, 301; and homosocial desire, 273

Scott, Joan, 153–54 n.27

Shockley, Ann Allen, 272, 291

Six Degrees of Separation, 237, 271

Six Feet Under, 239–40

Smith, Barbara, ix, 4, 36

Sociology: construction of sexuality, 52–54, 59; and ethnicity, 54–56

Spillers, Hortense, ix

Spin City, 238–39

Suburban Homosexual Outreach Program, 33

Sula, 146

Sullivan, Andrew, 63–64

Theory in the flesh, 135; definition of, 127

Tongues Untied, 133–135, 215–16, 240

Turner, Nat, 327–28

Turner, Victor, 138

Tyson, Mike, 143

Valente, Joseph, 126

Van Vechten, Carl, 174

Walker, Alice, 125, 151 n.1

Warner, Michael, 6, 22, 28, 128

Watermelon Woman, The, 12, 221–24

Weeks, Jeffrey, 162–63

Welcome to Africville, 91, 100–103

West, Cornel, 207–8

Wiegman, Robin, 164–68

Will and Grace, 245 n.38

Wilson, August, 341–42, 346 n.32

Wright, Richard, 74, 181. See also *Long Dream, The*

Library of Congress Cataloging-in-
Publication Data
Black queer studies : a critical anthol-
ogy / E. Patrick Johnson and Mae G.
Henderson, editors.
p. cm.
Includes bilbiographical references and
index.
ISBN 0-8223-3629-4 (cloth : alk. paper)
ISBN 0-8223-3618-9 (pbk. : alk. paper)
1. African Americans—Study and
teaching. 2. Gay and lesbian studies—
United States. 3. African Americans—
Race identity. 4. Gays—United States—
Identity. 5. Lesbians—United States—
Identity. I. Johnson, E. Patrick.
II. Henderson, Mae.
E184.7.B535 2005
306.76′6′072—dc22
2005009917

Cathy Cohen's "Punks, Bulldaggers, and Welfare
Queens: The Radical Potential of Queer Politics?," first appeared in *GLQ*, vol. 3, no. 4 (1997):
437–65. Permission to reprint courtesy of the
author and Duke University Press.

An earlier version of "Straight Black Studies: On
African American Studies, James Baldwin, and
Black Queer Studies" appears in Dwight A.
McBride's *Why I Hate Abercrombie and Fitch:
Essays on Race and Sexuality* (New York: New
York University Press, 2005), 35–58. Permission
to reprint courtesy of the author and New York
University Press.

Phillip Brian Harper's "The Evidence of Felt Intuition: Minority Experience, Everyday Life, and
Critical Speculative Knowledge," first appeared
in *GLQ*, vol. 6, no. 4 (2000): 641–57. Permission
to reprint courtesy of the author an Duke University Press.

E. Patrick Johnson's " 'Quare' Studies or (Almost) Everything I Know about Queer Studies I
Learned from My Grandmother," appeared in
Text and Performance Quarterly vol. 21, no. 1
(2001): 1–25. Permission to reprint courtesy of
the author and Taylor and Francis.

An earlier version of Mae G. Henderson's essay
"James Baldwin's Giovanni's Room: Expatriation, 'Racial Drag,' and Homosexual Panic," first
appeared in *Callaloo* vol. 23. no. 1 (2000): 313–
27. Permission to reprint courtesy of the author.

Faedra Chartard Carpenter's "Robert O'Hara's
Insurrection: 'Que(e)rying History,' " first appeared in *Text and Performance Quarterly* vol.
23, no.2 (2003): 186–204. Permission to reprint
courtesy of the author and Taylor and Francis.